D1545508

IRISH LITERATURE:

A Social History

FOR ROBERT AND ALISON

Irish Literature:
A Social History

Tradition, Identity and Difference

NORMAN VANCE

Basil Blackwell

© Norman Vance 1990

First published 1990

Basil Blackwell Ltd
108 Cowley Road, Oxford, OX4 1JF, UK

Basil Blackwell Inc.
3 Cambridge Center
Cambridge, MA 02142, USA

British Library Cataloguing in Publication Data

A CIP catalogue record for this book is available
from the British Library.

Library of Congress Cataloging in Publication Data
Vance, Norman, 1950–
Irish literature: a social history / Norman Vance.
p.   cm.
Includes bibliographical references (p.
ISBN 0-631-15629-1
1. English literature—Irish authors—History and criticism.
2. Irish literature—History and criticism.   3. Ireland—
Intellectual life.   4. Ireland—Social conditions.   5. Ireland in
literature.   I. Title.
PR8711.V3   1990
820.9′9415—dc20   90-431

Typeset in 10.5 on 12.5pt Imprint
by Hope Services (Abingdon) Ltd.
Printed in Great Britain by
T. J. Press Ltd., Padstow, Cornwall

Contents

Illustrations and Maps   vii
Preface   viii
Acknowledgements   x
Outline Chronology   xii

CHAPTER 1
Tradition, Ireland, Literature   1

CHAPTER 2
Seventeenth-century Beginnings: Archbishop Ussher and
the Earl of Roscommon   17

CHAPTER 3
The Eighteenth Century and Beyond: William Drennan and
Thomas Moore   65

CHAPTER 4
The Literatures of Victorian Ireland: William Carleton and
Thomas D'Arcy McGee   119

CHAPTER 5
Revival Reviewed: St John Ervine and James Joyce   165

CHAPTER 6
Contemporary Ireland and the Poetics of Partition: John
Hewitt and Seamus Heaney   209

Notes 261
Note on Unpublished Sources 297
Select Bibliography of Primary Texts 301
Index 305

Illustrations and Maps

Illustrations

1 Thomas Ryan, *The Flight of the Earls* (Dublin: Royal Hibernian Academy) 18
2 Daniel Maclise, *The Origin of the Harp* (for a poem by Thomas Moore) (Manchester: City of Manchester Art Galleries) 101
3 Sir John Lavery, *St Patrick's Purgatory* (Dublin: Hugh Lane Municipal Art Gallery) 138
4 T. J. Barker, *Queen Victoria* ('The Secret of England's Greatness') (London: National Portrait Gallery) 181
5 Colin Middleton, *September Evening, Ballymote* (Belfast: Ulster Museum) 248

Maps

1 The counties and provinces of Ireland. xvi
2 Principal physical features of Ireland. xvii

Preface

———

This book explores the ways in which perceptions and constructions of Irish literary tradition articulate contending, sometimes damaging, intuitions of identity in Ireland. It is an essay in revisionist literary history rather than a comprehensive formal survey. Conventional views of the course of Irish writing are interrogated by inspecting the tradition-forming process at different periods. There are case-studies of various writers, famous or unjustly neglected, whose work has contributed to or suffered from the operations of selective tradition. Contemporary Irish writing, responding to acute political and social tensions, often embodies creative reappraisals of the Irish literary heritage. It is time literary historians took a fresh look at the myths and realities of identity and difference in Ireland.

The present study has evolved from Brian Golding's invitation to read a paper in Oxford on literary aspects of Irish nationalism. I am grateful to him, and to New College, Oxford, where I was able to start work on the project as a junior research fellow. I have benefited enormously from the advice and practical help of many individuals and institutions. Special thanks are due to Sam Hanna Bell, John Boyd, Anthony Buckley, Tom Clyde, Lindsay and Muriel Green, Virginia Hardy, Margaret Harry, Finlay Holmes, Elizabeth Knowles, J. T. Leerssen, T. H. Mullen, Fiona Mullen, Kathryn Porter, William and Myrtle Vance and my long-suffering colleagues at the University of Sussex, particularly John Barrell, Colin Brooks, John Burrow, Alun Howkins, Maurice Hutt, Tony Inglis, Stephen Medcalf, Angus Ross and the late Allon White. For access to materials, I am grateful to the BBC (Northern Ireland), the Bodleian Library, the British Library, the Linenhall Library (Belfast), Marsh's Library (Dublin), the National Library of Ireland, the New York Public Library, the Presbyterian Historical Society of Ireland, the Public Record Office of Northern Ireland, the Royal Irish Academy, the Vanier Library of Concordia University, Montreal and the libraries of The Queen's University, Belfast and Trinity College, Dublin. I owe a special debt to the Sussex University Library and its inter-library loan office. My research was assisted by grants from the British Academy and the University of Sussex. My greatest debts are to my wife Brenda Richardson for her heroic tolerance and support and alert interest, and to our children, whose heritage is partly Irish and for whom in a sense the book is written.

Acknowledgements

———

Some of the material here has been published in different form in *Irish Historical Studies*; and in C. J. Byrne and Margaret Harry (eds), *Talamh an Éisc: Canadian and Irish Essays,* Halifax, Nova Scotia: Nimbus, 1985.

The author and publishers wish to thank the following for permission to use copyright material: Blackstaff Press for extracts from 'Gloss' and 'The Scar' from *Out of My Time*, 'Encounter 1920' and 'A Local Poet' from *Time Enough*, 1976, 'Below the Mournes in May' in *The Rain Dance*, 1978, 'The Twelfth of July', 'Going up to Dublin', 'Outside the Creeds' and 'Late Spring 1912' from *Kites in Spring*, 1980, 'Freehold' and 'The Bloody Brae' from *Freehold*, 1986, all by John Hewitt; 'Flight of the Earls now Leaving' and 'For the Centenary' in *Judy Garland and the Cold War* by James Simmons, 1976; and 'Sarah Ann' in *Livin' in Drumlister* by W. F. Marshall, 1983; Faber and Faber Ltd for extracts from 'The Woman in the House' from *Sailing to an Island* by Richard Murphy, 1963; 'Carrickfergus' from *Collected Poems* by Louis MacNeice, 1966; 'History' from *Why Brownlee Left* by Paul Muldoon, 1980; 'Requiem for the Croppies' from *Door into the Dark*, 1969, 'Traditions', 'The Other Side, 'Servant Boy' and 'The Tollund Man' from *Wintering Out*, 1972, 'Singing School', 'Viking Dublin: Trial Pieces', 'The Unacknowledged Legislator', 'Funeral Rites', 'Hercules and Antaeus' and 'Exposure' from *North*, 1975, (with Farrar, Straus & Giroux, Inc.) 'Casualty' and 'Glanmore Sonnet 2' from *Field Work*, 1979, 'Station Island', 'The First Flight' and 'Shelf

Life' from *Station Island*, 1984, 'Holding Course', 'Wolfe Tone', 'Clearances', 'Parable Island' and 'A Peacock's Feather' from *The Haw Lantern*, 1987, 'Belfast' and 'The Poetry of John Hewitt' from *Preoccupations*, 1980, 'The Death of a Naturalist', 'At a Potato Digging' and 'Blackbury Picking' from *Death of a Naturalist*, all by Seamus Heaney; Gallery Press for extracts from 'A Farewell to English' from *A Farewell to English* by Michael Harnett, 1978; Kate Middleton for 'Evening Ballmore' by Colin Middleton; Michael Longley for 'Landscape' from *Man Lying on the Wall*, Victor Gollancz, 1976; Tom Ryan for 'The Flight of the Earls'; the Society of Authors for extracts from *Mrs Martin's Man*, 1914, *Four Irish Plays*, 1914, *Sir Edward Carson*, 1915, and *Changing Winds*, 1917 by St John G. Ervine; and with The New York Public Library for extracts from a letter from St John G. Ervine to Lady Gregory, 5 May 1916, Henry W. and Albert A. Berg Collection, Astor, Lenox and Tilden Foundations.

Outline Chronology

1603	Surrender of rebellious Hugh O'Neill, Earl of Tyrone
1607	Flight of the Earls and collapse of old Gaelic order in Ulster
1609	'Plantation' of Ulster begins
1629–34	Geoffrey Keating, *History of Ireland*
1631	James Ussher, *A Discourse of the Religion Anciently Professed by the Irish and British*
1632–6	*Annals of the Four Masters*
1641	Outbreak of rebellion in Ulster
1649	Execution of Charles I; Cromwell's massacres at Drogheda and Wexford; John Milton, *Observations on Ormond's Articles of Peace with the Irish Rebels*
1684	Roscommon, *An Essay on Translated Verse*
1689	Siege of Derry
1690	Defeat of James II by William III at Battle of Boyne
1696	John Toland, *Christianity not Mysterious*
1719	Toleration Act improves position of Protestant Dissenters
1724	Jonathan Swift, *Drapier's Letters*
1725	Francis Hutcheson, *An Inquiry into the Original of our Ideas of Beauty and Virtue*
1735–7	George Berkeley, *The Querist*
1760–3	Poems of 'Ossian' published by Macpherson
1778	First Catholic Relief Act, which relaxed some provisions of the Penal Laws

1782   Dungannon Volunteer Convention; Grattan's Parliament

1784–5   William Drennan, *Letters of Orellana, an Irish Helot*
1789   Charlotte Brooke, *Reliques of Ancient Irish Poetry*
1790   Edmund Burke, *Reflections on the Revolution in France*
1791   Wolfe Tone, William Drennan and others found United Irishmen
1798   United Irishmen rebellion
1800   Act of Union
1803   Robert Emmet's Rising in Dublin
1808–34   Thomas Moore, *Irish Melodies*
1815   William Drennan, *Fugitive Pieces in Verse and Prose*
1829   Catholic Emancipation
1830–3   William Carleton, *Traits and Stories of the Irish Peasantry*
1840   Founding of O'Connell's National Repeal Association
1845   Beginning of Great Famine
1846   Thomas D'Arcy McGee, *Irish Writers of the Seventeenth Century*
1848   Young Ireland Rising; McGee escapes to USA
1853   Opening of Queen's Island shipyard, Belfast
1857   William Johnston, *Nightshade* (an 'Orange', anti-Catholic novel)
1859   Religious revival in Ulster
1866   Attempted Fenian invasion of Canada from USA
1867   Matthew Arnold, *On the Study of Celtic Literature*
1870   Gladstone's first Irish Land Act
1878   Standish Hayes O'Grady, *History of Ireland: Heroic Period*
1879   Thomas Witherow, *Historical and Literary Memorials of Presbyterianism in Ireland*
1882   Foundation of Gaelic League
1886   Gladstone introduces an Irish Home Rule Bill: strong opposition in Ulster
1889   W. B. Yeats, *The Wanderings of Oisin*
1890   Parnell divorce case (Parnell dies 1891)
1891   Oscar Wilde, *The Picture of Dorian Gray*
1892   Douglas Hyde, 'The Necessity of De-Anglicizing Ireland'
1904   Opening of Abbey Theatre in Dublin with plays by

	Yeats and Lady Gregory; G. B. Shaw, *John Bull's Other Island* (performed in London)
1907	J. M. Synge, *The Playboy of the Western World*
1911	St John Ervine, *Mixed Marriage*
1912	Ulster Covenant to resist Home Rule; sinking of (Belfast-built) *Titanic*
1916	Easter Rising
1919–21	Anglo-Irish ('Black-and-Tan') War
1920	Partition begins when Government of Ireland Act provides for separate northern and southern parliaments
1922	James Joyce, *Ulysses*
1922–3	Civil war in Ireland
1926	Sean O'Casey, *The Plough and the Stars*
1932	Sean O'Faolain, *Midsummer Night Madness*
1936	John Hewitt, *The Bloody Brae* (not published until 1957)
1937	New, effectively republican, Irish constitution
1939–45	Ireland maintains neutrality during World War II
1939	W. B. Yeats, *Last Poems;* Louis MacNeice, *Autumn Journal;* James Joyce, *Finnegans Wake;* Flann O'Brien, *At Swim-Two-Birds*
1942	Patrick Kavanagh, *The Great Hunger*
1949	St John Ervine, *Craigavon, Ulsterman*
1951	Mary O'Malley founds Lyric Players, Belfast
1955	Samuel Beckett, *Waiting for Godot* (French version 1953)
1956	Militant Ulster Protestant Action founded; IRA Operation Harvest campaign
1965	Terence O'Neill and Sean Lemass, northern and southern premiers, have talks
1966	Seamus Heaney, *Death of a Naturalist*
1967	Northern Ireland Civil Rights Association founded
1968	Thomas Kinsella, *Nightwalker and Other Poems*
1969	First fatality in worsening sectarian violence in Ulster; British troops take over responsibility for security
1972	'Bloody Sunday' riots in Derry; suspension of Stormont parliament
1973	Eire joins Common Market
1975	Michael Hartnett, *A Farewell to English* (poems)
1976	Collapse of Northern Ireland 'power-sharing' Executive

1980   Brian Friel, *Translations* (first Field Day production)
1981   Molly Keane, *Good Behaviour*
1985   Anglo-Irish Agreement concluded between London and
        Dublin governments
1986   John Hewitt, *Freehold and Other Poems*
1987   Seamus Heaney, *The Haw Lantern*

MAP I   The counties and provinces of Ireland

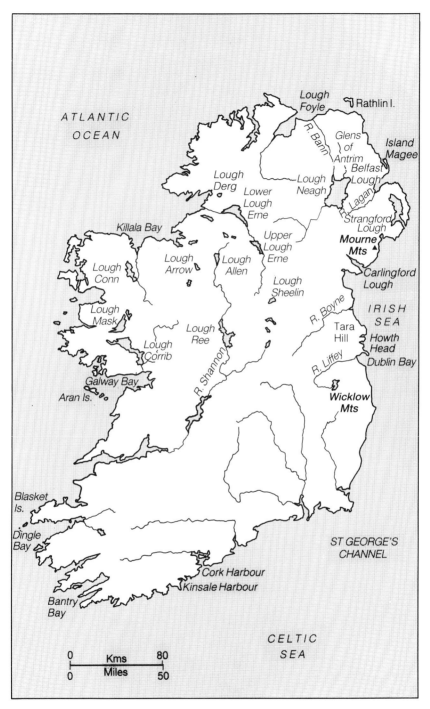

ATLANTIC
OCEAN

Lough
Foyle

Rathlin I.

R. Bann

Glens
of
Antrim

Island
Magee

Lough
Derg

Lower
Lough
Erne

Lough
Neagh

Belfast
Lough

R. Lagan

Killala Bay

Upper
Lough
Erne

Strangford
Lough

Mourne
Mts

Lough
Conn

Lough
Arrow

Lough
Allen

Lough
Sheelin

Carlingford
Lough

Lough
Mask

R. Boyne

IRISH
SEA

Lough
Ree

Tara
Hill

Howth
Head

Lough
Corrib

R. Shannon

R. Liffey

Dublin Bay

Galway Bay

Aran Is.

Wicklow
Mts

Blasket
Is.

Dingle
Bay

ST GEORGE'S
CHANNEL

Cork Harbour

Kinsale Harbour

Bantry
Bay

CELTIC
SEA

0   Kms   80
0   Miles   50

MAP 2   Principal physical features of Ireland

CHAPTER I

Tradition, Ireland, Literature

———

O UR UNDERSTANDING of Ireland past and present has benefited enormously from a generation of demythologizing historical scholarship. But the work of revisionist literary history has just begun.[1] There are comprehensive guides and surveys, but scholars and critics still tend to neglect or misrepresent particular periods of Irish literature, individual writers continue to languish in ideological exile, and significant new writing, particularly in Ulster, cannot be assimilated to conventional views of the Irish literary tradition.[2] Only by determined intrusion into the apparently invulnerable continuities of Irish tradition, only by taking Walter Benjamin's advice and blasting out of the continuum of history specific cultural and literary episodes, can adequate Irish literary history be written. The tradition-making process, the quest for origin and identity, is not necessarily as perniciously self-deluding as Michel Foucault has claimed, but it needs to be critically inspected.[3]

The sense of tradition continues to wield its ancient power to dramatize and moralize Irish history and experience. As long as the gable-ends of Belfast shriek 'Remember 1690' and patriots remember Easter 1916 no Irishman will forget his traditions. The positing of romantic continuities establishes hallowed identities, imparts righteousness and assuages the pangs of insecurity and disruption. If the great St Patrick had not existed it would have been necessary for Catholics and Protestants, separately, to invent him. In a sense they have, since there are rival hagiographical traditions.[4] Yeats and an anonymous medieval scribe both imagine dancing in the Holy Land of Ireland. Cuchulain seemed to join Patrick Pearse in the Dublin Post

Office.[5] In popular consciousness the 'boys behind the wire' imprisoned in contemporary Ulster shake hands with the eighteenth-century United Irishmen; nineteenth-century Irish folk-memory lined up Brien Boru and Lord Edward Fitzgerald against Oliver Cromwell and King William III.[6] Chronology, critical historiography and common sense are powerless against the emotional and imaginative force of such associations.

Irish writing naturally tends to reproduce and reinforce these potencies, sometimes in the very act of interrogating them. By its travesties of Irish political rhetoric, the 'Cyclops' episode of Joyce's *Ulysses* invites renewed interest in the myths of populist nationalism. Irish literature both conveys and is incorporated into Irish tradition. A distinction is needed between tradition as a pattern of continuity and development of form, manner, language and style, and tradition as an aspect of subject-matter. A further distinction proposes itself between tradition as theme (novels about the Big House in an established local community; poems about recovering ancient glories) and themes which may represent or evolve into a tradition of interest or concern (novels about Catholic education; poems about the Irish countryside). But the categories constantly overlap. Thomas Flanagan, himself a novelist, has argued for a tradition of the Irish novel defined by attentiveness to specific, tradition-laden concerns, notably the question of Shakespeare's Irishman Macmorris: 'What ish my nation?'[7] John Cronin's valuable study *The Anglo-Irish Novel* resembles F. R. Leavis's *The Great Tradition* in discussing a few important examples of the novel form, but he asserts continuities of theme as well as of form, language and tone.[8]

Other literary scholars have attempted to establish Irish traditions out of more intangible continuities. Vivien Mercier's *The Irish Comic Tradition* (1962) is a learned, question-begging *tour de force* which sweeps us from ancient Irish literature by way of the twelfth-century *Vision of MacConglinne* to *Finnegans Wake*. Richard Kearney introduces a recent symposium boldly entitled *The Irish Mind* by adventurously positing a special Irish logic which could link the prehistoric carvings of Newgrange with the theology of Erigena, the philosophy of Berkeley and the theatre of Samuel Beckett.[9]

An even more majestic notion of tradition for Ireland is available in T. S. Eliot's idea of a European tradition of cultural monuments proceeding from Virgil and Dante to reach and be modified by writers still unborn.[10] On Eliot's view *Ulysses,* which he knew, and Seamus Heaney's Dantesque 'Station Island', which he did not, are most importantly innovative works within the constantly-changing European tradition.

But no Irishman with any sense of his country's distinctiveness would be altogether happy in Eliot's Europe. On closer inspection Eliot's idea of tradition discloses traces of an anti-nationalist cultural imperialism which accepts Dante's doctrine of the literary dignity of the vernacular as a necessary consequence of the eclipse of Virgil's Rome and Virgil's Latin but holds out for a residual spiritual and cultural empire of the Christianized West.[11] Neither the Imperial Rome of Virgil nor the centralizing disciplines of the Roman Church had much direct impact on early Irish literature. The oldest surviving Irish translation of the *Aeneid* is in early modern Irish, in the fifteenth-century *Book of Ballymote*. The warlike paganism of the heroic cycles of pre-Christian Ireland was not colonized or suppressed by Rome or the Roman Church, but accommodated alongside the pieties of Christianity. The sometimes ironic juxtaposition is articulated in works such as the *Agallamh na Senorach*, or 'Colloquy of the Ancient Men', which brings St Patrick face to face with a resurrected Oisin.

The comparatively recent and constantly troubled alliance between Irish nationalism and the Roman Catholic Church might do something to reconcile the Irish cultural patriot to Eliot's cultural perspective. But no patriot could welcome the imperial powers Eliot is willing to confer on the major vernaculars: 'There can only be one English literature . . . there cannot be British literature, or American literature.'[12] Nor, by the same token, could there be a separate tradition of Irish literature.

Notions of tradition are problematic and selective for pragmatic as well as ideological reasons. Consciousness of tradition cannot be comprehensive or constant. It is perhaps a little unnatural. It represents an imaginative response, sometimes individual, sometimes collective, to particular circumstances and stresses. It is not possible for most people most of the time to keep in focus more than a few of the treasures and glories of the cultural past. Even then, there has to be a reason for thinking about such matters at all. The uprooting of apparently time-honoured habits of peace and civility in European war prompted Eliot to a selective vision of European literary tradition more robust because more intangible than demonstrably vulnerable political and national institutions. In Ireland a sense of cultural disclocation, or insecurity, or reviving national pride, or willed identification of colonizer with colonized, has at different times inspired different perceptions and constructions of Irish literary tradition.

Pursuing and recovering traditions, for whatever motive, is a creative act of the historical imagination. The Jewish critic Walter Benjamin, writing amid the dangers of Hitler's Europe in 1940, suggested that we do not recognize the past 'the way it really was' as Von Ranke and other nineteenth-century historians thought they could. Instead, we 'seize hold of a memory as it flashes up at a moment of danger . . . The danger affects both the content of the tradition and its receivers.[13] There is a close analogy with autobiography, the product of individual rather than corporate memory, often a response to a specific, topical urgency. John Stuart Mill artfully constructed his own past and his relationship with his father to promote his matured neo-utilitarian philosophy.[14] Autobiographies are notoriously tricky and unreliable as historical sources, which rather discourages the critical investigator of 'tradition' or communal memory. But recent historical analysis of the 'invention of tradition' in eighteenth- and nineteenth-century Europe and in the Victorian legal profession demonstrates the possibility and the historical value of understanding individual moments or episodes of tradition-seeking in themselves.[15]

Before proceeding to inspect particular episodes of this kind in the Irish literary past it is necessary to reflect a little on the idea of a literary heritage and on the pressures moulding rival constructions of Irish literary tradition. Recent developments in English studies have encouraged the interrogation of much that has customarily been accepted as 'given'. This has extended to notions of the English literary tradition, usually apprehended as some kind of canon of valuable texts capable of surviving sustained critical attention. The implied analogy with the canonical texts of Holy Scripture illustrates the authoritarian as well as authoritative aspects of 'canonicity', and the perils in store for 'heretical' or 'uncanonical' works.[16] Radical commentators have pointed out the dangers of unstated bias and ideological coercion in any canon, or in its attenuated derivative, the academic curriculum. Such bias and coercion can manufacture and deliver an artificial cultural consensus, effectively suppressing other possibilities.[17]

This insight urgently needs to be extended to Ireland. Unexamined notions of 'Irish literature' and the Irish literary tradition are inescapably coercive in a country notoriously lacking in consensus, where social, political, religious and cultural dissent are rife, particularly in the six northern counties. The problem is exacerbated by the marginal status of Irish writing in relation to the dominant British culture of Europe's western islands. Within the more conservative and restricted versions of the canon of English literature, pedagogically useful in Ireland and America as well as in England, only Yeats and Joyce, and now perhaps Seamus Heaney, tend to attract major attention as specifically Irish writers. Maria Edgeworth, Synge and Shaw might be added as afterthoughts. Beckett, Swift, Sheridan and Goldsmith are highly respected, but their Irishness is often overlooked.

This has two main consequences. For non-Irish readers all previous Irish writing tends to be anachronistically selected and filtered into a manufactured context for Yeats and Joyce and some of the more easily appropriated values or concerns of their work are identified as the stuff of Irish literature and the Irish experience. Raymond Williams has observed this process operating more generally in relation to the concept of 'literature' itself as a privileging and specializing category.[18] For the Irish reader this restricted, implicitly patronizing view provokes various forms of cultural-nationalist or regionalist reaction. Inevitably, 'Irish literature' is a category which frequently registers resistance to the imperialism of T. S. Eliot's European tradition and the awe-inspiring tyranny of a majestic English literary tradition depending on language rather than locality. But the anti-colonial, post-imperialist impulse behind this resistance is itself the locus of particular ideological pressures tending to limit the notion of 'Irish literature' to the literary expression of Irish national aspiration or a problematic Irish psyche.

The strains and tensions, and the problematics of identity, imposed on writers by this kind of resented marginalization have been seen as the characteristic dynamic of 'minor literature'. The concept was originally proposed by Kafka in relation to the Czech literature of Prague and the Yiddish literature of Warsaw. It has been extended and developed by Gilles Deleuze and Félix Guattari and has recently been explored by David Lloyd in relation to the Irish writer James Clarence Mangan, with very illuminating results.[19] But Mangan's chosen 'minor' status and his refusal to realize or enter into an authentic identity are not typical. Other Irish writers have evaded or sublimated their unease through the tradition-seeking process, and critics of Irish literature have done the same.

Selecting and manipulating traditions and hypothetical continuities, literary or otherwise, is often a tactic of insecurity, a feature both of colonial administrations and of anti-colonial resistance mythologies as recent research on Zimbabwe has demonstrated.[20] But yesterday's resistance mythology may easily pass over into today's post-colonial orthodoxy, legitimating a regime where once it inspired a revolution. Something of the kind seems to have happened in what is now

Tanzania. There is a Dar es Salaam 'school' of historiography founded on the assumptions that all past movements in that part of Africa must have been incipient national movements, that nationalism is the key to understanding all periods of Tanzanian history, and that all other factors may be disregarded.[21]

There is still a tendency for the Irish past to be understood in this way and for Irish literature to be read by this doubtful light. Sixteenth-century writing in Irish has been interpreted as the expression of a new and strident nationalism, to take one example. Nicholas Canny has argued convincingly that this view is misconceived, demonstrating that the poetic loyalties of the period were personal and local rather than national, seeking to uphold the dynastic ambitions of a patron rather than the cause of country.[22] Extreme colonialist representations of a pre-colonial past as bloody stasis, a tract of time without history or civility dominated by the 'wild Irish', can now be seen as obvious distortions. But nationalist tunnel-vision can be just as misleading. Distorted historical perspectives arise out of and reinforce sectarian, selective cultural traditions which obscure other, rival modes of relationship with the past and encourage the neglect of particular cultural treasures.

For traditions and continuities, however partisan and ahistorical, to be at least imaginable and negotiable there must be some underlying constant, some reliable vehicle of tradition. In the case of literature, language and genre seem to be the most promising possibilities. But the promise can be treacherous. Hans-Georg Gadamer insists that the mode of being of tradition is language, that language is the medium through which the texts or components of tradition are understood *as* a tradition.[23] But it may not always be the same language, and crossing language barriers can put the continuities of tradition under considerable strain even while the effective discontinuity stimulates the fabrication of encompassing tradition. The literature of a given area may have been expressed through different linguistic traditions: in Ireland Gaelic, Latin, Old Norse, Norman-French and English writings have at different times articulated different aspects of the unfolding Irish experience. All need to be considered if 'Irish literature' in the fullest sense of the term is to be properly understood. Even within a single language apparent continuities may be specious: the currency of particular linguistic forms in localities where literary language later developed has to be inferred in the absence of written records, and early forms for which there is documentary evidence may have no direct descendants in modern usage. Angus Wilson's *Anglo-*

Saxon Attitudes is written in an English which is not in direct line of descent from the Anglo-Saxon of King Alfred. The Munster dialect of the seventeenth- and eighteenth-century lyric poetry rediscovered by the Celtic revivalists is not directly descended from the Old Irish of the eighth-century tales of Cuchulain in the Ulster Cycle. The English of medieval Ireland is discontinuous with the Irish English of Yeats and Joyce moulded by the speech of later English immigrants.[24] There is much to be said for basing notions of Irish tradition not on language but on responses to topography and geographical location on the extreme western periphery of Europe. The map of Ireland's physical features and Ireland's place on the map of Europe are possibly the only constants in Irish affairs.

The continuities of genre are even more undependable. J. C. Beckett observes, with some justice, that in the eighteenth century, English-language 'novels, poems and plays that were distinctly Irish in character' were not in demand with the Irish reading public.[25] On this basis Beckett proceeds to classify eighteenth-century Irish writing in English as part of English rather than Irish literature, postponing the beginnings of a distinct 'Anglo-Irish' literature until the nineteenth century.[26] But 'novels, poems and plays' represent a distinctly modern understanding of the nature and forms of 'literature'. In eighteenth-century Ireland the novel, only recently established in England, had not yet come into being as a vehicle for exploring Irish experience, but there were other literary forms current and popular in Ireland which did: historical and topographical works, poems about politics, people and places, religious writings addressing distinctively Irish concerns. The implied distinction between 'novels, poems and plays' and other less obviously imaginative forms of writing is not one that would necessarily have commended itself to readers of the seventeenth or eighteenth century in England or in Ireland.

Even today there is some disquiet about such sharp distinctions between imaginative and discursive writing. Northrop Frye made some attempt to elaborate a more flexible concept of 'literature', allowing for varying proportions of creative or 'fictional' and expository or 'thematic' elements in individual 'literary' works. Even so, he felt obliged to propose a separate rhetoric of 'non-literary' prose, represented, for example, by political pamphlets which somehow 'insulate and conduct the current of history',[27] no mean imaginative and literary feat in itself, one might have thought.

The more generous, old-fashioned category of 'polite letters', 'polite literature' or even 'polite learning' is much more helpful in any discussion of literary tradition. It embraces scholarship and the more sophisticated forms of history as well as poetry and more familiar literary modes. 'Polite letters' were familiar to Archbishop Ussher and Geoffrey Keating, Jonathan Swift and Roderic O'Flaherty. The identifying characteristics were not obviously 'fictional' or 'imaginative' substance, but elegance of style and intellectual refinement. The suggestions of privilege implied in the epithet 'polite', however obnoxious in a democratic age, are actually very appropriate to the Irish situation in epochs of restricted literacy when the capacity to manipulate literary language (often archaic and artificial) was probably a mark of privileged status as a scholar, a representative of the non-Celtic ruling class, a religious, or a poet or historian of the old aristocratic Gaelic order now in terminal decline.

If neither language nor genre nor 'literature' as we tend to understand it today offers much support for sustained continuities in Ireland, do topographical and geographical permanences contribute much of substance to Irish literary tradition? They do. Poems of place have survived from the earliest times. Ireland's geographical location close to the British mainland entails an enduring Irish-English (or Irish-British) dialectic, institutionalized by conquest, obsessively explored in literature. This polarity has been explored from the perspective of comparative literature by J. T. Leerssen in his important study *Mere Irish and Fíor-Ghael* (1986). But simple polarities are too simple for the tangles of the Irish experience and Irish writing. In any case, it is not so much demonstrable continuity as resented discontinuity that stimulates the tradition-seeking process. As Eric Hobsbawm has observed, 'where the old ways are alive, traditions need be neither revived nor invented.' Where the old ways are no more, men set to work to create an 'ancient past beyond effective continuity'.[28]

In Ireland at different time different kinds of discontinuity have been sensed, different sorts of old ways have lapsed, different traditions have been established or implied. There is no single Irish literary tradition unless it is the tradition of abrasive yet often mutually parasitic interaction of different traditions. The traditions can be multiplied endlessly, and any given tradition can from a different perspective be assimilated to or redefined in terms of other traditions. One broad distinction may be helpful. There are historically and sociologically distinct modes of Irishness, each of which can lay claim to or periodically invent a specific cultural tradition. There are also different modes of selecting a general Irish literary tradition.

The different modes of Irishness, broadly speaking, are the Celtic and usually Catholic Irish mode (the 'mere Irish' of Tudor colonial discourse), the English-descended, usually Protestant Irish (sometimes called 'Anglo-Irish' and inexactly assimilated to the colonial ruling class or 'Protestant Ascendancy') and the Scots-descended Irish Presbyterians, largely confined to Ulster, sometimes called 'Scots-Irish'. Without ever fusing completely, these different strains have constantly intermingled and regrouped through cultural assimilation, intermarriage, political alliance or shared resentment. Any given Irish writer tends to operate in terms of this untidy, sometimes tense, sometimes sympathetic interaction rather than with reference only to his inherited or chosen mode of Irishness.

The modes of selecting a general Irish tradition, which overlap unevenly with the modes of Irishness, are, roughly, the moderate nationalist mode, incorporating both English-language and Gaelic writing, the non-nationalist, sometimes internationalist mode, chiefly concerned with Irish works in the English language, and the extreme Celtic nationalist mode, ostensibly concerned only with the Irish language though most of its propagandists have written partly in English. Against, behind and through all of this there is the pressure and stimulus of London and the dominant English literary tradition.

The moderate nationalist view of Irish literature is the most familiar and the most influential.[29] It traces the Irish literary genius from pre-Christian Celtic origins in the Mythological Cycle and the Ulster Cycle through a series of occlusions and suppressions (usually attributable to England) into nineteenth-century rediscoveries and renewals culminating in the literary 'renaissance' associated with Yeats and Lady Gregory. Since this coincided with and demonstrably interacted with the final stages of a separatist nationalist movement, it could be argued that the early years of the present century witnessed a literature of national consciousness triumphantly inaugurating the modern era of cultural and political independence. Unfortunately, the late Victorian and Edwardian Anglo-Irish literary enterprise which self-consciously annexed itself to a selective version of Gaelic culture compounded of heroic myth, legendary history, seventeenth- and eighteenth-century lyric poetry and the oral traditions of the peasantry was never satisfactorily representative of the cultural interests and heritage of either the Anglo-Irish socio-economic elite or of the increasingly urbanized, English-speaking Irish people. Nor did it do justice to the range and variety of the Irish cultural past in which Irish writers in Latin and Norman-French as well as English and Gaelic had played a part. In any case, despite their romantic Celticism, Yeats and Lady Gregory and their associates were modern writers in English with interests that did not stop at the 'national question', however loosely defined. Much the same can be said of most Irish writers since their day.

From the outset the moderate nationalist perspective was open to attack from at least three different directions, corresponding approximately to the non-nationalist (and largely Anglo-Irish) standpoint, the extreme Celtic nationalist position and the often overlooked Scots-Irish point of view.

The non-nationalist attitude is well represented by Yeats' school-friend W. K. Magee, who wrote under the name of 'John Eglinton'. Resenting a Celticism which devalued the non-Celtic cultural past of Ireland, Eglinton objected to the limiting criterion of nationally self-conscious 'Irishness' as the mark of worthwhile Irish literature in English. 'Nature' itself should be the concern of this and all serious literature, he felt.[30] He also deplored Yeats' partisan disdain for the cosmopolitan Anglo-Irish intellectual and cultural achievement embodied in Trinity College, Dublin.[31]

In fact, the later Yeats repented of this a little, fashioning a distinguished pedigree for himself out of an eighteenth-century succession of Trinity men, Swift, Berkeley, Goldsmith and Burke rather than the Gaelic poets of the same period. A book on Berkeley to which Yeats contributed a preface[32] actually cites a later article by John Eglinton discussing the post-1920 tendency to extend the range of Irish literature backwards to include earlier writing in English. In this Eglinton registers the possibility that the true origins of modern Irish culture lie not in the remote Celtic past but in Norman Ireland, where Norman and indigenous elements fused as they did in England to provide the basis for a rich composite literary tradition.[33]

This Anglo-Irish attitude repudiates cultural nationalism. It is not necessarily anti-Celtic or Anglophile though it may contain traces of the colonist's self-justifying debunking of the cultural state of the nation before his own arrival. It is characteristically anti-isolationist, pluralist and pragmatic, seeing residence rather than race as the definition of Irishness. Eglinton resented the tendency of seventeenth- and eighteenth-century English governments to snub and over-rule the Anglo-Irish, saw himself as a 'Modern Irishman' rather than as an ineffectually hybridized Anglo-Irishman, and yet felt 'as a good European' that he could accept Ireland's connection with Great Britain.[34]

George Bernard Shaw, more pugnaciously, took a similar line, complaining of Macaulay's attempt to steal Swift from the Irish and present him to English literature because he was not a Celt. Addison, he pointed out, did not stain himself with woad but that did not prevent him being a Briton.[35] Exasperated by what he saw as an inward-looking romantic Celticism in the new Ireland of 1923, he opposed to Celtic racialism the internationalist perspectives made available to Ireland through the world-wide currency of the English language:

> Let all the romantic ladies be engaged compulsorily as actresses in a national theatre . . . Let the fisherman who strays on Lough Neagh's bank when the clear cold eve's declining be thrown into it. And then Ireland will have a chance at last.[36]

The whimsical Irish novelist James Stephens was even more caustic about narrow notions of Irishness as they emerged in 'national' literature. Bizarrely anticipating the death of the author announced by Roland Barthes nearly fifty years later, he suggested that 'All books should be anonymous . . . and should be known only by numbers' since they represent the communal effort and feeling of whichever community the nominal author belongs to by sympathy. But it emerges that he is referring only to prose and very bad poetry. For him true poetry is individual rather than communal. Irish poetry, however, in so far as it articulates the themes of Irish nationhood cherished by sections of the community, is anonymous and very bad indeed. He then cites the nineteenth-century poets in English who usually feature in moderate nationalist accounts of Irish literature and in books about the literary background to Yeats: Davis, Mangan and Ferguson.[37] Stephens is unfair to his poets but not necessarily to the partisan spirit which claimed them rather than the Earl of Roscommon or William Drennan the Ulster poet for the Irish literary tradition.

For the extreme nationalists, however, not even Davis, Mangan and Ferguson were acceptably Irish. English-language Celtic revivalism was for them an aesthetic diversion rather than a genuine national movement. D. P. Moran, the most acerbic champion of Irish Ireland, condemned Yeats and the Celtic revival as a glaring fraud perpetrated upon the credulous Irish people and dismissed English-language cultural patriots such as Thomas Davis as owing allegiance not to Ireland but to 'Anglo-Ireland.[38] The term 'Anglo-Irish', acceptable to moderate nationalists when connected with national sentiment, bristles with difficulties which do not escape the attention of the more exteme nationalists. It continues to cause embarrassment at the conferences of the International Association for the Study of Anglo-Irish Literature. It tends to imply a residual colonialism which most modern Irish writers would repudiate. The trouble is that it tacitly conflates a frequently resented social grouping, the old Anglo-Irish 'Protestant Ascendancy' as it came to be known in the late eighteenth century,[39] with the strain of Irish literature in English to which many of the 'ascendancy' contributed though in the company of Roman Catholics and northern Presbyterians and other Irishmen who did not regard themselves as Anglo-Irish or 'Ascendancy Protestants'. The extreme nationalist position was that the increasing use of English all over Ireland was the most insidious imperialism of all. Thoroughgoing cultural patriots such as Daniel Corkery and Douglas Hyde, later first President of Ireland, felt like Nehru and the Indian nationalists at the same period[40] that the cultural dominance of the English language was so overwhelming that the only hope was to 'de-Anglicize',[41] to develop a sense of identity based on 'native' or 'pre-colonial' language and culture. On this view all previous Irish writing in English could be dismissed wholesale as culturally adulterated or inauthentically Irish. Some of the great Irishmen of the past, such as Archbishop Ussher, biblical chronologist, Irish historian and Protestant prelate, were indicted for crimes against the Irish cultural nation.[42]

This austerely racialist cultural politics was discredited even in the early years of the new state when young writers such as Sean O'Faolain, Frank O'Connor and Liam O'Flaherty, all of them steeped in the native tradition, abandoned 'Irish' Ireland to write in English about the contemporary Irish experience, urban as well as rural, in a cosmopolitan literary perspective owing more to Maupassant and Turgenev than to the traditions of the Gaelic past. But the extreme nationalist stance served to unsettle naive English-language claims to all or part of the Irish literary tradition and to suggest there was another medium in which Irish tradition could continue and flourish.

Assailed for being too Irish or for not being Irish enough, the moderate nationalist view of Irish literature had at least the merit of moderation and flexibility. Yeats' romantic perceptions of an Irishness linking aristocrat and peasant but effectively excluding the Dublin streets can be extended by Joyce's townscapes and sympathetic penetration of the lower-middle-class world of Leopold Bloom of Dublin. Joyce might have been complexly ironic about romantic Ireland and Irish politics but he engaged imaginatively with them, and for moderate men that was a sufficient entitlement to Irishness. It is not easy to ignore Dublin, but it is all too easy for the Dublin-based critic fed on Joyce and Yeatsian dreams of rural Ireland, moderate man though he be, to play down or ignore the cultural significance of non-Yeatsian northern landscapes and Ireland's second city, Belfast. Long before the partition of Ireland the Presbyterian north tended to be excluded or to withdraw itself from the cultural map of Ireland. County Down farmers and Belfast linen-merchants often felt they had better things to do with their time than write, or even read, and Belfast as a seaport and industrial city of the nineteenth century could not compete culturally with Dublin, a university city and administrative capital since the seventeenth century. But Ulster participation in the political and literary campaigns of the United Irishmen and Young Ireland in the late eighteenth century and in the 1840s need not be forgotten because Edwardian Belfast was, by a majority, unsympathetic to Celtic Ireland and Home Rule. In the twentieth century the literary history of Ireland has become increasingly a tale of two cities but aggressive nationalist perceptions of the Irish literary tradition, savagely pilloried by the Ulster dramatist and biographer St John Ervine,[43] take no proper account of the non-nationalist, non-Anglo-Irish, non-Celtic, non-Catholic cultural perspectives of Ulster.

But in what sense can the prosperous Presbyterian-influenced north-east be seen as Irish at all, a contributor to 'Irish literature'? Non-Presbyterian Ulster writers such as William Carleton (from Co. Tyrone) or Louis MacNeice (from Carrickfergus, Co. Antrim) lose their regional identities in the larger identity of Dublin-centred 'Irish literature' while the Co. Tyrone verses and stories of the Rev. W. F. Marshall, a Presbyterian minister, or the Co. Down novels of Sam Hanna Bell, may seem closer to the English regionalism of William Barnes or Thomas Hardy than the rural romanticism of Patrick Pearse or Padraig Colum.

This neatly illustrates the insecure identity of contemporary Ulster, geographically Irish, politically British though not by universal consent, dominated by a factious Unionist majority which cannot identify fully with either mainland Britain or the old Anglo-Irish 'Protestant Ascendancy'. But this very insecurity has produced its own forms of tradition-seeking as a mode of asserting identity. Scots-descended Ulster Presbyterians are the largest grouping in a far from homogeneous and relatively recently consolidated 'Protestant community'.[44] Largely Unionist in the 1980s, but not necessarily so in the 1880s and still less in the 1780s, 'Ulster Scots' can sense as great a physical and moral separation from would-be liberal, secularist, multi-racial England as the most unreconstructed Irish nationalist. The implacable hostility to the recent Anglo-Irish agreement of both hard-line Unionists and Sinn Fein nationalists in a sense illustrates the point. If Irish national literature and sentiment have enshrined Cuchulain and heroic conflict, Presbyterian Ulster breathes the atmosphere of heroic moral intransigence. The covenanting tradition within Scots Presbyterianism, exported to Ulster in the seventeenth century, permitted a distinction between loyalty to the person of the monarch and acquiescence in the policies of his government.[45] This tradition was invoked by radical Presbyterian United Irishmen in the eighteenth century and in the anti-Home Rule Ulster League and Covenant of 1912 and has continued to be a mainstay of unionist sentiment. But what are its literary consequences, if any? To some extent they have been negative: political and religious suspicion of the attitudes of the Dublin *literati* has combined with the literary philistinism associated both with residual puritanism and with industrial materialism. It cannot be seriously maintained that there is a distinctive and continuous Ulster Unionist tradition in Irish literature. But is is clear that the distinctive, ambiguous heritage of partly Presbyterian Ulster, radical and conservative-Unionist by turns, represents a powerful stimulant and irritant to contemporary Irish writers such as John Hewitt, Tom Paulin and Seamus Heaney.

Heaney, born of Catholic stock in Co. Derry, Northern Ireland, has reflected wryly on his curious status as an Irish, not British, English poet. He has drawn inspiration from Wordsworth, Hopkins and Ted Hughes as well as from Celtic Ireland, but insists, reasonably, that English politics in Ireland exert no rights over the English lyric,[46] whatever Douglas Hyde and the extreme nationalists might have said.

In an open verse-letter to the editors of *The Penguin Book of Contemporary British Poetry* (1982), Heaney wittily articulates his embarrassment at being included in the anthology and so classified as a 'British' poet. Twice before, he says, his muse had acquiesced, but not this time: 'British, no, the name's not right.' The problem of identity is elegantly complicated by the fact that Heaney grew up in the Irish nationalist tradition in controversially 'British' Ulster. But Heaney is no naive cultural nationalist. He acknowledges his British audience and his British publisher (Faber). Playing with the imperial concept of literary culture developed by Faber's most famous director, T. S. Eliot, Heaney proposes a post-imperial 'new commonwealth of art'. He deftly embodies in his poem snatches of Eliot's *Waste Land* and a medieval English lyric already parodied by Ezra Pound, a Yeats allusion, Ulster dialect speech, references to Latin and Gaelic literature, and a bare mention of Michel Foucault, representative of the European intellectual left.[47] This virtuoso performance lays out the complex allegiances of the modern Irish writer: international modernism, the English lyric, regional speech, modern Irish literature in English, the classical tradition underpinning European literary culture, Gaelic tradition. Much of this could have been picked up in a good library anywhere from New England to New South Wales. But the point is that Heaney picked it up chiefly in the northern part of Ireland. Heaney now enjoys international acclaim, but he is acclaimed as an Irish poet.

It evades the issue to insist that Irish utterance can be compounded of so many voices only in the late twentieth century, in an internationalist atmosphere where literatures of all kind are not only current but subject to rigorous academic analysis and discussion. Irish utterance, Irish literary tradition, in so far as it exists as a single entity, has always been constituted out of a disturbingly rich plurality. But cultural politics, colonialist and nationalist, have conspired to obscure this richness and variety. It is only in the light of this generous complexity that modern Irish writing and the actualities and potentialities of the contemporary Irish experience, stricken and divided as it is, can be fully understood. The origins of modern Irish literary traditions and tradition-forming, Celtic, Anglo-Irish and Scots-Irish, go back to the seventeenth century when the Scots and Cromwell completed the plantations of Ireland.

CHAPTER 2

Seventeenth-century Beginnings:

Archbishop Ussher and the Earl of Roscommon

———

THE SEVENTEENTH century, and particularly the first half of the century, might seem too early or too late as a starting-point for an enquiry into the nature and operation of literary tradition in Ireland. Literary historians of English literature in Ireland usually prefer to start later. Seamus Deane in effect begins in 1690, Norman Jeffares in the early eighteenth century, Patrick Rafroidi in 1789 and Richard Fallis in the middle of the nineteenth century.[1] Some scholars have started earlier. David Cairns and Shaun Richards look to the sixteenth century and the discourses of colonialism reflected in Shakespeare and Spenser as a natural starting-point. St John D. Seymour, anxious to emphasize the Anglo-Irish contribution to Irish culture against the trend of particularist cultural nationalism in the 1920s, harks back to the thirteenth century.[2] The modern poet Thomas Kinsella, committed to poetry in the Irish language but aware of Latin and Norman-French as well as of English elements in a complex, fragmented yet enduring tradition, begins his *New Oxford Book of Irish Verse* (1986) in the sixth century and includes English poems from the fourteenth century onwards.

But culturally as well as politically it is really the seventeenth century that establishes the pattern for modern Ireland and inaugurates the tradition-seeking process. Protestant Unionism and Catholic Nationalism alike have seventeenth-century roots.[3] Lloyd George

PLATE I Thomas Ryan, *The Flight of the Earls*

noted with exasperation that De Valera kept dragging him back to Cromwell when he wanted to discuss contemporary Ireland.[4] Even before Cromwell the pattern was set. The last resistance to the Tudor conquest of Ireland ended with the surrender of Hugh O'Neill on 30 March 1603, six days after the death of Queen Elizabeth I. Modern Irish cultural history effectively begins soon after, with the literary consequences of the 'Flight of the Earls' in 1607, when Hugh O'Neill and Rory O'Donnell, Earls of Tyrone and Tyrconnell, took ship for the continent. Further rebellion was futile: their traditional authority was at an end. Their departure marked the end of the aristocratic Gaelic social order in its last outpost, the wild north of Ireland, and facilitated the systematic 'plantation' of Ulster with English and Scottish settlers, in a sense completing the colonizing process inaugurated by the Normans. This brought gains and losses.

The losses are part of the patriotic legend of Ireland and so have had more attention than any possible gains. Romantic Irishmen lament the collapse of the old patronage system, the eclipse of the bards, the dispossession and dispersal of the hereditary learned families, the inability of the indigenous Gaelic culture to assimilate religiously alien New English and Scots as it had previously at least partly assimilated Vikings and Normans.

The disregarded positive consequences could be said to be enriched cultural awareness conveyed through the aggressive and defensive articulation and consolidation of various overlapping ideas of Irish tradition and identity, developed by colonists and natives, Protestants and Catholics. This was made possible by a sense of historical and cultural crisis and an interval of comparative peace, until 1641, almost unprecedented in recent Irish history.

Despite the dramatic abruptness of the Flight of the Earls things did not change overnight. The Gaelic scholar Aodh De Blácam has even claimed that 'The seventeenth century was the most brilliant, the most copious, and the most tragic century in the history of Irish letters.'[5] The eventual decline of the Gaelic culture associated with the old social order was slow and lingering and the process itself generated an indignation and an elegiac wistfulness which led to some of the finest lyric poems in the entire Gaelic tradition.[6] The corresponding rise of Ireland's modern English (and Scottish)-influenced culture was equally gradual. Anglophone and Gaelic Irishmen did not live in total cultural isolation from each other, as has sometimes been assumed. At least some of the surviving Gaelic scholars found interested English patrons. Throughout the seventeenth century and well into the eighteenth, the two cultures coexisted in intermittently abrasive but mutually energizing relationship. Irish cultural nationalists and English literary historians alike have failed to notice, partly because they have rather neglected the scholarly discourse, mainly historical and theological, within which much of this interaction took place. Many of the books were in Latin, the common tongue of European learning, some were published abroad and are now hard to come by, and some existed only in manuscript.

Access to such works was never easy. Writing in all the languages of Ireland had always been vulnerable to the endemic hazards of war, civil disturbance and social dislocation. The printing press should have made a difference, ensuring multiple copies, but printing did not come to Ireland until 1550 and even then it served only English and Protestant interests. The first Irish-printed book in the Irish language, a Protestant catechism, was published in Dublin in 1571. There was no printing outside Dublin until the 1640s, and no printing at all in Ulster until 1694.[7] In consequence there are few Irish-printed books until well into the seventeenth century. Manuscript collections in the keeping of great nobles or learned families such as the Mac Firbhisighs, hereditary custodians of the Great Book of Lecan, were seriously at risk in times of political upheaval and dispossession.[8] By the end of the sixteenth century, many valuable manuscripts had been destroyed.

It was to guard against further loss as well as to secure particular religious or political ends that new manuscript collections and printed compendia or digests of older materials were compiled in the seventeenth century. Ancient, medieval and sixteenth-century Irish writing, in Irish, Latin and English, was made more accessible and gathered into coherent patterns, the beginnings of usable traditions. Immemorial legends of Finn and Oisin were preserved in *Duanaire Finn*, an anthology of poems dating back to the fourteenth century compiled from manuscript sources at Louvain and Ostend in 1626–7.[9] The twelfth–century Latin works of Giraldus Cambrensis, the *Topographia Hibernica* and the *Expugnatio Hibernica*, considering Ireland from the uncomplimentary perspective of a well-born Welsh ecclesiastic who accompanied Prince John to Ireland, could now be seen as the inauguration of a continuing colonial discourse. Richard Stanihurst had made considerable use of these writings in his own work in the sixteenth century. Now they were conveniently incorporated into William Camden's massive *Anglica, Hibernica, Normannica, Cambrica, a Veteribus Scripta* (1602), a work which brought together different strands of an allegedly British rather than merely English past. Sir James Ware, Irish auditor-general under Strafford, gathered together earlier English accounts of Ireland in his *History of Ireland* (1633). He also commissioned transcripts of English and Irish manuscripts to facilitate his own researches into Irish church history and antiquities, leading eventually to works such as *De Hibernia et Antiquitatibus ejus Disquisitiones* (1654).

The revival of interest in Giraldus Cambrensis and the emergence of an English tradition of writing about Ireland provoked a predictable Irish reaction. Séathrún Céitinn (Geoffrey Keating) produced his *Fora Feasa ar Éirinn* ('Basis of Knowledge about Ireland', more usually rendered 'History of Ireland') in 1629–34. Keating made a distinction between the 'Sean Ghaill', the old foreigners or Normans, from whom he was in fact descended, and the 'Nua Ghaill' or new foreigners, the new English of the sixteenth and seventeenth centuries. He observed of the latter, 'Every one of the new Galls who writes on Ireland writes . . . in imitation of Cambrensis who is as the bull of the herd for them for writing the false history of Ireland.'[10]

Keating took issue with English-centred works, such as Spenser's *View of the Present State of Ireland* (1596), Richard Stanihurst's *Description of Ireland* (1577), Meredith Hanmer's *Chronicle of Ireland* (just published in Ware's *History of Ireland*) and Fynes Moryson's *Itinerary* (1617). But Keating was able to make good use of the recent work of non-Gaelic scholars such as Ware and James Ussher, Protestant Archbishop of Armagh. He also alluded to the philological speculations, published in Latin, of European polymaths such as J. G. Becanus, author of *Origines Antwerpiae* (1569), which belonged with the international community of learning in which planter and Gael both participated.[11]

Keating's work was perhaps the last important historical work to circulate only in manuscript: it was not printed in full until the Celtic Revival took the matter in hand with the Irish Texts Society edition of 1902–14. But from the outset it was of interest to Anglophone Irishmen as well as to native speakers. An English translation was published in 1723, ostensibly by Dermot O'Connor though there are grounds for ascribing the project to the notorious Donegal deist and learned adventurer, John Toland.[12] Before this there were seventeenth-century manuscript translations, including a Latin one by John Lynch, sometime Roman Catholic archdeacon of Tuam, completed at St Malo some time before 1674. There was an English version owned since before March 1689/90 by Sir Robert Southwell,

Secretary of State for Ireland. Another translation was apparently made by Timothy Roe O'Connor for Lord Orrery about 1668.[13] Though this version seemed to have disappeared it is at least possible that it has survived unidentified in Archbishop Marsh's library in Dublin. The manuscript translation *A Defence of the True History of Ireland . . . by Jeffery Keating* preserved there certainly bears no resemblance to Dermot O'Connor's published text.[14]

As well as translating Keating, John Lynch was engaged on his own account in refuting Giraldus Cambrensis and patriotically celebrating the ancient dignity of the indigenous language and culture against English detractors. His Latin treatise *Cambrensis Eversus* (1662), dedicated to Charles II, professes loyalty to the Stuart kings of Ireland while criticizing Giraldus and Stanihurst as Keating had done. But Lynch can also quote Stanihurst with approval and he makes use of Ware and other non-Gaelic sources. Sir John Davies' *A Discoverie of the True Causes why Ireland was never Entirely Subdued* (1612) is cited as an historical authority and (highly selective) use is made of Spenser's *View of the Present State of Ireland* to substantiate Lynch's commendations of the old Gaelic poets.[15] Lynch was a friend of the historian Roderic O'Flaherty, and O'Flaherty's Latin treatise *Ogygia* (1685), dedicated to James, Duke of York, soon to be James II, draws on *Cambrensis Eversus* as well as other Latin, English and Irish sources to vindicate the antiquity of Ireland and the title of the Stuart dynasty to the throne of Ireland in virtue of their ultimate descent from the Gaelic kings of Munster.[16]

The royalist aspect of *Cambrensis Eversus* and *Ogygia* had been anticipated in the *Annals of the Four Masters* (1632–6), more correctly the *Annals of the Kingdom of Ireland (Annála Ríoghachta Éireann)*. This work set out to record the history of the kingdom of Ireland from early times down to 1616. John O'Donovan's epoch-making edition and translation (1848–51) amounted to a rescue operation on fast-fading Gaelic tradition and legend stretching back to pre-Christian times.[17] But the same could be said of the original compilation, drawn from scattered sources. It is in effect a massive collection and digest of old chronicles. The work was undertaken by a team of scholars directed by Michael Ó Clérigh, an Irish Franciscan at St Anthony's College, Louvain, though he had been sent back to Ireland to collect manuscript materials for various historical and hagiographical projects. Ó Clérigh, a Donegal man, came from one of the old learned families, hereditary chroniclers to the O'Donnells. St Anthony's had been founded in 1606 by Florence Conroy, from the learned family of

Ó Maelconaire, and from the beginning the friars included men from bardic families, some of them of bardic training, who endeavoured to preserve and consolidate the traditions of Celtic and Catholic Ireland and promote the work of the Irish Counter-Reformation in response to aggressively Protestant English rule.[18] The *Annals of the Four Masters* mingles biblical history with traditions of national origins, but this is not sectarian propaganda. In the seventeenth century all Christendom bowed to the authority of the biblical record and this logically entailed acceptance of national descent from one of the sons of Noah. The *Annals* begin with Noah's flood and the legend of Noah's grand-daughter coming to Ireland. The earliest section in effect turns the legendary matter of the old *Leabhar Gabhála* or *Book of Invasions* into annalistic form.[19] But legend gradually yields to reliable history. The annalistic method and the titular emphasis on the kingdom of Ireland posit a seamless continuity and essential unity of Irish history and tradition from earliest times, asserted against the threatened dislocations of an insecure present.

This work, and Ó Clérigh's manuscript collections, as well as Ware's published researches, provided a solid basis for other historical projects at Louvain. Among the most distinguished were John Colgan's *Acta Sanctorum Veteris et Majoris Scotiae seu Hibernicae* (Louvain, 1645) and his lives of the principal Irish saints, Patrick, Brigid and Columba, published as *Trias Thaumaturga* (Louvain, 1647). Colgan's cumbersome description of Ireland as the 'ancient and greater Scotia' reflects a controversy which had been rumbling since the 1620s. It could be argued that the true source of modern Irish cultural nationalism is not the romantic antiquarianism of the nineteenth or eighteenth centuries, nor even the Irish counter-reformation of the seventeenth, but the profound irritation generated by the reckless Scottish chauvinism of Thomas Dempster. A colourful and quarrelsome Catholic polymath and adventurer who taught humanities and law in various places in the Low Countries, France and Italy, Dempster exploited the notorious ambiguity of the Latin term 'Scotus', which usually but not invariably means 'Irish' rather than 'Scots' in ancient and medieval texts. Arguing that if it could mean 'Scots' then it did, Dempster made extravagant claims for the Scottish contribution to the history of European letters and the Church. In *Nomenclatura Scotorum Scriptorum* (1620), *Scotia Illustrior* (1620) (placed on the Index) and the posthumous *Historia Ecclesiastica Gentis Scottorum* (1627) Dempster and his assistants amassed enormous quantities of misinformation about nearly 1300 people of arguably Scottish antecedents, including England's Alcuin and Boadicea, a Cypriot, a Frisian, at least one Frenchman, several Italians, many Irishmen and a few 'ghosts' who never actually existed.[20]

Among Dempster's worst offences from an Irish Franciscan point of view were depriving Ireland of the honour of nurturing the Franciscan philosopher Duns Scotus, the famous 'subtle doctor', and claiming that the ninth-century neo-Platonist theologian, Johannes Scotus Erigena, was another Scot.[21] Modern scholarship suggests Dempster was right about Duns Scotus and wrong about Erigena, but the Irish were unwilling to give up the subtle doctor. The great Irish Franciscan historian Luke Wadding, founder of St Isidore's in Rome, the other important Irish Franciscan college on the continent, defiantly edited the works of Duns Scotus in sixteen volumes.[22] His labours encouraged, and were encouraged by, his fellow countrymen such as David Rothe, Catholic Bishop of Ossory, who patriotically challenged Dempster's contentions. As Rothe observed in 1631, in a letter to Wadding, 'Dempster's insolencie with his nameless crue did whetten somwhat to make a discovery of their errors with a recovery of our ancient renowne acquired by the sweat of our ancestors.'[23]

Rothe had already challenged the insolent Dempster in his powerfully rhetorical polemic *Hibernia Resurgens,* published in Rouen in 1621. This alluded to the serpent in the garden of Eden in the biblical epigraph on the title-page and denounced Dempster's work as the venom of the old serpent while vindicating the Irishness of the Irish saints. After 300 pages of abuse and historical argument, Rothe concludes that Ireland will rise above Dempster's calumnies and piously prays for his greater temperance, faith, honesty and common sense.[24]

There were other replies to Dempster, including an anonymous vindication of Ireland as the older Scotia, published in Antwerp in 1621. In the course of a detailed discussion of the vexed question of nomenclature, the author concludes that his contention that Ireland was originally called Scotia is common ground with 'every kind of author, sacred and secular, ancient and modern, at home and abroad, Catholic and heretic' (or Protestant).[25] This large claim is supported not only in the learned investigations of the Protestant Archbishop Ussher but in the work of his protégé Sir James Ware. One of the earliest poems praising Ireland was written in Latin by the Irishman St Donatus of Fiesole, ninth-century scholar, teacher and biographer of St Brigid. One of the main sources of bibliographical information about Donatus is in fact Dempster's *Historia Ecclesiastica*. Sir James Ware's encyclopaedia of Irish writers, *De Scriptoribus Hiberniae* (Dublin, 1639), the first work of modern Irish literary history, makes use of Dempster's material while firmly classifying Donatus as an Irish, not a Scottish writer. A little later the Franciscan John Colgan quotes Donatus' poem twice in his *Trias Thaumaturga*, prefixing it to the Life of St Brigid and pointing out that Donatus' reference to the absence of snakes in Scotia proves that Scotia must be Ireland.[26]

The politics of Irish antiquarianism need to be discussed with caution. There is a continuous antiquarian discourse from Ware to the Celtic Revival but the accompanying enthusiasms for the country or the nation of Ireland do not have the same continuity. Eighteenth-century patriotism is not the same as nineteenth-century nationalism, as J. T. Leerssen has shown in his studies of antiquarian research in both periods.[27] In the seventeenth century the simple claim to be Irish could provoke storms of protest from different kinds of Irishmen or Irish residents. Keating's distinction between the old and the new foreigners, or Luke Wadding's distinguishing among the old Irish, the mixed Irish (or old English) and the Anglo-Irish (or recent English settlers) point to embittered divisions, even within Irish Catholicism, though writers from every grouping had contributed to Irish historical discourse.[28] The entire Anglo-Irish family had been ferociously denounced to the Congregation of Propaganda in Rome in 1659 for tolerating Protestant heresy under Elizabeth and for ruining the cause of Catholic Ireland by temporizing conduct during the 1641 rebellion. 'Anglo-Irish' in this case turns out to mean 'of English descent', however remote. John Lynch's polished and dignified reply, *Alithinologia*, defended Anglo-Irishness as a valid way of being Irish. He accepted the reality of bitter differences in Ireland but suggested that these could be differences within the same family. His epigraph condenses two verses from the Psalms: the Latin could be translated 'You were speaking against your brother; you were slandering your own mother's son. I will rebuke you and settle matters before you.'[29]

Beneath all the divisions, however, whether regarded as fraternal strife or racial animosity, there ran a common interest in the geographical and historical circumstances of Ireland and in the traditions of Irish learning.. Among the manuscripts in the library of Trinity College, Dublin are genealogical notes on Irish kings extracted 'out of an Irish booke' owned by 'Tho: Stafford eq.'. This was the Sir Thomas Stafford, secretary to Sir George Carew, who wrote or was credited with *Pacata Hibernia* (1625), a detailed account of the

Elizabethan Irish wars especially in Munster under Carew's presidency.[30] Collecting and studying Irish books and manuscripts and discussing them with others of possibly different backgrounds was a way of bridging differences and establishing some kind of Irish identity.

Sometimes affinities underlying apparent cultural differences could be found in the manuscripts themselves. A few Irish medieval texts in English and Norman French have survived, some collected in the volume once owned by George Wise, mayor of Waterford in 1571. This is now in the British Library as MS Harley 913.[31] The contents include *The Land of Cokaygne,* a lively satirical poem probably written by a Goliard or disrespectful wandering scholar. It is about a tranquil and opulent glutton's paradise far out in the sea west of Spain. The theme is European, represented, for instance, in Pieter Brueghel's painting *Luilekkerland* (1567), now in Munich. French and Dutch analogues have been noted.[32] But like the thirteenth-century Irish prose satire *Aislinge Mac Conglinne* ('The Vision of Mac Conglinne'), which may even be a direct source, the poem burlesques the ancient Irish other-world visions deriving from the mythological cycle and the later fantastic island-paradises reported in voyage-narratives (Immrama) such as *The Voyage of Bran, Son of Febal.* These medieval Anglo-Irish connections have never been systematically explored.[33]

Other items in the same manuscript include the Norman-French poem *The Entrenchment of New Ross,* and a song about the redoubtable Sir Piers de Birmingham. These were transcribed for Sir James Ware in the seventeenth century. The manuscript volume containing the transcripts was in the possession of Henry, Earl of Clarendon, Viceroy of Ireland, in 1697. It is now among the Lansdowne manuscripts in the British Library.[34]

The already complex literary tradition indicated by surviving manuscripts and published works in Irish, English and Latin was first charted in Sir James Ware's *De Scriptoribus Hiberniae.* Ware made a distinction between writers born in Ireland and writers who had made some later contact with the place but generously classified both as writers of Ireland. This compilation in effect attempted a sort of cultural legitimation of the English in Ireland by assimilating their writings to a partly purpose-built, pluralist Irish literary tradition. But such an enterprise had practical utility and influence. Two hundred years later Walter Harris's augmented English version, *The Writers of Ireland* (Dublin, 1746), was invaluable to Thomas D'Arcy McGee in the writing of his *Irish Writers of the Seventeenth Century* (Dublin, 1846), a work designed to heal national divisions stemming from the seventeenth century. Ware's book was not the only one of its kind. Dubhaltach Mac Firbhisigh, last survivor of the learned family who had been hereditary historians to the Ó Dubhda, compiled an unfinished and unpublished treatise, *Ughdair na h-Erend* ('The Authors of Ireland') (1656).[35] This can be seen as a defensive and protective consolidation of an already vulnerable and vanishing native tradition. But it was prepared in an atmosphere of collaboration with rather than isolation from the English in Ireland. Mac Firbhisigh almost certainly knew of Ware's work and may have made use of it since he was working closely with Ware from 1655 to 1666, assisting in the work of transcribing and translating Irish manuscripts. It is likely that he was also in contact with Archbishop Ussher and his antiquarian researches since the Great Book of Lecan, once owned by the Mac Firbhisighs, is known to have been in Ussher's keeping at a time when Dubhaltach Mac Firbhisigh made considerable use of it.[36]

Seventeenth-century Irishmen and others concerned with Ireland were also brought together despite religious and political differences by questions of language. All over Europe in the seventeenth century the gradual eclipse of Latin as the common tongue of scholars, churchmen and diplomats gave rise to a new interest in the nature of vernacular languages. It also stimulated attempts to invent, or perhaps reconstruct from antiquity, some alternative universal language. The potential tension between these impulses was reflected in Ireland. The establishment of an Irish printing-press at Louvain encouraged devotional writing in the Irish language such as *Scáthán Shacramuinte na haithridhe* ('The Mirror of the Sacrament of Penance') (Louvain, 1619) by Aodh Mac Caghwell or Mac Aingil. To assist unlearned Irish readers with the bewilderingly rich vocabulary of the language, Michael Ó Clérigh, principal author of the *Annals of the Four Masters,* compiled the first published Irish glossary, *Foclóir no Sanassan Nua* (Louvain, 1643). An Irish Grammar, which circulated in manuscript, was prepared by Cornelius Flagerty, Lector to the Irish College in Rome, in 1653.[37] A little later Francis Molloy, a Franciscan at St Isidore's College, published his *Grammatica Latino-Hibernica* (Rome, 1677). Richard Plunket had meanwhile completed the first Irish–Latin Dictionary at Trim in 1662, a work which assisted the pioneering Celtic researches of the Welsh antiquarian Edward Lhuyd.[38]

Serious philological investigation of the Irish language seems to have begun with the researches of Richard Creagh, a politically turbulent Catholic Archbishop of Armagh who was arraigned for treason and died in the Tower of London in 1585, not without suspicion of poisoning. His treatise *De Lingua Hibernica* has not survived, though a brief Latin summary of the contents of twenty chapters has been preserved in a seventeenth-century manuscript.[39] But the propagandist David Rothe had had access to the complete work in 1631 and wrote to Luke Wadding, 'I have the *authographum* of the blessed martyr primat Craegh [sic] his history and etymologicall deduction of our Irish languadge oute of the Hebrewe etc, which I doe much valye, as being the worke of so worthy a man.'[40] The alleged connections with Hebrew were also mentioned by Richard Stanihurst, a Dubliner of ultimately English descent, in *De Rebus in Hibernia Gestis* (Antwerp, 1584). John Lynch noticed this and quoted the passage in *Cambrensis Eversus*: 'the Irish . . . is, in fine, connected with the Hebrew language by a common bond of affinity.' Lynch himself claimed the authority of the great Renaissance scholar Joseph Scaliger for the view that Irish was one of the eleven original languages of Europe.[41]

Patriotic pride in the antiquity of the Irish language and an apparently perverse determination to demonstrate connections with Hebrew can be traced through the long evolution of European comparative philology.[42] The enthusiasm survived into the nineteenth century: Francis Crawford was contributing papers to the *Proceedings of the Royal Irish Academy* on 'Hebraeo-Celtic Affinities' in 1849 and 1850.[43] Scaliger's posthumously published *De Europaeorum Linguis* (1610) had stimulated philological enquiries which were often motivated by national pride rather than scholarly objectivity. Improbable connections between Hebrew and various European vernaculars were pursued by enthusiasts not simply because Hebrew was the sacred language of the Old Testament but because St Jerome had authoritatively stated that Hebrew was Adam's tongue, the original language of all mankind before the confusion of tongues at the tower of Babel. Dante in *De Vulgari Eloquentia* had accepted St Jerome's view but resisted the temptation to make extravagant claims for the primacy of the Italian vernaculars.[44] In the seventeenth century other commentators were less restrained. Adrianus Scrieckus, for example, tried to flatter the peoples of the Low Countries by proving to his own satisfaction that in antiquity Gauls, Celts and Teutons were all different names for the same Celtic people whose language differed from Hebrew only as one dialect might differ from another.[45]

It was probably in order to challenge romantically patriotic philology associated with incipiently anti-English myths of origin that Sir James Ware tried to insist that there was scholarly agreement that the earliest Irish language was Britannic, introduced by British colonists. He did admit, however, that there was no conclusive proof.[46] The political resentment, confusion, inefficiency and mutual incomprehension generated by earlier English hostility to the Irish language and by brutal attempts to impose an Anglophone administration upon a largely Irish-speaking population had come to be recognized before the end of the sixteenth century. Both Protestant and Catholic Churches became aware of the need to maintain contact with the people through the medium of Irish. In 1595 Henry Ussher, uncle of the more famous James Ussher discussed later in this chapter, was recommended for the position of Archbishop of Armagh because he was 'very perfect in the Irish language'. In 1626 Luke Wadding urged the appointment of an Irish-speaking Roman Catholic Primate, instead of an Anglophone Anglo-Irishman who would be unable to cope convincingly with Irish-speaking clergy and would be more likely to abscond to the heretics (Protestants).[47] Queen Elizabeth expressed an interest in the Irish language and commissioned an Irish New Testament, published in 1603. The scholarly William Bedell, brought to Ireland by James Ussher and promoted to be Bishop of Kilmore, initiated a translation of the Old Testament into Irish eventually completed after many delays in 1685.

But Bedell had more radical projects for healing partly linguistic divisions and restoring the religious harmony of mankind which seemed to have been lost at Babel. Why not devise a new common language which would circumvent petty differences and directly express universal realities? Was there, could there be, such a thing as a 'natural' language which could restore, or procure, an intimate relationship between words and things? There were many universal language schemes in seventeenth-century Europe, some of them scientific, rationalist projects associated with the new Royal Society in England. One of the most important was John Wilkins' long-meditated *Essay towards a Real Character and a Philosophical Language* (1668), intended to assist the 'general good of mankind'. But there was a more mystical tradition, associated with the German sage Jacob Boehme, stretching back into the Middle Ages and drawing on Cabbalism and Raymond Lull's systematizing of all knowledge in terms of a universal symbolized set of divine attributes or perfections.[48] Wilkins was rather contemptuous of this tradition, but Bedell was more sympathetic. He was in contact with the religous and educational ideas of the Moravian bishop Johann Amos Komensky, better known as Comenius, which had been influenced by the mystical tradition, and he shared Comenius' vision of a universal language as 'the universal carrier of light', instrumental in renewing contact with the divine harmony of the universe and reconciling men in religious peace.[49]

Bedell was associated with Comenius' London-based disciple and popularizer Samuel Hartlib, a friend of John Milton, and through Hartlib both Bedell and Ussher contributed to the expenses of another British Comenian, John Dury, a kind of roving ambassador for European Protestant unity.[50] Hartlib had links with other Irishmen, including the Dublin scientist Gerald Boate, one of Ussher's protégés, and saw Boate's *Irelands Naturall History* (1653) through the press.[51] While the cohesion and importance of the so-called Irish Hartlib circle has been called in question,[52] it is clear that Hartlib knew about Bedell's 'universal character' project and encouraged it, trying hard to get it printed. The actual detailed work was undertaken at Bedell's instigation and to his specification by a Rev. Mr Johnston, tentatively identified as Rev. John Johnston, Fellow of Trinity College and skilful engineer and architect who had supervised major building works for the Earl of Strafford.[53]

The ultimate fate of Bedell's and Johnston's scheme, to be called *Wit-Spell*, was disconcerting. The work was virtually complete and plates had been engraved when the 1641 Rebellion broke out. In the ensuing confusion it seems that the manuscript fell into the hands of Franciscan friars who suspected heresy in a scheme to reverse the confusions of Babel and tore it up. The plates were used by tinkers to mend kettles. A rough draft of an early version survived and was brought to Oxford by Johnston's widow about 1650, but it attracted little interest there[54]

The destruction of the manuscript of *Wit-Spell*, all the more poignant because Bedell was on genial terms with the friars in his neighbourhood and worked hard for the Irish-speaking community in his diocese, seems to signal the end of an era. From this point, inter-communal understanding deteriorated sharply and whatever shared concerns and common discourse there might have been in Irish letters collapsed amid the horrors of civil war. The horrors of 1641, real and imagined, encouraged settlers to expect the worst from the native Irish during the Williamite wars (quite needlessly) and contributed both to the fortitude with which the Siege of Derry was resisted and to the entrenched siege-mentality generated by insecurity which has characterized Ulster Protestant attitudes ever since.

But the Rebellion, the Cromwellian administration of Ireland, the Restoration and the Williamite wars had the effect of highlighting unexpected similarities as well as unbridgeable differences between the different modes of being Irish. Irish Presbyterians and Irish Catholics alike became more embattled and developed a much sharper sense of their distinctive identities. Presbyterianism was formally organized for the first time when Presbyterian chaplains arrived with General Munro's army in 1642. Irish Catholicism became a political and military cause in the 1640s, assisted with arms and money brought from Rome by the papal nuncio Rinuccini in 1645.

In the nineteenth century the liberal Presbyterian scholar Thomas Croskery was irritated by the use and abuse of seventeenth-century Irish history to inflame contemporary antagonisms. He noted the rival historiographical traditions, Catholic and Protestant, and observed how 'the events of 1641–2 have . . . had the effect of sustaining a most persistent hostility in the minds of a large class of Irish Protestants towards their Catholic countrymen.'[55] The remark is just, but also a little misleading. It collapses a bewilderingly complex problem of conflicting allegiances and divided communites into a simple polarity.[56] At least in the early stages of the rising rebel leaders made important distinctions between English and Scottish settlers. The Scots were in effect protected since the rebels had no quarrel with them. To begin with, selective action was taken only against English settlers, not with the intention of undoing the plantation or overthrowing the king's authority but at least nominally to uphold the king's authority and to frustrate anticipated radical changes in official English attitudes towards Catholics.[57]

The Scots of Ulster had their own curiously parallel dissatisfactions, not with the king but with the king's administration in Ireland. By 1630 they already numbered 4000 families or more.[58] They worshipped rather uneasily in Presbyterian form but within a loosely administered episcopalian structure of church government. Laudian-inspired attempts to tighten up ecclesiastical administration precipitated resentment and stimulated a sense of imperilled identity. By 1637 many of the Scottish ministers had been deprived of livings and returned to Scotland. When Charles I tried to impose the prayerbook on Scotland, the Scots banded together in a renewed National Covenant expressing loyalty to the king and determination to preserve true (or Presbyterian) religion. This covenant came to be seen as a contract between God and His people to which the king also was or ought to be a party. The Scots in Ulster naturally wished to share in the Covenant, but Thomas Wentworth the Lord Deputy tried to stop this by administering the notorious 'Black Oath' of 1639. This required everyone over sixteen to swear on the Gospels that he abjured the

Covenant. The measure was counterproductive: when the Solemn League and Convenant concluded between parliament and the Scots, an extension of earlier convenants, was administered to the army in Ulster in 1644, people from all over the country associated themselves with it in defence of their religion.[59]

One consequence of all this was interesting similarities between the rhetoric of seventeenth-century Irish Presbyterians and dispossessed Catholics. Insecurity and external challenge encouraged the Presbyterian covenanting ideal with its implicit identification with the Children of Israel, the wandering but covenanted people of the Old Testament. Insecurity also prompted Gaelic poets to make the same identification: the indignities of lost leaders, dispossession and exile could be transformed by assimilation to the plight of Israel in Egypt or in the wilderness of Sinai. The theme is almost a commonplace, illustrated in the Co. Down poet Fear Dorcha Ó Mealláin's 'An Díbirt go Connachta' ('Exodus to Connaught').[60]

The parallel sense among Presbyterians and Catholics of actual or impending persecution by the king's administration (or each other), coexisting with formal allegiance to the person of the king, established a curious pattern of similarity if not sympathy at the politico-religious margin, a pattern that persisted well into the nineteenth century. The execution of Charles I was welcomed by neither Presbyterians nor Catholics in Ireland since hopes of religious toleration had been vested in the king's person. This was a grave embarrassment to the new English republic: Irish Presbyterians and Catholics alike were quickly denounced by John Milton, no less, writing as an official propagandist. Like many subsequent English commentators on Ireland, Milton rather suggested that the different sorts of Irish were as bad as each other. Consistent with his distrust of old priests and new presbyters, he condemned Irish Catholicism as a manifestation of Antichrist and condemned Irish Presbyterians in the persons of the 'blockish Presbyters of Clandeboye' who had publicly condemned regicide for daring to intervene in secular matters.[61]

Every modern war is fought over again in print and the resentments engendered become the commonplaces of partisan discourse. Protestant episcopalians, Presbyterians and Catholics could all lament lost happiness from the middle of the seventeenth century. In a sense modern Irish literature began as it was to continue with a mingling of elegy and a sense of outrage. Sir John Temple's lurid and dismissively anti-Catholic work *The Irish Rebellion* (1646) invokes and perpetuates an uncharitable tradition by drawing on Giraldus Cambrensis' disparaging remarks about the 'native' Irish. His sensational narrative may have contributed to the grotesquely violent imagery of his son's protégé, Jonathan Swift.[62] But Temple also describes a golden age of English and Scottish settlement among the Irish with 'many thousands of men, women and children peacably setled and securely intermixed among them', only to be barbarously murdered or subjected to horrid cruelties when war broke out.[63] These cruelties, polemically exaggerated rather more than the peacefulness preceding them, were to provide a notional justification for the severity of Cromwell's proceedings in Ireland.

The same golden-age motif is present in Lord Anglesey's *Letter to the Earl of Castlehaven* (1681). This is both a Puritan, New-English response to Castlehaven's Catholic royalist *Memoirs of the Irish Wars* (1680) and a kind of trailer for his own rival *General History of Ireland,* never published and probably never completed. Anglesey recalls how, before the war, Ireland 'never enjoyed a more profound, and more like to be lasting Peace and Prosperity, Commerce and Trade . . . there never was more Unity, Friendship, and good Agreement, amongst all sorts and degrees.' He adds that he himself had lent most of his silver plate to entertain the Roman Catholic Bishop of Ferns during his visitation of the County of Wexford 'and had it honestly restored'.[64]

Presbyterians were different. They were unlikely to have any silver plate to lend, or to know many Catholics who might wish to borrow it. For them the golden age was not a co-operative past so much as a godly future to be achieved through earnest ministry. In the meantime, they too turned to writing Irish history as a necessary mode of legitimation in territories where they felt insecure. By the 1670s the Presbyterian Church in Ulster was in effect the main Church in the Scots-dominated areas, unobtrusively subsidized by a royal grant (the *regium donum*) first paid by Charles II in 1672. Against this background the Belfast minister Patrick Adair was commissioned to write *A True Narrative of the Rise and Progress of the Presbyterian Government in the North of Ireland,* controversially claiming effectively Presbyterian jurisdiction over part of Ireland under the king.[65] Like Thomas Witherow, a nineteenth-century historian of Irish Presbyterianism, Adair found a natural starting-point in 1623, the year that Robert Blair relinquished the teaching of moral philosophy at Glasgow University for the pastoral care of Bangor in Co. Down. Blair corresponded to someone like St Brigid in early Irish Presbyterian hagiography, hailed as 'a star of the first magnitude' by another Presbyterian writer in the seventeenth century.[66]

But Presbyterian history and tradition-formation faced special difficulties in Ireland. Roman Catholic and Gaelic Irishmen could easily demonstrate ancient continuities, freshly documented by the Louvain hagiographers or by Keating, and Protestant episcopalians could make a counter-claim of continuity with an ancient Irish and British Church independent of Rome. Documenting this claim was one of James Ussher's major scholarly projects. The Scots Presbyterians had to align themselves with a different kind of tradition, the tradition of missionary adventure. All they could look back to in Ireland itself was a brief period of practical toleration under Archbishop Ussher. The godly among them felt that they were confronted with an untamed wilderness, morally as well as geographically. Their justification for being in Ireland at all was that by disrupting rather than sustaining established continuities they might improve matters. Neither the native Irish nor the first Scottish planters, some of them outlaws and unscrupulous adventurers, showed much sign of true religion, they felt. As Adair put it, 'The case of the people throughout all the country was most lamentable, being drowned in ignorance, security, and sensuality, which was Mr Blair's great discouragement to settle in these parts.'[67] The only continuity was the God of Abraham and of Isaac and of Jacob, the God of a covenanted people who unexpectedly filled Blair's heart with 'sweet peace and extraordinary joy' on the road to Bangor so that he 'was forced to lie down upon the grass to rejoice in the Lord who was the same in Ireland as he was in Scotland'.[68]

The uncivilized ignorance and immorality alleged of Irish priests and English and Scots settlers ('the scum of both nations', according to a contemporary) prompted not nostalgia but prophecy and optimistic visions of a transformed and godly country. Official and episcopal disapproval of Presbyterian Church government and the persecution of individual Presbyterian prophets, mainly in Scotland, encouraged hopes for a better future free from bishops and tyrants. While the historian D. W. Miller has distinguished sharply between 'prophetic' and individualistic 'conversionist' strands in Irish Presbyterian history, seeing the latter predominating only in the nineteenth century,[69] the two cannot be altogether separated. The vision of a transformed and righteous (Presbyterian) nation implies the conversion to righteousness and civility of its individual citizens through Presbyterian ministry and preaching the gospel. Rev. John Livingston had ministered under difficulties in Killinchy, in Co Down, in 1630–2 before being obliged to return to Scotland. Persecution of Irish Presbyterians continued and effective ministry lapsed. When Livingston came back with General Munro's army in 1642 he noted a spiritual decline and falling from grace among individuals. He heard public expressions of grief from those who had been weak enough to abjure the Covenant by taking the Black Oath, and saw how

> many of those who had been civil before, were become many ways exceeding loose; yea, sundry who, as could be conceived, had true grace, were declined much in tenderness; so as it would seem the sword opens a gap, and makes every body worse than before, an inward plague coming from the outward.[70]

This mingling of outer and inner, the national-prophetic and the individualist-conversionist components of Presbyterianism, encouraged and reflected an ambivalent sense of identity. This became manifest not only in later ecclesiastical schism but in the apparently incompatible ideological stances of Presbyterian Irishmen, resisting and identifying with the political nation, Dissenters and beneficiaries of royal subsidy, rebels and king's men, liberals and conservatives, scholars and writers of imaginative historical vision and philistine fundamentalists. Prophetic and national Presbyterianism looked to the Old Testament God of history; conversionist Presbyterianism looked beyond history and public discontents to eternity, and so was often effectively conservative in social and political terms. The former attitude, more important for this period, can be illustrated from Presbyterian psalmody. Psalm 124, 'If it had not been the Lord who was on our side', was translated and adapted for congregational singing by the French Calvinist Theodore Beza for the *Genevan Psalter* in 1551. This version was translated into English to fit the same tune by William Whittingham, in *The Anglo-Genevan Psalter* (1561), and it was soon in regular use in Scottish and Irish Presbyterian worship, again to the same tune: 'Now Israel may say, and that truly'. More than four centuries later, it is still in use.[71]

For seventeenth-century Presbyterians, as for persecuted Catholics, there were saints and martyrs, unrepresentative extremists who nevertheless acquired a moral radiance within their particular tradition. The prophet and pastor Alexander Peden is a case in point, important in both Scotland and Ulster because he took refuge from Scottish religious persecution in the north of Ireland. Peden and other Scottish 'Covenanters' denounced their Irish brethren for their meekness under episcopacy and royal authority in the 1680s.[72] This may have planted or fertilized the seeds of militant disaffection which eventually grew and bore wild fruit among the Presbyterians who fought against England as United Irishmen in 1798.[73] Four years before the famous siege of Derry, Peden prophesied 'hunger, hunger in Derry, many a black and pale face shall be in thee', seeing this as a judgment on the 'formality and security of Ireland'. He looked forward to the time when *'Britain* and *Ireland* shall be overthrown with judgements, and drowned in blood' and the 'children of the persecuted captivity' would come into their own.[74]

Lurid prophecy apparently verified by the historical record was not a Presbyterian perquisite: it was part of Ireland's general popular culture, a function of her endlessly troubled history. It could be found in Gaelic tradition from the alleged prophecies of St Columcille and St Bercan anticipating the Vikings[75] to the nineteenth-century prophecy-men described in the fiction of William Carleton. While the scholarly Archbishop Ussher was properly sceptical of irrational and alarmist 'prophecy' and could offer a reasoned critique of extravagantly prophetic biblical exegesis,,[76] one of his own sermons was retrospectively deemed to have predicted the 1641 rebellion and the ultimate downfall of Rome. It was reprinted alongside other popular 'prophetic' writings down to the nineteenth century.[77]

Demoralized Catholics in Cromwellian Ireland might reasonably have turned either to golden-age nostalgia or to prophetic visions of ultimate triumph over the oppressor. There are traces of this in Catholic and Celtic discourse but what sometimes emerges is a strange mingling of the two modes, the rhetoric of heroic sacrifice with apocalyptic overtones. The words and deeds of Patrick Pearse, the best-known of the rebel-martyrs of Easter 1916, demonstrate the atavistic potency of this rhetoric. The best seventeenth-century example comes from Nicholas French, Roman Catholic Bishop of Ferns, who sees defeated (Catholic) Ireland as a sacrificial victim like Agamemnon's daughter Iphigenia: 'a noble ancient Catholic nation clad all in redd robes, not to bee now offered up as a victim; but already sacrific'd, not to a profane deity, but to the living God for holy religion.'[78]

The response of the Gaelic poets to political disaster of this magnitude has been explored by recent historians who have detected local and pragmatic poetic resentments and escapist responses rather than the incipient Celtic nationalism which has sometimes been alleged.[79] The rhetorical force of Gaelic idiom can confuse the issue. It is necessary to distinguish a conventionally exaggerated poetry of lamentation and regret for a lost poetic order from a formal manifesto for cultural separatism. Late Victorian and Edwardian

Celtic Revivalists sentimentally concluded that political adversity and dispossession confirmed and strengthened the splendid isolation and immaculate cultural purity of the Irish literary tradition, 'impregnable to the assaults of foreign literatures'.[80] This cultural myth seemed to be substantiated by a seventeenth-century lyric 'Milis an teanga an Ghaedhealg' ('Sweet is the Irish tongue'), unreliably attributed to Geoffrey Keating. The poet celebrates the rare beauties of the Irish language, free from the influence of Latin or Hebrew or the taint of any other language.[81] This pleasing fancy has not survived philological scrutiny. Scholars have argued for at least some Viking loanwords, particularly in relation to shipbuilding, and ecclesiastical and administrative influences have contributed traces of Latin, Norman-French and English to the Irish lexicon. The claim to splendid isolation has been successfully challenged for the Irish Middle Ages by scholars such as Robin Flower.[82] It is even harder to sustain for the seventeenth century. The issue can be debated on aesthetic as well as political grounds. What the cultural nationalist might regard as the adulteration of uncontaminated native tradition can also be seen as a species of enrichment. It can be argued that the old bardic tradition was actually aesthetically moribund and that the incursions of the 'new foreigners' and the collapse of traditional, aristocratic Gaelic society in a sense revitalized and eventually democratized Irish letters in Irish and in English. Reformation, Counter-Reformation and plantation were stimulants as well as irritants, fostering the European and British dimension of Irish tradition even while provoking enduring animosity.

Language and form as well as substantive literary content register the political disruptions of the epoch. The archaic Irish used in the *Annals of the Four Masters* (though not in Keating) was the medium of recondite traditional learning rather than of popular culture. The same could be said of the elaborate syllabic metres or *Dán Díreach* ('direct compositions' or 'poem structures') used by the old professional poets. From the end of the sixteenth century the popular accentual metre (*amhráin* or 'songs') used by humbler versifiers began to take over, so that a haughty aristocratic poet of the old school like Daibhi Ó Bruadair could both disparage the new verse as the work of 'street poets' and demonstrate his own mastery of it.[83]

Some of the more important political poems of the seventeenth century are written in the metre and speech of the people, the emerging idiom of a race deprived of aristocrats and traditional elites. Dialect forms and English loanwords abound. The terms 'transplantation' and 'Parliamentárians' tell their own story in *An Síogaí Romhánach* ('The Roman Sprite') (1650), an *aisling* or vision-poem. This describes how a beautiful maiden representing suffering Ireland appears to the poet in Rome as he lies on the tomb of the exiled princes Hugh O'Neill and Rory O'Donnell.[84] Back in Ireland the common people, the small tenants and labourers left without their traditional overlords, were not necessarily inconsolable. At least a few of them had begun to prosper on their own account as a result of confiscation and resettlement, particularly in Cromwellian times. The poets' aristocratic scorn for the base-born English-speaking *arrivistes,* whom they labelled 'Clan Thomas', is directed not just against Cromwellian settlers but against upwardly-mobile Irishmen who in a different political rhetoric might be deemed to have triumphantly cast off the shackles of feudalism. The aristocratic scholar-priest Brian Mac Giolla Phadraig was not impressed by the new social order:

> beggarwomen's sons with curling locks,
> white cuffs around their wrists, and fancy rings,
> like Ireland's one-time princes of Dal gCais.

They even smoked tobacco ('tobac'), word and thing a foul English importation.[85]

But effective condemnation calls for sound knowledge of the enemy and all his works, an element of participation in the same discourse. Directly or indirectly Ó Bruadair had had some contact with the English poet Samuel Butler's *Hudibras* (1663–80). Butler's anti-Cromwellian satire in a sense parallels Ó Bruadair's retrospective condemnation of Cromwellian military adventurers. In a poem written in 1690, Ó Bruadair generically labels the Cromwellians 'Ralph', after the name of Hudibras's clerk.[86] The traditional names of Deirdre and Eimhear, wife of Cuchulain, are juxtaposed for satirical purposes with 'Gammer Ruth' and 'goodman Cabbage' in another poem.[87]

The extended satire in verse and prose, *The Parliament of Clan Thomas*, is in Irish and about the Irish, but it too gestures towards wider horizons. It participates in the European tradition of estates satire and the English and European genre of quasi-parliamentary debate represented, for example, by Chaucer's *Parlement of Foules* and the *Senatulus* of Erasmus. It has connections with English pamphlets such as *Martin Mark-All, Beadle of Bridewell* (1610) as well as with the specifically Irish tradition of prose-burlesque.[88] The first and earlier part of the work includes a linguistically jumbled conversation between the young Englishman Roibín an Tobaca, a tobacco-seller, and Tomás an Trumpa (Thomas the parasite).

All of this points to an unacknowledged cultural pluralism, tentative and perhaps involuntary but not negligible. Ó Bruadair's despairing review of recent Irish history, *Suim Purgadóra bhfear nEireann 1641 – 1684* ('Summary of the Purgatory of the Men of Ireland') was an important poem. There are numerous early, possibly authorial, marginal annotations, mainly in English, in the surviving manuscripts, offering terse historical commentary and indicating a cross-cultural readership.[89] But as always in Ireland, cross-cultural adventure is likely to collide with narrow insularity. Ó Bruadair's moving lament for Elizabeth Aherne, sister of Sir Edward Fitzgerald, originally had nine stanzas of English followed by four of Irish. But in the only manuscript which has survived the eighteenth-century scribe, John Stock, took partisan exception to the English verses and left them out, apologizing for 'having soiled my book in the beginning with English'.[90]

English and Latin soiled or decorated many Irish-language books in the seventeenth century because these were the languages of the British and European cultural heritage in which the Irish tradition already creatively participated. The European tradition of satire against women stemming from St Jerome's polemic against Jovinian and represented in Chaucer's prologue to the *Wife of Bath's Tale* produced seventeenth-century English works such as *The Parliament of Women* (1640) and *The Parliament of Women, with the Merrie Lawes by them newly enacted* (1646). The same tradition led to the Irish *Párliament na mBan* ('Parliament of Women') (? 1670), which has obvious links with *The Parliament of Clan Thomas*. Latin elegiacs and Irish quatrains appear side by side in this work: all Europe knew how Adam, Sampson, Peter, David and Solomon were deceived by women and the famous names fitted the verse-forms of Latin and Irish equally well. They were, after all, part of what Ireland shared with the rest of Europe.[91]

Classical as well as biblical lore was the common currency of literary Europe, including England and Ireland. Caesar and Achilles, Agamemnon and Croesus, were part of a common heroic and legendary lexicon in the seventeenth century so it is not surprising to find such glittering names invoked in Sheaffraidh Uí Dhonnchadha's formal elegy for Maurice Fitzgerald.[92] The better-read Anglo–Irish gentry and some Scots-educated Presbyterian Irishmen had access to the same classical learning and the same courtly idiom as Irish poets such as Uí Dhonnchadha, though they may not always have realized it.

Seventeenth-century Irish letters reveal a pattern of cultural pluralism and tense cultural interaction coexisting with embattled cultural and political difference. Separate yet parallel and related traditions and identities begin to emerge. Some of the implications for later Irish writing can be traced in the life and work of Archbishop Ussher.

ARCHBISHOP USSHER (1585–1656)

James Ussher, Protestant Archbishop of Armagh and Lord Primate of Ireland, an important and controversial figure in his own time, is remembered today only for the splendid folly of dating the creation of the world at 4004 BC. His career as a churchman and man of learning has not been completely ignored by specialist historians but they have not enhanced his reputation.[93] The scholar respected by Gibbon and saluted by Dr Johnson as 'the great luminary of the Irish church' has recently been condemned as an intellectual reactionary.[94] The great Irishman admired by the Young Ireland radicals of the 1840s has been dismissed as the sworn enemy of the Irish language and the Irish people. This last indictment, resting on slender evidence which has been misinterpreted, has survived almost unchallenged ever since Douglas Hyde's Protestant and Anglo-Irish guilt-complex prompted his rash judgement that Ussher and his associates were anti-Irish bigots animated by 'strong social prejudice and race hatred'.[95] Modern Irish literary historians have virtually ignored him because he is not obviously relevant to the narrowly defined nineteenth- and twentieth-century narrative they pursue. Even an authoritative survey of 'Irish literature in Latin, 1550–1700' can spare only a paragraph for Ussher.[96] But Ussher is an interesting and distinguished figure in his own right. His massive learning, at once generous and partisan, his intellectual and ecclesiastical contacts with Scots Presbyterians, Oxford Anglicans, Irish Counter-Reformation historians and European humanists and his strained and ultimately unsuccessful attempt to serve both England and Ireland all make him the first significant embodiment of the complex affiliations and tensions which characterize modern Irish writing.

Ussher was born into an important and influential family, established in Ireland at least as long as the families of more accredited Irish writers such as Geoffrey Keating and John Lynch, of English descent like himself though still faithful to the old religion. But unlike the Keatings and the Lynches, the Usshers had stayed in the area of greatest English influence, and this made them sympathetically responsive to the new Protestantism of England. They had served English interests ever since Edward I appointed John le Ussher Constable of Dublin Castle in 1302. Ussher's father, Arland Ussher, was one of the six clerks of Chancery in Dublin. Together with Luke Challoner, later James Ussher's father-in-law, he took a prominent part in the foundation of Trinity College, Dublin. Arland Ussher's brother Henry became Archbishop of Armagh in 1595, in succession to his brother-in-law John Garvey, and was specially recommended for the post because of his competence in Irish, as noted earlier. Ussher's mother was Margaret Stanihurst, daughter of the Recorder of Dublin. Her brother was Richard Stanihurst, the writer who had incurred the anger of Keating for his unsympathetic *Description of Ireland* (1577).[97]

He might also have expected the anger of his nephew for his Catholicism. Under the influence of his former tutor Edmund Campion (later famous as a Jesuit conspirator), he had become a Roman Catholic and eventually took orders as a priest. But Ussher, harsh and implacable against the Roman Catholic Church in his published writings and official pronouncements, remained on friendly terms with individual Catholics inside and outside his own family, asking his uncle Richard to procure books for him from the Catholic libraries of Louvain.[98] His own mother may have been a Roman Catholic like her brother, though this claim ('si non patre, certe matre Catholica') is rather suspect since it is made in the violently partisan *Commentarius Rinuccinianus* (1658) which attacks Protestantism and the English in Ireland with equal vigour.[99] Certainly there were other Catholics in the family. His maternal grandmother Anna Fitzsimons was a relative of Henry Fitzsimons the Jesuit controversialist, professor of philosophy at Douai. Fitzsimons was imprisoned in Dublin Castle for sedition for some years and while he was there, in 1603, he was invited to take part in a public religious controversy. His Protestant adversary was his precocious young kinsman, James Ussher.[100]

This family division was not unusual during Ireland's and Britain's first Protestant century. William Shakespeare's father may have been a Roman Catholic, which has fuelled speculation that Shakespeare himself had Catholic leanings. John Donne, poet and Protestant divine, was brought up a Roman Catholic and numbered persecuted Catholics among his family, including Sir Thomas More. John Milton's father was born a Catholic and his brother Christopher apparently became one.[101] Religious divisions in Irish families, potentially more destructive than in English families because of the graver and more embittered political dimension, hold out the promise of high tragedy. But there is also the possibility of the comedy of confused identities. In the late sixteenth and early seventeenth centuries Protestant and Catholic divisions cut across rather than neatly coincided with racial, political and social groupings, the Old (or Norman-descended) and the New English and the 'meere Irish'. It was only later that an Irishman's religion became a (not invariably reliable) guide to his political loyalties. Ussher's Catholic uncle Richard Stanihurst, continuing the debunking tradition of Giraldus Cambrensis, is actually more anti-Irish than his Protestant nephew. It is not Ussher but Stanihurst who is described as a writer of lampoons and a slanderer ('Sillographi et sycophantae') in *Commentarius Rinucinnianus*.[102]

Because of later political identifications of Catholicism with anti-English feeling in Ireland, a legacy of the troubles of the 1640s, Ussher's staunch Protestantism has been taken to identify him automatically with English rather than Irish interests. But this is too simple. Irish Protestants had interests and concerns which sometimes bound them closer to Ireland than to anyone in England. The strains and insecurities felt by the Protestant 'English-Ireish' (Ussher's term) are illustrated in Ussher's most important political speech, delivered at Dublin Castle in 1627 before the Lord Deputy. Charles I, trying to rule without parliament, was in financial difficulty in Ireland as well as in England. The Catholic gentry of English descent, still technically liable to recusancy fines and other legal penalties, were understandably reluctant to contribute financially to the support of the army in Ireland. Some measure of formal religious toleration might be politically expedient to stimulate contributions, but George Downham, Bishop of Derry, and Ussher himself, embarrassed by a conflict of loyalties, felt they could not acquiesce in such barefaced cynicism.[103]

On the one hand, as a militant and convinced Protestant, Ussher believed that bishops who connived at the toleration of recusants would be little better than atheists inviting divine vengeance. On the other hand, as a king's man and an Irish Protestant who remembered Spanish landings at Kinsale, Ussher feared a renewed alliance of Irish rebels and Spain against which a strong army in Ireland was the only protection. Without actually saying that recusancy fines did not matter, Ussher dwelt on the practical leniency of the king in this matter and urged the Catholic gentry to contribute to the royal coffers as a *quid pro quo*. But the roles of king's man and Irishman sat together a little uneasily. In anticipation of numerous later resentments, Protestant and Catholic, of exploitative, intrusive or insensitive English administration in Ireland Ussher went on to call for the employment of loyal Irishmen, including 'some of the natives', in the service of the king alongside the Englishmen who seemed to have a monopoly of such positions. He also urged the Lord Deputy to arrange for greater economic investment to develop Irish natural resources and deplored the extent to which money was being taken out of Ireland to pay for imports from England. There runs through this later part of the speech something of the bewildered sense of rejection and alienation characteristic of later Irish and, specifically, Ulster 'loyalism' in relation to England. Ussher records the dissatisfaction of the 'English-Ireish' 'that they are not truly distinguished fro[m] the meere Irish' and are 'no better thought of in their loyaltie than the meere Irish'.[104]

This edginess arises in part from the isolated position of Irish Protestants at this period. Ussher was born into an embattled minority religion which was different in kind from the religion of the Church of England as it was to develop under Archbishop Laud. The early provosts of Trinity College, Dublin, were Cambridge puritans rather than proto-Laudians and Ussher was a kind of puritan himself. He grew up in 'an atmosphere of minimal conformity and of Calvinist doctrine'.[105] Despite the common bond of scholarship, Ussher's relations with Laud were strained and unsatisfactory. As far as he was able, Ussher tried to resist Laudian anti-puritan innovations in Trinity College and in the Irish Church, but without much success.[106] While the Church of England under James I and Charles I was increasingly opposed to puritans within and Presbyterians without, the Irish Protestant episcopal church, confronted with a hopeless missionary task, ineffective and insecure, had more to fear from Roman Catholicism and tacitly and pragmatically tolerated Presbyterianism, at least for a time.

What was Ussher's own attitude? The nineteenth-century Presbyterian historian James Seaton Reid may have exaggerated Ussher's unAnglican, unEnglish sympathy for the Presbyterian forms of worship and church-government. After all, Ussher had written *The Apostolical Institution of Episcopacy* (1641) and this had provoked Milton's *Of Prelatical Episcopacy* (1641) which identified Ussher as a principal upholder of bishops rather than presbyters. Milton savagely if wrong-headedly attacked Ussher's use of letters controversially but, it now appears, correctly attributed to St Ignatius, first-century bishop of Antioch, which supplied evidence of the importance of bishops in the early days of the Church. Though Ussher was invited to take part in the Presbyterian Assembly of Divines at Westminster after the Civil War, he refused.

But against this should be considered Ussher's enthusiastic practical support for the schemes for European Protestant union promoted by John Dury, himself of Scottish Presbyterian antecedents. Ussher also had his own abortive project for reconciling Presbyterian and episcopal church government. He was in contact with Hugo Grotius the scholarly Dutch jurist and advocate of Christian unity. All of this was largely irrelevant to and perhaps even subversive of the insular traditional Anglicanism of England but it reflected and rationalized some of the ambiguities of Scottish and Irish practice at the time. The Scottish Bishop of Dunblane claimed that he functioned as a member of a Presbytery rather than as an autonomous prelate. In Ireland Bishop Knox of Raphoe and Bishop Echlin of Down ordained Scots Presbyterians, the latter with the encouragement of the local magnate James Hamilton, first Earl of Claneboy, son of a Scottish Presbyterian minister.[107]

In an earlier existence, functioning with James Fullerton as a secret agent of James VI of Scotland, Hamilton had been a schoolmaster in Ship Street, Dublin, and later one of the first fellows of Trinity College. His most famous pupil was James Ussher, who numbered Hamilton's teaching among 'the providences of God towards himself'.[108]

Hamilton seems to have studied under Andrew Melville, the great Scottish educational reformer and Presbyterian leader. Melville had been a revitalizing force at the universities of Glasgow, Aberdeen and Edinburgh and this had an effect on the new college in Dublin in conjunction with the puritan influence imported from Cambridge. Trinity College soon adopted the simplified revisionist approach to Aristotelian rhetoric and logic associated with Melville's teacher Pierre de la Ramée, or Petrus Ramus. The Ramist method tended to replace the elaborately syllogistic logic of scholastic tradition with a sometimes drastically reductive system of dichotomies, dividing and subdividing complex issues into binary oppositions of an allegedly self-evident kind. Ramism exerted some influence on Ussher and his associates and on the origins of the modern Irish literary tradition, but perhaps less than has been assumed.

The influence and importance of Ramism have been much discussed and, as it now begins to appear, somewhat exaggerated.[109] John Milton prepared a textbook of logic on Ramist principles, though there is some dispute about the extent to which he can be described as a Ramist poet.[110] Christ's College, Cambridge, which was Milton's college, was known as a centre for Ramist ideas and one of its fellows, George Downham, had compiled a commentary on Ramus (1610) which provided a basis for Milton's work. Milton was still a child when Downham accepted preferment in Ireland as Bishop of Derry. In this capacity he became one of Ussher's closest allies, associated with him in opposition to the proposed toleration of Catholics in 1626–7, as we have seen. It is curious that, despited acrimonious public differences on the question of bishops, Milton and Ussher had a great deal in common, sharing a common Protestant, even puritan, perspective on the thought and scholarship of their day. Both men were exposed to Ramist ideas but neither was taken over by them. Hugh Kearney has observed that Ussher's notebooks indicate the extent to which a potentially radical Ramism dominated the early arts curriculum at Trinity, as it did in some Cambridge colleges. To illustrate Ramist influence Kearney points to some of Ussher's sermons. Even when preaching before the king Ussher avoids the traditional notion of natural hierarchy and prefers the simple dichotomies of godly and ungodly.[111] But any divine of puritan leanings would have done the same: this is not conclusive evidence of Ramism. The dichotomies of heaven and hell, Catholic and Protestant, or indeed, 'English-Ireish' and 'meere Irish' in Ussher's thought do not require a Ramist explanation. It is actually difficult to trace much manifestly Ramist influence in Ussher's writing despite Hugh Trevor-Roper's undemonstrated assertion of its sustaining but cramping effect upon him.[112] Even if Trinity had introduced new fashions in logic, Ussher's mind naturally favoured traditional modes of thought and demonstration, and in any case it was good tactics to meet Counter-Reformation propaganda on its own ground and attack it with its own weapons of traditional syllogistic logic and historical precedent. The surviving notes relating to Ussher's early controversy with his kinsman Fitzsimons the Jesuit indicate a rigorously Aristotelian scholastic and syllogistic mode of argument where one might have expected the smart dichotomies of the Ramist logic just coming into fashion.[113]

The social and political context in which Ramism seems to have been favoured is more interesting and illuminating than its alleged literary influence. It draws attention to differences between the milieu of Ussher and that of the Oxford scholars to whom he is often rashly assimilated. Democratically-minded urban puritans, distrustful of the power of the court and the country gentry, welcomed the dogmatic simplifications of Ramist method which seemed to pay more attention to the apparently innate or inherent properties of things than to the persons, institutions or traditional authorities associated with the status quo but not necessarily or self-evidently worthy of respect. This made Archbishop Laud uneasy and he opposed Ramism in Trinity College. At this early stage Trinity was still a town college like Glasgow or Edinburgh rather than a national institution like Oxford or Cambridge drawing from the ranks of the landed gentry. Many of the Irish gentry were still Catholic at this time and not attracted by the new Protestant university.[114] This suggests that the Protestant Irish intellectual elite were bourgeois to begin with, discontinuous with the later so-called 'Protestant Ascendancy' associated with country estates. But W. J. McCormack has argued that the rural and patrician connotations of 'Protestant Ascendancy' in the nineteenth century have a mythical dimension helping to obscure the largely middle-class and urban sources of Protestant power.[115] The Trinity of Ussher's day, serving a middle-class urban elite, can be seen to have inaugurated and fostered the real intellectual and cultural strengths of Protestant Anglo-Ireland, based not at Castle Rackrent but in the counting-houses and courtrooms of Dublin and in the country rectories.

Ussher and urban Dublin embodied religious and political opposition to a largely Catholic and Gaelic countryside, but the extent of the opposition must not be exaggerated: Irish was spoken in the streets of Dublin as well as English, and Ussher's uncle had been able to learn it. In any case, Ussher's characteristic ploy as a writer and controversialist is to combine opposition with a legitimating rhetoric which annexes and assimilates aspects of the religious and political 'other'. His most important polemical works strain after unity rather than division. If he had no love for Rome he had no hatred for individual Roman Catholics. The tediously anti-English Catholic historian Philip O'Sullevan Beare, followed by the equally partisan authors of *Commentarius Rinuccinianus,* had dismissed all Protestants in Ireland as obdurate heretics and representatives of the English yoke. They were condemned alongside those misguided Irish Catholics, often of Anglo-Irish extraction, who fought for their sovereign against Spanish aggression and Irish rebels in the last years of Elizabeth's reign.[116] By comparison Ussher's tone is almost bland. He took issue with O'Sullevan and paid tribute to his loyal fellow Irishmen of different religion. Instead of indulging in sectarian denunciations he concludes a major work of Protestant apologetic with a prayer for general enlightenment and religious peace and unity:

> The lord likewise grant (if it bee his blessed will) that *Truth* and *Peace* may meet together in our dayes, that we may bee all gathered into *one fold* under *one shepheard,* and that the whole earth may be filled with his glory. Amen. Amen.[117]

Ussher's pioneering researches into early Irish church history, much valued by later historians both Catholic and Protestant, had the partisan, polemical intention of inventing tradition, demonstrating non-Roman pre-Reformation antecedents for the Protestant episcopal church in Britain and Ireland. But the effect of this work was also to show unity in difference and to establish a common ecclesiastical heritage as well as a common Saviour for British and Irish Christianity, despite ancient and modern tensions and divisions. Even in the midst of demonstrating grave differences on issues such as the dating of Easter he could find space to emphasize the exemplary mutual respect between contending parties in an earlier age:

> Neither is it here to be omitted, that whatsoever broyles did passe betwixt our *Irish* that were not subject to the See of *Rome,* and those others that were of the Romane communion, in the succeeding ages, they of the one side were esteemed to be *Saints,* as well as they of the other; *Aidan* for example and *Finian,* who were counted leaders of the Quartidecemian party [opposed to the Roman dating of Easter] as well as *Wilfred* and *Cuthbert,* who were so violent against it. Yet now adayes . . .[118]

This pattern of mutual respect is reproduced in Ussher's own relations with Irish Catholic scholars involved in parallel researches into Irish ecclesiastical history. Some of his overtures were received with great caution, for the Protestant primate had the power to expose Catholic dignitaries such as David Rothe, Bishop of Ossory, to the most extreme legal penalties if they even set foot in Ireland. But Ussher acknowledged scholarly assistance from Rothe in his treatise *Britannicarum Ecclesiarum Antiquitates* (1639) and offered Rothe access to his unrivalled manuscript collections.[119] Thomas Strange, guardian of the Franciscan convent in Dublin, wrote in 1629 to his cousin Luke Wadding at St Isidore's College in Rome that Ussher had offered his assistance for Wadding's proposed *Historia Ecclesiastica Hiberniae,* and had helpfully observed that for the period before Pope Gregory VII there were better materials available in Dublin than in Rome. In return Ussher would be grateful if Wadding could search in the Vatican library for information on several uncertain matters. This arrangement seems to have worked well. Another Franciscan, Didacus Grey, wrote to Wadding from Limerick that books despatched to Ussher had arrived safely:

> Your 2 volumes came to my lord primate's hands (I meane Ussier the Protestant) wheare they are better wellcome then to many other in the kingdome that are not soe sensible of the common good of our kingdome as hee, notwithstandinge his profession [religion].[120]

It may have been because of these contacts and a sense that Ussher's learning was more profound than his Protestantism that Ussher the Protestant champion was secretly offered a modest pension by Cardinal Barberini if he settled in Rome and wrote against the theologians of the Church of England.[121] Ussher was described as being 'in great want' at this time since he had had to abandon his see and take refuge in England after the 1641 rebellion,[122] but it seems unlikely that he was seriously tempted. He resisted a more attractive offer conveyed through Cardinal Richelieu, who admired his work on ecclesiastical antiquities, which would have installed him as King's librarian in Paris with guaranteed freedom of religion. These curious overtures demonstrate that Ussher's staunch Protestantism did not confine his learning in partisan channels or remove him from participation in a European literary culture common to Reformation and Counter-Reformation in Dublin and Oxford, Paris and Rome. The propagandist authors of *Commentarius Rinuccinianus* claimed that it was only worldly self-interest that had postponed Ussher's open profession of Catholicism. With more justice they observed that in his major work *Britannicarum Ecclesiarum Antiquitates* there was little except the dedication to Charles I as 'fidei defensor', defender of the faith, which was directly heretical or antagonistic to Catholic sensibilities.[123]

Ussher somehow contrived to be irenical and polemical, Irish, British and European, all at the same time, though not without strain. His learned treatise *Gottescalci et Praedestinatianae Controversiae* (1631) could be seen at one level as a characteristic attempt to find support in the earlier, pre-Reformation history of the Western Church for his own particular brand of Irish Calvinistic Protestantism, viewed askance in England and soon to come under threat in Ireland through Laudian innovation. But Ussher corresponded with Laud about this project. One of his major sources was the *Historia Pelagiana* (1618) of Gerhard Jan Voss or Vossius, a Protestant scholar at Leiden well known to both Laud and Ussher. But as Ussher told Laud, he was able to supplement Vossius with two previously unpublished 'confessions' or doctrinal statements of Gottschalk made available to Ussher by the French Jesuit Jacques Sirmond (Sirmondus) who had referred to them in his recent work *Concilia Antiqua Galliae* (1629).[124]

The element of special pleading involved in gratuitously reviewing ninth-century predestinarian controversies turns out to be less partisan than might have been expected. Gottschalk of Orbais was a Benedictine theologian and poet who advocated double predestination, insisting that the damned as well as the saved were chosen from all eternity. This incurred the displeasure of his metropolitan Hincmar of Rheims and brought condemnation for heresy at a series of synods and at national councils at Savonnières (859) and Toucy (860).[125] Ussher sided neither with Gottschalk nor with Hincmar, but noted the divided mind of the Church on the issue and paid particular attention to the moderation of Archbishop Remigius of Lyons who disliked Gottschalk's doctrine but disapproved of Hincmar's extreme systematic refutation of Gottschalk. He looked for some intermediate position and at the synods of Valence (855) and Langres (859) promoted a moderate predestinarian doctrine more in keeping with the teaching of St Augustine.

Ussher regretted that Remigius' moderation had not been observed by later controversialists who had institutionally divided the Church. A sense of proportion and a respect for diversity of opinion were perhaps the most important lessons to be learned from past controversy, Ussher implied, perhaps hoping that the doctrinaire Laud could take a hint. As he wrote to him,

> although my special drift in setting forth this historical declaration was to bring either side to some better temper; yet I thought it fitter to publish it in the Latin tongue than in the vulgar, because I held it not convenient that the common people should be troubled with questions of this nature.[126]

One of the principal theologians contributing to these predestinarian debates was the Irishman Joannes Scotus Erigena who had eloquently assailed Gottschalk's double predestination in his treatise *De Divina Praedestinatione,* seeing in it a fatal blindness to the nature of God's eternal love ('aeterna caritas').[127] Ussher the Irishman devotes a whole chapter to Erigena and warmly endorses the verdict of contemporary Irish Catholic writers such as John Colgan and David Rothe that, despite the claims of Thomas Dempster, Erigena was indeed an Irishman and not a Scot. As Ussher observes, 'Hibernia nostra', 'our Ireland' is known as 'Eri' and 'Erin' by Irish-speakers, whence, 'Erigena'.[128] But even in this matter Ussher does not wish to be divisive, and in his *Discourse of the Religion Anciently Professed by the Irish,* published in the same year as his work on Gottschalk, he reminds us of his British as well as Irish allegiances by observing that, while Ireland was known as Scotia, he does not want to quarrel with modern Scots on this issue: 'I will not follow the example of those that have of late laboured to make division betwixt the daughter [Scotland] and the mother [Ireland], but account of them both, as of the same people.[129]

Erigena, like the other controversialists, made frequent reference to Augustine's work on predestination and free will. Augustine's great adversary Pelagius, traditionally regarded as a British theologian, was a potential embarrassment to Ussher's reconstructed British and Irish Church and his own Augustinian and Calvinist theology since he embodied the heretical rival doctrine of salvation by works. Jerome had suggested that Pelagius was of Scottish descent but Ussher adroitly sidestepped the possibility of a Scots-Irish heretic by accepting the view that he was Welsh.[130] That at least kept him a safe distance from Ireland. Ussher's account of Pelagian heresy is followed with acknowledgement by Gibbon who sees it as a major trial to the early British clergy, something they 'abhorred, as the peculiar disgrace of their native country'.[131]

It was all the more important to disown Pelagius because Ussher, like other Protestant apologists, took the view that Roman Catholicism with its penitential disciplines was a religion of works rather than faith. He described contemporary Catholics as 'this proud generation of Merit-mongers' descended from the Pelagians of old.[132]

Augustine rather than Pelagius, faith rather than works, the operations of divine grace rather than the merits and actions of the natural man, represent a major theme in Ussher's sermons, published after his death. These sermons reportedly lacked the elaborate rhetorical graces and 'strong lines' of John Donne and Jeremy Taylor and this plainness is probably exaggerated in the unauthorized reported versions in which they survive. Even allowing for this it is clear that Ussher laid heavy emphasis on the stern justice as well as the mercy of God. 'The Natural Man is a Dead Man' was his own title for an Oxford sermon of 1620. His subject was the appalling fate of the fearful and unbelieving as set out in Revelation. For those who had refused God's grace, the good things of life, the learning and the material advantages which Trinity College and ecclesiastical preferment and association with the scholars and libraries of Oxford had bestowed on Ussher himself would vanish away:

There is a kind of degradation of the soul, it is depriested as it were, and become like a degraded Knight that hath his honour taken from him. All the rich talents, and all the rich prizes, that were put into the fool's hand, shall be taken from him . . . You that have abused your learning and gifts that God hath given you, do you think that they shall go with you to hell? No such matter, you shall be very sots and dunces there. All your learning shall be taken from you, and you shall go to hell arrant blockheads.[133]

The degraded knight image, which Ussher used more than once, sums up the insecurity and the sense of uncomfortable responsibility overshadowing the glittering privilege of his class and his own position in seventeenth-century Ireland. The strain of serving the king as a faithful knight, while also preserving the honour of his sacred calling (involving Protestant witness), has already been noted. The king was not the only problem. Degradation, the loss of function as well as of privilege, was a constant threat for the priests and prelates of the insecure and resented Protestant episcopal church. The forces of the Counter-Reformation could easily triumph if another Spanish-supported Irish rebellion broke out. As it happened Ussher did lose both function and privilege in the wake of the 1641 rebellion, when he was obliged to abandon his see and his magnificent library to seek refuge in England.

This pervasive insecurity can be seen as a major energizing force in Protestant Irish writing down the centuries, variously tinged with guilt, sublimated in cultural nationalism, smothered in Orangeman's bluster or airily transformed into the serene cosmopolitanism of the Anglo-Irish intellectual who belongs everywhere because he is not quite sure he belongs in Ireland. Ussher's own assiduously international correspondence and intellectual curiosity perhaps inaugurates the tradition represented also by the European historical vision of the

Trinity historian J. B. Bury or the broad cultural horizons of essayists such as W. K. Magee ('John Eglinton') or Hubert Butler, our contemporary, who writes about Russia, Greece, Spain and Yugoslavia while thinking all the while about Ireland.[134]

English and Scottish planters in Ireland were usually required to build a bawn or fortified dwelling for security. On the foundation of Protestant belief and confidence in the authority or scripture Ussher built to procure some measure of mental and emotional security in a dangerous country. He raised formidable edifices of biblical, patristic, classical and antiquarian learning to reassure as well as to instruct his contemporaries. The lonely and vulnerable Protestant found shelter in the ancient non-Roman Irish and British Church resurrected, indeed partly created, from the fragmentary surviving evidence.

But vaster and more comprehensive structures might be possible. Beyond political and religious divisions, beyond the tensions of Church and world, Christian and pagan, classical and biblical tradition, there lay the immense and shadowy unity of world history proceeding majestically from creation to apocalypse under the eye of the one almighty God. Ussher had read Sir Walter Ralegh's *History of the World* (1614) which continued the work of early universal historians such as Eusebius and Orosius, beginning like them with the creation as historical event. But much was still dark and obscure, as Ralegh admitted.[135] A small step towards uncovering and apprehending the stupendous structure of world history would be the establishing of a reliable chronology down to the reign of the Emperor Vespasian. This was a formidable undertaking which involved reconciling different histories and traditions and resolving imperfect and contra-dictory evidence into a single table of dates. There had been earlier attempts, ranging from the sketchy 6000-year chronological scheme attributed to Rabbi Kattina in the Babylonian Talmud to Scaliger's detailed and sophisticated work in *De Emendatione Temporis* (1583). Ussher's labours were eventually crowned with the publication of *Annales Veteris Testamenti* (1650) and *Annalium Pars Posterior* (1654), soon available in English as *Annals of the World* (1658). The problems had been immense: indications of date might be in accordance with the Julian calendar or the Gregorian calendar, not yet followed in Britain, so these needed to be carefully adjusted; historical events dated only in relation to each other needed to be transferred to a reliable absolute scale; astronomical evidence in the biblical record and in secular sources needed to be evaluated and elucidated in the light of modern knowledge.

Even before Ussher embarked on his Herculean task he had felt the need for some agreed starting-point to the history of the world to which all other dates could be referred. The crucial interval was the period between the creation and the birth of Christ since the chronology of the Christian era was comparatively well established. Ussher's first estimate seems to have been that this period lasted 4,000 years. This was a traditional view adopted by Melanchthon and Luther and obtained by dividing the Jewish 6000-year chronology into three equal epochs, the last of which was the present age of the Messiah.[136] But this provisional dating of the creation at 4000 BC appeared in an early work, *A Body of Divinity* (? 1614 but published only in 1645), for which Ussher had no great regard. It is in the form of a catechism, intended to accompany and expound the Calvinist doctrine of the Irish Articles of 1615 for which Ussher was largely responsible. Detailed scholarly discussion would have been doctrinally irrelevant and out of place in such a work. Ussher's later and more considered view took account of Scaliger's *De Emendatione Temporis* which had established that the death of Herod the Great must have happened in 4 BC so Jesus must have been born four or five years earlier than the traditional date. If the creation had indeed happened 4000 years earlier it must have been in 4004 BC and Ussher's careful calculations confirmed this date. But what time of the year? There was no agreement among commentators, and Sir Thomas Browne sensibly dismissed the whole issue as a fruitless question in *Religio Medici*;[137] but with a characteristic combination of obsessive precision, arcane learning and literal-mindedness, Ussher addressed the problem. He rejected the suggestion in the Talmud that it must have been spring and decided on the autumnal equinox as the season corresponding to the third day of creation when herbs already yielding seed and trees yielding fruit were created. The spatial as well as temporal concreteness of Ussher's understanding of creation is disclosed characteristically in an archi-tectural metaphor: he concluded that on Sunday, 23 October 4004 BC, the first day of creation, God created Highest Heaven and the Angels, the roof of the building, and then turned to the foundations, the Earth and the Deep.[138]

The smoothly interlocking pieces of Ussher's chronological structure had been supplied by a host of witnesses from all times and places. But in the uncomfortably specific time and place of early seventeenth-century Ireland Ussher had to prop up a less well-founded edifice. His participation in the edgy, defensive aggression of an unfairly privileged minority religion which claimed to be the true religion of the whole country earned him the title of 'Heresiarch' among Catholic propagandists and strained the scholarly friendships he managed to establish with individual fellow Irishmen of the old religion.[139]

But this religious hostility has been regularly confounded with social and cultural hostility to the language as well as to the faith of the majority of Irishmen, all the more because as a man of the Pale, Ussher was not himself a native Irish speaker. But his writings show that unlike most of the Protestant Irish bishops of his time (many of them Englishmen) he knew some Irish and could discuss the etymologies of place-names.[140] It is both anachronistic and seriously misleading to see him as a kind of anti-type to Douglas Hyde and the Gaelic League, as Douglas Hyde did. His Irish manuscript collections generously made available to other scholars, and his active support of Sir James Ware's fundamental researches into Gaelic antiquities indicate a stronger sympathy for his country's Celtic traditions than he has usually been credited with. The relationship with Ware was reciprocal: Ussher facilitated Ware's work by commending him to English scholars such as Sir Robert Cotton, and in return Ware let Ussher have sight of 'all such old manuscripts concerning the affairs of this kingdom which come unto me', passing on the Leinster Annals from the Book of Leinster and asking for the Ulster Annals and the Annals of Innisfallen.[141] The Book of Lecan which had come into Ussher's hands was made available to Irish scholars who needed to use it: Michael Ó Clérigh, principal compiler of the so-called *Annals of the Four Masters,* was able to draw on it for his genealogical researches.[142]

On the negative side, Ussher did temporarily close down some Irish-language schools, including the flourishing Galway academy of Alexander Lynch, father of the author of *Alithinologia* and *Cambrensis Eversus.*[143] This was early in his career, in 1615, when he was Chancellor of St Patrick's Cathedral in Dublin and a government commissioner. But the closures were not because the schools were Irish-speaking but because they were Catholic and it was government policy that education at all levels should be in Protestant hands.

It has been suggested, by Norman Sykes and others, that Ussher's alleged hatred of the Irish language was greater than his hatred of Catholicism, impaired the missionary outreach of his Church and led to friction with Bishop Bedell of Kilmore, instigator of the Irish translation of the Old Testament.[144] But the evidence, critically considered, points to a different conclusion. Bedell, an Englishman, had been appointed Provost of Trinity College in 1627 on Ussher's recommendation and with his full approval. Bedell's establishing an

Irish lecture at Trinity, so far from alienating Ussher, had helped to procure his promotion to the see of Kilmore in 1629. It emerges from Ussher's correspondence with Bedell, misconstrued by Ussher's biographer and editor C. R. Elrington, that while grave differences developed between the two men in 1629 and 1630 these were partly based on a misunderstanding and had to do with attitudes towards Roman Catholics and ostensibly Catholic practices rather than with Bedell's translation project.[145]

Bedell, less anti-Catholic than Ussher, had lived in Catholic Italy as chaplain to Sir Henry Wotton, and had become friendly with the Venetian churchman Paolo Sarpi, sometime Provincial of the Servite order but excommunicated by the pope for defending the Venetian Church against the ultramontane aspirations of Cardinal Bellarmine and the papacy. This exposure to what might be described as liberal Catholicism had encouraged Bedell to keep on friendly terms with the Irish Catholics all about him on the grounds that 'differences between us and the Church (or Court rather) of Rome were not in Faith (which we had common) but in certain additions foreign to it'.[146] The obnoxious Dean of Kilmore, Nicholas Bernard, who was Ussher's chaplain and protégé, had denounced Bedell to Ussher for 'coming near to Papists' through laxity against Catholics in the church courts and in allegedly Romanist eucharistic practice. Ussher hastily construed this as undermining the Protestant presence in Ireland, but Bedell was able to show that he had the authority of Ussher's own mentors William Perkins, the English Puritan, and John Calvin himself for his liturgical preferences.[147] Bernard's mischief-making seems to have been prompted by spite because Bedell had been unwilling to present him to the living of Kildromfarten, in addition to the three he already held, on the grounds that an Irish-speaker was urgently needed for this Irish-speaking locality.[148]

In this matter Bedell was acting in accord with the official instructions to the Lord Deputy 'concerning the State of the Church of Ireland' which had been issued in 1623. These guidelines, requested by Ussher himself, confirmed the original instructions of James I. They directed the primate to take special care to ensure Irish-language services, and 'that the New Testament and Book of Common Prayer, translated into Irish, be hereafter frequently used in the parishes of the Irishrie'.[149] Ussher's own sympathy with the spirit of these instructions is demonstrated by his agreeing to depart from established custom and ordain to the priesthood a man who had not had a liberal education but who did know Irish, 'being satisfied that such an ordinary man was able to do more good than if he had Latin without any Irish at all.'[150]

The source of Ussher's difficulties in his own country was not the Irish language or the Irish people but the ultimately incompatible demands of Protestant staunchness, the financial needs of the king and the devastatingly thoroughgoing policies of the Lord Deputy Strafford and Archbishop Laud which Ussher could do little to modify. Left to himself, as scholar rather than prelate, he was as much Irish as Protestant, champion of the Irishness of Erigena along with the Irish Franciscans, custodian of the Great Book of Lecan in succession to the Mac Firbhisighs because like them he treasured and made literary use of the riches of the Irish past.

But the Irishness of Ussher found no resting place in Ireland. The 1641 rebellion drove him from his own country, never to return. It is a tribute to the catholicity of his learning, rising above considerations of sect and party, that Oliver Cromwell honoured this champion of the king's authority and defender of episcopacy and contributed to the expenses of his funeral, for which the stern prohibition of the Anglican liturgy was relaxed.[151]

Ussher's exile and death in England might seem to vindicate the claims of extremists such as his adversary Philip O'Sullevan Beare that there could not be such mongrels as the 'Anglo-Ibernici': those of English descent were still English under the skin, he claimed, with no claim to be regarded as Irish.[152] But Ussher had not wished to leave Ireland. Dying abroad in spite of one's country is almost a mark of the Irish writer, from Erigena to Joyce. The country cannot always contain or limit the imaginative and intellectual energies released or stimulated by its distinctive problems of allegiance and identity. Ussher's importance in Irish letters has been played down by posterity because of his angular political Protestantism and because he so visibly participated in English and European literary and cultural discourses, the worlds of Milton and Vossius. But in the international world of Reformation and Counter-Reformation, still linked by the common possession of Latin learning, Irish distinctiveness could be perceived, asserted and vindicated only in the context of Western Christendom.

The necessary internationalism of the Irish writer, apparent even in William Carleton's sense of himself as an Irish Gil Blas, can be seen in a more secular form in the work of Ussher's protégé Wentworth Dillon, Earl of Roscommon, poet, translator and critic.

THE EARL OF ROSCOMMON (?1637–85)

If Ussher held in finally unresolved tension the multiple identities of the Irish writer, Irish, British and European, the Earl of Roscommon might be held to have resolved the issue by virtually excluding the Irish dimension. Roscommon's polished translations and his prescriptive *Essay on Translated Verse* (1684) are recalled today only in footnotes to Dryden and Pope. The Ireland he largely rejected has long since rejected him. But his career illustrates the difficulties and the compensating strategies of the Irish writer caught up in the catastrophic politics of his country.

Wentworth Dillon, later fourth Earl of Roscommon, was at risk in Ireland from the moment of his baptism, which helps to explain his preference for the life and culture of England and the continent. His mother, Elizabeth Wentworth, sister of Thomas Wentworth the Lord Deputy, could not have realized how odious the name of Wentworth would be in the last years of Charles I and in Cromwellian Ireland or she would have called him something else. On his father's side the young Dillon inherited the political and religious tensions of the Irish Reformation and Counter-Reformation.

The Dillons were an important family of Norman-Irish descent.[153] Their history indicates unstable religious allegiances in the seventeenth century which serve as a corrective to the model of absolute religious and cultural division between Catholic and Protestant suggested by later Irish history. Sir Lucas Dillon, Chief Baron of the Exchequer in Ireland, was faithful to the old religion to the extent of petitioning against religious persecution in 1605. He was briefly imprisoned for his pains. His grandson Robert Dillon, Wentworth Dillon's grandfather, had become at least nominally Protestant by 1622 as this was mentioned as a reason for advancing his father James to the dignity of first Earl of Roscommon.[154] Ussher has been credited with converting Robert Dillon,[155] but if he did he made a poor job of it. It is clear from the state papers that by 1641 Robert Dillon was identified as a Catholic noble, bringing to the king in Scotland 'an offer signed by the Papist nobility and gentry of this kingdom to put down the rebellion without help from England'.[156]

Such lukewarm Protestantism ran in the family. Robert Dillon's sister Jane had married into another prominent family of Dillons, and his nephew Thomas Dillon, fourth Viscount Dillon, had been brought up in this family as a Roman Catholic, became a Protestant in 1630 on succeeding to the viscountcy, but was reconciled to Rome in 1646. In 1651 the Parliamentary commissioners in Ireland reported that 'he hath been always eminently active in the counsels, wars and actions of the Irish Papal and Royal party in this nation against the Protestant and English interest'.[157]

Though the identification of Protestant and English interests was not yet absolute in the 1620s, Ussher would have had a political as well as a personal and religious interest in fostering the Dillons, to whom he was apparently related, in their rather ambiguous new-found Protestantism. He ensured that Robert Dillon's son James, on whom the future fortunes of the family depended, was sent to Exeter College, Oxford, to be treasured as 'a jewel of price' and given a soundly Protestant education under the direct supervision of the distinguished Dr John Prideaux, Rector of the College.[158] After the fall of the Lord Deputy in 1641 and the collapse of the king's cause in Ireland, the Wentworths and the Dillons were obviously in danger in Ireland. On Ussher's recommendation young Wentworth Dillon, son of the 'pearl of great price', was educated in the house of Samuel Bochart, Protestant pastor at Caen and a distinguished professor at the Protestant university in that place.

Bochart and Ussher had corresponded on abstruse scholarly matters: both belonged in the same European tradition of biblical and historical scholarship. Bochart's great work *Phaleg* (1646–51) was a monumental treatise on biblical historical geography, using historical and linguistic evidence to relate the Book of Genesis to contemporary theories and apparently established facts of population dispersal. Ussher's own *Geographical and Historical Disquisition Touching . . . Asia* (1641) was a minor exercise in a similar vein. Bochart's importance for Irish letters goes beyond his tutelage of Wentworth Dillon. His interest in semitic philology and, specifically, possible links between the defunct Phoenician tongue and the Celtic languages encouraged philological speculations which issued in the bizarre Celtomania of the eighteenth century.[159]

Bochart's influence on the young Dillon is difficult to assess. The often unwieldy erudition of Bochart, Ussher and early seventeenth-century scholarly discourse procured its own nemesis in the burlesque pedantries of *Tristram Shandy* in the next age, to which Dillon also seems to belong spiritually if not chronologically. He seems to have acquired an education in polite letters rather than solid Protestant learning from his sojourn on the continent, first in Caen and later in Italy, where he lingered until the restoration of Charles II. The moral influence of Bochart's Protestant household may have had some effect, if the praise of Alexander Pope is anything to go by:

> In all Charles's days
> Roscommon only boasts unspotted Bays.[160]

Certainly Roscommon rather severely stipulated that in poetry at least

> Immodest words words admit of no defence
> For want of Decency, is want of Sense.[161]

In translating Horace he improved on his author's unflattering vision of the coming age, 'Progeniem vitiosorem' (*Odes* 3.6), by commenting with parenthetic dryness on the morals of his own time:

> next age shall see
> A race more profligate than we
> (With all the pains we take) have skill enought to be![162]

But Pope's tribute is perhaps as much a condemnation of the lax morals of the Restoration court as solid evidence of Roscommon's personal qualities. For all his high moral tone he seems to have had an inordinate passion for gambling.[163]

A more indirect consequence of the Irish and French Protestant matrix of Roscommon's work is perhaps a kind of displaced puritanism evident in his narrow fastidiousness and neoclassical commitment to rules or aesthetic commandments for the wholesome government of the muses. Addison paid tribute to his

> Rules, whose deep sense and heavenly numbers show
> The best of critics, and of poets too.[164]

Rules, a fascination with uncovering or creating solid intellectual and imaginative structures, and a translator's commitment to continuities despite cultural, historical and linguistic difference are the salient features of Roscommon's work. All can be related at some level to Ireland. The nephew of the Lord Deputy who had failed to reduce Ireland to law and order sought the safer role of poet and unacknowledged legislator, maintaining that 'True poets are the Guardians of a State' (*Essay*, p. 23). Ussher's harmonious intellectual structures, imposing historical continuity and coherence upon the insecurities of

Protestant life in Ireland, find their secular, aesthetic counterpart in Roscommon's admiration for the magnificent concreteness and magisterial architecture of *Paradise Lost* and in his notion of a poem as something built, not merely spoken or written:

> On sure Foundations let your Fabrick Rise
> And with attractive Majesty surprise,
> Not by affected, meretricious Arts,
> But strict harmonious Symetry of Parts
>   (*Essay*, p. 10)

Roscommon's understanding of translation incorporates the classical notion of *translatio* as cultural transfer, diffusion and migration: France's translators had made the literary treasures of Greece and Rome their own, but now England and the succinctly vigorous English language had emulated and surpassed the French, making possible feats of cultural assimilation. Roscommon's own efforts in this direction run parallel to the annexation of Irish traditions attempted by Ussher and Ware. He translated Horace's *Art of Poetry* (1680) and tried to be an English Horace. He also translated the ancient Latin hymn the *Dies Irae* and Dr Johnson piously records that with his dying breath he recited from it:

> My God, my Father, and my Friend
> Do not forsake me in my end.[165]

This final act of willed identification with the tradition of the whole Western Church can be seen as a symptom of the loneliness and isolation of an almost permanently exiled Irish Protestant.

The legacy of Roscommon is perhaps most apparent in Pope's virtuoso *Essay in Criticism* (1711) which draws on the *Essay on Translated Verse* and represents a wittier and more enduring exercise in the same vein.[166] Addison's praise of Pope's *Essay* in the *Spectator* (20 December 1711) concluded by placing it on a par with Roscommon's *Essay* and Sheffield's *Essay upon Poetry*. When Addison wished to complain about translations of Italian opera into English he selected examples which demonstrated the specific errors Roscommon had warned against.[167] Eighteenth-century critics were confident that Roscommon's rules were immutable and would last as long as poetry was written.[168] Some of Pope's most famous normative phrases such as the 'ruling passion' and 'the Sound must seem an Echo to the Sense' are borrowed from Roscommon, who speaks of 'the Ruling Passion of your mind' and observes that in Virgil, 'The sound is still a comment to the Sense' (*Essay*, pp. 7, 22).

Something of the implicit politics of prescriptive aesthetics is implied in Pope's nomination of Roscommon as one of those who knew better than the xenophobic libertarian Englishmen 'unconquer'd and unciviliz'd' who resisted neoclassical decorum. Roscommon, in continental exile during the Commonwealth and Protectorate when English liberties were discussed more noisily than ever before, returned at the Restoration and helped also to restore 'Wit's Fundamental Laws'.[169] In the interests of purifying and fixing the standard of the English language, Roscommon wished to form an Academy like those he had encountered abroad in France and Italy. Little is known about this project, though it seems to have involved a number of prominent wits and writers, including the young Daniel Defoe.[170] In this unsuccessful venture, deplored by Dr Johnson, Roscommon had Dryden's support, and Dryden paid tribute to his work in a significantly political metaphor:

> The Muses Empire is restor'd agen
> In *Charles* his Reign, and by Roscomon's Pen.[171]

The connection between restored rules for poetry and the restored rule of the Stuarts is not fortuitous. Roscommon was a beneficiary of the Restoration and became Master of the Horse to the Duchess of York, sister-in-law of the king. He also translated into French William Sherlock's treatise on the Divine Right of Kings, *The Case of Resistance of the Supreme Powers* (1684), as if in homage to the martyred Stuart his family had tried to serve in Ireland. His conservative respect for order and permanence, political, linguistic and poetic, relates to the substance of things hoped for and not seen in his native Ireland during years of civil war and imperilled civility in which neither English nor Irish letters could flourish. Dryden's elaborate compliment to Roscommon almost suggests an Irish cultural revenge upon imperial England, eerily anticipating contemporary observations of the high proportion of non-English (including Irish) writers prominent in English letters today. The whimsical conceit is resolved by invoking the Norman-Irish rather than Gaelic heredity of the Dillon family:

> 'Tis well for us his generous bloud did flow
> Deriv'd from *British* Channels long ago.[172]

Roscommon's close association with the English court and his reluctance to visit his Irish estates even when it was safe to do so seems to rob Dryden's whimsy of its point since he seems so much more British than Irish. But it is worth remembering that seventeenth-century Irishmen of all persuasions looked to the person, if not the policies, of the king as their ultimate source of security.

Just because of this it seems curious that the Irish royalist poet should have been one of the first critics to pay tribute to the republican John Milton's *Paradise Lost*. The second edition of the *Essay on Translated Verse* praises the authentically classical blank verse of the poem by modulating into blank-verse Miltonic pastiche rehearsing the shaking of the foundations of heaven with Satan's revolt and then the triumph of 'God's Victorious Son' over 'th' old Original Rebels'. But as we have seen Milton's mingled classical and theological erudition belongs in the Protestant tradition of Ussher and Bochart, the tradition in which Roscommon was brought up. Aesthetically, it was a relatively small step from Miltonic hierarchies and deplored rebellious angels to Roscommon's dreams of order and the deplorable rebellious Irish who had disrupted his childhood.

Despite all the evidence to the contrary exemplary peace and order was a possibility even in Ireland. In his only specifically Irish poems, verses written for the Dublin performances of the tragedies *Pompey* and *Alexander the Great,* Roscommon paid tribute to the peace of Ireland which (allegedly) flourished when Caesar was busy staining the Thames, the Danube and the Nile with blood. Ireland had stayed at peace much more recently during the Scottish Covenanters' rising of 1679 (described in Scott's *Old Mortality*), though trouble had been expected from the Ulster Presbyterians:

> Yet let us boast, for sure it is our pride,
> When with their blood our neighbour lands were dyed
> Ireland's untainted loyalty remain'd
> Her people guiltless, and her fields unstain'd.[173]

But the dream of order and peace could not survive an actual visit to Ireland: Roscommon was set upon by three ruffians in Dublin, though providentially rescued by a passing disbanded officer.[174] Ireland's peace and loyalty, protested too much, were to emerge as even more problematic in the following century. Cosmopolitan, English and Irish, prescriptive and insecure, devoted to a classical ideal of art, civility and transhistorical permanence as a mode of refuge from Irish realities and a troubled century, Roscommon, like Ussher before him, embodies some of the perplexities and aspirations of the Irish English writer down the ages. He stands at the head of the Irish mode of thought and feeling which culminates in Yeats' sailing to Byzantium in pursuit of the artifice of eternity.

CHAPTER 3

The Eighteenth Century and Beyond:

William Drennan and Thomas Moore

T HE URBANE neoclassicism of the Earl of Roscommon, much admired by eighteenth-century men of letters, might seem an appropriate prelude to what has been regarded as the most gracious Irish century, memorialized in the dignified volumes of W. E. H. Lecky's *History of Ireland in the Eighteenth Century* (1892). Yeats assiduously promoted this highly selective, characteristically Anglo-Irish, perception of the period, celebrating Berkeley and Burke, Goldsmith and Swift, to dignify his own literary ancestry and cast haughty aspersions on what he saw as the cultural and spiritual degeneracy of contemporary urban Ireland.[1] In defiance of Lecky, Daniel Corkery's romantic nationalist counter-myth of the disadvantaged 'hidden Ireland' elegized the doomed aristocratic Gaelic culture as it lingered in exile and among the neglected poets, the oral traditions and the fugitive erudition of the Irish countryside.[2] This embodies a similarly seductive and equally misleading vision of a period and an increasingly pluralist culture which are still inadequately understood.

After the Williamite wars the seventeenth-century categories of planter and Gael gradually modulated into 'Protestant Ascendancy', so-called, and downtrodden Catholicism, with largely Presbyterian Protestant dissent, also disadvantaged, uncertain of its identity, floating uneasily somewhere between the two. The tense coexistence of these groupings, and of the writers they produced, all in uneasy relationship with the politics and culture of mainland Britain, led to a less serene but culturally more interesting epoch than is usually realized. Eventually, under the stimulus of the Irish Volunteer movement, all the uncertainties and resentments, the coterie loyalties and circumscribed perspectives of different kinds of Irishmen came together into something fleetingly approximating to broadly-based patriotism, cultural pride and national consciousness. The finest hour of culturally pluralist Ireland was in the brief interval between Grattan's Parliament (1782) and the overthrow of the United Irishmen (1798), swiftly followed by the Act of Union (1800). But even here one must beware of sentimental exaggeration and myth-making. The cultural and religious hostilities of the eighteenth century have probably been overstated, but so have its episodes of communal harmony.

The Irish eighteenth century was in many ways the creation and victim of the previous century, inheriting and perpetuating its bitter divisions. The legends of the 1641 rebellion cast a dark shadow during the Williamite wars and in the subsequent settlement. Folk memory and political rhetoric cherished the horrors of 1641, Drogheda and Wexford and soon added to them tales of Protestant resistance and Catholic defeat at Derry and Aughrim, Enniskillen and the Boyne. The partisan heritage of this epoch was ultimately embodied in the formation of Orange Lodges in rural Ulster in the 1790s. The Orangemen institutionalized the siege mentality of truculent defiance by annexing the motto of the House of Orange, 'Je Maintiendrai', as one of their slogans.[3] But sloganizing sectarianism could exist alongside a measure of mutual toleration and a sense of common identity as Irishmen. A recent study of popular culture in Ulster suggests that in the eighteenth and nineteenth centuries, Irish popular culture was the common possession of Catholic and Protestant to a considerable extent. For example, John Ashton's Drydenesque heroic tragedy *The Battle of Aughrim* (1756), a polished piece rather misleadingly described as a 'folk play', was constantly performed by amateur players to popular audiences, Catholic and Protestant, though it is concerned with a Protestant victory.[4]

This is at least as much a tribute to the author as to the community, for the play is scrupulously even-handed. The balance and antithesis of its Augustan heroic couplets extend to characterization and plot. There is no evidence to suggest that Colonel John Michelburn's much cruder drama *Ireland Preserved* (1705), reflecting his experiences with the Derry garrison during the siege, enjoyed the same wide popularity in performance, or indeed was ever performed, though both plays were reprinted, sometimes together, well into the nineteenth century.

Even so, it seems likely that in the eighteenth century, as at other periods, different kinds of Irishmen shared an often unenchanted sense of their own place and other elements of a common heritage even if harsh economic, political and religious animosities constantly threatened to set them at odds with each other. The more benign legacy of the seventeenth century can be illustrated in the subsequent fortunes of historical works such as those by Keating, Ussher, Ware and Lynch respected and constantly used by later scholars and writers of varying persuasions. Eighteenth-century Irish historiography is not free from sectarian bias either in its enthusiasms or in its moments of scepticism, but it provides a meeting-ground for different Irish traditions to a surprising extent. Keating's *General History of Ireland* in the 1723 translation of O'Connor (or was it Toland?) seemed to provide evidence of Ireland's early independence from Roman ecclesiastical domination, an emphasis comparable to that of Ussher. It used the word 'Catholic' rather less and 'parliament' rather more than Keating himself had done. It supplied ancient (if only arguably historical) precedents for autonomous Irish parliamentary institutions, a point of great interest to Protestant Irishmen seeking greater constitutional independence for their country. Scots-descended Irish Presbyterians also began to take a general and patriotic interest in the history of their country. One of the most important new works, building on seventeenth-century scholarship (particularly Ware), was by the Strabane minister, William Crawford. His *History of Ireland from the Earliest Period to the Present Time* (1783) was dedicated to the Earl of Charlemont.[5] Crawford and Charlemont, from different backgrounds and traditions, were both Irish constitutional patriots. Crawford managed to combine Ussher's Protestant antiquarianism with a patriotic, even chauvinistic, truculence. He described the papal reorganization of the Irish Church at the Council of Kells in 1152 as subjecting the Church to 'the usurped power of a foreign dominion', and he praised those who 'contended with spirit in support of their ancient constitution'.[6] A Dissenter himself, he was glad to acknowledge that the apparently more tolerant atmosphere of the 1780s was allowing Catholics and Dissenters alike to share in the renewed national life.[7]

Catholics certainly shared in the historical discourse of the period. The learned Dr John Lanigan, the greatest Catholic historian of his time, drew heavily on Ussher and Ware as well as *The Annals of the*

Four Masters in his *Ecclesiastical History of Ireland,* begun in 1799
and published in 1822. Ware's great-grandaughter's husband, Walter
Harris, a topographical writer and historian in his own right,
translated and expanded Ware's Latin works for the benefit of his own
age, publishing them as *The Whole Works of Sir James Ware
concerning Ireland* (Dublin, 1739–46; new edition 1764). John
Lynch's younger contemporary Roderic O'Flaherty published his
Ogygia in Latin in 1685, drawing extensively on Ware and on Ussher
as well as on Lynch himself. The accumulated seventeenth-century
erudition in this work was made available to later ages not only in
James Hely's English translation (1793) but in a supplement posthumously published as *Ogygia Vindicated* (1775), edited by Charles
O'Conor. O'Conor's friend Dr Sylvester O'Halloran, a distinguished
surgeon and, like O'Conor, a patriotic Irishman and a Roman
Catholic, was able to use all this work in his own published researches,
particularly his *Introduction to the Study of the History and Antiquities
of Ireland* (1772). O'Halloran and O'Conor were among Crawford's
sources for his *History of Ireland.* They were also used by O'Halloran's
Protestant god-daughter Charlotte Brooke. This neglected writer was a
friend of the scholarly antiquarian Bishop of Dromore, Thomas Percy.
Her volume of translations from the Irish, *Reliques of Ancient Irish
Poetry* (1789), was undertaken with Percy's encouragement and on the
analogy of his *Reliques of Ancient English Poetry* (1765). All this
historical learning, Catholic and Protestant, was used a little later by
the poet Thomas Moore, who made patriotic poetry and almost
unreadable historical narrative out of the rediscovered Celtic past.

Ussher was the best known of the seventeenth-century historians
outside Ireland. His pioneering work on ecclesiastical origins was
taken up by an Englishman, Edward Stillingfleet, later Bishop of
Worcester, whose *Origines Britannicae, or, the Antiquities of the
British Churches* was published in 1685. The rather sceptical account
of Irish antiquities in the fifth chapter alludes to Keating, Ware and
the *Annals of the Four Masters* as well as *Ogygia,* but not in a manner
of which any of the authors would have approved. The book was
vigorously attacked by the Donegal Deist John Toland in his
aggressively anti-clerical treatise *Nazarenus* (1718). Stillingfleet was
also attacked in O'Flaherty's *Ogygia Vindicated,* specifically for his
dismissive claim that there was no Irish literature before St Patrick. As
O'Flaherty informed his prospective patron Samuel Molyneux (son of
the writer William Molyneux who had helped with the publication of
Ogygia),[8] such errors demanded refutation assisted by patriotic

'Candour and Sincerity, such as was practisd by Primate Usher & Sr Ja: Ware who grounded their Dictates deliver'd to publick view on ye Authentick Antient Monum[en]ts of their Country.'[9] Molyneux would have appreciated the artful compliment to Ussher, not just as another Irish Protestant but because the Molyneux and Ussher families were linked by marriage. For family reasons, or because of a shared interest in Irish antiquities, or both, two of Ussher's works were in his library.[10]

The materials Stillingfleet had collected came to Ireland after his death in 1699 because Archbishop Narcissus Marsh of Dublin acquired them for his excellent library. Marsh's Library, still useful to Irish scholars, helped to facilitate the late eighteenth-century Celtic revival associated with Bishop Percy and the foundation of the Royal Irish Academy. It was in Marsh's Library that Percy observed an Irish manuscript being copied for the use of his eccentric antiquarian friend, General Vallancey.[11]

There are other more directly political continuities from the seventeenth century. The political ascendancy of the Anglo-Irish Protestant episcopalians had its intellectual dimension, annexing the antiquarian legacy of Ussher and Ware and establishing a distinctive tradition of largely economic and scientific discourse, linked with yet separate from the traditions of mainland Britain. While W. J. McCormack has called in question the aristocratic glamour with which the idea of 'Protestant Ascendancy' has been invested,[12] the importance of well-born gentlemen in eighteenth-century Ireland cannot be denied. O'Flaherty's patron William Molyneux is a case in point. A descendant of Queen Elizabeth's Chancellor of the Exchequer of Ireland, a friend of Locke and a prominent member of the Dublin Philosophical Society, he applied Lockian notions of government to the question of Irish constitutional liberty in his famous tract *The Case of Ireland . . . Stated* (1699). The political philosophy came largely from Locke but the argument from history came from the earlier researches of Molyneux's father-in-law, Sir William Domville, a former Attorney-General of Ireland, who had collected legal precedents from medieval times allegedly demonstrating the former legislative independence of the Irish parliament. The antiquarian aspect of the work, so typical of the Irish seventeenth century, did not stop there. Molyneux also made use of an old treatise, *Modus Tenendi Parliamenta in Hibernia,* which had been published in 1692 by his brother-in-law Anthony Dopping, Bishop of Meath.[13]

Molyneux's work was to be an inspiration to Anglo–Irish constitutional patriots seeking to improve the terms of their unequal association with Britain. Henry Grattan reputedly introduced the new constitutional freedoms of 'Grattan's Parliament' in 1782 by saying, 'Spirit of Swift, spirit of Molyneux, your genius has prevailed; Ireland is now a nation.' There is, however, some evidence that this represents a late and considerably 'improved' version of the speech and that Grattan's oratory owed little to either Swift or Molyneux.[14] Even so, the 'patriot tradition' stemming from Molyneux is not a complete myth. Swift's brilliant and influential Irish pamphlets owe more to Molyneux and other Whig theorists than is usually recognized.[15] In 1782, Grattan's great year, Molyneux's *Case of Ireland . . . Stated* was reprinted in radical Belfast at sixpence a copy because of its perceived contemporary relevance.[16] William Molyneux's progressive great-nephew Sir Capel Molyneux paid tribute to his illustrious kinsman in 1782 in indifferent verse as 'the pride of last devolved age/ Who singly dar'd to stem his country's doom'.[17] In the spirit of his great-uncle and in pursuit of constitutional liberties, he chaired the meetings of the Dublin Constitutional Society in the 1780s. It was at one of these meetings, in 1784, that the libertarian *Letters of an Irish Helot* were formally approved and adopted for publication. The author was William Drennan the Ulster poet and later a founder of the United Irishmen.

Lecky and Yeats were to develop their own versions of eighteenth-century (Anglo-) Irish tradition, not so much excluding as failing to notice the Roman Catholics and Dissenters who were not specifically included in the large ideas and ultimately unrealized aspirations to constitutional freedom from English parliamentary interference. The 'Irish political nation' of the early eighteenth century was a Protestant episcopalian preserve. But the rhetoric used to defend this narrow ground and to try to protect the beleaguered Irish economy, at the mercy of powerful English interests, was eventually invested with a wider and more genuinely national significance. Some of Swift's economic writings detailing the crippling restrictions on Irish trade, and selections from Bishop Berkeley's book of practical Irish questions *The Querist* were republished by the Young Ireland radical John Mitchel in 1847 under the title *Irish Political Economy,* with additional notes to update 'the statistics of beggary'. Thomas D'Arcy McGee, another Young Ireland propagandist, paid tribute to Molyneux as a precursor of his own nationalism, the man who 'relumed the fading light of Irish nationality'.[18]

The tradition stemming from Molyneux, Berkeley and Swift was as much economic and scientific as political. The young Berkeley encountered the works of Locke as an undergraduate of Trinity College through the influence of William Molyneux. His first important work was *An Essay towards a New Theory of Vision* (1709). This was a study of the psychology of visual perception which commented on the 'Molyneux Problem' of the heterogeneity of sight and touch, a matter first discussed by Molyneux and Locke. Berkeley also made considerable use of Molyneux's pioneering treatise, *Dioptrics* (1692). His work on vision was enthusiastically disseminated, particularly by the philosophers of the Scottish Enlightenment who educated Ireland's Presbyterians throughout the eighteenth century.[19] Berkeley's undergraduate friends included Molyneux's son Samuel and his nephew Samuel Madden. It was in the spirit of Molyneux's patriotism and in association with Madden and Swift's publisher George Faulkner, members of the Royal Dublin Society, among others, that Berkeley attacked extravagance, squalor and sloth. He campaigned for the economic, agricultural and industrial improvement of his diocese of Cloyne and Ireland generally. He also explored the practical questions which he listed in the *The Querist* (1735–7), furthering the movement towards national betterment and economic independence which had been stimulated by Swift's *Proposal for the Universal Use of Irish Manufacture* (1720), the *Drapier Letters* (1724) and other works.[20]

But strenuous native-born speculation and practical concern about Ireland's wretched economic plight stop some distance short of the aggressive nationalism and the truculently independent mind of 'We Irish men' with which Yeats invested Berkeley.[21] The characteristic publication of the economic patriots is perhaps Samuel Madden's *Reflections and Resolutions proper for the Gentlemen of Ireland* (Dublin, 1738) which suggested Ireland's best interests might be served by an Act of Union with England. Berkeley anticipated later progressives not in his nationalism so much as in his comparative lack of sectarianism. He insisted less than most on the privileges of his Church in a country where Catholics and Presbyterian Dissenters significantly outnumbered Anglicans like himself. He asked whether 'it may not be right for us also to admit Roman Catholics into our college [Trinity]? (It was not until 1793 that Roman Catholics were permitted to take degrees.[22]) Addressing the Catholics of Ireland he asked, 'why should disputes about faith interrupt the duties of civil life, or the different roads we take to heaven prevent our taking the same steps on earth?'[23]

Despite Berkeley's tolerant common sense, legal and practical toleration was long resisted in Ireland for political reasons. The sufferings of Irish Catholics under the Penal Laws after the Williamite wars are the most cherished legend of the Irish nationalist tradition. Seventeenth-century confiscations of land and the civil disabilities which minimized Catholic power and influence locally and nationally were understandably much resented. Catholics were excluded from parliament, the parliamentary franchise and (until 1793) the town corporations. Little was done about this until the later eighteenth century when a series of Catholic Relief Acts in 1778, 1782 and 1793 brought some improvement. In song and story, and in actuality, there were graphic accounts of Catholic suffering. Roderic O'Flaherty, the author of *Ogygia*, was born a gentleman in Moycullen Castle in Co. Galway and could claim (remote) descent from an Irish King, but he lost much of his land in the Irish wars. Despite recovering some of his patrimony on appeal in 1653, he led a life of learned poverty, obliged in the end to sell even his books and manuscripts.

But recent research suggests that the Penal Laws were not always effectively enforced, that their material consequences have been exaggerated, and that a Catholic interest survived and even flourished, particularly in the west of Ireland, during the Penal period.[24] Since sentiment is more potent than revisionist history, literary historians have not yet found it necessary to pay much attention to these findings. They still tend to limit the Gaelic literary tradition of this period to a proto-nationalist poetry of resentment and rebellion summed up in the English title of Seán Ó Tuama and Thomas Kinsella's valuable anthology, *Poems of the Dispossessed* (1981). An anonymous quatrain preserved in a manuscript written in 1745 somewhere on the Ulster-Leinster border seems to say it all:

> The world laid low, and the wind blew—like a dust—
> Alexander, Caesar, and all their followers.
> Tara is grass; and look how it stands with Troy.
> And even the English—maybe they might die.[25]

This poem is much prized by patriotic translators and anthologists but it is not always noticed that it is as much a European as an Irish poem. It is a classic example of the 'ubi sunt' motif in the European literary tradition, elaborated with classical as well as Irish allusions. The wider horizons of Irish poetry in this period, minimized by cultural nationalists, should not be ignored.

Diminished aristocratic patronage and hospitality were stridently deplored by the eighteenth-century Irish poets whose living had depended on them. Romantic daydreams of the Gael's deliverance from the bondage of foreign churls ('daoithe Gall') became a commonplace among poets such as Aogán Ó Rathaille. But even in Ó Rathaille other themes are possible. He celebrates the hospitality of the English-descended Browne family and the nuptials of Valentine Browne with the ceremonious elaboration of the old bardic tradition.[26] The contacts between planter and Gael in the eighteenth century, as in the seventeenth, have been played down and too little explored. But there is evidence that the Gaelic poets sometimes wrote for an audience which included English- as well as Irish-speakers. A poem now in the British Library laments the supplanted McCarthy family which had supported James II against William. The lament is presented in alternating, parallel stanzas of English and Irish.[27]

In the eighteenth century the tradition of epigram descending from the Latin of Martial was available to English and Irish alike: well-turned English rhyming stanzas or Irish quatrains could both serve as vernacular equivalents. An epigram of Martial, Englished by Addison in 1711 in the *Spectator*, was also translated into Irish. All three versions are transcribed in the same Irish manuscript which would have circulated among a bilingual community.[28] An early nineteenth-century manuscript, written in Limerick 1818–22 by Malachy O'Curry, brother of the Gaelic scholar Eugene O'Curry, includes a collection of lively epigrams in parallel English and Irish versions, at least one of which is also found in a Latin and Irish version in a different manuscript.[29] The English versions are more than limping glosses on the Irish. To take one example, Daniel O'Brien seems to have been a wit and a poet in both languages. His wife was a gift of the gods,

> But if your providence divine
> For greater Bliss design her,
> To obey your Will at any time
> I am ready to resign her.[30]

In the late eighteenth and early nineteenth centuries the most important embodiment of the still coexisting and interacting English and Gaelic traditions was Dan O'Connell, the 'Liberator'. A Catholic and a Celt, he came from a distinguished family still prominent in Derrynane, Co. Kerry, despite the Penal Laws. His aunt had composed the greatest Irish elegy of the eighteenth century, the much-anthologized 'Lament for Art O'Leary' ('Caoineadh Airt Ui Laoghaire'). But his political career benefited from the Anglo-Irish influences represented by education at Trinity College, Dublin, and practice at the Irish bar. His great political campaigns were conducted through the medium of English. Given this biculturalism, it is appropriate that his fame was acknowledged in Peadar Dubh Ó Dálaigh's macaronic verse in Irish and English:

Tabhair lámh le Domhnall cleibh [join hands with darling Daniel]
To gain Erin's sons their liberty.[31]

Liberty was restricted for Presbyterian Dissenters as well as for Catholic Irishmen for most of the eighteenth century. Though dissenting disabilities were not so severe, they fostered an interestingly parallel tradition of periodically articulated discontent. Long before Catholic emigration began, Ulster Presbyterians were emigrating in droves to the New World, driven by high rents, economic distress and the oppression of an episcopalian establishment disposed to equate their formal 'schism' with 'sin'. A meagre legal toleration of Presbyterian worship was not granted until 1719 and even then it was bitterly opposed by most of the Irish bishops.[32] So many Protestant Ulstermen, or 'Scots-Irish' as they were sometimes called, became prominent in colonial America that after the American Revolution the Irish politician Lord Mountjoy remarked (with some exaggeration), 'We have lost America through the Irish.'[33] In their own country, at least until the second half of the eighteenth century, Presbyterian Irishmen had been effectively excluded from the Anglican Trinity College, Dublin, and had to look for higher education in Scotland. They were also excluded from the corporations (until 1780). While not formally barred from the Irish House of Commons they seldom had the wealth or political connections then necessary for a political career.

Some prominent Presbyterian families found that the only way to succeed in public life was to conform to the Protestant episcopal church. Robert Stewart, later the famous Viscount Castlereagh, was baptized a Presbyterian but prudently educated as an Anglican and sent to Cambridge.

Less pliable Presbyterians engaged in controversy and formed combative alliances, usually with radical English Dissent. Though his specifically Presbyterian credentials are a little suspect, the republican deist John Toland went to the Presbyterian University of Glasgow after renouncing the Catholicism of his early life. He associated with English Dissenters and his sustained attack on the institutions and doctrines of (Anglican) orthodoxy has been linked with Presbyterian polemic though it was much more extreme.[34] A much more conservative Presbyterian, the scholarly William Bruce of the Belfast Academy, produced an expanded Irish edition of the English dissenting classic by Micaiah Towgood, *A Dissenting Gentleman's Answer to . . . Mr White's three Letters* (1746–8), published in Newry in 1816.

A specifically Irish Presbyterian discourse gradually emerged in response to repeated attacks from Anglican controversialists, Jonathan Swift among them.[35] Much of this writing is unreadable today, but it is important in that it confronted the ambiguities of the Presbyterian position, consistently loyal to the Crown, as Presbyterian defenders of Derry had demonstrated, but deeply resentful of, and deeply suspected by, the Anglican-dominated political establishment. The classic works were Rev. Dr James Kirkpatrick's massive *Historical Essay upon the Loyalty of Presbyterians in Great Britain and Ireland* (Belfast, 1713) and Rev. Dr John Abernethy's *Reasons for the Repeal of the Sacramental Test* (1733). As late as 1794, 'Abernethy' was still one of the set books for ordination candidates in the progressive Presbytery of Antrim.[36]

Though many Presbyterians confined their attention to the special problems of the Presbyterian community Abernethy at least was also concerned about his Catholic countrymen, though chiefly because he wanted to convert them. By the 1790s Presbyterianism was more outward-looking. After the passing of the Catholic Relief Act of 1793, the General Synod of Ulster added to its loyal address to the king a Declaration congratulating 'their Roman Catholic countrymen on their being restored to the Privileges of the constitution'.[37] But the Declaration was not unanimous, and more conservative counsels soon prevailed. The Moderator of the 1793 Synod, Rev. Dr Steel Dickson, was imprisoned in Fort George for his part in the United Irishmen's rising. After this the Synod presented another address in which they found it politic to disown their radical and disaffected brethren and nervously to reassert their traditional loyalty to the king.[38]

The two ministers who conveyed this loyal address were Robert Black and Patrick Vance. Black had taken part in the Volunteer movement and Vance had preached to the Belfast Volunteers in 1793.[39] Volunteering had been a milder and safer form of patriotism. Presbyterian involvement in the movement brought Dissenters into closer contact with the patriot tradition of the episcopalian 'Protestant

Ascendancy'. The Volunteers had been formed by the upper and middle classes to protect Ireland from foreign invasion and local disorder while regular troops were withdrawn from the country to fight the American war. Military enthusiasm proved infectious and the parades soon stimulated unprecendented and broadly-based Irish national feeling and self-respect. Irishmen marching under arms demonstrated what William Drennan called 'the buried majesty of the people'.[40] There was some cautious Catholic participation and many Protestants wished for more. Aspirations to Irish constitutional independence received a fresh impetus. The English government grew alarmed. A disciplined force of thousands of armed men in Ireland, some of them aggressive radicals who later became United Irishmen, was an obvious threat to the status quo. There were clashes with the military in Dublin and Belfast in 1793 and the volunteers were finally disbanded[41]

Patriots and prudent conservatives, resentful of the old 'Protestant Ascendancy' yet associated with it sometimes through a common Protestantism, sometimes through a common patriotic Irishness, opposed to popery but sharing Catholic civil disabilities, the Irish Presbyterians, and Irish Presbyterian writers, had a complex and unstable sense of their identity.

This problematic sense of identity is characteristic of other kinds of Irishman. The identity of the eighteenth-century Irish writer, shaped by his imaginative participation in a particular religious and cultural tradition but complicated and enriched through interaction with other traditions, can be explored by considering the careers of the Presbyterian thinker Francis Hutcheson, the Anglican Dean Jonathan Swift and the Roman Catholic antiquarian Charles O'Conor.

Francis Hutcheson (1694–1746) was the son of a Presbyterian minister. After attending the dissenting academy at Killyleagh in Co. Down he proceeded to Glasgow University where, like the famous Abernethy and Kirkpatrick,[42] he studied under the progressive or 'New Light' theologian John Simson. This set him apart from the Calvinistic conservatives of his father's congregation, but launched him on his career as an innovative thinker. The slight relaxation of the law represented by the Toleration Act of 1719 allowed the Presbyterian Dissenters of Dublin to set up an academy and about 1721 Hutcheson was invited to take charge of it. His assistant, who became his life-long friend, was Thomas Drennan, later minister of the first Presbyterian congregation in Belfast and father of the poet William Drennan.[43]

Hutcheson left Dublin for the Chair of Moral Philosphy at Glasgow in 1730. He exerted an enormous influence on the subsequent development of Scottish philosophy, particularly the aesthetics of Lord Kames, the ethics of Thomas Reid and Dugald Stewart and the political thought of his student Adam Smith.[44] This has encouraged commentators to see him in a Scottish rather than an Irish context. But he was important in his native place in several ways, some of them curiously indirect.

Historians of American political thought have observed the popularity of Hutcheson's published works at Princeton and at the College of William and Mary in Virginia. Thomas Jefferson's reading in Hutcheson had an influence on the framing of the American Declaration of Independence. The excitements of the American Revolution, mediated by Tom Paine and others, stimulated the patriotic radicalism of the United Irishmen.[45]

More directly, Hutcheson's influence was felt by Irish Presbyterians preparing for the ministry. Hutcheson's ideas, and Hutcheson's disciples, were prominent in the Scottish universities where many of them studied. In the 1790s ordination candidates for the Presbytery of Antrim still needed to know their Hutcheson.[46] This was natural enough, in view of the often neglected Irish matrix of Hutcheson's work. He wrote his first and most important book, *An Inquiry into the Original of our Ideas of Beauty and Virtue* (1725) while he was still in Dublin. His ideas were formed in the atmosphere of progressive Dissent and Irish Whiggery. His Dublin associates included the liberal Presbyterian James Duchal, Abernethy's biographer, and the liberal episcopalian Edward Synge, from a famous literary family, who was then acting as Dean Swift's precentor at St Patrick's Cathedral. But his most influential friend was Viscount Molesworth, the Shaftesburian philosopher and sometimes nervous patron of John Toland, who was a radical or 'Real Whig' political theorist best known for his *Account of Denmark* (1694).[47]

The Molesworth circle, as it has been called, brought together men of genius and talent, including, on the fringe, Dean Swift himself. Though Swift sneered at Molesworth as a Deist and shared in the violent ecclesiastical and political hostility to Toland's *Christianity not Mysterious* (1696), he shared Molesworth's 'patriot' views on Irish politics and praised his *Considerations for Promoting Agriculture* (1723).[48] Molesworth encouraged Hutcheson to assimilate and develop Shaftesburian ideas and in his *Inquiry* he developed an optimistic moral theory which linked virtue and benevolence with beauty. He propounded the notion of a quasi-aesthetic moral sense functioning independently of the rational faculty. In later works this was supplemented with a libertarian political theory: the state of nature before the institution of Civil Government was not anarchy, as Hobbes and Pufendorf had claimed, but liberty. This imposed special responsibilities on government: 'when the common rights of the community are trampled upon . . . then as the governor is plainly perfidious to his trust, he has forfeited all the power committed to him.'[49]

Hutcheson seems to have impressed Irish radicals and conservatives alike. In the posthumously published *System of Moral Philosophy* (1742) he discussed 'The private rights of man' and 'the natural equality of man' in a way that commended itself to the United Irishmen intoxicated with Tom Paine's *The Rights of Man* (1792–3). But Hutcheson the Dissenter also impressed the dignitaries of the established Church. Archbishop King of Dublin, usually no friend of Dissenters, resisted clerical pressures to close down Hutcheson's academy in the 1720s. He and Archbishop Boulter of Armagh, a personal friend of Hutcheson's, were among the subscribers to Hutcheson's posthumously published *Collected Works* (1755). So was Edward Synge, now Bishop of Elphin. Synge's sermon on toleration, preached to the Irish House of Commons in 1725, has been ascribed to Hutcheson's influence since toleration was not in fashion among episcopalians at the time.[50]

Since Hutcheson's *Inquiry* was among other things one of the most important works on aesthetics before Edmund Burke's *Philosophical Enquiry into the Origin of Our Ideas of the Sublime and the Beautiful* (1757) it is tempting to claim direct influence and infer a specifically Irish aesthetic tradition. But Burke never mentions Hutcheson. The two writers have some points of similarity but they contribute independently to a common British discourse. Hutcheson and Burke stand in a similar relation as political thinkers. Despite some interesting speculation by Seamus Deane[51] no direct connections can be demonstrated. But there are probably indirect links. Burke's general debt to some of the Scottish 'common-sense' philosophers who developed Hutcheson's concept of the 'moral sense' is now established. Burke particularly admired the work of his friend Adam Smith, whose early Hutchesonian *Theory of the Moral Sentiments* resembles Burke's grounding of morality in the natural affections.[52]

The case of Hutcheson demonstrates the extent to which Irish writing and Irish tradition persist in relation to the larger context of British and European letters. Hutcheson was taken up by the French *philosophes* who could read the *Inquiry* and the *System of Moral Philosophy* in the rather inadequate translations of M.–A. Eidous, the associate of d'Holbach and Diderot. Before Bentham and Mill Hutcheson had considered 'a mathematical calculation in subjects of morality', a way of working out 'the greatest happiness of the greatest number', and this idea found its way into the *Encyclopédie*, without Hutcheson's name on it, in Louis de Jaucourt's article on 'Gouvernement'.[53]

Irish and British, influential in Scotland, respected in France and America, the libertarian Dissenter befriended by bishops, Hutcheson's identities as an Irish writer were as various and paradoxical as those of his contemporary Jonathan Swift. Swift was famous as an English satirist and as the 'Hibernian patriot', but he had bitterly resented having to return to Ireland. Through the Dublin Molesworth circle he had some contact and even political sympathy with dissenters like Hutcheson but he contributed to the official Anglican rhetoric of disapproval with venomous relish.

Irish churchmen had been obliged to come to terms with the Revolution settlement or to leave Ireland: there was no other legitimation for an established Protestant Church in a largely Catholic country.[54] But this practical Whiggery, reinforced by fear of Catholic Jacobitism, stopped short of liking the Dissenters, who were popular only with English Whigs. These 'brother-Protestants' threatened the precarious privilege of the Irish Established Church almost as much as the Catholics. Swift wrote prose pamphlets upholding the Test Act which disadvantaged the Presbyterians. He also wickedly mocked the rhetoric of outraged Dissenters. His poem 'On the Words–Brother Protestants, and Fellow Christians' insists insultingly that these 'Fanatic Saints' are different in class, creed and kind from the members of Swift's church, parasites at best:

> Thus all the Footmen, Shoe-boys, Porters
> About St James's, cry, *We Courtiers* . . .
> Lice from your Body suck their Food;
> But is a Louse your Flesh and Blood?[55]

But for different purposes a different rhetoric applies. Swift the economic patriot claimed allies spurned by Swift the churchman. His celebrated *Drapier's Letters* (1724) were provoked by William Wood's purchase of a potentially very profitable patent for minting copper coins for Ireland. It was alleged that 'Wood's halfpence' could and would bring economic disaster to the whole nation. Swift described Whigs and Tories, Conformists and Presbyterians (but not Catholics) united to resist this monstrous imposition.

It is this capacity to supply—indeed to invent—an Irish national voice that justified the title 'Hibernian Patriot' which Swift assumed in the *Drapier's Letters*. But though Swift could incorporate the Catholic Irish in the lethal irony through which he discloses Irish degradation in his *Modest Proposal* and other works, he tends to keep his distance from the 'mere Irish'. This is apparent in a poem attacking Wood:

> I hear among Scholars there is a great Doubt
> From what Kind of Tree this WOOD was Hewn out.
> *Teague* made a good PUN by a *Brogue* in his Speech,
> And said: By my Shoul he's the Son of a BEECH.[56]

The pun, such as it is, depends on a stage-Irishman's non-standard pronunciation, assimilating 'beech' and 'bitch' to a single sound rhyming with modern English 'itch'. Swift's joke is phonologically accurate.[57] It was his ambivalent situation as an English Irishman, more English than most because of prolonged English residence and English parentage, that made him peculiarly aware of the idiosyncratic pronunciation, idiom and syntax of the English language as colloquially spoken in Ireland among people often uneasy and uncertain about their identity in a divided country at the British margin.

Swift's Irish experience, in conjunction with his early service in the household of the patrician Sir William Temple, enhanced his sense of the normative value, instability and precariousness both of the standard literary English of his time and of the problematic civility and metropolitan attitudes which it endeavoured to voice. The relativizing perspectives of *Gulliver's Travels* partly reflect this. So do less familiar writings, such as his brief tract *On Barbarous Denominations in Ireland* or his *Proposal for Correcting, Improving and Ascertaining the English Tongue* (1712), presented in the form of a letter to Robert Harley. Like the Earl of Roscommon in the previous generation, and like Roscommon's friend Dryden to whom Swift was related, Swift noted the example of the French academy and insisted on the need to rescue the English language from the barbarous encroachments and constant change which made past literature and historical records almost unintelligible a century later. Writing English history, he says, is 'like employing an excellent Statuary to work upon mouldring Stone'.[58] The monumental image, which seems to derive ultimately from Horace's boast 'exegi monumentum aere perennius' ('I have completed a monument more lasting than bronze') (Odes 3.30), implies a yearning for timelessness, a characteristically Irish, especially Anglo-Irish, desire to escape from the vicissitudes of history altogether. Roscommon, Dryden and Swift all participate in the discourse of British and European neoclassicism but Swift's neoclassical civility is partly defined by implied contrast with the Irish experience of turbulence and instability.

A later work on language seems at first to be an exercise in the uncritical patriotic philology of the sixteenth and seventeenth centuries. In *A Discourse to prove the Antiquity of the English Tongue. Showing . . . that Hebrew, Greek, and Latin, were derived from the English* (after 1727) Swift apparently changes his mind and claims English has changed very little in the last 2634 years. He purports to prove his contentions by etymology, offering sounder evidence than earlier scholars such as Camden and Pezron. The outrageous mock-etymologies which follow disclose his satiric intention. Interestingly, Pezron (Paul-Yves Pezron (1639–1706), Abbé of Charmoye) was a Celtic philologist convinced that the Celts were the children of Japhet and the ancestors of the whole of Europe. This was an early example of the eighteenth-century European Celtomania which fuelled the patriotic Celtic revivalism of the 1790s and led to uncritical extravagances, such as Charles Vallancey's fantasies about Irish–Carthaginian connections.[59]

Swift's vision of a pure and timeless English, important for his own practice as an English writer, is tinged in its Irish aspect with an implicit cultural imperialism. But this coexists with, and is perhaps undermined by, a certain unacknowledged sympathy with the vitality of the Gaelic tradition around him. Vivien Mercier has discussed the Irish original of Swift's verse-translation 'O'Rourke's Feast' and a possible Irish source lying behind *Gulliver's Travels*.[60] Swift seems to be denigrating Irish speakers of English in his fragmentary *Dialogue in Hybernian Stile,* but the comic vigour of the piece derives from the creative interaction of English and Irish syntax and idiom. Possible social contexts for this interaction have still to be fully explored,[61] but Swift was aware of cross-cultural influences and seems to have had some contacts himself with Irish-speakers, probably through his friend Anthony Raymond, a Fellow of Trinity College and an Irish scholar.[62]

Despite these Irish connections Swift remains as much a British as an Irish writer. There are probably incidental Irish allusions in parts of *Gulliver's Travels,* particularly in the third book,[63] but no comprehensive Irish reading is really possible. Wolfe Tone, the United Irishmen's leader, enjoyed the narrative, but as a British rather than as an Irish text. He alluded incidentally and inaccurately to Blefuscu, the rival empire to Lilliput, and its sacred book or Koran the *Brundecral,* when he called Tom Paine's *Rights of Man* the 'Koran of Blefescu', meaning Belfast.[64] But that was only his whim: the connection is purely phonetic.

Swift's major legacy to Irish letters is the lethal iconoclastic wit and the savage indignation he contributed to the patriot tradition, later assimilated to and appropriated by nationalist discourse. But his edgy concern with language is also important. His godson and biographer was Thomas Sheridan the younger, actor-manager, father of R. B. Sheridan the creator of Mrs Malaprop, great-grandson of Denis Sheridan, the Irish-speaker who helped Bishop Bedell translate the Old Testament into Irish. Stimulated by his godfather, Sheridan developed an implicitly coercive theory of the moral importance of a standard elocution, set out in works such as *British Education: or, The Sources of the Disorders of Great Britain* (1756). He also published an English pronouncing dictionary in 1780. It was widely used at a time when Ireland was becoming a largely English-speaking country.

The rapid decline of Irish is well documented. In the 1720s Tadhg Ó Neachtain could name twenty-six Irish scholars from all over Ireland known to him in Dublin,[65] but by 1786 Bishop Percy was lamenting that hardly anyone could be found to read an Irish manuscript. No Irish type was available to print Gallagher's *Irish Sermons* (1795) or *Bolg an tSolair* (1795), a pioneering anthology of Irish poetry with verse translations.

The situation was saved by a Celtic revival, less well-known than the later revival associated with Yeats and Lady Gregory but a remote cause of it. The Irish antiquarian enthusiasms of Percy and others led to the establishment of the Royal Irish Academy in 1785. The European craze for Ossianic primitivism coincided with and assisted this development for Ossian, allegedly Scottish, was actually Irish, Yeats' Oisin in a different guise. Charles O'Conor of Balenagare (1710–91) was important in this Celtic revival and in the apparently hopeful political developments which accompanied it. He was a founder member of the Royal Irish Academy, a Catholic in a mainly Protestant body, and a founder member of the Catholic Association. Impoverished though of noble and ancient family, he was the friend of 'Ascendancy' landlords and noblemen and of starving Catholic peasantry. He moved easily between these two worlds and helped to make available to enthusiasts such as the English army officer Charles Vallancey what survived of the traditional learning of Gaelic Ireland.[66]

O'Conor's lineal descent from 'the last unfortunate native prince who ruled that island [Ireland]', was extravagantly asserted in the obituary notice his son contributed to the (English) *Gentleman's Magazine* for August 1791. This rather pandered to the sentimental romanticism, soon exploited by Thomas Moore, which even then made the English interested in a largely mythologized Ireland. There are surer grounds for claiming that the O'Conor family tried to keep up the traditions of hospitality and artistic patronage characteristic of the old Gaelic order. Turlough O'Carolan, one of the last of the great Irish bards, was entertained in O'Conor's father's house and seems to have taught the young O'Conor to play the harp. Lessons in Irish history were given by Dominic O'Duigenan, a surviving member of one of the famous families of hereditary historians.[67]

O'Conor's own commitment to Gaelic learning is demonstrated in his attempts to continue and expand seventeenth-century compilations of historical and literary materials. He tried hard to get sponsors for an edition of the *Annals of the Four Masters*, but to no avail. He had more success in tracking down the manuscript of Roderic O'Flaherty's sequel to *Ogygia, Ogygia Vindicated,* which had been preserved in a private library, and this was published in 1775.

Some of O'Conor's most successful endeavours were as a kind of gentlemanly research assistant to historians and antiquarians who could not cope with Irish manuscripts. He worked hard for General Vallancey and contributed to his *Collectanea de Rebus Hibernicis* (1770–86). He helped Joseph Cooper Walker, a Treasury official at Dublin Castle, with his *Historical Memoirs of the Irish Bards* (1786) and assisted Ferdinando Warner, an English clergyman, with his *History of Ireland* (1763). Thomas Leland, librarian of Trinity College, Dublin, benefited from O'Conor's advice in purchasing manuscripts and in compiling his disappointingly partisan *History of Ireland from the Invasion of Henry II* (1773).[68]

O'Conor's other activities as a Catholic publicist might seem inconsistent with his position as a protégé of the Protestant Ascendancy. He attacked Henry Brooke's anti-Catholic *Farmer's Six Letters to the Protestants of Ireland* (Dublin, 1746) which had been prompted by fears of Catholic Jacobitism. But his dignified *Cottager's Remarks on the Spirit of Party* (1754) caused no offence to Brooke, who enlisted

O'Conor's help for later works such as a rather uncritical *Essay on the Antient and Modern State of Ireland* (1760).[69]

The rhetorically effective contrast between a glorious ancient Ireland and a degraded modern Ireland, not yet hackneyed, was sometimes developed by 'economic patriots' such as Broke, but O'Conor could make the point better himself. Taking advantage of the current controversies about the authenticity of the poems of Ossian, O'Conor's *Dissertations on the History of Ireland* (enlarged edition 1766) made strong claims for an Irish source for Ossianic traditions and developed a kind of cultural nationalism. The eighteenth-century cult of civility which had seemed to Swift and Hume to exclude the native Irish altogether[70] could be adapted to incorporate them. The disruptions of the Normans, tactfully doing duty for the English and Scottish interlopers of later ages, could not destroy the spirit of the nation:

> Poetry preserved the Spirit of our Language, the force of Elocution and in some Degree the antient Genius of the Nation, even in Ages of Anarchy. In Conjunction with its Sister-art, Music, it must have produced much more powerful Effects in better Times: In the worst, it preserved the People from degenerating into Savages. Their Manners approached nearer to those of Citizens, than of Barbarians.[71]

The combination of poetry, music and national sentiment posited here anticipates Thomas Moore's *Irish Melodies:* both Moore and O'Conor were cautiously eloquent in articulating for a non-Celtic audience diplomatically distanced racial feeling sanitized but also crystallized into historical myth.

Humiliated national feeling and the problems of Catholic disabilites were addressed more directly by O'Conor and his physician friend John O'Curry in their pamphlet *Observations on the Popery Laws* (1771). Originally published anonymously, this work contrasts the dramatic social and economic development of the American colonies over the past ninety years with the lack of improvement in the condition of Ireland under British rule in five centuries. It sourly reflects that a consequence of this is the flood of Irish emigration to the New World even in time of peace. Why lighten the ship of state in a calm? The ship of state metaphor has a classical pedigree going back to Demosthenes and Plato, and there are more overt classical allusions in the book. The Latin epigraph on the title-page comes from Livy, and is very apt. It is from the speech of Lucius Furius Camillus urging the Roman senate to secure lasting peace by admitting the defeated peoples of Latium into full citizenship.[72] And why, one might ask could the English not do the same with Irish Catholics? The easy classical reference bespeaks gentlemanly education. Montesquieu, whose *Esprit des Lois* was much admired by the Irish constitutional patriots, was similarly given to Roman precedents lifted from Livy. The pamphlet could easily have been penned by a liberal-minded, well-informed, Anglo-Irish Protestant and the authors may have calculated that its anonymity would foster this impression and make it seem more disinterested and persuasive.

O'Conor was a shrewd tactician. He deliberately linked his specifically Catholic concerns with the Ossianic and romantic tastes of the Anglo-Irish gentry and the progressive aspirations of the Anglo-Irish patriot tradition which culminated in the Volunteer movement and Grattan's parliament. He was a subscriber to Charlotte Brooke's *Reliques of Ancient Irish Poetry* (1789): Miss Brooke was the daughter of the economic patriot Henry Brooke with whom he had associated in the past. Though the Volunteers were led by Protestants, and though Grattan's Parliament was a Protestant triumph, O'Conor in 1783 was sure that Catholics would now share in the re-emerging Irish nation: 'Very lately we became a free and independent people, and that description alone comprises the happiest revolution we have had here for 700 years past . . . We are united in a single creed of politics.'[73]

O'Conor's optimism was premature, but when the Royal Irish Academy was founded in 1785, this seemed to be a continuation of the patriot tradition and the new sense of national self-respect by other means. Grattan was a member, and so was the Earl of Charlemont, the 'volunteer Earl'. Economic patriotism, antiquarianism and volunteer bravado all seemed to come neatly together in Charlemont's contribution to the *Transactions* of the Academy on 'The Antiquity of the Woollen Manufacture in Ireland, proved from a passage of an ancient Florentine Poet'.[74] O'Conor was one of the first Catholics to be a member of the Academy but others soon followed, joined with Protestants in a new and non-sectarian intellectual enterprise.

The sequel is disheartening. O'Conor's son carried the patriotic cross-cultural links forged by his father one stage further by becoming a United Irishman. But there seemed to be little future for Catholic patriots in Ireland after 1798 and he emigrated to the United States, where his own sons were already established.[75]

The wild and doomed enthusiasm of the United Irishmen, the

bloodshed and bitterness of 1798 and the resented jobbery associated with the passing of the Act of Union in 1800 all seem remote from the scholarly O'Conor and the Royal Irish Academy, and more distant still from the Irish and British world of Hutcheson and Swift. But the Academy, and intellectual interchange among Irishmen from different and conflicting traditions, survived 1798. The former United Irishman and poet William Drennan was a member and so was the poet Thomas Moore (an honorary member).[76] In the work of Drennan and Moore, a Presbyterian and a Catholic, the interplay of traditions and the invention of tradition which is still with us can be explored.

WILLIAM DRENNAN (1754–1820)

William Drennan, Ulster poet and pamphleteer, physician and United Irishman, is largely forgotten today, though he does not deserve to be. He coined the phrase 'the Emerald Isle', for which he seldom gets the credit, and he was a founder of the Society of United Irishmen, though Wolfe Tone is the only founder posterity has remembered. His political pamphlets and the letters he exchanged with his sister have enlightened a succession of historians and biographers. One or two of his political songs appealed to Thomas Davis and Young Ireland[77] and continue to appear in the more comprehensive anthologies of Irish verse. The Belfast Academical Institution which Drennan helped to establish still stands, a well-known school ('Inst'), though long since deprived of its ambitious collegiate department by the foundation of a university in Belfast.

Drennan's first literary work was the indignantly libertarian *Letters of an Irish Helot* (1784), published in Belfast and then in Dublin, written to and for his 'Fellow Slaves', the people of Ireland. But the people of Ireland have proved partisan and ungrateful. Drennan is excluded from the Dublin poet Thomas Kinsella's *New Oxford Book of Irish Verse* (1986). He is scarely mentioned in recent general accounts of the Irish literary tradition. The only serious account of his work is a few perceptive pages in Terence Brown's *Northern Voices* (1975), a study confined to Ulster poets. One effect of this neglect is to perpetuate Irish divisions by reinforcing particularist versions of the Irish cultural heritage, excluding or marginalizing not only Drennan but the contribution of Ulster Presbyterian Dissenters to the national discourse. Another consequence is the undeserved obscurity of some illuminating and thoughtful poetry and prose: Drennan can still help to explain modern Ireland to itself.

Drennan's eclipse can be partly explained by the accidents of time and place. Though he published poems and pamphlets piecemeal in the 1780s, and 1790s, his collection of *Fugitive Pieces in Verse and Prose* did not appear until 1815, in Belfast. At that time Ireland under the Union was on the whole anxious to repudiate the revolutionary 1790s and the United Irishmen with which Drennan had been associated. When Irish national sentiment found a new outlet in Daniel O'Connell's campaigns for Catholic Emancipation and Repeal of the Act of Union this was largely discontinuous with the earlier movement which had been led by Protestant radicals. Early in the nineteenth century romanticism inaugurated a new aesthetic intolerant of Drennan's deistic rationalism, his neoclassical verse and his sometimes caustic negotiations of the heady matter of Irish antiquity. Thomas Moore, with a base in London rather than provincial Belfast, had emerged as the leading Irish poet. Moore's famous *Irish Melodies* were more sentimental, but they were also more musical and more metrically adventurous than Drennan's 'Verses for Old Irish Melodies' (*Fugitive Pieces,* pp. 5–8) which confined patriotic indignation within the octosyllabic quatrains or 'Long Metre' of seventeenth- and eighteenth-century Presbyterian psalmody. Drennan worked from the same sources as Moore: both were influenced by Edward Bunting's published collections of *The Ancient Music of Ireland* to which Drennan contributed a translation from the Irish.[78] But for Drennan the national music was a means to a national end, while for Moore it was really an end in itself. Where Drennan had been a political activist before the Union, Moore, the younger man, made his career after the Union by successfully passing off aggressive nationalism as wistfully entertaining nostalgia. This guaranteed him a wider audience than Drennan. Moore's conceit 'The cold chain of silence' in his poem 'Dear Harp of my Country' is adapted from Drennan's phrase 'The dark chain of silence', but Moore's acknowledgement does not mention Drennan by name and preserves a diplomatic distance from the 'rebellious but beautiful Song "When Erin first rose"' which contains these words.[79]

Moore's popularity helped to set Irish poetry on a course of sentimentality and romantic nationalism leading to the bad verse poured out by Thomas Davis and the Young Ireland propagandists of the 1840s. By a natural process of reaction this provoked a more fastidious aesthetic which shrank from overtly political verse of any

kind, good or bad, and so perpetuated Drennan's obscurity. While
Yeats was one of the subscribers to D. A. Chart's edition of *The
Drennan Letters* in 1931 he had not found room for Drennan in his
earlier *Book of Irish Verse* (1895; revised edition 1900), perhaps
deeming him to fall into a limbo somewhere between his rather
contradictory principles of 'the traditions of Thomas Davis' and 'the
traditions of good literature'. The mists of the Celtic twilight almost
obliterated the Enlightenment poet altogether by ignoring every aspect
of his work except its relatively unimportant 'Celtic' dimension. At a
meeting of the Irish Literary Society in London Eleanor Hull
overpraised the translations from the Irish, anxious to be compli-
mentary in the presence of Drennan's great-grandaughter. Robert
Farren, blind and tone-deaf to Drennan's real merits, eventually
managed to find a redeeming 'hint, no more, of Gaelic influence' in the
heptasyllabic rhythms of his restrained and moving 'Wake of William
Orr'.[80]

Drennan is important not as a rush-light of the Celtic twilight but
because he was the most effective literary exponent of the radical
nationalist possibilites within Irish Presbyterianism. He created from
them a usable tradition which modern Ulster poets, such as John
Hewitt and Tom Paulin, have tried to refurbish and annex.[81] He is
interesting because this distinctive voice, terse and caustic, was
synthesized from many sources, classical and modern, English,
Scottish and European as well as Irish. In this he represents the
multiple contexts and the multiple identity of the modern Irish writer.

The name Drennan comes from the Irish 'draighnean' ('blackthorn')
and is common in Connaught, particularly in Co. Galway, where
Scottish and English Protestant settlers had comparatively little
impact. But these impeccably 'nativist' antecedents were overlaid with
Scottish influences and further complicated by immersion in a
specifically English literary culture. William Drennan was the youngest
son of Rev. Thomas Drennan, educated at Glasgow University,
minister of the First Presbyterian Church in Belfast since 1736,
formerly a colleague of his lifelong friend Francis Hutcheson in a
dissenting academy in Dublin. Drennan himself studied at both
Glasgow and Edinburgh and became a close friend of the celebrated
Dugald Stewart, philosopher in the Scottish 'common-sense' tradition
inaugurated by Hutcheson. Drennan's mother's family were connected
with the Scottish Hamiltons who settled in Ulster early in the
seventeenth century as a result of royal favour shown by the king to his
agent James Hamilton, once Ussher's schoolmaster.

Thomas Drennan was theologically and politically among the more liberal members of his Church, aligning himself with the English tradition of Protestant Dissent rather than with the establishment attitudes of the Presbyterian Church of Scotland. He associated himself with the Presbytery of Antrim which differed from other Presbyteries in not requiring subscription to the Calvinistic and Trinitarian Westminster Confession of Faith. William Drennan's sense of identification with his father's outlook was most fully expressed in the brief apologia he prepared in his own defence when he stood trial for seditious libel in 1794. Because he was a late child (his father was fifty-eight when he was born), Drennan's appropriation of the tradition in which his father stood links him with a much earlier period of Presbyterian Dissent. Thomas Drennan's friends had been the veteran Presbyterian controversialists Abernethy and Duchal. He had taken his stand on dissenting classics such as Towgood's *Dissenting Gentleman's Answer to . . . Mr White* (1746–8). William Drennan was aware that he inherited the radical independence of the Protestant Dissenter and the cherished principle of private judgement guided only by 'nature and the New Testament'. Like his father he was interested in the English dissenters such as Philip Furneaux, author of *An Essay on Toleration* (1773) and Joseph Priestley the radical scientist.[82] The ultimate source of much English and Irish Dissenting argument, apart from nature and the New Testament, was Locke's *Letters concerning Toleration* (1689–92). It was on Locke's political philosophy as well as on the Lockian *Case of Ireland . . . Stated* by the Anglo-Irish William Molyneux that Drennan based his libertarian politics in his early *Letters of an Irish Helot*, written to capitalize on the patriot enthusiasm generated by the Volunteer movement.

The French Revolution, Jacobinism and Tom Paine gradually introduced wider perspectives. In 1791 Drennan proposed for the revived Volunteers a motto from Rousseau, 'Tout homme doit être soldat pour la défense de sa liberté'.[83] He was obviously delighted when Richard Edgeworth (father of the novelist Maria Edgeworth) told him that he had the voice of Rousseau and he tried (unconvincingly) to identify himself with the Rousseau of the *Confessions,* a stern republican but all too human (*Letters*, p. 215). The Girondin novelist Jean-Baptiste Louvet had written a lurid 'Hymne de Mort' when he was on the run from his political enemies the Montagnards, intending to sing it on the way to the scaffold if he was arrested.[84] Drennan's spirited translation appropriates the defiantly republican sentiments for his own country: Louvet's denunciation of 'Des vils oppresseurs de la France' becomes less specifically

> Oppressors of my native land!
> In vain have I denounc'd your crimes–. . .
> Our country lost, the slave MAY live;
> Republicans MUST die.
>
> (*Fugitive Pieces,* p. 71)

In his own voice Drennan approached Irish oppression in the spirit of enlightened rationalism rather than martyrdom. His first sketch of what was to become the United Irishmen is contained in a letter of May 1791 in whch he advocates a Brotherhood committed to 'Real Independence to Ireland' and 'The Rights of Man and the Greatest Happiness of the Greatest Number' (*Letters,* p. 54). Tom Paine's contemporary *Rights of Man* vindicating the principles of the French Revolution was widely circulated in Ulster[85] but the concept of the rights of man was obviously older than Paine and the French National Assembly. Francis Hutcheson, for one, had discussed the rights of men and the formula 'the greatest happiness of the greatest number' probably comes directly from Hutcheson.[86]

The greatest number of Irishmen were in fact Catholic, and one of Drennan's motives in promoting the United Irishmen was to bring all creeds and classes together in the common cause of radical political reform. The Declaration or Test of the United Irishmen which Drennan composed pledged members to 'forward a brotherhood of affection, an identity of interests, a communion of rights, and an union of power among Irishmen of all religious persuasions' (*Letters,* p. 66). Drennan was prepared to live and die a United Irishman and gave instructions that his coffin should be carried by six Catholics and six Protestants. His wish was respected.[87] But the Protestant leaders of the United Irishmen found theoretical sympathy with Catholic oppression an inadequate basis for practical co-operation, particularly when the government seemed disposed to grant further concessions to keep Catholics from uniting with Protestant radicals. Wolfe Tone complained that the Catholic priests were 'men of low birth, low feelings, low habits and no education'.[88] Drennan's misgivings sprinkle his letters. The Catholics were self-centred, timid and divided, he claimed. The Protestant radical saw the world differently. Catholics had had to be cautious and conservative to survive and avoid hostile attentions during the Penal era, and it was a sometimes autocratic priesthood as

much as any democratic popular will which had sustained the faithful
in their ancestral religion. The ex-Catholic John Toland had bitterly
condemned the priesthood as a superstitious imposition. Drennan felt
much the same about it, at least in his private letters:

> I believe the priesthood in all ages has been the curse of
> Christianity, and I believe there never will be happiness or virtue
> on the face of the earth until that order of men be abolished . . .
> (*Letters*, p. 293)

The torpor and helpless passivity of priest-ridden Ireland is a
recurring object of Drennan's angry scorn. Ireland as the 'Shan Van
Vocht' or 'poor old woman' celebrated in the ballads associated with
1798 makes an unexpected earlier appearance in the *Letters of an Irish
Helot*. Drennan felt the Volunteer enthusiasm had not lasted: 'the
honest gentlewoman awaked from a trance' but she soon 'threw off her
warlike attire and sunk down again—a wretched woman'. The first
Helot letter ends 'awake, arise—for if you sleep you die!'[89] With
patriotic exasperation and savage geographical wit Drennan addresses
his country:

> My Country! shall I mourn, or bless,
> Thy tame and wretched happiness? . . .
> At the back of Europe, hurl'd—
> A base POSTERIOR of the world.
> (*Fugitive Pieces*, p. 12f)

Drennan's indignation was not just with Catholics, The eccentric
Irish MP Francis Dobbs, a millenarian, quite seriously associated
Ireland's ecclesiastical capital Armagh with Armageddon, and saw St
Patrick's banishing of the snakes as a foretaste of the final overthrow
of that great serpent Satan, destined to happen on Irish soil.[90] This
prophetic enthusiasm led Dobbs into the volunteer movement and
Grattanite constitutional patriotism. But Dobbs spoke so warily and
ineffectively at the Dungannon Volunteer meeting of 1782 that neither
Ireland nor the Volunteers were much the wiser. The exasperated
Drennan wickedly parodied his long-winded bumbling in a verse-satire
enclosed in a private letter and not published until long after. After
making Dobbs say

> We said and I say—the Repeal is Enough—
> And let all say Amen or Grattan will—puff—

the poem reviews the prospect of wholesale slaughter and ends in bathos:

> Ah! see–there they lye–all Dying or Dead–
> Sir–I move–Sir–'tis better to dye in one's Bed.[91]

Drennan had withdrawn from active participation in the United Irishmen before this ironic prospect had become a grim reality in the bloodshed of 1798.

In anger and in gentler mood, Drennan's muse sang of Irish realities in the literary idiom of England. The Dublin Constitution Society which adopted and republished the *Letters of an Irish Helot* was modelled on the English Society for Constitutional Information, founded in 1780. This body was later associated with Tom Paine and with the eccentric English radical Horne Tooke, whom Drennan knew and regarded as a friend of the United Irishmen in the 1790s (*Letters*, pp. 141, 217, 274–6). Tooke (then known as John Horne) had featured in some of the famous anonymous *Letters of Junius* (1769–72). These scathingly effective attacks on the Duke of Grafton and his administration provide a literary model for the Helot letters, also anonymous when they first appeared. Not surprisingly, Drennan was delighted when the Irish Helot was explicitly compared with Junius (*Letters*, p. 49).

In poetry as well as in prose, Drennan looked to English models. His sensitivity to historical and emotional as well as pictorial possibilities in landscape is characteristic of the late eighteenth-century sensibility sometimes vaguely described as 'pre-romantic' and associated in particular with the poetry of Thomas Gray.[92] It is not surprising that Drennan regarded Gray's poem 'The Bard', which embodies Celtic (Welsh) history, tradition and landscape, as 'that very first of lyric poems' (*Letters*, P. 277). The homage was made even more explicit when Drennan, like others before him, tried his hand at translating Gray's Latin Alcaic Ode about the Alps, 'O tu, severi religio loci'. Naturally enough, Gray's Latin is rendered as a competent pastiche of Gray's English poetry. The influence of Gray is clear in Drennan's original verse. Like Gray, Drennan was imaginatively responsive to the diction and melancholy possibilities of Milton, and his poem 'To a friend. Written at Mallow' seems to hover somewhere between Milton's 'Il Penseroso' and Gray's 'Elegy written in a Country Churchyard'. Milton's 'Come, pensive nun, devout and pure', becomes in the similar calm movement of Drennan's verse

Thee, pensive nun! thy vot'ry hails,
In twilight walks, thro' lonely vales,
Where, melted by the Western breeze,
The moon-beams trickle thro' the trees;
(*Fugitive Pieces*, p. 28)

In Roman religion and Latin poetry the sense of the numinous in particular places was conveyed in the notion of the *genius loci* or guardian-god of the locality. The *genius loci* is invoked in Gray's poems of place and in Milton's 'Lycidas'. It appears also in Drennan's verse, most effectively in his epitaph for his little son Thomas Drennan, which concludes,

Where lov'd in life, and humanly ador'd,
Here, let thy presence shed a sainted grace;
Thy courteous form to these known walks restor'd,
Be its good Genius still, and sanctify the place!
(*Fugitive Pieces*, p. 151)

Like Milton and Gray, Drennan was well versed in the themes and conventions of Latin poetry. The old Latin culture of Europe still persisted in attenuated form. Scottish medical dissertations were still written in Latin in the 1770s and Drennan's MD treatise on the treatment of fevers concludes with an elegantly appropriate tag from Catullus on the joys of returning home.[93] He had decided that the rest of his career would be in Ireland. Literary doctors with classical interests were not uncommon: Smollett's acquaintance and satiric victim Dr James Grainger had translated Tibullus, and Drennan tried his hand at Tibullus too (*Fugitive Pieces*, p. 43).[94] He also paid homage to Horace, imitating the famous Ode (3.30) on the permanence of poetry, 'Exegi monumentum'.

His most substantial translation, a version of Sophocles' *Electra*, is more than a literary diversion: it identifies in the play a moral and political theme continuous with Drennan's concerns as 'Irish Helot' and United Irishman. Drennan's Electra has radical aspirations. In a rather free expansion of his original he make the chorus wonder in Miltonic tones if she can

Reverse the common laws of fate
And force the adamantine gate
Closed on the prisoner of the tomb
And bid him live in time to come?

The Enlightenment vision crystallized in Pope's epitaph on Newton,

> Nature and nature's laws lay veiled in night:
> God said, let Newton be, and all was light.

is imposed on the conclusion of the play: the chorus intones,

> O! race of Atreus, well redeemed from woes,
> By prudence first, then valour, at the close!
> For crime o'er Argos hung, in horrid night,
> But LIBERTY arose,–and all was light.

The liberty is Sophoclean, but not the implied achievement of an eighteenth-century rational polity. The antithesis of night and light is supplied by Drennan and so is the specific mention of an afflicted country. In the immediately preceding speech, the heroic avenger Orestes promises the usurping Aegisthus that his imminent death will be a warning to other

> Who mount o'er law, and by their crimes, grow great–
> Better will mankind be, and better ruled the state.

The punishment of lawlessness is in the original Greek, but Sophocles says nothing about the improvement of mankind or government. Drennan stops short of appropriating the *Electra* as an Irish political fable, but the reformist and libertarian aspirations of the United Irishman are projected on to and derive general stimulus from the tangle of private obsession and public legitimacy explored in the play.[95]

Enlightenment values, a classical literary education and the formal disciplines of eighteenth-century English verse inform two of Drennan's most important Irish poems, 'Glendalloch' (1802) and an imitation of Juvenal's eighth satire, of uncertain date. There is an ancient tower in Glendalloch in Co. Wicklow which Drennan characterizes as

> A mighty grave-stone, set by Time,
> That, 'midst these ruins, stands sublime,
> To point the else-forgotten heap,
> Where princes and where prelates sleep.

On the face of it, the poem seems to combine the already old-fashioned mode of eighteenth-century topographical poetry, typified by John

Dyer's 'Grongar Hill' (1726), with the melancholy commonplaces of the so-called 'graveyard poets', such as the Anglo-Irish Thomas Parnell, author of 'A Night-Piece on Death' (1721). But Drennan uses the topographical and melancholic modes only as a starting-point. He has no tears to shed for princes or prelates, only for the Ireland they have helped to ruin. Mysterious Glendalloch is represented as the home of an exiled prophetic Arch-Druid who is first cousin to Gray's Bard. But unlike Gray's protagonist, the Arch-Druid has a crisply optimistic Enlightenment vision, derived perhaps from Pope's *Essay on Man*. For him Nature is less the occasion of wistfulness than the mirror of the eternal mind imperfectly perceived:

> To view of superficial eyes,
> In broken points this mirror lies . . .
> From beams of truth distorted, cross'd,
> The image of our God is lost.

But Justice will not annihilate what Goodness has created: reason and morality can be the attributes of Irishmen as well as of God, and 'light' is self-consciously rhymed with 'right'.

Unfortunately for this prophecy, St Kevin and his ascetic and superstitious monks took over the ancient site of Glendalloch:

> Envelop'd in their cowls, they move,
> And shun the God of Light and Love.

The coming of the Danes and the ensuing bloodshed further hampered the spread of light and liberty. The ecclesiastical aspect of English conquest from the time of Giraldus Cambrensis to the Penal Laws prompts the tart remark in the spirit of Toland's libertarian anti-clericalism that

> Conquest was then, and ever since,
> The real design of priest and prince.

The melancholy historical review continues. Grattan's Parliament seemed to hold out hopes for science and art, religious toleration and political autonomy, but the Act of Union put paid to all that. By the end of the poem mysterious Glendalloch can be seen as the memorial and mausoleum not so much of the ancient glories of Ireland and her Church as celebrated by antiquarians from Ussher to Charles O'Conor

but of the Enlightenment vision of light and liberty found and lost in
the last decade of the Irish eighteenth century. Where O'Conor and
others had seen in the Danish incursions a model and metaphor of later
English conquest and Irish ruin, Drennan tartly suggests that the Irish
cause was already on the road to ruin through the pride and wilfulness
of the Irish themselves:

> A land, by fav'ring Nature nurs'd,
> By human fraud and folly curs'd,
> Which never foreign friend shall know,
> While to herself the direst foe!

The stern censure and the refusal to sentimentalize Ireland's harsh
history spring from the former United Irishman's despairing sense of
the acutual disunity of his countrymen which had just procured their
humiliating defeat. The Irish politician Edmund Burke, sympathetic
to Irish Catholics and critical of British colonial policy but the
eloquent assailant of political revolution in France, was one of the
Irishmen Drennan held to blame.

Critics such as W. J. McCormack and Seamus Deane have made
much of Burke the Irishman in recent years. McCormack has culled
from his rhetoric metaphors of fragmentation and a romantic
incompleteness which he sees as characteristic of, and a source for,
the dominant, tragic discourse of Irish writing in the nineteenth
century. Deane sees him as the voice of Catholic Ireland and a
grandparent of the Irish Literary Revival.[96] But Drennan's sharp
hostility to Burke, aesthetic as well as political, draws attention to the
narrow inadequacy of any construction of Irish literary tradition which
gives Burke such unchallenged prominence. Burke's proto-nationalist
credentials are impressive, but only on a very restricted and partisan
definition of the Irish nation. He loathed the rapacious privilege of the
Anglo-Irish 'Protestant Ascendancy' ('that junto of robbers') and he
was associated with the movement to secure relief of Catholic
disabilities. But his British parliamentary career kept him from close
contact with Irish realities and he had neither interest not sympathy to
spare for the radical Presbyterian tradition represented by Drennan.
The publication of *Reflections on the Revolution in France* (1790)
revealed the extent of Burke's hostility to the English-based Jacobins
and radical Dissenters, from Toland to Priestley, with whom the more
militantly libertarian Irish dissenters tended to identify themselves.
Burke's *Letter to Sir Hercules Langrishe* (1792), on the subject of

extending the franchise to Irish Catholics, bluntly stated that the alternative would be an alarming and subversive combination of Catholics and Dissenters.[97] His son Richard Burke, appointed as agent of the Irish Catholic Committee in 1790, visited Ireland in 1792 on Committee business, but Wolfe Tone was unimpressed. Drennan was distinctly wary of Richard Burke, as he was of his father, noting that the elder Burke 'hates Presbyterians as he hates the devil, and I firmly believe he is now only a spy of Pitt's' (*Letters*, p.98).

The suspicion was unjustified, but the Burke family sank even lower in Drennan's esteem when Edmund Burke was awarded a Civil List pension of £1200 per annum in 1794, followed a year later with annuities from the Crown's reserved revenue totalling £2500.[98] The pension infuriated radicals and Foxite Whigs already outraged by Burke's invective against Dissenters and Jacobins. Burke's majestic and withering response, his *Letter to a Noble Lord* (1796), rebuked his critics and reiterated his opposition to subversive Jacobinism at home and abroad. But Drennan, predictably, if unfairly, was contemptuous of the *Letter*. For one thing, the autobiographical passages in which Burke publicly mourned the recent death of his son Richard showed a lack of delicacy and restraint, he felt, almost an error of literary tact by Drennan's old-fashioned standards. The whole thing was 'written in the very dotage of his wit . . . in his invective he is as coarse and vulgar as one of Robespierre's hirelings' (*Letters*, p. 233). Drennan was convinced that Burke had been 'bought off' and was now a spent force as far as reform in Ireland was concerned. His savage indignation, honed in the tradition of Swift and Juvenal before him, took appropriately Juvenalian form in an imitation of Juvenal's eighth satire.

This poem attacks empty pride of family. For Juvenal 'nobilitas sola est atque unica virtus' (8.20), virtue is the one and only source of nobility. A noble name meant nothing in itself. As Drennan put it,

> Puppies well-bred, are Caesar'd into fame,
> And TOMMY TOWNSHEND takes great SIDNEY's name.

As a reward for political services the Whig MP Thomas Townshend had been raised to the peerage as Baron (1783) and later Viscount (1789) Sydney, but he had no claim to the glories of earlier Sidneys such as the courtly Sir Philip Sidney or his great-nephew Algernon Sidney, the republican political theorist and Whig martyr who was one of the toasts of the United Irishmen.[99] If Burke was elevated to the peerage as his final reward for attacking dissenting radicals,

> how could wash of heraldry efface
> The name of BURKE, and dignify disgrace!
> Could peerage blazon o'er the pension'd page,
> Or give a gloss to ignominious age!

The theorist of the sublime and the beautiful, the great political moralist of his age famous for his sustained attack on Warren Hasting's corrupt administration in India, was now fatally compromised:

> Himself, the prime corrupter of his laws,
> Himself, the grievance which incens'd he draws;
> He lives, a lesson for all future time,
> Pathetically great, and painfully sublime.
>
> *(Fugitive Pieces,* p. 89f)

Perhaps the great name of Burke would soon be only a name. In Juvenal's Latin the corresponding passage concerns the worthless Rubellius Blandus, a proud descendant of Tiberius, about whom absolutely nothing else in now known.

Drennan's poem then departs from its classical original to develop a characteristically angry apostrophe to Ireland. The glory and the sorrow of Ireland in earlier times were already a commonplace of Irish verse, newly responsive to the patriotic antiquarianism of the later eighteenth century and the related enthusiasm for Ossian and all his works. In 1796 the Belfast radical paper the *Northern Star* published a poem entitled 'Tara':

> Glorious Tara! Ireland's pride,
> Seat of ancient heroes, hail![100]

Joshua Edkins's 1801 anthology *A Collection of Poems* (all of them 'strictly and purely Irish'), which included many of Drennan's earlier poems, gave generous space to Tara and to Ossianic melancholy. The inevitable rhyme of 'tomb' and 'gloom' in William Preston's 'Tale from Ossian' is found also in W. B.'s pseudo-Scandinavian 'Hialmar and Hyrinda'. Thomas Robertson's 'Ossian's Last Hymn, Versified' projects a contemporary sense of national demoralization on to the mythic past as the dying hero says 'Then farewell life–and thou, my harp, farewell'.[101] But Drennan's scorn in his Juvenal imitation cuts through romantic langour, lassitude and mystification to the present realities of poverty and potatoes: in glorious Ireland

misery sits, and eats her lazy root,
There–man is proud to dog his brother brute!
In sloth, the genius of the Isle decays,
Lost in his own, reverts to former days . . .
Through all, extends one sterile swamp of soul,
And fogs of apathy invest the whole.

(*Fugitive Pieces*, p. 93f)

Drennan's concern is with the political present and future rather than the mythologized past. In this he had more in common with the practical and sceptical rationalists Richard and Maria Edgeworth than with the romantically conservative Burke. Even in elegy, in 'The Wake of William Orr', Drennan observes classical restraint and looks beyond the ruin of his country. William Orr, a young Presbyterian farmer from Co. Antrim, had been convicted of administering the oath of the United Irishmen and was executed in 1797, 'the first real martyr of the United movement'.[102] But instead of wallowing in martyr's blood Drennan articulated an Enlightenment confidence that order and justice would eventually prevail over primal chaos. Taut stanzas and the imagery of creation and resurrection discipline sorrow into aspiration:

God of mercy! God of Peace!
Make this mad confusion cease;
O'er the mental chaos move,
Through it speak the light of love. . . .

Here we watch our brother's sleep;
Watch with us, but do not weep;
Watch with us thro' dead of night,
But expect the morning light.[103]

As a doctor and as a reformer Drennan was pledged to attack avoidable evils, physical and political, by rational and scientific means. He encountered the like-minded Richard Edgeworth at the Volunteer conferences in the 1780s and made a considerable impression on his young daughter Maria, then aged fifteen and described in a letter as Drennan's chief admirer (*Letters*, p. 401). Despite differences of social background, the eccentric Anglo-Irish engineer and educationalist from Longford and the Belfast doctor had common interests and a similar intellectual background. As Marilyn Butler has shown, the moral and social philosophy of the Scottish Enlightenment had considerable influence on the outlook of Edgeworth and his circle. Dugald Stewart was a friend and mentor to the Edgeworth family as he was to Drennan.[104] Not surprisingly, Drennan took an interest in Maria Edgeworth's literary career and as early as 1807, after *Castle Rackrent* and *Belinda* but with *The Absentee* (1812) and *Ormond* (1817) still to come, he told his sister she was 'by far our finest female writer' (*Letters*, p. 375).

In Drennan's own later career in Belfast, as editor and promoter of the progressive *Belfast Monthly Magazine* (1803–13), as a founder of the Academical Institution, and as an active member of the Linen Hall Library and Society for the Promotion of Knowledge, Drennan continued to embody the positive and practical reformist qualities which had first interested the Edgeworths. These qualities, and the sceptical voice, cool but angry in season, which went with them, have been edited out of the Irish literary tradition to make more room for romantic melancholy, decaying big houses and peasant vitality.

Only in Ulster (itself in danger of being edited out of Irish literary tradition until rediscovered as a context for Seamus Heaney) has Drennan been much valued. In 1847, in increasingly industrial and conservative Belfast, the heterodox liberal churchman Henry Montgomery paid tribute to him as 'a philosopher, a statesman, an orator, a poet, and in all that gives dignity to the name, a MAN!'[105] His own estimate was more modest:

> Man of taste, more than talent; not learn'd tho' of letters;
> His creed without claws, and his faith without fetters.

Another unassuming political dissenter, the modern Ulster poet John Hewitt, took on the mantle of Drennan and applied these words to himself when he was awarded the freedom of Belfast in 1983.[106] Hewitt's increasing stature may at last allow Drennan to come into his own again. But for much of the nineteenth century Irish letters were dominated by the much better-known figure of Thomas Moore.

THOMAS MOORE (1779–1852)

The contrasts between Moore and Drennan seem to demonstrate crucial cultural divisions in Ireland, different modes of Irishness. It is almost fatally easy to oppose Dubliner and Belfast man, Catholic and Protestant, dreamy elegist of heroic Ireland and practical organizer, talented entertainer and stern reformer, romantic melodist and Enlightenment satirist. Moore's popularity and Drennan's obscurity in the nineteenth century and since can be seen as cultural symptoms

PLATE 2   Daniel Maclise, *The Origin of the Harp* (for a poem by Thomas Moore)

of increasingly triumphalist Celtic and Catholic nationalism. But the antithesis can be overworked. Moore at his best resists and transcends the stereotyped Irishness he helped to invent; Moore at his worst has never escaped censure.

Moore's catchpenny charm and immense popular success provoked hostile reactions even in his heyday. The lilting anapaestic rhythms, facile national sentiment and soft-focus nostalgia of his celebrated *Irish Melodies* (1808–34) have been savoured and scoffed at since the poems first appeared. The rhythm and the sentiment went with the musical settings. The fastidious could complain of the very tunefulness and accessibility of Sir John Stevenson's arrangements, heavily simplified from the traditional airs currently being collected by Edward Bunting and others. Hazlitt observed that Moore had turned the 'wild harp of Erin into a musical snuffbox'.[107] The *Irish Melodies* attracted the ambiguous compliment of parody long before the series was complete. In 1812 Horace and James Smith tried their hand at the already familiar lilting stanza:

> For Erin surpasses the daughters of Neptune
>   As Dian outshines each encircling star;
> And the spheres of the heavens could never have kept tune
>   Till set to the music of Erin-go-bragh![108]

Joyce also parodied 'tummy moor's maladies',[109] as if to measure his distance from the self-indulgent complaint of romantic melancholy. But the musician in him loved the songs: he incorporated snatches from virtually all the *Irish Melodies* into the rich ironic counterpoint of *Finnegans Wake*.[110] For most of the nineteenth century Moore had been so much identified with Irish national sentiment that to dislike him could be seen as a kind of treason. But the tone-deaf Yeats was not much impressed, finding the poems 'artificial and mechanical' without the music, for which he had no ear anyway. He made exceptions only for 'The Light of Other Days' and 'At the Mid Hour of Night'.[111] Patrick Kavanagh, in full retreat from self-deluding sentimental Irishness, sourly remarked of Moore that

> The cowardice of Ireland is in his statue,
> No poet's honoured when they wreathe this stone.[112]

Thomas Kinsella, committed, like Kavanagh, to a harsher and more discordant perception of Ireland, is glibly dismissive, certain that all agree Moore is 'not an important poet'.[113] He might be right, but a stream of recent studies seems to suggest otherwise.[114]

For better or worse, Moore is stubbornly memorable: the cadences and images linger in the subconscious, as Dickens and Poe discovered.[115] Even the austere Ulster poet John Hewitt responds to the haunting note of national and spiritual aspiration sounded in Moore's 'Song of Fionnuala'. In Moore's poem Lir's lonely daughter has been turned into a swan until Christianity dawns over Ireland's darkness and the mass-bell is heard. She wonders plaintively

> When will heaven, its sweet bell ringing,
> Call my spirit from this stormy world?

In 'An Irishman in Coventry' (1958) Hewitt is more stubbornly secular, harshly reviewing the long disaster of Irish history, but concluding

> Yet like Lir's children banished to the waters
> our hearts still listen for the landward bells.[116]

Not all the *Irish Melodies* are merely melodious, and Moore's importance is not confined to them. He was a religious poet, a love poet, an imitator of the classics, an effective political satirist, a painstaking historian and biographer, a novelist (or sorts) and a staunch campaigner for religious toleration. His European reputation, which spread to Poland and Russia, owed much to the *Melodies,* frequently translated and well known in the French version of 1823 by Louise Swanton Belloc, Hilaire Belloc's grandmother. Hector Berlioz set some of them as *Neuf Mélodies Irlandaises* (1830). But it was one of Moore's *Sacred Songs*, 'This world is all a fleeting show', that formed the basis of the first number of Berlioz' *Tristia* (1830–1), a religious meditation for voices and orchestra. Moore wrote for the *Edinburgh Review,* not only on poetry and Ireland, as one might expect, but also on the Fathers of the Church and on German Protestantism,[117] displaying taste and learning as well as a robustly disrespectful attitude towards ecclesiastical traditionalism.

An Irish adventurer whose reputation was made in England, a friend of rebels and establishment figures, a Catholic educated alongside Ireland's Protestant gentry, a romantic and a convinced Christian who relished Voltaire, Moore spans different traditions and encompasses different identities like so many Irish writers before and since. His *Memoirs* were edited (badly) by an English Prime Minister,

Lord John Russell, but he has been claimed by the cultural nationalists as a poet in the authentically Celtic (and so unEnglish) tradition. He sings of Tara and Brien Boru, Red Branch Knights and Lir's lonely daughters, with some sensitivity to the word-music as well as the matter of an older Ireland. Robert Farren points out that his rhythms, not as mechanically regular as parody or familiar anthology-pieces (such as 'The harp that once through Tara's halls') might suggest, are innovative in English prosody. He claims they reflect at least something of the intricate patterning and varied pulse of the Gaelic *amhrán* or popular accentual verse. One of the best examples is 'Oh ye dead', where Farren detects 'the voice of Gaeldom breaking in'. The title, the widening perspectives and the bleak feeling of Joyce's story 'The Dead' (in *Dubliners*) come from this poem:

Oh ye Dead! oh ye Dead! whom we know by the light you give
From your cold gleaming eyes, though you move like men who live,
Why leave you thus your graves,
In far-off fields and waves,
Where the worm and the sea-bird only know your bed,
    To haunt this spot where all
    Those eyes that wept your fall,
And the hearts that wail'd you, like your own, lie dead?[118]

It is also true that Moore often sounds the bogusly Celtic note of romantic melancholy, at least in *Irish Melodies*. Ossianic gloom misled G. K. Chesterton, following Matthew Arnold, into the belief that

the great Gaels of Ireland
Are the men that God made mad,
For all their wars are merry
And all their songs are sad.[119]

Moore must take some of the blame for perpetuating the melancholy mode and convincing a credulous public that this was the very soul of Ireland. In extreme youth Moore had attempted explicitly Ossianic verse himself. In his heyday it was the European cult of Ossian reflected in the wistfulness of romantic poets such as Alphonse de Lamartine which helped to create the taste for the *Irish Melodies* in France. Lamartine's Ossian and his inevitable harp contribute to the historian Augustin Thierry's fantasies about Ireland. In a reverie prompted by the *Irish Melodies* Thierry imagines downtrodden Irish peasants in their villages and along the lake-shores listening to songs accompanied by the harp which tell of ancestral oppression and wrong.[120]

But Moore is often jollier than this. While he stops well short of the ribald exuberance of Gaelic poems such as Brian Merriman's *Cúirt an Mheadhon Oidhche* ('The Midnight Court') (1780), his earlier love poetry attracted prudish censure because of its coy but enthusiastic sensuality.[121] Traces of the goliardic vitality of the *Aislinge Mac Conglinne* ('The Vision of Mac Conglinne') or the probably related *Land of Cokaygne* can be found in some of his satirical writing. Edward Irving's ponderously prophetic *Babylon and Infidelity Fore-doomed of God* (1826) provoked Moore's poem 'The Millennium' (1826) which mocks the lunatic fringes of Protestant 'enthusiasm' in sound eighteenth-century style. Moore derides not only the Irvingites but also Francis Dobbs, who had exasperated William Drennan. In his robust common sense Moore can be much more like Drennan than one might expect on the basis of *Irish Melodies*. He regards extravagant millennial expectation as almost literally 'pie in the sky':

A City, where wine and cheap corn shall abound,–
A celestial *Cocaigne,* on whose buttery shelves
We may swear the best things of this world will be found,
As your Saints seldom fail to take care of themselves!

. . . .

There was Counsellor Dobbs, too, an Irish M.P.,
Who discours'd on the subject with signal *éclat*,
And, each day of his life, sat expecting to see
A Millennium break out in the town of Armagh!
(*Poetical Works*, p. 410)

Moore the satirist seems to belong in a different context and tradition from Moore the elegist of Ireland or, as Shelley put it, 'The sweetest lyrist of her saddest wrong'.[122] In his poem 'A Case of Libel' the Devil hoofs about in the guise of a metropolitan dandy frequenting White's and Crockfords's. The Regency world of prize-fighting, Byron and Bonaparte is indicated in the boxing slang of the 'Epistle from Tom Crib to Big Ben' which alludes to Bonaparte's transportation to St Helena. Politically, Moore sided with the English Whigs, which made it natural for him to share in Byron's political and poetic vendetta against the High Tory poet laureate Robert Southey. Moore's 'The

Three Doctors' attacks Southey's verbosity ('writes books by the yard') and his diehard anti-Catholicism ('Seven millions of Papists, no less,/ Doctor S-th-y attacks like a Turk') (*Poetical Works*, pp. 329f, 411).

Moore's Englishness goes beyond his metropolitan satire and his friendship with Byron. He had been educated at Samuel Whyte's English Grammar School in Dublin before proceeding to the still overwhelmingly Protestant Trinity College, Dublin, and then the Middle Temple in London. These experiences had taught him the English cultural idiom of well-to-do Anglo-Ireland. The curriculum of Whyte's school emphasized spoken English and was unusually literary, affected by Whyte's own literary interests and by the speech-theories of his friend Thomas Sheridan, the godson and biographer of Swift. Dramatic performances by Whyte's pupils had included Nicholas Rowe's *Jane Shore* (1714) and a version of Milton's masque *Comus* (1637) with a special epilogue written by Henry Grattan, no less. This kind of schooling taught Moore that literature could be a performance art, but the literature was old-fashioned and very English.[123]

It was the mark of an English or Anglo-Irish gentleman to be conversant with the classics. Moore's first substantial literary work, a verse-translation of the Greek lyrics attributed to Anacreon (published 1800), established him as an English poet in the tradition of Cowley and Herrick who had translated some of the same poems. He projected himself as a scholar and a gentleman in the English mode, effortlessly (if superficially) aware of the relevant scholarship and of other translations in several languages. By keeping this cosmopolitan company the young Moore proclaimed himself a man of letters. By mediating to the Greekless English public ancient songs of love and fleeting pleasure, postponing or evading graver subjects, he inaugurated his risky but successful career as a popular entertainer. Anacreon's songs, performed at public banquets in antiquity, anticipate the nineteenth-century parlour-song. The *Irish Melodies* are in a sense Moore's Irish Anacreontics, translating but strategically softening and sugaring partly alien material. If Irish tradition is both harsher and funnier than Moore is sometimes willing to make it, the Greek of Anacreon and the subsequent Anacreontic tradition is also crisper, simpler and less sentimental than the winsome English of Moore's drawing-room versions.

What Moore actually translates is already at several removes from the fragmentary surviving lyrics by Anacreon written in the sixth century BC. Like other translators before him, Moore works from the *Anacreontea*, later Greek poems in the same vein written at various periods, finally collected in a tenth-century manuscript which was eventually printed by Henri Estienne in 1554. Anacreon himself had written of thinning hair, old age and inexorable death in a wry little poem preserved in an ancient anthology of lyrics about mortality.[124] But the grimness of the original lyric was already considerably modified by the later adaptation, translated by both Cowley and Moore, which begins, in literal translation, 'The women say, Anacreon, you are old. Take a glass and look at your thinning hair and your bald forehead'.[125] In Moore this becomes, more floridly and copiously,

> The women tell me every day
> That all my bloom has past away
> 'Behold', the pretty wantons cry,
> 'Behold this mirror with a sigh;
> The locks upon thy brow are few,
> And like the rest, they're withering too.'

Moore's original concludes by suggesting that old men should play the more as Death approaches but Moore's version turns the sharp paradox into banal commonplace. The last word of the Greek is *Moires,* 'doom', but Moore buries his word 'death' in the middle of a line three lines from the end and concludes blandly

> And had I but an hour to live,
> That little hour to bliss I'd give.
> (*Poetical Works,* p. 9)

Moore's method, symptomatic of his misleadingly winning ways with his Irish materials, can be illustrated by another Anacreontic poem. The original playfully introduces the poet's almost countless loves with a simple conditional sentence: 'If you can count all the leaves of the trees, if you can discover the sands of the entire ocean, I will make you sole reckoner of my loves'.[126] Moore complicates the simple images, suffusing them with romantic languor:

> Count me on the summer trees,
> Every leaf that courts the breeze:
> Count me, on the foamy deep
> Every wave that sinks to sleep . . .
> (*Poetical Works,* p.12)

A similar fluent fuzziness blurs and generalizes diction and feeling in Moore's version of the poem attributed to Tibullus which Drennan had previously translated. Drennan's economical and slightly more literal version, as abrupt as the original, begins

> Yes–'twas the vow that clos'd the happy night–
> None of thy sex shall taste such dear delight!
> (*Fugitive Pieces*, p. 43)

But Moore sacrifices economy and precision on the altar of vapid charm:

> 'Never shall woman's smile have pow'r
> To win me from those gentle charms!'–
> Thus swore I in that happy hour
> When Love first gave thee to my arms.
> (*Poetical Works*, p. 379)

The erotic rhyme of possibly voluptuous 'charms' and embracing 'arms', unwarranted by the original, is unnecessarily repeated in the final stanza of Moore's version. This is really indistinguishable from the love-lyrics he composed in his own right for *Irish Melodies*. In 'Believe me, if all those endearing young charms' one finds the same inevitable rhyme, as the charms 'fleet in my arms', and the same Anacreontic note of evanescent eroticism (*Poetical Works*, p. 149).

But Moore at his best rises above marketable charm and sentimental pseudo-classicism. He belongs among the English romantics. Romantic rebellion and romantic emotion recollected in tranquillity impart depth, tension and seriousness to the best of the *Irish Melodies* and some of his later work. In verse and prose he consistently derided militant Protestantism and the repressive Tory administrations which opposed Catholic Emancipation. Imaginatively, if not practically, he gradually came to identify himself with Ireland's struggle for national freedoms, a struggle already approximating to the Ossianic and Wordsworthian condition of 'Old unhappy far-off things/ And battles long ago', though the most recent instalment, in 1798, was still a painful memory.

The matter of Ireland was a natural romantic theme. Patriotic history and legend, assembled by Charles O'Conor and the other eighteenth-century antiquarians, provided a rich and accessible store of noble feeling and heroic example, and the same could be said of the great days of the Volunteers and Grattan's Parliament, already lost to all but memory and myth. De Quincey had witnessed that last session of the old Irish Parliament before it disappeared with the Union and had been indignant at its passing without 'the protesting echo of a sigh'.[127] Shelley had been fascinated by the revolutionary ardour of the United Irishmen and admired their eloquent defence counsellor John Philpot Curran. Curran's rhetoric drew sustenance from the new libertarian atmosphere of the 1780s. In 1790 he told the Irish Privy Council that 'The condition upon which God hath given liberty to man is eternal vigilance'. The famous statement was explicitly connected with Grattan's triumph in 1782, for Curran remarked that it was but eight years since his 'degraded country' had acquired the dignity of a free people.[128] Inflamed by Curran's stirring defence of Drennan's friend Archibald Hamilton Rowan and of the radical printer Peter Finnerty, Shelley dashed off his wild, revolutionary *Address to the Irish People* (1812) and tried to make Ireland's cause his own.[129]

Moore, on the other hand, more or less had Ireland's cause thrust upon him. The older generation of English romantics, Wordsworth, Coleridge and Southey, had found it bliss to be adolescent in the first dawn of the French Revolution in 1789. But Moore encountered revolutionary ardour only in 1798, the United Irishmen's would-be 'Year of Liberty'. He was a student at Trinity College, where opinion was divided. The Dean of Trinity, Whitley Stokes (grandfather and namesake of a great Celtic scholar), had been a United Irishman, though never a combatant: even so, he had been temporarily suspended from his post. Moore's own behaviour at the time seems to have been fairly cautious, but his college friend Robert Emmet belonged to an ardently patriotic family which was deeply involved. In the aftermath of military defeat and the corruptly engineered Act of Union, in 1803, Robert Emmet tried to lead another rebellion. It collapsed into a brief affray in the Dublin streets and Emmet was arrested and executed. This would have been the end of the matter except that Emmet made a stirring and defiant speech from the dock which is one of the great set-pieces of Irish nationalist rhetoric. Though the evidence is defective and highly suspect,[130] Emmet is usually represented as concluding: 'when my country takes her place among the nations of the earth, then, and not till then, let my epitaph be written.'

Moore apparently preserved Emmet's draft of the speech, intending to incorporate it in his projected *History of Ireland,* but he never did. Instead he combined his personal recollections with folk-memory and used Emmet as a point of contact between mythic history and contemporary oppressed Ireland, though Emmet himself largely disappeared into legend in the process. In 'Oh! breathe not his name' Moore wrote Emmet's epitaph while ostensibly respecting his wish that no man should until Ireland was a nation.

> Oh! breathe not his name, let it sleep in the shade,
> Where cold and unhonour'd his relics are laid:
> Sad, silent and dark be the tears that we shed,
> As the night-dew that falls on the grass o'er his head.
>
> But the night-dew that falls, though in silence it weeps,
> Shall brighten with verdure the grave where he sleeps;
> And the tear that we shed, though in secret it rolls,
> Shall long keep his memory green in our souls.
>   (*Poetical Works*, p. 144)

The name of Emmet is both absorbed into and silently irradiated by unvoiced national sentiment, participating in the paradox of life-renewing martyrdom which characterizes national as well as religious ideologies. Emmet's body has already become the 'relics' associated with saints and martyrs. The hope of awakening to resurrection is implied in the verb 'sleeps' which rhymes with but softens 'weeps'. The weeping has already been mythologized by transfer from individual mourners to the night-dew of encompassing nature. In biblical idiom dew is a symbol and instrument of divine grace and renewal for God's people,[131] and in Moore's poem patriot tears assume a similar mystical function, transformed into the dews which refresh the green grass of Ireland.

Emmet could be seen as the successor and representative of all the dead heroes of 1798 (including Lord Edward Fitzgerald whose biography Moore later wrote). By extension he could become the type of all Irish national heroes. Memories of Emmet and of 1798, which Moore could not obliterate if he wanted to, suffuse 'Forget not the field where they perished', though both the field and the vanquished 'they' are historically unspecific. The spirit of Emmet is vindicated in the contrast of crudely triumphalist tyranny and indomitable patriotism:

> Could the chain for an instant be riven
>   Which Tyranny flung round us then,
> No, 'tis not in Man nor in Heaven,
>   To let Tyranny bind it again!

> But 'tis past – and tho' blazon'd in story
> The name of our Victor may be,
> Accurst is the march of that glory
> Which treads o'er the hearts of the free.
>   (*Poetical Works*, p. 166)

Romantically illogical hope wells up in the poetry. The incoherence but spiritual vitality of patriotic aspiration is registered in fractured syntax miming broken chains ('No, 'tis not . . .'). The relation between tyranny and victory is artfully confused by the delayed resolution of the reader's uncertainty about the application of the pivotal 'But 'tis past' and about whether patriot or tyrant is 'blazon'd in story' and touched with some kind of ambiguous glory. The effect of this momentary mystification is to subvert the opposition of victory and defeat and to invest death with the possibility of triumph.

A similar process is at work in 'Remember the glories of Brien the brave'. This poem, only formally about the long-dead hero of Clontarf who defeated the Danes, is actually about the lost liberties and disappointed hopes of recent Irish history, imaginatively recoverable in the reflected light of legendary victory which transforms dead companions like Emmet into conquering heroes:

> Forget not our wounded companions, who stood
>   In the day of distress by our side;
> While the moss of the valley grew red with their blood,
>   They stirr'd not, but conquer'd and died.
>   (*Poetical Works*, p. 144)

The historically displaced heroic sentiment, powerfully vague, was set to the music of Berlioz and triumphed on the Paris barricades during the July revolution of 1830, we are told,[132] yet it entertained rather than disturbed the Whig establishment in their London drawing-rooms. It is easy to condemn Moore for sanitizing sedition and playing safe with his English public, but this misrepresents the risks he was prepared to take and the hostility he constantly encountered from conservative opinion, notably in the *Quarterly Review* and *Blackwood's Edinburgh Magazine*. It also trivializes the tensions and ambivalence of his poetry, encompassing without reconciling rebellion and quiescence, hope and despair, atavistic blood-sacrifice and the rational prospect of daylight and liberty.

These tensions were accommodated within Moore's most ambitious venture, the narrative poem *Lalla Rookh* (1817). Byron had helped to create a taste for the romantic East, and Francis Jeffrey in the *Edinburgh Review*, previously hostile to Moore's work, made amends by acclaiming this as 'the finest orientalism we have had yet'.[133] Not realizing that *Lalla Rookh* was an exotic Persian tale, the Whig hostess Lady Holland complained, 'Mr Moore, I have not read your 'Larry O'Rourke". I don't like Irish stories.'[134] In a sense she was right: it *is* Irish at bottom. Moore rather lost his way with it since his poetic gift was for lyrical intensities rather than extended narrative. But in the inset story 'The Fireworshippers' he found an opportunity to rework the Emmet story and this gave him the stimulus to complete the poem. Emmet is represented by the heroic young Hafed. The placing of the tale of Hafed within the frame-narrative distances the Emmet story as myth but also provides an audience and a social context to demonstrate, or at least test, its affective power and its posthumous significance.

At one level the narrative is an enlightened plea for toleration. One of its models is a play by Voltaire, mercifully never performed, which is entitled *Les Guèbres, ou La Tolération* (1769). The Fireworshippers or Ghebers were Persian Zoroastrians whose religion and country were threatened first by the Roman Empire and then by Islam. Voltaire used imperilled Zoroastrianism as a metaphor for Jansenism, which the French authorities had signally failed to tolerate. Eventually the Roman Emperor of the play learns the lesson Voltaire has to teach and proclaims

Les persécutions
Ont mal servi ma gloire, et font trop de rebelles.
Quand le prince est clément, les sujets sont fidèles.

(The persecutions have ill served my glory and make too many rebels. When the prince is merciful the subjects are loyal.)[135]

Moore's Ghebers also stand for a modern oppressed people, in this case Irish Catholics. Moore's Hafed, like Emmet, is really too late to turn back the tide of history. The story is set in the seventh century when Iran has already become an Islamic province and Zoroastrianism has been supplanted as the state religion. The parallel with Catholic Ireland under Protestant English rule is not hard to find, though since Emmet was actually a Protestant, Moore is in effect simplifying the Irish struggle into a crudely sectarian affair. The increasing tendency to identify Catholic and national causes was to have disastrously divisive consequences later on. But Moore's fable can sustain a more general reading. Voltaire had noted that Christianity had been as much at risk as the religion of the Ghebers under Roman tyranny,[136] and Christians, like the Ghebers, had always seen Islam as a threat. The implied association of Zoroastrianism with Christianity is perhaps strengthened by some remarks by Sir William Jones, one of Moore's historical sources for his poem. Developing the view that ancient Iran was the seat of the Indo-European peoples, the cradle of European civilization, Jones suggested that in its earliest form ancient Iranian and Indo-European religion was monotheistic, anticipating if not directly continuous with Christianity.[137] On this view the Iranian religion of the poem could be not merely the type but almost the prototype of persecuted Christianity down the centuries and, specifically, of penally oppressed Irish Catholicism.

Moore's fable dignifies and aestheticizes resentment and revolt by means of romantic primitivism, a mode successfully adopted in other patriotic Irish works of the immediately post-Union period such as Lady Morgan's novel *The Wild Irish Girl* (1806) and its derivative, Charles Maturin's *The Wild Irish Boy* (1808). The fireworshippers are wild, rebellious, almost demonic figures determined 'To break our country's chains, or die!' (*Poetical Works*, p. 299). Moore uses the frame-narrative to head off conservative misgivings among his readers: the poet-narrator Feramorz radiates imaginative enthusiasm for his theme, which encourages Lalla Rookh to fall in love with him, while the preposterous self-important chamberlain Fadladeen is shocked and apprehensive, expecting to hear of treason and abomination. Within the tale, romantic rebellion is powerfully attractive across cultural and political boundaries. Hinda is the daughter of the bigoted and repressive Arab Emir Al Hassan, but she is soon in love with Hafed.

The tragic outcome is inevitable, as it nearly always is in Irish tales of Catholics and Protestants embarked on inter-communal adventure or passion. The implied argument for toleration is shouldered aside by the more atavistic rhetoric of blood-sacrifice. Hafed's revolt is unsuccessful. Mortally wounded in hopeless battle he and a single companion flee to one of the mountain shrines of their religion where the sacred fire is kept burning. His companion dies. Defying 'Moslem chains' and probability alike Hafed shouts 'Now, Freedom's God! I come to Thee', vaults on to the sacred pyre with a smile of triumph, and

> In that last effort, ere the fires
> Have harm'd one glorious limb, expires!
> (*Poetical Works*, p. 314)

Triumph and despair, glory and defeat, coexist in that artfully contrived confusion which is almost Moore's stock in trade. Hinda arrives to discover that 'Iran's hopes and hers are o'er'. She plunges into the sea where the Peris of the Ocean sing an anapaestic elegy (remarkably like one of the *Irish Melodies*) saying almost nothing in ten stanzas except

> Farewell – farewell – until Pity's sweet fountain
> Is lost in the hearts of the fair and the brave,
> They'll weep for the Chieftain who died on that mountain,
> They'll weep for the Maiden who sleeps in this wave.
>   (*Poetical Works*, p. 316)

The fair Lalla Rookh and the brave Feramorz are as affected as the Peris could wish. All this emotion recollected in tranquillity not only advances their union but has implications for Iran: it emerges that Feramorz is really the king in disguise and his imaginative sympathy with the hard-driven rebel of his tale bodes well for a humane and tolerant reign.

Moore's ideal state, like Moore's poetry, contains and improbably harmonizes noble subversive energies and immemorial pieties within a rational enlightened polity. In this respect he is less a romantic dreamer, more a creature of the European and Scottish Enlightenment like Drennan, than is usually realized. His direct contacts with Ireland's Presbyterian and dissenting tradition were minimal. But he had his own copy of the Rev. Dr William Steel Dickson's autobiographical *Narrative* (1812), describing the adventures of the Glasgow-educated minister who became commander-in-chief of the Co. Down United Irishmen. He also owned Thomas Reid's Glasgow lectures *Essays on the Active and Intellectual Powers of Man* (1785–8) in the 1790 Dublin edition. This was a major text of the 'Common Sense' tradition of Scottish philosophy inaugurated by Francis Hutcheson. It seems likely that Moore had used it as a textbook at Trinity, where he would also have encountered Locke. William Molyneux' Lockian argument *The Case of Ireland . . . Stated* (1776 edition) was in his library. As a Catholic increasingly involved in the battles for Catholic Emancipation, Moore was also familiar with the urbanely enlightened pamphleteering of the Irish Catholic *literati*. His own fictionalized review of Irish Catholic disablilities, *Memoirs of Captain Rock* (1824), draws on the historical material assembled by Charles O'Conor and John Curry among others.[138]

This ecumenical intellectual background, drawing on eighteenth-century Scots-Irish, Anglo-Irish and Catholic Irish traditions, encouraged the later Moore to defend a specifically Catholic position on the broad ground of general moral and Christian principle. His marriage to a Protestant wife may also have been a factor. His prose-satire *Travels of an Irish Gentleman in Search of a Religion* (1833), glancing at the piously Protestant Hannah More's popular tale *Coelebs in Search of a Wife* (1809), challenges the traditional Anglo-Irish association of gentlemanliness with Protestantism alone. This had continued in places such as Trinity College even after Catholics like Moore and O'Connell began to study there. Moore's Catholic protagonist, himself a Trinity man, contemplates adopting the seemingly gentlemanly religion of the Protestant Ascendancy. With the eventual granting of Catholic Emancipation in 1829 no special worldly advantage was involved so disinterested religious enquiry was a genuine possibility. The enquirer reads widely but comes to the conclusion that the bizarre Gnostic heretics of the past were proto-Protestants. He decides to stay a Catholic.

In a less sophisticted but more entertaining polemic, 'The Petition of the Orangemen of Ireland' (1826), Moore, like Burke before him, denounces the moral and religious foundations of 'Protestant Ascendancy' in its militant, 'Orange', aspect. The poem impersonates the indignation of supposed political grievance while illustrating the real grievances of Ireland's Catholic majority, obliquely resurrecting enlightenment debates about government and the rights of man:

> To the people of England, the humble Petition
>   Of Ireland's disconsolate Orangemen, showing –
> That sad, very sad, is our present condition –
>   Our jobbing all gone, and our noble selves going; –
>
> That, forming one seventh, within a few fractions,
>   Of Ireland's seven millions of hot heads and hearts,
> We hold it the basest of all base transactions
>   To keep us from murd'ring the other six parts; –
>
> That, as to laws made for the good of the many,
>   We humbly suggest there is nothing less true;
> As all human laws (and our own, more than any,)
>   Are made *by* and *for* a particular few; . . .
>   (*Poetical Works* p. 413)

One of Moore's least-regarded late works is a short novel called *The Epicurean* (1827), originally written as a long poem but never finished in that form. It concerns a pagan philosopher's search for truth and religion and is set in the third century (in poetically exotic surroundings) so that the humanistic, even deistical Christianity he eventually embraces is that of the ante-Nicene Church from which both Catholic and Protestant traditions ultimately derive. The shift from narrative poem to novel as an appropriate vehicle for a serious subject is itself of historical interest, heralding the eclipse of the long poem and anticipating the Victorian novel of high seriousness, not to mention Walter Pater's interestingly parallel *Marius the Epicurean* (1885) which may owe an unacknowledged debt to Moore.

But *The Epicurean* also looks back to the Irish eighteenth century. The protagonist is Alciphron, a leading Epicurean from Athens possibly named after an obscure second- or third-century sophist whose *Epistles* the younger Moore had justly described as 'that dull book' (*Poetical Works*, p. 10 n). But the name is just as likely to have come from a religious dialogue by Bishop Berkeley, *Alciphron: or the Minute Philosopher* (1732). Berkeley's Alciphron is a freethinker or 'minute philosopher' eventually persuaded by the Christian Euphranor that the natural course of ideas is itself the language or handwriting of God. The specific link with Berkeley may be coincidental, though Moore would have come across at least some of Berkeley's work at Trinity. But Moore and Berkeley, the Catholic and the Protestant, share a vision of a common Christianity which satisfies the questing intelligence and is more fundamental and important than the sectarian attitudes which bedevilled their country.

At one level Moore seems to offer straightforward exotic romance: Alciphron comes to faith through love for the Egyptian maiden Alethe who suffers martyrdom. But Alciphron's pilgrimage possibly owes something to Bunyan's *Pilgrim's Progress*, which also underpins one of Moore's *Sacred Songs*.[139] 'Alciphron' is Greek for 'stout-hearted' and 'Alethe' means 'truth': the novel can be read as an allegory of courage and truth brought together by love to encounter the suffering and serenity of Christian faith.

Moore's Sacred Songs (1816–24) express the same non-sectarian religion. They redirect to more conventionally religious ends the language of death and renewal, desolation and hope, which is characteristic of *Irish Melodies*. Some, such as 'War against Babylon' and 'Sound the loud Timbrel o'er Egypt's dark sea', renew the patriotic rhetoric of righteous warfare and liberation, effectively following if not acknowledging the old Irish tradition of associating oppressed Ireland with oppressed Israel. But the best of the *Sacred Songs*, and the best of Moore's writing, rise above oppression and narrowly national feeling and speak to the universal spirit of man of fulfilment and peace:

> Come, ye disconsolate, wher'e'er you languish,
> Come, at God's altar fervently kneel;
> Here bring your wounded hearts, here tell your anguish –
> Earth has no sorrow that Heaven cannot heal.
>
> *(Poetical Works,* p. 205)

Maynooth professors such as Patrick Aloysius Murray and George Crolly revered the national spirit of Moore.[140] Young Ireland propagandists such as Thomas D'Arcy McGee found in his songs the soul and aspirations of Ireland. Ireland's parliamentary leader Charles Stewart Parnell was not literary, but the only two poetic quotations he is known to have attempted (and bungled) were both from Moore.[141]

But Moore, with all his faults and limitations, belongs to a wider audience. In the music of Berlioz, in the adaptations of Frenchmen and Italians, Russians and Poles, he speaks out of the complexity of the Irish experience and the traditions of Ireland to the condition of all mankind.

CHAPTER 4

The Literatures of Victorian Ireland:

William Carleton and Thomas D'Arcy McGee

WITH THE passing of William Drennan and Thomas Moore Irish literature seemed to change direction, or even to begin again as if they had never been. A new and different sense of tradition, dominated by the tastes of W. B. Yeats and Celtic Revivalism, eventually ensured that Drennan in particular almost disappeared off the map. Ulster radicalism and the possibilities of a distinctively Ulster Protestant contribution to Irish writing seemed to disappear along with him. Moore remained popular with politicians and sentimental nationalists, but he never meant much to Yeats and his circle. The Irish poetic ancestors Yeats himself selected were Mangan, Ferguson and Davis.[1] Davis, the best nationalist but the worst poet of the three, as Yeats had to admit,[2] was the only one to show much interest in either Drennan or Moore. Even then, the tradition was hardly direct. Davis actually knew very little about Drennan and he had first encountered Moore only indirectly, in the romantic essays of the French historian Augustin Thierry.[3]

The problem is compounded by the fact that the Irish novel comes to prominence in the nineteenth century, and that in itself poses problems of continuity with earlier, non-fictional forms. Yeats and his contemporaries read novels, and the Irish Literary Revival found significant expression in fiction as well as poetry and plays as John Wilson Foster has recently demonstrated.[4] Yeats's own anthology of

Representative Irish Tales (2 vols, 1891) registers the importance of this emerging fictional tradition, in which William Carleton has an important place. Maria Edgeworth's *Castle Rackrent* (1800) represents a convenient starting-point and Irish rural life represents a recurring theme imparting coherence to a now-familiar and well-documented history.[5] But Drennan and Moore are essentially university wits and urban poets with rhetorical rather than realist designs upon the countryside. While connections between Drennan and the Edgeworths have been noted in the previous chapter there are no other obvious links between the enlightenment poet and the fiction of nineteenth-century Ireland. Moore was sometimes used by the novelists as a source of patriotic quotations,[6] and romantic propagandists and bad poets found in him a dubious inspiration, but his aristocratic and heroic legend of wistful Irishness had actually little direct bearing on the poverty and vanishing folkways of the Irish poor recounted by Carleton and others.

This seeming discontinuity can be related to the larger discontinuities of nineteenth-century Irish life occasioned by the Act of Union and its aftermath. Belfast was emerging as an important manufacturing centre within the newly United Kingdom and the social and sectarian tensions this engendered gradually marginalized both literature and radical politics. Dublin was dead without its parliament and viceregal court. More than ever before urban intellectuals and landed gentry alike looked to London for professional and social opportunities, a phenomenon already noted in the career of Thomas Moore. The increased proportion of absentee landlords did nothing to improve conditions in the countryside, which soon became the locus of political discontent and the main object of attention in the literature of the period.

But 'literature' can be too narrowly defined and discontinuity is itself a powerful stimulus to the tradition-seeking process. In religious polemic and political tracts, historical and topographical works, poems and novels, different kinds of nineteenth-century Irishmen set about trying to write themselves into significant relationship with the past, and past writing, as a way of establishing or affirming identity. Past ages, particularly the seventeenth and eighteenth centuries, were not so much revisited as recreated. Long before Joyce, the ambition to forge the uncreated conscience of the race was stirring in the smithies of Irish souls. The ambition was doomed to varying degrees of disappointment. What, after all, *was* the 'race'? There was no agreement about whether the essential Ireland of the nineteenth century was or should be British or Irish, Protestant or Catholic, a progressive modern country or a Gaelic outpost, an industrializing and culturally pluralist society or a homogeneous collectivity of peasant farmers.

In this confusion Drennan and Moore themselves largely disappeared. But the traditions they annexed or invented, the Enlightenment and romantic attitudes they embodied and the stirring times through which they had lived were absorbed into the various discourses of tradition and identity. The mantle of Drennan was in a sense divided between historically-minded liberal Presbyterians and Dan O'Connell, the 'Liberator', whom Drennan respected. The great O'Connell was a far more successful political organizer than Drennan, but his outlook can be traced back to some of the same Enlightenment sources, notably Paine and Voltaire.[7] The Young Ireland radicals such as Thomas Davis and John Mitchel who broke away from O'Connell can also be linked with Enlightenment traditions, particularly in their grasp of the dismal science of political economy. Romantic antiquarianism, prominent in Moore, did not end with him but passed through a series of transformations in the more scholarly atmosphere of the nineteenth century, culminating in the enthusiasms of the Irish Literary Revival.

Carleton and D'Arcy McGee are not the direct and obvious literary descendants of Drennan and Moore. Carleton the countryman seems rather to look forward to Seamus Heaney, who put him in *Station Island* (1984). But the Carleton of *Traits and Stories of the Irish Peasantry* (1830–3) was a romantic: like Moore, and even more like Sir Walter Scott, in his recreation of an already vanished or vanishing mode of life and feeling. On the other hand, Carleton the ambitious Protestant attacking the Catholic 'superstition' of his upbringing recalls both the iconoclastic rationalism of Drennan and the problematic relationship between Catholicism and social status explored in Moore's *Travels of an Irish Gentleman in Search of a Religion*. McGee, a now forgotten writer, was another romantic, stimulated by the continuing interest in Celtic antiquities. He lectured enthusiastically on Moore and wrote patriotic Irish ballads partly in Moore's idiom. But as a Young Ireland propagandist, historian and political visionary he was also a United Irishman of the nineteenth century, committed like Drennan, though without Drennan's consistency, to a dream of nationhood spanning different traditions, incorporating and transcending religious and cultural diversity.

Carleton and McGee lived and wrote in the long shadow of 1798, like all their countrymen. For better or for worse, until mid-century at least, nineteenth-century Ireland was obsessed with the United Irishmen. As actual memories faded folk-memory and heroic myth took over, assisted and sharpened by the publication of R. R. Madden's three series of lives of the United Irishmen (1842–6). This provoked its own reaction: conservative opinion in the columns of the *Dublin University Magazine* deplored the United Irishmen as the wicked adversaries of legitimate government; the ultra-Tory *Blackwood's Edinburgh Magazine* saw in O'Connell's agitation to repeal the Act of Union a resurgence of the

> jackasses of Ireland . . .
> Whose ears, though cropp'd in ninety-eight
> Now flout our skies again.[8]

For the more conservative of the Ulster Presbyterians, typified by the Rev. Henry Cooke, the events of 1798 were an unmitigated disaster: Presbyterian involvement in them had jeopardized the relatively favourable position of their Church under an English government which subsidized ministerial salaries with a small grant or *regium donum* going back to the seventeenth century. But liberal and radical opinion tried variously to revive either the sense of national unity or the separatist politics of Irishness retrospectively attributed to the earlier movement. The Young Ireland republican extremist John Mitchel, a Presbyterian from Co. Down, founded a paper called *The United Irishman* in 1848. Henry Montgomery, a heterodox liberal Presbyterian, saluted O'Connell's fight for Catholic Emancipation in 1829, which he thought was in the best traditions of the United Irishmen. But he stopped well short of separatist nationalism and denounced O'Connell and Repeal in 1831.[9] This usually tempered and politically circumscribed nostalgia for 1798, particularly strong in Ulster, finds an echo even today in the work of the Belfast poets John Hewitt and Tom Paulin.

But after the United Irishmen and the Act of Union, Irishmen had to find imaginative and practical ways of living in the present, in an Ireland now formally the western extremity of a legislatively united kingdom. The term 'West Briton', which has persisted as a dismissive label for anti-nationalist attitudes, actually makes an early appearance as a positive descriptive term. In 1816 John Giffard, a Dublin customs official, noted the demoralization and economic decline of Dublin since the disappearance of parliament and viceregal court. He made the novel suggestion that the British parliament should meet sometimes in Edinburgh or Dublin so that North Britons and West Britons might breathe the atmosphere of government and observe at first hand the formulation of policy affecting every part of the United Kingdom.[10]

This defensive local patriotism coexisting uneasily with acceptance of a larger British identity points to poles of tension both political and cultural, still registered in almost every region of Britain and most acutely in Northen Ireland. Interestingly, the shrewdly pragmatic Daniel O'Connell could sound rather like John Giffard at times. In 1836 he felt that there was a chance at least that Ireland might after all benefit from the Union,

> a union of prosperity, and the rights of justice and of benefits . . .
> The people of Ireland are ready to become portion of the Empire,
> provided they be made so in reality and not in name alone; they
> are ready to become a kind of West Britons, if made so in benefits
> and justice; but if not, we are Irishmen again.[11]

The insecurity of this political vision, underscored by the syntactic shift from hypothetical 'they' to practical 'we', has its counterpart in contemporary Ulster, where conflicts of Britishness and Irishness, centre and periphery, are still unresolved. The debate was developed and extended by the writers, notably the Ulsterman Samuel Ferguson. Also writing in 1836, he spelt out the problem of identity and difference and the cultural imperatives entailed by the political status quo. While many famous Irishmen were also 'British all by blood', 'we cannot all be Britons, and though we would gladly be even West Britons in wealth and tranquillity, we must be Irish in mental achievements or we are nothing . . .'[12] The implication was that a British polity and an Irish culture could coexist and Ferguson's own scholarly and creative work proceeded on those terms.

A certain narrowness and an intermittent sense of strain resulted from this view. Celtic antiquarianism and sensitivity made Ferguson the poet of 'The Burial of King Cormac' and 'Deirdre's Lament for the Sons of Usnach' but Ferguson complained in 1868 that Celtic antiquarianism was 'almost the only species of literature now cultivated in Ireland which can properly be called native.'[13] Ferguson may have exaggerated a little, but this limited realization of the possibilities of Irish literature was matched by a critical tendency, exemplified by Matthew Arnold in *On the Study of Celtic Literature* (1867), to identify Irish culture exclusively with Celtic culture, and a selective, romanticized version of Celtic culture at that.

As famine darkened the land the British aspect of Ferguson's British Irishness became more problematic. The 'wealth and tranquillity' West Britons might expect in a United Kingdom were conspicuous by their absence. For a time Ferguson was a member of the Protestant Repeal Association. He was persuaded to associate with Gavan Duffy and the Young Ireland group in a short-lived Irish Council uniting Irishmen of all kinds at a time of national crisis.[14]

Things did not look quite so black in Belfast, unprecedentedly prosperous in the 1840s. The conservative Presbyterian Henry Cooke was fully aware that the wealth of the city derived from participation in the British Industrial Revolution and urged sceptics to look at the teeming warehouses and 'be a repealer–if you can'.[15] O'Connell's campaign for repeal of the Act of Union made little headway in Ulster among those Irishmen who were benefiting from the Union.

It was in this atmosphere of divided opinion and unequally distributed prosperity that Thomas Davis began to reinvent the notion of a single Irish nation, telling the Trinity College Literary Society, 'Gentlemen, you have a country.' With more political fervour and less literary tact than Ferguson, he inaugurated an ambitious programme of cultural nationalism. By 1845, the year of his death, he had temporarily secured the services of Carleton's errant pen for the Library of Ireland which was to express a new unity of national spirit arising out of cultural diversity. But largely Protestant and increasingly industrial north-east Ulster was not greatly interested.

Victorian Ulster and its writers have been little explored, perhaps because of a suspicion that the most British province could not possibly be authentically Irish. The Ulsterman Ferguson's attempts to sustain both a British and an Irish identity illustrated rather than resolved the problem, compounded by aggressive and restrictive definitions of Irishness forged in the bitter famine years. But it is absurd to infer a consciously unIrish, or even anti-Irish, tendency in nineteenth-century Ulster when Ulster, like the rest of Ireland, was sharply divided against itself religiously and politically. One could almost say that the legacy of division was the most Irish aspect of Victorian Ulster.

Even within the Presbyterian community there were deep-seated tensions between liberals and conservatives, arising from the dual identity of their Church, at once an embattled dissenting body and a (meagrely) subsidized state church, the Irish extension of the established Church of Scotland. The conservative tendency was well represented by the formidable and influential Dr Henry Cooke who, in

1834, rather presumptiously and prematurely proclaimed banns of marriage between Irish Presbyterianism and the episcopalian Established Church, all in the interests of upholding the political status quo of 'Protestant Ascendancy'.[16] The more liberal, sometimes radical, tendency, with which William Drennan had identified, continued among Presbyterians aware of a tradition of past sufferings at the hands of a (comparatively) wealthy and arrogantly imperious established church.

The Presbyterian historians James Seaton Reid and Thomas Witherow, who took a prominent part in the public affairs of their Church, periodically invoked and refurbished this tradition. Reid's moderatorial sermon to the Synod of Ulster in 1828 was an extended history lesson. In 1849 he challenged Ussher's Anglican biographer C. R. Elrington on the issue of Ussher's alleged puritan leanings and friendliness to Presbyterians which Elrington had denied against the evidence. Reid's indignation articulated the hereditary Presbyterian resentment of Anglican privilege and contempt for Dissenters which he detected in Elrington.[17] Witherow, like many Irish Presbyterians, had studied in Scotland. He confessed he was more impressed by the traditions of convenanting martyrdom at the hands of episcopacy which he encountered in Edinburgh than by the older traditions of monastic piety associated with Iona.[18] For Witherow the open-air masses of Penal days recalled in Catholic tradition had their counterpart in Presbyterian tradition. The covenanters had been obliged to hold open-air services or 'conventicles' in seventeenth-century Scotland. In Ulster there had been starlit services in the glens near Comber held in defiance of persecuting bishops and billeted soldiers seeking to exterminate Presbyterian worship.[19]

The Presbyterians wrote up their traditions in 1842, on the two-hundreth anniversary of the foundation of their Church. This coincided dramatically with a renewed outbreak of Anglican persecution, or something very like it. At the official celebrations one speaker referred to 'These days of supreme ecclesiastical arrogance, when one small sect [the episcopal church] has the impudence to unchurch and excommunicate the whole Christian world'.[20] The Irish bishops did not like non-Anglican marriage services. While marriages between Presbyterians conducted by a Presbyterian had been legal in Ireland since 1737, there was some uncertainty about the status of Presbyterian marriages where one party was not a Presbyterian. The Archbishop of Armagh, Lord John George Beresford, the 'living symbol of the Protestant Ascendancy',[21] took an interest in the issue in 1842. It was rumoured in the press that he had contributed £6000 to the legal fees of defendants charged with bigamy who were trying to convince the courts that their Presbyterian marriages had been illegal and invalid. For all that Dr Cooke had appeared as the friend of the Anglican establishment, in 1834 he felt this was an outrageous situation and worked hard to get the law changed.[22] He had an unexpected ally: though Cooke and Presbyterian Belfast had spurned O'Connell in 1841, the Liberator magnanimously badgered the Commons on this issue until new legislation was enacted in 1844.[23]

This was not the only occasion on which Irish Presbyterians and Roman Catholics had combined against the resented Anglican ascendancy. The Synod of Ulster had supported the cause of Catholic Emancipation since 1793 despite the hostility of Cooke and other ultra-Protestant diehards.[24] Emancipation was granted in 1829, but the vexed question of the land, the stock theme of nineteenth-century Irish writing, continued to trouble rural Presbyterians and Catholics alike. There were too many small tenant-farmers trying to make a living on the land, burdened with rents and insecure tenure. Carleton's novels and later works have made us almost over-familiar with the sufferings of starving Catholic peasantry ground down by absentee landlords and their wicked agents. Presbyterian tenants suffered too, though not usually so severely. The Devon Commission set up in 1843 to investigate the problem took evidence from Presbyterian ministers as well as Catholic priests about the misfortunes of their people. In the past farmers in the eastern counties of Ulster had fared better than most because of the long-established custom of 'tenant-right'. This required an incoming tenant to pay his predecessor a capital sum in respect of improvements to the property. Improvements thus secured benefits to the tenant as well as the landlord, which encouraged good farming and long tenancies. But in the early 1840s times were hard and Ulster landlords began to discontinue the custom, secure in the knowledge that it did not have the force of law. The consequences were disastrous. Agrarian outrages multiplied. In at least one case in Co. Down the landlords backed down and reinstituted tenant right. A sense of looming catastrophe on the land encouraged Ulstermen to think in national terms. In 1847, in its loyal address to the Lord Lieutenant, the Presbyterian General Assembly urged that the Ulster custom of tenant right 'should be universally extended and legally confirmed'.[25] A worried land-agent told the Devon Commission that any curtailment of tenant right would make Ulster as unsettled as other parts of Ireland: 'You would have a Tipperary in Down.'[26]

The Devon Commission evidence reveals resentment of landlordism and defensiveness about Ulster tenant right, which were cultural and national as well as economic. Rev. Dr John Brown, Presbyterian minister of Aghadowey in Co. Londonderry, was one of the best-informed witnesses before the Commission. He observed that

> what has proved very injurious to the country is, that persons coming from England apply English customs to us . . . A gentleman coming from London does not understand the *patois* of our northern people, who speak a kind of Scotch; and on the other hand, they understand as little of his cockney English.[27]

This linguistic and cultural distinctiveness is interestingly parallel to the distinctiveness of Irish-speaking rural communities which still persisted in the south and west of the country. Dialectologists have charted the incidence of Scots-related dialect-forms in Ireland, unevenly distributed through parts of the northern province.[28] The dialect-literature associated with them has been surveyed by the Ulster regionalist poet John Hewitt, who published an anthology of Ulster dialect poems, *Rhyming Weavers,* in 1975. The strangeness of this idiom and the politically subversive literary use to which it could be put is illustrated in the work of James McHenry of Larne, a Presbyterian minister who emigrated to Philadelphia. In his novels about eighteenth-century Ireland and the United Irishmen, he used Ulster dialect to demonstrate the cultural difference between Ulster people and the English. But this bewildered and alienated a snobbish New England reviewer who complained of the 'language we do not understand', 'an unknown tongue'.[29]

The Ulster dialect poets, like the cultural patriots of the Gaelic League, often used language to register cultural and political dissent, to measure their distance from England as well as from standard English. The Ulster rhyming weavers who looked to Burns rather than to English poets for literary models were equally unsympathetic to English or Anglo-Irish landlordism. David Herbison, the 'bard of Dunclug' (near Ballymena, Co. Antrim), was a radical Presbyterian whose father had stood bail for four United Irishmen and forfeited eighty pounds in consequence. He walked to Belfast to buy copies of the works of Burns and Allan Ramsey but he learnt to write verse not just from books but from a lively local tradition: his mother had sung or recited ballads to him in childhood and his father and elder brother were poets. In 'The Pauper's Lament', 'The Pauper's Death' and 'The

Pauper's Burial' he angrily denounced the inhuman operations of the
Poor Law and the process of industrialization which drove handloom
weavers such as himself upon its tender mercies. His poems were
much admired locally and attracted the interest of the conservative
Anglo-Irish intellectuals. A favourable review in the *Dubin University
Magazine* brought him introductions to the literary establishment in
Dublin and London. Inevitably, perhaps, the prospect of a wider
audience encouraged him to conform to standard idiom and conventional literary fashion, which gradually impoverished his work.[30]

Herbison's career illustrates the cultural and social pressures of the
era. The distinctive voice of Ireland's dissenting Presbyterians was
constantly being neutralized or assimilated in an increasingly polarized
society. Eventually the binary oppositions of Catholic and Protestant,
nationalist and Unionist, obliterated other distinctions and procured
the partition of Ireland. This development would have dismayed the
liberal Thomas Witherow. Witherow's political hostility to the
'Protestant Ascendancy' and his sense of common purpose with
disadvantaged Catholics owe somethng to his upbringing as a
Presbyterian in a largely Catholic area where such schools as there
were for underprivileged Catholics and Presbyterians made no
religious distinctions and prepared boys for the ministry or the
priesthood as required.[31] But Witherow's experience and outlook were
not typical. All too often Presbyterian alliances with Catholic opinion
were merely tactical and brittle. The sense of common disadvantage
which linked Presbyterians and Catholics was easily shattered by the
sense of common Protestantism which linked Presbyterians and
Anglicans.

Sectarian tensions increased in nineteenth-century Ireland because
of missionary enthusiasm. Instead of tolerating or despising Catholics
from a distance, Protestants wanted to convert them. Early Protestant
activities in Catholic areas promoted by Baptists and Wesleyan
Methodists had been tactful and socially beneficial, on the whole,
though there had been some opposition. But the situation deteriorated
after 1822 when the Protestant Archbishop of Dublin, William Magee,
declared religious war on the Catholic Church. In what came to be
called the 'Second Reformation' Protestant episcopalians tried hard to
make their Church the church of the whole people of Ireland, the
never-fulfilled intention with which it was originally established in the
wake of the English reformation.[32] Plans for national education in a
religiously divided country foundered because of Anglican insistence
on specifically Protestant biblical instruction. Father Mathew's much-

needed temperance movement in the 1840s, endorsed by Protestant Dissenters, was regarded with suspicion by Anglicans who disliked any movement supported by priests and Presbyterians. The Vatican was not entirely happy either, troubled by Father Mathew's non-Catholic allies.

Religious tension and mutual suspicion were most acute in Belfast. The rapid expansion of the city as a port and an industrial centre drew Catholic labourers from the surrounding countryside into what had previously been a largely Protestant community. The more prosperous artisans, on the other hand, were often Protestant, and some of them had acquired their skills in the industrial and shipbuilding centres of England and Scotland. Friction was perhaps inevitable, but evangelical clergymen made it worse. The Rev. William MacIlwaine, Rector of St George's, always lectured during Lent on the errors of Rome. On one occasion, in 1849, he suggested 'in love' that Catholicism was to the Church what leprosy was to the human body.[33] Inflammatory open-air preaching by well-known figures such as the Presbyterian 'Roaring Hugh' Hanna and the Anglican firebrand Thomas Drew, an ardent Orangeman, eventually helped to spark off sectarian rioting. This was so serious in July 1857 at the time of the Orange parades that a worried government set up a commission of inquiry.

The Ulster Evangelical Revival of 1859, the 'year of grace' for sympathizers, the 'year of delusion' for sceptics,[34] might well have made matters worse. The political implications of this episode have been carefully studied, but its cultural significance not just for Ulster but for the whole of Ireland has been overlooked. It has been suggested with some justice that the revival may have helped to consolidate the aggressive political Protestantism which still distinguishes Ulster Unionism.[35] It is interesting that the Protestant leader Ian Paisley wrote a very sympathetic if uncritical study of the revival early in his career.[36] There were outbreaks of mass hysteria at overcrowded meetings and rather undignified endeavours to 'rescue' Roman Catholics for the (Protestant) gospel. The Catholic press warned the faithful to keep well away from it all. An anonymous Belfast novelist dashed off a tale about *Flora Verner; or, the Sandy Row Convert*, rehearsing familiar sectarian themes. There is a 'Cruel Romish Stepmother', a young girl whose conversion involves her in appalling ordeals, and a cohort of scheming 'priests and their dupes' who try to put down the revival by underhand means.[37]

But there is plenty of evidence to suggest that the revival actually improved inter-communal relations. Contemporary observers noted a general improvement in public morality. There was a marked drop in the crime rate and aggressive Protestants became more considerate of their Catholic neighbours. The Orange processions of 1859 were entirely peaceful. Orangemen touched by the revival moderated their drinking, which obviously helped. As one commentator noted, 'amidst the triumphs of temperance and Revival, party spirit died and was buried, without strong drink at its wake or funeral'.[38] William Gibson, the Presbyterian historian of the revival, even suggested that the revival might hasten the decline of Orangeism and its 'ignorant bravado'. It was noticeable that the politically conservative Established Church, to which most of the Orangemen belonged, was distinctly equivocal about the revival. The Bishop of Down was sympathetic but the Dean of Down was not. Anti-Catholic clergy such as William McIlwaine professed themselves sceptical about its religious value.[39] Liberal Presbyterians, on the other hand, were generally enthusiastic.

The literary significance of the revival is complex. On the one hand, it is tempting to lay at its door the blighting philistinism and religious narrowness which is still a feature of Ulster life and until recently encouraged a view of the Irish literary imagination which ignored or rejected Protestant Ulster almost completely. On the other hand, it can be shown that the improved community relations attributable to the revival, short-lived as they proved to be, still had the effect of liberalizing the Presbyterian sense of tradition. The most important continuity could now be seen not as a continuity of embattled principle but a more outward-going continuity of Christian witness and participation in the moral life of the country as a whole.

Industrial Belfast, epicentre of the revival, might almost have been invented to illustrate what Matthew Arnold meant by Philistines in *Culture and Anarchy* (1869). Arnold's Celts were not Philistines: the essay *On the Study of Celtic Literature* (1867) which helped to encourage the Dublin-based Irish Literary Revival had nothing to say about unCeltic and apparently unliterary Belfast. Arnold's cantankerous commercially-minded puritanical Dissenters constituting the philistine enemies of culture are not hard to find even in modern Belfast or in any other large city. The revival seemed to reawaken the old-fashioned evangelical distrust of the secular imagination. One revival pamphleteer saw in Dickens 'the most insinuating foe the youthful reader has to meet with'. A Belfast tradesman's daughter was so spiritually benighted that she had read only 'novels and works of fiction' until she was converted.[40] But this is only one thin strand among many. Some of the better-written revival pamphlets show that enthusiasm for the revival was not incompatible with knowing and liking the work of Scott or Milton. Protestant Ulster was not particularly supportive of literary men trying to live by their wits and their pens, but this was true of Ireland as a whole, as William Carleton was to discover with some bitterness. If anything, prosperous and serious-minded Belfast became more generous to writers from the 1840s onwards. Thomas Beggs, a bleach-worker and former sailor who wrote poems about the sea and the landscapes of his native Antrim, had a long struggle with poverty and disappointment, but things improved shortly before his death in 1847. He was able to publish his poems in the *Belfast Newsletter* and in the Presbyterian newspaper *The Banner of Ulster*[41]. Its principal founder, Rev. Professor William Gibson, went on to write the fullest and most sympathetic contemporary account of the 1859 revival.

Writing about the 1859 revival inevitably recalled an earlier revival, the Six Mile Water Revival of 1626. Was this an outbreak of ignorant and undisciplined fanaticism and hysteria or was it a mighty outpouring of the spirit of God in a place and at a time sadly in need of it? Enthusiasts for the later revival recreated the earlier one in the same image. It was pleasant to identify one's hereditary enemies not so much as Catholic or tyrannical Anglicans as the wicked and the unregenerate.

The historian Thomas Witherow was sympathetic to the 1859 revival and contributed an account of its progress in his part of Co. Derry to Gibson's *Year of Grace*.[42] The moral and communal benefits of the revival prepared the ground for his most popular and important work, a revisionist history of *Derry and Enniskillen in the Year 1689* (1873). This work revisits two of the Orangeman's holy places, heroically defended against King James' besieging army during the Williamite wars. But in keeping with the spirit of the revival, Witherow substitutes the language of social co-operation for that of atavistic sectarianism and notes that

> conscientious and honest difference of opinion in religion is not inconsistent with kindly feeling, with friendly intercourse in daily life, with mutual help in distress and difficulty, with harmony of action on all questions touching the common good.[43]

The common good of Ireland concerned most of the writers of Victorian Ireland in varying degrees. It did not need to involve moral earnestness or historical seriousness. The different traditions which contributed to the literatures of Victorian Ireland were repositories of wit and humour, fantasy and grave, formal beauty as well as religious and political insight. All these qualities helped to enrich the national life and to disclose to an unhappy and divided country aspects of its best or better self. James Clarence Mangan's version 'from the Irish' of 'O'Hussey's Ode to the Maguire', bleak and desolate though it is, does more than offer a very free paraphrase of a seventeenth-century elegy by Eochaidh Ó hEoghusa.[44] In its unconventional syntax and rhythm, its artful assonance and alliteration, it surprises the reader into awareness of the dignity and grace of other difficult days in Ireland:

Large, large affliction unto me and mine it is,
That one of his majestic bearing, his fair, stately form,
Should thus be tortured and o'erborne—that this unsparing storm
Should wreak its wrath on head like his![45]

A more familiar Anglo-Irish note is sounded in William Allingham's critique of landlordism, 'Laurence Bloomfield in Ireland' (1864), sombrely formalizing indignation into old-fashioned iambic couplets. But Allingham could also celebrate the Irish attachment to particular places (in 'The Winding Banks of Erne') and Irish whimsy about 'the little people' (in 'The Fairies') which cross political and sectarian frontiers and relate to the common popular culture.

To an unrecognised extent the writers produced by the traditions of Protestant Ulster make a similar contribution to the culture and consciousness of their country. The poets Francis Davis the Belfastman (as he called himself) and William McComb, a Belfast bookseller, have been too easily forgotten.

Davis was actually born in Cork in 1810 and worked as a muslin weaver in Hillsborough, Co. Down. A Presbyterian like William Drennan, he had something of Drennan's radicalism and nationalist spirit, campaigning for Catholic Emancipation as a very young man. He settled in Manchester for a time but returned to Belfast in 1843. Soon after this he was deeply moved by the preaching of Rev. John Radcliffe, Presbyterian minister of Castledawson (1841–8), and later a minister in Jamaica.[46] By 1848 Davis had begun to write for the Young Ireland organ *The Nation*, for which he interviewed William Carleton.[47] Like his associates on the paper, he wanted to revive a sense of unanimity and national purpose among all Irishmen. With this in mind he celebrated the patriotic excitements of the Volunteer movement and Grattan's Parliament, claiming

Our island has wakened to freedom again;
"Twas only in slumber she thought of a chain!
(*Miscellaneous Poems*, p. 1)

A prophetic sense of economic and social as well as religious division
between the north and south of Ireland prompts Davis to a poetry of
reconciliation in 'My Southern Brother' which comments on the
loneliness of divisions and offers liberty and landscape as a basis for a
common Irishness, concluding

Now, love, we'll away to the green mountain heather,
And sing our wild anthems of freedom together.
(*Miscellaneous Poems*, p. 37)

Something of Drennan's furious scorn for his enslaved countrymen's
timidity can be found in Davis's poetic exploration of the military
fiasco of Young Ireland in 1848, yet another frustrated nationalist
revolt. He begins

Crawl on, ye worthless reptile race,
Crawl on in tearless degradation;

and concludes,

Oh! where's the soul it would not shame,
To own the hapless land that nursed ye;
Ye wrangled round the gates of fame
Till Freedom's bleeding god has cursed ye![48]

There are gentler poems, of love and local landscape, and a direct
and sensuous paraphrase of the opening verses of the *Song of Solomon*
which represents a point of intersection between poetic instinct and
Bible-reading Presbyterianism. But Davis knew about the Celtic and
Anglo-Irish traditions of his country as well and was anxious to share
his knowledge, particularly among working men. He founded a weekly
magazine grandly entitled *Francis Davis, the Belfast Man's Journal,
and Magazine of Miscellaneous Literature; comprising Tales and
Sketches of Ireland, its localities, history, traditions, manners, sufferings,
and virtues.* Despite serial features such as 'Jenny Ramsay – A Tale of
Ulster' and 'The Power of Love! A Tale of '98' and patriotic 'Walks
Among the Graves' of John Philpot Curran and Jonathan Swift the
magazine could not be sustained and Davis returned to his loom.

John Hewitt has seen in Davis a precursor of his own poetic isolation in philistine Belfast.[49] There may be some truth in this, but the causes of his isolation were probably as much political and personal as cultural: an angular radical in an increasingly conservative city could not expect popularity. We cannot know exactly why he became a Roman Catholic just before his death in 1885, but secular reasons might include a sense of solidarity with relatively disadvantaged Catholics in Belfast's burgeoning prosperity and an inkling, not unknown among nationally-minded Presbyterians, that Roman Catholicism was the original and somehow natural religion of the Irish people. whatever the cause, it suggested ultimate despair of the Presbyterian way of being Irish.

Davis's radical sympathies were shared by fewer and fewer Presbyterians as the nineteenth century progressed. William McComb, as a shrewd bookseller, understood his market and achieved greater commercial success through more conservative allegiances and a greater religious self-consciousness. This was perhaps appropriate for the publisher of Dr Henry Cooke's journal *The Orthodox Presbyterian* and, later *McComb's Presbyterian Almanac*. McComb is often specifically, even aggressively, Protestant and Unionist in his outlook, anticipating the downfall of the papacy and poetically commemorating 'The Fleet in Belfast Lough' and 'Victoria and Albert and loyal Belfast'.[50] But he is at least fleetingly aware of the whole range of his country's imaginative heritage, English, Scottish and European as well as Irish. He is able to draw on Anglo-Irish, Scots-Irish and Celtic traditions and on aspects of Ireland's general popular culture.

The results are sometimes a little bizarre. In trying to emphasize the importance of Burns to Irish as well as Scottish readers and writers, he claims the Ayrshire poet was 'dear to his country and Erin go bragh' (*Poetical Works*, p. 290). An ambitious elegy for England's hero, the Anglo-Irish Duke of Wellington, carries an epigraph from Ossian and makes Ireland speak in the consciously Celtic tones of Thomas Moore, rather preposterously lamenting the passing of a nursling whose manhood affections were given to England:

> He is gone! and the Banshee in Dangan is wailing;
>   The music is still in the court and the hall;
> The hearts of the strong one with sorrow are failing
>   And the warrior's scabbard has dropped from the wall.
>   (*Poetical Works*, p. 318)

Ossian and Moore were more usually annexed by nationalists such as Dan O'Connell.

Predictably enough, there are poems about the 1859 revival and the Six Mile Water revival. McComb's Scots-Irish heritage is spelt out in lines still occasionally quoted in Presbyterian pulpits in 'Two Hundred Years Ago', written for the Presbyterian bicentennial in 1842. The more radical strand in the Presbyterian heritage is not ignored as one might expect: one of his most popular ballads celebrates the Co. Down folk-heroine of 1798, Bessie (or Betsy) Grey the blacksmith's daughter.

McComb's evangelical piety and philanthropy and his early career as a teacher brought him into contact with the Dublin Kildare Place Society and the milieu of Anglo-Irish evangelicalism in which the newly-Protestant William Carleton found employment. This, more than his inherited Presbyterianism, seems to have influenced the apocalyptic Protestantism of his long poem about the European revolutions of 1848. Was the collapse of the papal states the beginning of the end for the papacy as seventeeth-century prophecy seemed to imply? The enthusiasm for prophecy, characteristic of an insecure and old-fashioned religious society, is found among Catholics as well as Protestants in Irish tradition and features in Carleton's fiction. It is an aspect of the general popular culture.

Men more educated and privileged than McComb were touched by the prophetic strain. William Johnston of Ballykilbeg, son of a Co. Down landlord, was a staunch upholder of 'Protestant Ascendancy', later notorious as an Orangeman and maverick politician. He saw God's hand in the events of 1847–8, just before he began his studies at Trinity College, and noted in his diary that the effect of reading the news from Italy and the Book of Revelation was to be convinced that the end was near for Rome.[51] Johnston's anti-Catholicism was linked with a biblicist piety in the evangelical tradition of the episcopal church to which he belonged. But Ballykilbeg was in a largely Presbyterian county and Johnston's political ambitions required Presbyterian support. A major function of the fiction Johnston wrote from time to time seems to have been to flatter Presbyterian Dissenters and align Presbyterian tradition with a more general Protestant heritage.

The novels are blatantly anti-Catholic. But for all their manifest prejudices and absurdities they are quite well written. Evangelical piety had not prevented Johnston from learning narrative technique from the English fiction of Dickens, Thackeray and Bulwer Lytton.

Nightshade (1857), a novel of contemporary life, is an exercise in general-purpose British anti-Catholicism with the full panoply of nunneries and Jesuits and secretly Romanizing Oxford High Churchmen. It is in the same tradition as Charles Kingsley's *Westward Ho!* (1855) which Johnston admired so much that he sent Kingsley a copy of *Nightshade*.[52] But the religious animus is Irish, displaced into an English and French setting.

Under Which King? (1872), an historical novel set in the 1680s, is entirely devoid of the fairmindedness of Witherow's *Derry and Enniskillen* (1873). The British and Irish context of Protestant triumphalism is sketched in with references to the defeat of the Spanish Armada and the 1641 rebellion. A fierce old Cromwellian puritan, Elijah Brown, provides continuity between the 1640s and the 1680s, opposing the Protestant Lord Protector Cromwell to the papist James II. Specifically, Presbyterian heroism is recalled through allusion to Margaret Wilson, falsely accused of being at the battle of Bothwell Bridge described in Scott's *Old Mortality*. She was condemned to death at Wigtown assize in 1685, tied to a stake in the Solway estuary and left to drown as the tide came in. Even as the waters rose around her she refused to abjure her covenanting faith. Johnston may have been reminded of this story by Millais' painting 'The Martyr of the Solway' (1871) which has been frequently reproduced on Orange banners, particularly for Scottish lodges, but he could have read it in Macaulay. Johnston read the *History of England* carefully enough to detect a trivial error, which he pointed out to the author. Schomberg, King William's general, was described as landing in Antrim in 1689 but Johnston insisted, correctly, that it was Groomsport in Co. Down. Later editions of the *History* have the carefully vague statement 'Schomberg had landed in the north of Ireland'.[53]

William Johnston was hardly a major novelist, but his literary Orangeism embodies and demonstrates the Victorian accumulations of tradition from which militant Irish Protestants could reinforce their sense of identity. His work also illustrates the mentality by which William Carleton felt oppressed as an Irish peasant.

WILLIAM CARLETON (1794–1869)

William Carleton, author of *Traits and Stories of the Irish Peasantry* (1830–3), was hailed by Yeats as 'a great Irish historian', 'the great novelist of Ireland, by right of the most Celtic eyes that ever gazed from under the brows of story-teller'.[54] The poet John Montague took a similar view, claiming that 'almost singlehanded he effected a literary discovery of the Irish people'.[55] Irish poets have been kinder than English critics: Donald Davie and Walter Allen were uneasy about the language, form and fictional status of the stories.[56] Carleton's life and work have been widely discussed,[57] but critical enthusiasm has had to accommodate a steady stream of unfavourable comment which goes back to the earliest reviews. Specifically political criticisms can probably be discounted as prejudice, but it has to be conceded that Carleton can be both tiresomely didactic and offensively partisan in religious matters. Patrick Murray of Maynooth admitted as much in 1852 in a generally sympathetic assessment. Murray also observed that Carleton was better understood and appreciated in his native Ulster than in other parts of Ireland.[58]

This comment, and Murray's awareness that the economic and social conditions of Carleton's own claim to manifest 'a truly Hibernian spirit' and to 'exhibit Irish life' as if this were a single entity.[59] Was he the national writer saluted by Yeats and Montague, or was he at bottom a local-colour regionalist, confined imaginatively to the Clogher valley of Co. Tyrone where he was born? Carleton's uneven literary output supplies evidence to support either view. His identity as a writer is unstable and elusive, drifting between rural and metropolitan, Catholic and Protestant, conservative and progressive. The harsh conditions of authorship in early nineteenth-century Ireland were his own excuse for his literary shortcomings. But the social and political conditions which presented the Irish writer with such polarized possibilities actually worked to Carleton's advantage. His multiple literary personality commended him at various times to almost every sector of Irish society. Carleton in a sense united his country: the list of eminent persons who petitioned the government to grant him a pension in 1847 represents all the different ways of being Irish. Nothing else could have brought together the President of the Catholic College at Maynooth and Colonel Blacker, the Orange leader, in the presence of Maria Edgeworth, Dan O'Connell's son, Oscar Wilde's father and Rev. Dr Henry Cooke from Belfast.[60]

But Carleton the comprehensively national writer is in constant tension with Carleton the time-server, pandering to sectional interests as occasion offered. He was born a Catholic but found his first literary opportunities as a Protestant, writing for the anti-Catholic *Christian Examiner*. Even so, some of his best work could find points of contact

PLATE 3　Sir John Lavery, *St Patrick's Purgatory* (see p. 142)

with most Irishmen of good will. A good example is his early story 'The Poor Scholar' (1833), written for the second series of *Traits and Stories* and not previously published in the *Christian Examiner*. The ingredients seem familiar, but only because the famine of the 1840s and subsequent writing have made them so. There is a corrupt agent and an absentee landlord, a father evicted for no good reason and a son obliged to set off on foot to seek education, and eventual advancement to the priesthood, in a distant province. The son, Jemmy McEvoy, is Carleton by another name. He is desperately poor and harshly treated by a mercenary schoolmaster, but he is befriended by field labourers and Protestant clergy. He comes to the attention of the landlord who is so impressed that he resolves to pay more attention to his estates. This leads to the sacking of the agent and the restoration of Jemmy's father to his land.

As is often the case in Carleton, the plot is the least important aspect of the story. Carleton shrewdly demonstrates the distinction, common in Ireland, between abstract sectarian animosity and the sense of mutual obligation, kindliness and good will procured by personal contact among people of different religion. The old-fashioned super-stition that priest's money is unlucky because it is the price of sin paid over to secure absolution would have been sternly treated in the *Christian Examiner*. But here it is a joke: the priest offers two guineas to help young McEvoy on his way and the father accepts, thinking he can always change the actual coins with 'some o' these black-mouthed Presbyterians or Orangemen' and they can have the benefit of any ill-luck that might ensue (*Traits*, p. 498f). Protestants were as generous to Jemmy as the priest, some turning up at mass to make their contributions, others, uneasy about 'idolatrous' worship, sending money with a Catholic neighbour. The language is diplomatic: Protestants unhappy about the mass have scruples rather than prejudices and the word 'idolatrous' is their word, not Carleton's, neither endorsed nor repudiated. The political and sectarian violence endemic in the Irish countryside is both acknowledged and evaded: 'we will venture to say that had political excitement flamed up even to rebellion and mutual slaughter, the persons and property of *those* individuals would have been held sacred' (*Traits*, p. 506). This generates a peculiar and unnerving tension between hope and despair, local and individual harmony and conciliation and national disaster.

Liberal hope and conservative anxiety come together in Carleton's sense of himself as 'a liberal conservative, and, I trust a rational one . . .

knowing no party but my country'.[61] But in *The Emigrants of Ahadarra* (1848) the benign landlord, a liberal conservative of patriotic instincts, is placed in an awkward position. His very name recalls Ireland's English dimension: he is called Chevydale, recalling the English ballad of 'Chevy Chase'. Presumably of Anglo-Irish stock, he takes the conservative view that Ireland is not yet ready for Repeal of the Act of Union with England, but as a liberal and a patriot he realizes that it is the duty of Irish landlords ' "to prevent Irish interests from being made subservient to English interests, and from being legislated for upon English principles" '.[62] This denied the ultimate identity of English and Irish interests which was the formal rationale of the Act of Union and of the political status quo on which Irish conservatives took their stand.

Across the political, economic and religious divisions of Carleton's Ireland there ran a further division between the old and the new. Ireland was simultaneously a traditional and a modernizing society, and even Presbyterians and Orangemen who may have thought of themselves as agents of modernization were themselves subject to the modernizing process.[63] As the son of Irish-speaking parents well-versed in the folk-ways and oral traditions of the countryside, Carleton seemed to belong to the unchanging old Ireland. In an earlier generation he would probably have had a secure place in the local community as *seanachaidh* or story-teller, a role he could have combined with that of farmer or hedge- schoolmaster, perhaps, or even parish priest. As it was, new ambitions stirred and he became a struggling writer and sociologically displaced person. The new Ireland inaugurated in a sense by the Act of Union brought schemes for popular education and improved communications. The country was surveyed and mapped by English military engineers (with Irish help), quasi-scientifically investigated by English commissions of inquiry, subjected, unevenly, to the industrializing process (mainly in the north-east), evangelized by an established national church awakened to missionary responsibilities and spiritually transformed by what has been called the 'devotional revolution' within Irish Catholicism.

This movement possibly affected a majority of the Irish people more profoundly than any other. It reformed abuses and irregularities, improved standards of worship and pastoral care, outlawed the more superstitious elements of folk religion in the Church and brought wayward priests more effectively under the control of an efficient episcopate more directly answerable to Rome. It changed the world that Carleton left behind him when he left home.[64]

Like his Poor Scholar, Carleton had left home in search of the education that might eventually take him into the priesthood. Instead, he eventually settled in Dublin, worked for the Protestant evangelical Sunday School Society under the patronage of James Digges La Touche (a friend of the Belfast poet William McComb), and entered the marketplace as a professional writer. Imaginatively, he stayed with the unreformed Catholicism, the traditions and the communal bitterness of his youth, but rationally he rejected the ignorance and irregularity of the old ways. Becoming a Protestant was one of the ways of doing this, though the Catholic Dan O'Connell's Enlightenment reformism achieved the same ends.

In 1845, Carleton's most prolific year as a writer, Thomas Davis signalled the advance of the modernizing process by observing, 'the fairies and the banshee, the poor scholar and the ribbonman, the Orange Lodge, the illicit still, and the faction fight are disappearing into history.'[65] But his source for this colourfully disorderly vanishing world was the work of Carleton himself. Less of the old Ireland disappeared into history than either Davis the Young Ireland enthusiast or Carleton the rational liberal conservative might have wished. The trouble was that while the idea of an ordered Irish national consciousness was a function of modernization and mass communication (mainly in the English language) the content of that consciousness was inescapably drawn from the disorderly dying past which consequently clung to life beyond its natural term.

The *Irish Penny Journal*, to which Carleton contributed most of the pieces republished as *Tales and Sketches* (1845), illustrates this phenomenon, awkwardly refurbishing aspects of the past while trying to deliver the readership from past ignorance and superstition, manufacturing sanitized tradition. The sanitizing process was obtrusive and officious to the point of being counter-productive. The magazine was aimed at a popular readership and devoted much space to the Celtic literature and antiquities accessible to English-speakers since the late eighteenth century. But the divisive politics and the heritage of disadvantage associated with the eclipse of the old Gaelic order were firmly excluded since it was editorial policy to avoid 'the exciting and profitless discussion of political or polemical questions'. The remorselessly didactic and improving tone of the paper, more apparent in Mrs S. C. Hall's stories of Irish life than in those contributed by her rival Carleton, indicates a secular version of the Protestant evangelical assault on unreconstructed Catholicism, an onslaught parallel to and part cause of the reformist movement within the Irish Catholic Church.

The secular and the religious attacks on the bad old days are sometimes hard to disentangle. Caesar Otway, author of the well-informed *Sketches in Erris and Tyrawley* (1841), was one of the leading spirits in the *Irish Penny Journal* but he is usually pilloried, a little unfairly, as the fanatically anti-Catholic Mephistophiles who made Carleton sell his soul to Protestantism and the *Christian Examiner*. Carleton seems to have become disenchanted with Catholicism before he met Otway, but more because he disliked the social and political influence in the community of sometimes unruly priests than because of specifically religious misgivings. In a letter of 1826, admittedly written to try to curry favour with the government, he denounces the priesthood in terms which recall Toland and the anticlericalist aspect of the Enlightenment: 'Oh! let not the guardians of the British Constitution and human liberty give these men power!'[66]

There is at least as much emphasis on liberty and reason as on the more specifically evangelical themes of sin and the Bible in Carleton's *Christian Examiner* stories. The first and most notorious, 'A Pilgrimage to St Patrick's Purgatory', describes Carleton's pilgrimage to a famous shrine on an island in Lough Derg, Co. Donegal (see Plate 3). Lough Derg, or the red lake, was allegedly red with the blood of a dragon slain by Fingal on its shores. When Christianity came to this myth-laden place further legends sprang up, associating it with St Patrick, assimilating pre-Christian Celtic traditions of visits to the Otherworld to the concept of Purgatory. By the early Middle Ages St Patrick's Purgatory was famous all over Europe: it has been suggested that tales about it may have influenced the imagery of Dante's *Divine Comedy*. It was a site of intermittent abuses and excess and this led to its being shut down by the pope for a time, rather confirming the deep-rooted Irish suspicion that the pope is a Protestant.[67] The place has been much written about, before and after Carleton's day. Carleton's own response to the traditions of the spot is to detach himself from what he sees as the superstition and abuses surrounding it. As he observes with intellectual rather than religious priggishness, superstition 'is as natural to the mind not enlightened by true knowledge as weeds are to a field that has ceased to be well cultivated'.[68]

The agricultural metaphor, appropriate to Carleton's country background, entwines the religious with the secular attack on the bad old days and serves to link Carleton's new-minted Protestantism with his enduring concern to promote much-needed national improvements. Well-cultivated fields free of weeds require hard work and modern farming methods and these were commended in Carleton's *Parra*

Sastha; or, the History of Paddy Go-Easy and his Wife Nancy (1845), the story of an idle farmer. The volume was padded out with didactic 'Observations on Farming, etc.' extracted from a popular manual promoting scientific agriculture.

Fortunately for his readers, Carleton's severe disapproval of superstition is enlivened by a sense of humour and a sharp eye for Irish types. His Lough Derg pilgrims include a humorist, a classical schoolmaster, a rake and a hypocrite, as well as kindly and unaffected religious people. The vividly rendered privations of penitential discipline on the island, and the acute physical pain involved in going round the 'stations', pass over into knockabout when a pious busybody brutally awakens the drowsy pilgrim with a blow to the head from a blackthorn stick. The narrator retaliates in kind, 'the most meritorious act of my whole pilgrimage'.[69] The brutality, disorder and grotesque serio-comic excesses of the pilgrimage experience are officially laid at the door of Catholic traditionalism but they are part of the deplorable but vital old Ireland which Carleton's imagination never left.

'Father Butler', Carleton's next *Christian Examiner* story, pursues the libertarian rather than rationalistic aspect of his very secular Protestantism. The enslaving moral degradation of the Irish peasantry, variously attributed in later stories to alcohol (*Art Maguire*, 1845), Orangemen (*Valentine McClutchy*, 1846), Ribbonmen (*Rody the Rover*, 1845) or Whiteboys (*The Tithe-Proctor*, 1849), is associated here with 'the unlimited authority which their clergy, in the name of religion, exercise over them in all the circumstances of life'.[70] The narrative is sentimental and amiably absurd: Father Butler, of good family as the Anglo-Irish name implies, was in love with the fair Ellen in youth but was cajoled into the priesthood during a dangerous illness by emotional blackmail and unscrupulous and corrupt priestly pressure.

Like much of Carleton's work, this tale is flawed by the stiffness of the language and the artificial and condescending note of an inadequately impersonated gentility. Carleton may have hoped to please, and eventually to join, the Protestant gentry. He aspired (in vain) to study at Trinity College, which might have equipped him for a learned and gentlemanly profession. Later in his career he was able to satirize social pretension in the would-be elegant English 'pro-nonsensation' of Buck English, the villain of *The Tithe Proctor*. But he had to struggle for the right sort of English in every book he wrote, searching for a style that was rational and intelligible to the educated reading public but sensitive to the idiom of Irish people for whom

English might be a second language and whose relation with English speech and social norms was often strained and eccentric. Donald Davie intriguingly suggests a parallel in the lifeless dignity of late eighteenth-century English prose which has been blamed on the influence of Scots authors obliged to write in an idiom alien from their everyday speech.[71] Thomas Hardy provides a possibly closer parallel, resolutely regional in his fiction yet proud of an acquired metropolitan culture which he regarded as his point of contact with a sophisticated reading public.

Sometimes Carleton is able to make good literary use of the social or intellectual gulf between formal educated discourse and racy local dialect. The narrator of 'Wildgoose Lodge' in *Traits and Stories* (the original title was 'Confessions of a Reformed Ribbonman') speaks like his fellow countrymen at a meeting of the Ribbonmen, an agrarian secret society dedicated to exacting rough justice by extra-legal means. He lards his speech with casual piety, tags of Irish and 'broad' pronunciations. Refusing a drink he says,

'I'll jist trust to God and the consequences for the cowld, Paddy, ma bouchal; but a blessed dhrop of it won't be crossin' my lips, avick; so no more ghosther about it – dhrink it yourself, if you like.' (*Traits*, p. 589)

But the speaker is much more formal and conventional as narrator, asserting both a linguistic and a moral norm. The refusal of the drink is prelude to withdrawal from Ribbonism and dissociation from a particularly vindictive act of arson and murder, based on an actual event, which is then described in a standard English which implies outraged standards of behaviour:

The faces of those who kept aloof from the slaughter were blanched to the whiteness of death: some of them fainted, and others were in such agitation that they were compelled to lean on their comrades. They became actually powerless with horror; yet to such a scene were they brought by the pernicious influence of Ribbonism. (*Traits*, p. 598)

Awareness of different linguistic registers, thrust upon Carleton by his circumstances as a writer, gives rise to some of his best as well as some of his worst writing. Pretentious awkwardness is sometimes spotted in time and turned to comic effect. Carleton is good at impersonating the hedge-schoolmaster or the precious aspirant to the priesthood who represent other possible selves. The schoolmaster's tendency to be remorselessly informative, from which Carleton is not exempt, is parodied in owlish discourse on faction fights or the art of being a professional purveyor of alibis. The energetic futilities of scholastic debate, an aspect of the Maynooth training until well into the nineteenth century, are splendidly travestied in the gladiatorial dialectics of 'Denis O'Shaughnessy going to Maynooth' when Denis 'proves' to a bewildered neighbour that black and white are the same colour, particularly if your eyes are shut (*Traits*, p. 656–8).

For all Carleton's love of his native place and the idiom of his own people the dialect speech of the stories is not quite the language Carleton grew up with. Specifically, he admits he has 'studiously avoided that intolerable Scots–Hibernic jargon which pierces the ear so unmercifully', though this would often have been heard in the countryside: it would have been the speech of Carleton's Belfast mother-in-law. Not an easy or frugal son-in-law, Carleton resented what he felt was her mean-souled 'northern sharpness' and that seems to have set him against Scots-Irish sharpness in manner and speech for the rest of his life.[72] In his stories he edited it out but 'preserved everything Irish, and generalized the phraseology, so that the book, wherever it may go, will exhibit a truly Hibernian spirit' (*Traits*, p. vii).

The rather problematic 'Hibernian spirit' and artificially nationalized idiom involve various suppressions and simplifications. In one story a ghost is called a 'fetch' though Carleton acknowledges that in Northern Ireland as in Scotland the term 'wraith' would be used. 'I have adapted the other as more national,' he blandly observes (*Traits*, p. 96). The Scots influence on the idiom and culture of the north of Ireland is deliberately marginalized in Carleton, though if his reviewer Patrick Murray is to be believed, this still failed to make the stories genuinely national and equally intelligible in all parts of Ireland. Carleton's Ireland, already more or less confined to rural districts and small farmers, is further specialized and stylized by wilfully minimizing the Scots-Irish. This has had immensely damaging consequences, encouraging the cultural fragmentation of modern Ireland which has been allowed to coincide with and exacerbate socio-economic and political fragmentation. When the Irish muse eventually condescended to notice the city, at Joyce's prompting, it was the southern city of Dublin where the Scots-Irish were thin on the ground. The artificially selected Irish nation of the literary imagination is indicated by the northern poet Derek Mahon, who observed in 1973, 'A lot of people who are regarded as important in Irish poetry cannot accept that the Protestant suburbs in Belfast are a part of Ireland.'[73]

Protestant, including Presbyterian, Irishmen have from time to time been deemed to forfeit their title to Irishness either through conscious 'West Britonism' and sedulously aping the English or, more damningly, through hereditary involvement in colonial rapacity. The latter indictment underpins Carleton's atavistic resentment. He often uses the formula 'Protestants and Presbyterians' ('Protestants' alluding to the Protestant episcopalians of the Established Church) to describe as a single body privileged interlopers who allegedly drove indigenous Catholics to the hills and took possession of the best land (*Traits*, pp. 175, 492). This cherished myth has been challenged by the Tyrone Presbyterian novelist W. F. Marshall, in *Planted by a River* (1948).[74] True or false, its prominence in Carleton's fiction gives Catholics the monopoly of disadvantage, turns a blind eye to joint Presbyterian and Catholic hostility to the Established Church and 'Protestant Ascendancy', and artificially polarizes the world of his childhood.

Presbyterian and Scots-Irish influence in Tyrone seems to have been greater in the northern part of the county than in south Tyrone where Carleton was born, if the dialect evidence is anything to go by.[75] But Carleton had plenty of contact with Presbyterians who were far from privileged. His parents were on friendly terms with Presbyterian neighbours and selected one as Carleton's godmother, though the Catholic Church insisted in such cases on a second, Catholic, godmother (*Autobiography*, p. 22). Carleton's father considered sending the boy to a classical school at Augher run by a Presbyterian clergyman called Wiley (or Wylie), a dwarf of ferocious strength and temper. In the end he decided not to, not because he was a Presbyterian but because of his reputation for 'unnatural cruelty' (*Autobiography*, pp. 44, 60). Wiley may have been as much a misfit as Carleton himself: he was licensed to preach by the Presbytery of Tyrone in 1806 but there is no record that he was ever ordained or installed in a charge. His odd appearance and uncertain temper would have been a disadvantage in the pulpit, as they proved to be in his school. It did not last long.[76]

Carleton's comparative neglect of Presbyterian Irishmen represents a failure of imagination and social vision, but it is also attributable in part to the ruthlessly simplifying tendency of sectarian politics. William Johnston of Ballykilbeg promoted the fusion of Presbyterian and episcopalian traditions into a common triumphalist Protestantism for political ends. Carleton's rhetoric of ancestral disadvantage, identifying Presbyterian with episcopalian as the oppressor, achieves the same effect from the opposite point of view. There are some fragmentary intuitions of Presbyterian distinctiveness in Carleton's fiction but he lacks energy and interest to sustain them. In 'The Poor Scholar' there is a thumbnail sketch of a 'humorous little Presbyterian with a sarcastic face, and sharp northern accent'. The type is recognizable, even today, but the accent is perfunctorily and inadequately rendered and interest in him lapses after a page (*Traits*, p. 568).

Carleton may have intended a satiric portrait of a Presbyterian in the religious attorney Solomon M'Slime in *Valentine McClutchy*. The Scots-sounding prefix M' (or Mc) is too common in Irish names like McCarthy to be a guide in itself, but M'Slime's combination of offensively evangelical characteristics and the manner of a canting Dissenter could well be Presbyterian. Possibly the hope that a few (liberal) Presbyterians might buy the book prevented Carleton from making the identification too explicit. M'Slime is crudely presented as a hypocrite in the antinomian tradition travestied in James Hogg's novel about a Scots Presbyterian, *Confessions of a Justified Sinner* (1824), which Carleton may have read. Though M'Slime's loveless religion 'was often known to smack strongly of law', his Presbyterian legalism took second place to a high-minded disregard for any moral obstacles the law of the land might present to his plans. He sings metrical psalms at family prayers ('long measure, eight lines, four eights and two sixes') in Presbyterian fashion, though Carleton's impressive-sounding technical detail makes no sense. 'Long measure' settings use only eight-syllable lines: Carleton seems to have muddled 'Long measure' with 'Common measure' which alternates eight- and six-syllable lines. Less reconditely, Carleton makes him give a hungry messenger Rev. Vesuvius M'Slug's tract *Precious Puddings for Saintly Stomachs* instead of his breakfast (chapter 3).

Later in the novel the political dimensions of Presbyterianism is glimpsed for a moment. There are two newspapers in the Castle Cumber area, which has a population 'about one half Roman Catholic, and the other half Protestant and Presbyterian'. Both papers are non-Catholic. The *Castle Cumber True Blue* is Orange, Tory and Episcopalian in outlook while its rival, the *Genuine Patriot, and Castle Cumber Equivocal*, 'equivocal' presumably implying some kind of non-aligned liberalism, 'gives an occasional lift to the Catholics' and has a Presbyterian and dissenting readership (chapter 15). It sounds rather like the Belfast *Northern Whig* which enjoyed liberal Presbyterian patronage and supported Catholic Emancipation. But this distinction is not really sustained. Both editors are members of the local Orange lodge, though historically there was little Presbyterian interest in the Orange order until later in the nineteenth century. The two editors disagree within the lodge but drunkenness and anti-Catholic sentiment easily submerge their differences (chapters 19, 20).

There is something curious about Carleton's animus against the largely undifferentiated 'Protestant and Presbyterian' community. He was, after all, some kind of liberal Protestant himself, by conviction as well as from convenience, it appears. Certainly there is evidence to suggest that he died a Protestant despite Catholic traditions of deathbed repentance.[77] But Carleton's residual tribalism, his reversion to the social and political resentments of his childhood sharpened rather than softened by the passing of time, can be explained in terms of his equivocal status within the Irish Protestant establishment. Carleton discovered the hard way that there was a difference between being Protestant by religion and being part of the 'Protestant Ascendancy'. When he was employed in the Sunday School Office in Dublin and trying to prepare himself for a place at Trinity College by private study, he seriously annoyed Thomas Parnell. This meddling and unreasonable gentleman was a powerful member of the committee, partly because of his connections: he belonged to an important Anglo-Irish family and his brother Sir Henry Parnell was Secretary for War in 1831. Charles Stewart Parnell, the future Irish parliamentary leader, was his great-nephew. Tom Parnell seems to have thought that Carleton should be kept in his place and eventually contrived to have him dismissed without hope of appeal (*Autobiography*, pp. 199–203, 206–8). Even as a Protestant, Carleton was to remain an underdog, and the rhetoric of oppression came naturally to an ambitious man who could not always feed his wife and family. The only escape was through fantasies of benign paternalism which occasionally became realities when one or two of Carleton's well-placed Protestant friends were able and willing to help him. These fantasies are reflected in the ending of *Valentine McClutchy*. The greedy, dissolute and irresponsible absentee landlord is killed in a duel and is succeeded by his brother. It turns out the brother has already been living in the area, disguised as an artist: he understands his responsibilities to the local people and has already engineered the dismissal of the tyrannical land-agent, Valentine McClutchy.

The progressive paternalist landlord derives from the progressive and optimistic aspect of Carleton's imagination. One part of him continued to believe in a better and less sectarian future when Ribbonism and Orangeism alike would pass away along with priestly tyranny and the Protestant tyranny of the tithe-proctor. The good landlords of his liberal pipe-dreams would thrive under the benign and efficient government which might one day take over from prevailing incompetence and repression. By setting most of his novels and stories in the recent past of his own childhood, he can indicate improvements already under way, however patchy and inadequate. But the technique can rebound on itself because Carleton's early memories and atavistic sense of tradition anchor him imaginatively to an older Ireland so vividly rendered in its disorderly stagnation that it is hard to believe that new and better ways will ever triumph.

The constants of the old ways are the sense of place, family and community, poverty and religion. In the *Emigrants of Ahadarra* the outrage of undeserved eviction from the land is heightened by the sense of immemorial continuity of settlement upon it. There is a happy ending: the luckless M'Mahon family, father and son, are allowed to keep their holding after all. They stand for all the fathers and sons in endless succession who have lived in the same area and have formed a settled (and stagnant) community. The land in Carleton's Ireland is always ominous with resurrected tradition and history. *The Tithe-Proctor* opens on *Esker Dearg* (the Red Ridge), red, according to legend, because of 'a massacre which had taken place upon it during one of the Elizabethan wars'. Carleton's rationalizing comment that in fact the vegetation was reddish-brown fails to dissipate the effect. The Red Ridge still hints at endlessly renewed bloodshed and violence in the locality, and indeed the rapacity of the unreformed Established Church on the one hand, and the Whiteboy conspiracy against it on the other, rather confirm the suggestion.

Carleton describes his birthplace at the beginning of *Traits and Stories* as the 'valley of the "Black Pig", so well known in the politico-traditional history of Ireland' (*Traits*, p. 1). This alludes to the so-called prophecies of St Columkille, part of the largely oral tradition of rural Irish communities and mixed up with the folk religion not yet outlawed by new rigorism in the Catholic church. The legendary battles in this particular area of Tyrone were destined to come to a grand conclusion with a general massacre of the Irish, or Irish Catholics, some 40,000 in all. The remote origins of such prophecies seem to be not the historical Columkille or Columba of Iona but the forebodings and sense of looming catastrophe associated with Viking raids. Respectable educated opinion disapproved of the prophetic strand in popular culture but failed to extinguish it.[78] Carleton's work brought it before a wider audience: he makes many allusions to prophecies and the prophecy-men who retailed them in variously garbled forms. The tale 'Barney M'Haigh the Irish Prophecy Man' (1841) and the novel of famine *The Black Prophet* (1847) are the most obvious examples.

The cultural and social consequences of prophecies of disaster were unfortunate. They tended to reinforce the sense of heroic melancholy and elegiac futility inflamed by Ossianic romanticism at the end of the eighteenth century, to the exasperation of energetic radicals and reformers such as William Drennan. Carleton the reformer was too easily taken over by Carleton the gloomy romantic. The traditional prophecies promised general disaster in such general terms, including hunger and bad weather, endemic in Ireland, that they were almost unfalsifiable. Carleton's sensitivity to physical and emotional atmosphere as famine threatens allows him to write convincing speeches for his shrewd prophecyman in *The Black Prophet*:

> 'Look about you, and say what is it you see that doesn't foretell famine – famine – famine! Doesn't the dark wet day an' the rain, rain, rain, foretell it? Doesn't the rottin' crops, the unhealthy air, an' the green damp foretell it? Doesn't the sky without a sun, the heavy clouds, an' the angry fire of the West foretell it . . .? The airth is softened for the grave, an' in the black clouds of heaven you may see the death-hearse movin' slowly along. (chapter 2)

Carleton's interest in 'prophecy' as an art-form, a combination of received materials, a lively adaptive imagination and a gift of language and imagery which can stimulate 'a kind of wild and turbid enthusiasm' as the Black Prophet does, seems to indicate a parallel with his own art. His fictions are part documentary, recording traits as well as telling stories, and part creative and manipulative. Their effect can resemble the effect of the prophecies, reducing the flow of history to archetypal, timeless pattern. *The Black Prophet* actually draws on Carleton's memories of famine in 1817 and 1822 but appeals to a readership witnessing the contemporary horrors of the Great Hunger of the 1840s. An unusually strident dedication to the Prime Minister, Lord John Russell, more or less challenges him to prove himself a friend of Ireland by reversing the 'long course of illiberal legislation and unjustifiable neglect' of successive British governments. But this sharp topicality is blurred by the melodramatic and mythic overtones of the novel. The setting is an earlier season of famine, some twenty years previously, but the plot concerns murder and deceit going back twenty years before that. Unending famine and disease, represented as a recurring if not annual blight upon the land, become metaphors for the age-old blight of murderous conspiracy, violence and greed. The villains of the novel are not the government, or not directly, but the profiteers and hoarders among the people themselves who make a bad situation worse and increase tension and unrest.

One of the grimmest aspects of *The Black Prophet* is the detailed account of the operations of Darby Skinadre the meal-miser who exacerbates shortages by hoarding and then begins to realize his investment by extorting the last farthing out of emaciated and starving people (chapter 6). Darby is so obviously a general type rather than an individual that the scene in which he sells his meal does not fully come to life. But the very fact that he is a general type common in Ireland and in Carleton's fiction reveals the extent of Ireland's degradation. In *Art Maguire* the avaricious Jemmy Murray and his associate Corney Finigan have laid up reserves of meal and hay in expectation of crop failure and they positively want a bad harvest to ensure high prices and profits. The worst example of the type is Fardorougha the miser in the novel of that name (1839).

The most depressing feature of the plot is that Fardorougha's miserliness stimulates wickedness in others. When he ruthlessly forecloses on a debt owed by the Flanagan family he brings on himself an elaborately plotted revenge masterminded by Bartle Flanagan in conjunction with the local Ribbonmen. This makes the conventionally good and beautiful Una O'Brien cross herself devoutly and say she will ' "pray to God to forgive Bartle Flanagan, an' to turn his heart" ' (chapter 12). Whether the combination of Catholic gesture and (Protestant?) conversionist language is tactfully ecumenical or fortuitous is unclear, but the pious hope seems no better founded than Carleton's pious hope of effective reform. Most of Carleton's rascals and Ribbonmen are moral incurables, victims and agents of a hopelessly diseased social order. It sometimes seems that the only hope arises from the possibility that one piece of villainy may be frustrated by another. In the end Fardorougha is ruined by the absconding of the county treasurer who had acted as his banker. As Carleton notes in his Preface, this was based on an actual incident when the highly respectable treasurer of Co. Louth decamped to the Isle of Man.

Even when Carleton goes back to the more distant past his fiction has the timeless bleakness of the old prophecies or old ballads. The

Ulster ballad of 'Willie Reilly and his Dear Coolen Bawn' was pieced together by Carleton from various versions and contributed to the Young Ireland anthology of *Ballad-Poetry of Ireland*. Much later, Carleton made a bad but successful novel out of it. Willie is a Catholic and his love a Protestant: the story is set in the Penal days in the middle of the eighteenth century when such love was doomed, but the theme of 'mixed marriage' seems as timeless as Ireland itself. Squire Folliard is an archtypal blustering Protestant swearing by King William but kind to his Catholic servants. His daughter elopes to avoid marriage with the knock-kneed and villainous Sir Robert Whitecraft and is eventually able to marry her Willy Reilly. The most disturbing character in the story is not Whitecraft but the notorious Red Raparee, afraid of no man living except Willy Reilly himself. Both Whitecraft and the Raparee are eventually sentenced to death for complex villainies, but the Raparee at least rises from the dead in the numerous Whiteboys and Ribbonmen of Carleton's other fiction.

Ribbonmen and secret societies are involved with another, more optimistic strand of popular prophecy in Carleton's fiction. Naturally enough, prophecies of catastrophe were balanced by prophecies of rebellion and liberation. Examples can be multiplied from the late sixteenth century when the Elizabethan conquest began to take hold.[79] In Carleton's time the prophecies of 'Pastorini' were the best known. Charles Walmisley's *General History of the Christian Church* (1771), from which they were excerpted, actually surveys the history and condition of the Roman Catholic Church all over the world, from America to Japan, and says little about Ireland. But in a prophecy suggested by the eighteenth chapter of Revelation, Walmisley estimated that the fifth vial would be poured out about 1825 and urged the faithful to flee from the countries of wrath and perdition as the territories affected by the Reformation were reduced to darkness and pain.

Tendentiously selected extracts culled from Walmisley's lengthy treatise circulated among country people and secret societies, often by word of mouth, until the continued health of Protestantism after the mid-1820s discredited them. Rebels and Ribbonmen saw themselves as agents of apocalyptic Catholic triumphalism, or pretended to, but responsible clergy were not impressed. J.W. Doyle, Catholic Bishop of Kildare, denounced Ribbonism and prophecy in a pastoral address of 1822 and again in 1825.[80]

Carleton's characters knew about Pastorini, often grouped with pseudo-Columkille as a repository of arcane learning. In an imperfectly literate society all book-learning is arcane and not clearly differentiated, so the impact of Pastorini among the uncritical was understandable. But Carleton's point is harsher and more general than this. In his early story 'The Hedge School', he claimed that the rudimentary education available in the countryside encouraged rather than disciplined credulity and partisan bitterness, not least because the hedge-schoolmasters were sometimes involved with the secret societies. What little reading matter there was tended to be inflammatory rubbish like the selections from Pastorini: 'With this specimen of education before our eyes, is it at all extraordinary that Ireland should be as she is?' (*Traits*, p. 232f).

The later Carleton put the matter round the other way. Perhaps the appetite for prophecy stemmed from political disaffection rather than created it? His most Satanic (but also grimly Byronic) villain is the Black Prophet Donnel Dhu M'Gowan, who has murdered his wife's brother and twice tried to blame it on an innocent man. But the sense of menace and gloom which surrounds him and is reflected in his prophecies is part of the general dehumanized hopelessness of a famine-stricken land. Columkille and Pastorini are left some way behind as the incidental accoutrements of a study in despair. In the last chapter his daughter claims he was not altogether bad, was even a good man in early life. He dies refusing religious consolation, 'firmly, but sullenly, and as if he despised and defied the world and its laws' (chapter 32). With such a world, and such laws, who could really blame him?

Carleton's hope for a better life for the people of Ireland and for himself kept foundering in a mesh of contradictions and unresolvable tensions. He was trapped between ancestral and modern forces, between a sense of Catholic community and Protestant iconoclasm, between imaginative despair and rational optimism. None of the identities he assumed as a writer really worked for very long. He drew strength from, reinforced and was intellectually hampered by an atavistic sense of tradition. In this at least he was like Thomas D'Arcy McGee.

THOMAS D'ARCY MCGEE (1825–68)

McGee was born in more comfortable circumstances than Carleton. He read more, travelled more and took part in public affairs from which Carleton felt excluded. Carleton had seen himself as too cautious and too sensible for conspiracy, too poor and too uncommitted for conventional politics. McGee's greater breadth of experience did not make him a better writer: he never approached the stark imaginative intensities of *The Black Prophet* or *Valentine McClutchy*. But it did make him more versatile and better-informed, able to pursue dimensions of Irish literary culture ignored or neglected by Carleton. Our understanding of the possibilities of Irish tradition is extended and enriched by his work, which does not deserve its present obscurity.

McGee was a competent poet and a popularizer of genius, but at different times he was too liberal and too conservative for his own good, which is why he has been edited out of conventional Irish literary history. In his earlier Irish career his eclectic and pluralist literary nationalism was enthusiastically Celtic, but not quite Celtic enough. It was both ahead of its time and old-fashioned, at once an anticipation of post-Yeatsian enlarged perspectives and a throwback to the spirit of the United Irishmen. In his later career in North America he procured his own eclipse both by disapproving of Fenian extremism and by developing a narrowly Catholic definition of essential Irishness which managed to offend Irish-American Catholic opinion. His life is at least as interesting as his uneven and controversial writing.

The bare outline of his career is startling.[81] As a boy he spoke at Father Mathew's temperance meetings, already an orator. At seventeen he left Ireland for New England and immediately made a name for himself as an O'Connellite spokesman and publicist. He was appointed editor of the Irish-American *Boston Pilot* at the age of nineteen. He next appears as the London correspondent of the Dublin *Freeman's Journal* but soon switched to the Young Ireland organ *The Nation*. In 1847 he became secretary of the Young Ireland 'Irish Confederation'. He took an active part in the Young Ireland rising of 1848 and hid out in various parts of Derry and Donegal before taking ship once again for America. He was still only twenty-three, but he had already written copiously about Irish history, literature and politics and had tried his hand at patriotic verse and an incomplete ballad-history of Ireland. He then embarked on a new career in Irish-American publishing and adult education in Boston, Buffalo and New York before moving to Canada. There he represented Montreal in parliament, became Minister of Agriculture and Immigration in 1864, campaigned for Canadian federal union and when this was achieved (in 1867) was noted as the youngest of the 'Fathers of Confederation'. In 1868 he was assassinated in Ottawa by an Irish-American extremist, six days before his forty-third birthday.

McGee was not just a politician but a popular poet, historian and biographer devoted to the cause of Ireland and the Irish throughout the world. His *History of the Irish Settlers in North America* (Boston, 1851) ran through six editions in four years. He has been hailed as a founding father of Canadian literature and discussed at length in the American section of the standard history of Irish Catholicism,[82] but in Ireland he is a shadowy and enigmatic figure, faintly praised by Yeats[83] but still a fugitive lurking unobtrusively in a few anthologies. His work represents a point of access to the endlessly vexed question of the political and cultural identity of Ireland, variously perceived in Belfast, Dublin and London not to mention Boston, Montreal and Ottawa. But the very geographical spread of McGee's career and the consequent scattering of his published work and his private papers have made it difficult to come to grips with the whole man.

From the outset different identities were possible. His family background reveals the different modes of Irishness which he later sought to harmonize as a Young Ireland publicist. He was born in Carlingford, Co. Louth, the son of a coastguard, though holidays were often spent in Wexford which still preserved bitter memories of sectarian carnage in 1798. His father's family was of Ulster stock, claiming descent from one of the Scottish soldiers who came with General Munroe's army in 1642, commissioned to stamp out Irish rebellion and incidentally to organize and consolidate the Presbyterian presence in Ulster. But McGee grew up a Roman Catholic, profoundly influenced by his mother whose own father, a Dublin bookseller, had been imprisoned and financially ruined after joining with the United Irishmen in 1798. The heritage of bookishness and Irish national enthusiasms led naturally to hero-worship of the most celebrated Irishmen of his early years, Tom Moore the poet and Dan O'Connell the Liberator. Though O'Connell himself had made political use of the facile national sentiment of Moore's verse,[84] O'Connell and Moore came to represent sharply conflicting impulses in McGee's career, giving rise to some of the contradictions which have made him such an enigmatic figure.

In 1842 he took his literary and political enthusiasms to Boston. It was an awkward time to be Irish and Catholic in America. Conservative elements in the country, feeling threatened by the presence of several million foreign-born and often Roman Catholic residents among them, were beginning to form 'Know-Nothing' secret societies to oppose

these 'outsiders' politically and socially. The Germans and the Irish
were their particular targets. Two Roman Catholic churches were
burnt down in Philadelphia and 'Paddy' became a term of abuse and
contempt.[85] From his editor's chair at the *Boston Pilot* the young
McGee strenuously opposed this 'Know-Nothing' movement while
simultaneously spreading the O'Connellite gospel of Repeal throughout New England. His first book, *Historical Sketches of O'Connell and
his Friends* (Boston, 1844), like his public speeches, was a piece of
passionate partisan rhetoric seeking to counteract the patronizing scorn
of the 'Know-Nothings' by instilling a sense of national self-respect
among the Irish-born and promoting a vision of a new nation to be
made after Repeal. Thomas Moore, inevitably, was included among
O'Connell's 'friends'.

But McGee's grasp of Irish affairs was already a little out of date. In
a speech at Watertown, Massachusetts in November 1843, he
celebrated O'Connell as 'the advocate of the Dissenter, the friend of
the Quaker, the panegyrist of the Covenanters, the eloquent supporter
of the legality of Presbyterian marriages . . . The party for whom he
labours is his country and humanity.'[86] It was all more or less true, but
it was not quite the whole truth. The New England audience, some of
Puritan descent, no doubt, were expected to thrill to the celebration of
O'Connell as the Liberator of Protestant dissent in Ulster, as well as of
Catholic Ireland. But if the earlier O'Connell had worked with liberal
Dissenters for Catholic Emancipation, if English political writers such
as William Cobbett could be numbered among his friends for their
support of the cause, the later O'Connell's crusade for Repeal of the
Act of Union had a narrower basis of support and was rapidly
becoming a specifically Irish Catholic cause. The other problem about
McGee's O'Connell was that he was too much a passionate idealist
created in the image of the youthful McGee, too little the seasoned
pragmatist he really was. The Liberator probably never read *O'Connell
and his Friends*, never reprinted in England or Ireland. If he had he
would have been disconcerted to see himself keeping company with the
romantic rebel Robert Emmet as an opponent of the Union: 'No two
men of the present century more truly recognized the great principle of
disinterestedness; none so closely approached the ideal of patriotism.'[87]
All his life O'Connell deplored political violence and steered clear of it.
But McGee's other hero, Thomas Moore, was imaginatively if not
practically involved with the Irish tradition of armed struggle which he
helped to perpetuate at the level of myth. He had written the life of the
United Irishman Lord Edward Fitzgerald and had poetically mourned

the passing of Robert Emmet. O'Connell, on the other hand, had actually enrolled in the Yeomanry in Dublin in 1798 to resist the United Irishmen. McGee's bookseller grandfather had been (technically) his enemy.

Partly for these reasons O'Connell would not have liked McGee's only work of fiction, a short tale entitled *Eva Macdonald. A Tale of the United Irishmen and their Times* (Boston, 1844).[88] It is very romantic and very bad, an incoherent and inflammatory nationalist tract. Wolfe Tone and Napper Tandy make guest appearances, though the actual military engagements of 1798 take place offstage. The hero is Sir Cahir O'Doherty of the Glens of Antrim, named after a seventeenth-century rebel but 'a perfect Gentleman of the Old School' (p. 47) and so a standing rebuke to the monopoly of civility claimed by Protestant Ascendancy. An 'intrepid Knight', he stands in marked contrast to Captain Sinclair, an English naval officer, 'a singular compound of cruelty and cunning, cowardice and impertinence' (p. 5) who is his rival for the hand of the Scots-descended Irishwoman, Eva Macdonald. Ireland triumphs in love if not in war. In the spirit of the United Irishmen the different traditions of Ulster and of Ireland generally come together when Eva and Sir Cahir are married, and joy echoes through Castle O'Doherty 'like fairy music' (p. 46).

McGee's immature romance, influenced by his grandfather's experience of '98, owes something also to Moore's literary habit of mingling love and national sentiment. Moore had celebrated the glories of Brien the Brave, culminating in the battle of Clontarf, to elaborate the dream of ultimately triumphant nationality. O'Connell tried to exploit the romantic resonances of this famous victory over the Danes by organizing a monster rally at Clontarf in October 1843 in support of Repeal. But the pragmatic politician in him won an easy victory over the strictly rhetorical warrior when the government banned the rally and O'Connell cancelled it. This humiliation bitterly disappointed some of his younger supporters associated with Thomas Davis and the *Nation* newspaper. Eventually, as O'Connell's political obstinacy and the ever-increasing horrors of the famine seemed to call in question the practical effectiveness of the Repeal movement, this 'Young Ireland' group broke away from O'Connell. For his part O'Connell had to disown them when the *Nation* took to discussing terrorist tactics and sabotage.

Soon after his return from America, McGee had met Thomas Davis and Charles Gavan Duffy, adopted them as heroes more sympathetic to a youthful imagination than the ageing O'Connell, and identified himself with the Young Ireland cause. His employers on the *Freeman's Journal* became understandably annoyed. Their London correspondent was spending his time not in the press-gallery of the House of Commons but in the Reading-room of the British Museum, studying Irish history and antiquities with a patriotic enthusiasm caught from George Petrie's recent investigations of round towers and ancient churches and from the scholarly poetic recreations of old Ireland by Samuel Ferguson. The pioneer Gaelic scholarship of Eugene O'Curry and of John O'Donovan, editor of the *Annals of the Four Masters*, was also an important factor. McGee wrote elegies for O'Curry and O'Donovan. Recollections of Celtic keening and lament, Ossianic gloom and political despondency seem to have combined to make the elegy a popular Victorian Irish verse-form. Thomas Davis's 'Lament for the Death of Eoghan Ruadh O'Neill' and Samuel Ferguson's 'Lament for Thomas Davis' are among McGee's models. The patriotic antiquarian endeavour to secure national possessions from the ravages of time is paralleled in the writing of commemorative elegy. O'Donovan was a co-worker with McGee, one who

> toiled to make our story stand
> As from Time's reverent, runic hand
> It came, undeck'd
> By fancies false, erect, alone,
> The monumental arctic stone
> Of ages wreck'd.[89]

Logically, the wreck must be of the vanished ages rather than the monumental stone but the faint ambiguity and the emphatically final 'wreck'd' are ominous and disconcerting, as if neither national history nor cultural monuments could have any security except in romantic verse. But it was still possible to recover the Irish past from books, and this became McGee's new objective. The fruits of his voracious reading began to appear in the pages of the *Nation*, not the *Freeman's Journal*. McGee soon found he was writing for the *Nation* alone.

Some of these *Nation* pieces appeared in book-form early in 1846 as *The Irish Writers of the Seventeenth Century*, part of the patriotic 'Library of Ireland' series and perhaps McGee's most important work.[90] The effect of this pioneering study is to extend the Irish literary tradition in time and scope. Catholic and Celtic Ireland is well represented: Geoffrey Keating's *History of Ireland* and the *Annals of the Four Masters* are discussed, predictably enough, together with the works of Lynch, MacFirbis, Rothe and O'Flaherty. What is less expected is a fairly sympathetic account of Archbishop Ussher, saluted despite politics and Protestantism as a pioneer of the great tradition of Irish antiquarianism continuing down to O'Curry and O'Donovan. The historian Sir James Ware, courtier and placeman as he was, is celebrated as the presiding genius of Anglo-Irish cultural interaction, facilitating, even procuring, 'the confluence of our ancient and modern literature' (p. 73). William Molyneux is discussed, a little anachronistically, as 'the father of our modern struggle for Parliamentary Independence' (p. 239), an apostle of nationality. The tradition-seeking process has ruthlessly assimilated the gentlemanly concerns of Molyneux and the eighteenth-century Anglo-Irish political nation to the populist agitation of Dan O'Connell. The book illustrates the process deplored by Walter Benjamin and Michael Foucault, discussed in the first chapter of the present work, in that it fabricates illusory continuities to produce a plausible but unreal identity, an unchanging Irish nation. Though McGee acknowledges the prevalence of divisive dogmatism and bigotry the 'strongly national character' he attributes to the writers of the period tends to unite them into Young Ireland prototypes and conflates the different Irelands of Ussher and MacFirbis and the English-descended Catholic John Lynch.

But not all continuities are illusory. McGee shrewdly identifies seventeenth-century Ulster as a problem area, awkwardly different. His interest is more cultural than political, though the two cannot finally be separated: he was writing well before perceived religious and cultural differences brought the 'Orange card' into play and initiated the partition of Ireland. His comments rely on an anti-Puritan and rather English romantic aesthetic, encouraged by Schlegel on Shakespeare and anticipating Matthew Arnold's attacks on the Philistines of English Dissent. Ireland's north-eastern province, artificially homogenized, is described as 'sunk under the sickly shade of Knoxism. Scottish and English Puritanism produced disastrous effects upon the native genius of this kingdom' (p. 249). One might wish to argue the point and to suggest that McGee lacks appreciation of the historical consciousness and moral intensity of the Ulster Puritan imagination, but his observation is aesthetic rather than sectarian. Of partly Ulster descent himself, McGee took Ulster seriously. With all its ahistorical simplifications and special pleading, McGee's *Irish Writers of the Seventeenth Century* proposes a geographically and culturally comprehensive definition of Irishness, more generous than that of the cultural patriots of the Celtic Revival half a century later.

This pluralist vision of the Irish nation, buttressed by invented tradition, had its counterpart in the varied backgrounds of the Young Ireland leaders. William Smith O'Brien was proud of his ultimate descent from Brien Boru though educated among the English élite at Harrow and Cambridge. Thomas Davis, a Trinity Protestant, was the son of an Irishwoman from Cork and an English army surgeon. Some had northern connections. Charles Gavan Duffy was a Monaghan Catholic who briefly attended a Presbyterian school and then worked as a journalist in Belfast. John Mitchel, the angriest of the young men, was a solicitor from Down, son of a Presbyterian minister.

It was this northern dimension that had been rather neglected by O'Connell, whose appeal was more to the priests and people of the rural south-west than to the largely Protestant and industrializing north-east. McGee accompanied the Young Ireland mission to Belfast in September 1847 in an attempt to redress the balance. The plan was to involve the northern community in the national cause as they had been before the Union, both in the United Irishmen and in the Volunteers. McGee was proposed as editor of a new Belfast paper to promote national enthusiasms along the same lines as the Dublin-based *Nation*. Excitement mounted. As McGee wrote to William Smith O'Brien just before they went to Belfast: 'There is a great curiosity abroad about our Belfast meeting and you will see in Saturday's *Nation* some extracts from Ulster papers which will surprize and delight you.'[91]

Opposition was expected, particularly from the Orangemen. But in the event, the main criticisms came from the conservative Roman Catholic community, loyal to O'Connell and 'Old Ireland' and suspicious of angry Young Ireland. The Church authorities were unhappy with the notion of Young Ireland: it seemed uncomfortably like the Young Italy movement of Mazzini which had fought the temporal power of the pope in the cause of Italian nationality.[92] Neither Irish Catholicism nor Irish Protestantism was as homogeneous as sectarian myth implied. From this point on the Catholic McGee's plans suffered from tensions within Catholicism.

The Belfast Young Ireland expedition had little lasting impact and the proposed newspaper came to nothing. McGee returned to work for the cause in Dublin. But his poem in the *Nation*, 'The man from the north countrie', is a legacy of this episode: the lovely maiden who so often represents Ireland finds happiness and fulfilment with the northerner who stands for the northern province (*Poems*, p. 484f). Other poems testify to the aspiration to, if not the achievement of, whole-hearted Ulster involvement in a national ideal expanded to incorporate specifically northern and Protestant traditions and allegiances. The time-honoured Orangemen's cry of 'No Surrender' was audaciously adopted as the slogan of all four Irish provinces in the coming time:

> Heard in Dublin's dimmest alleys,
> Heard in Connaught's saddest valleys –
> In our night-time, from the North,
> Came a voice to stir the earth,
>   With its watchword, 'No Surrender!'
> . . . .
> On Slieve Donard plant your banner
> Let the mountain breezes fan her.
> Ireland feels its dawning splendor,
> Hoping, chiding, guiding, tender,
>   Shining on us, 'No Surrender!'
>   (*Poems*, p. 83f)

A later poem 'To the River Boyne' acknowledges that the river has 'Seen fraternal forces clash in anger' but emphasizes fraternity rather than anger, seeks to purge the Boyne water of its bitter sectarian aftertaste, and ingeniously sees in the river's position as 'blue bound of Ulster and of Tara' a fit emblem and setting for the Young Ireland Confederation, a pact 'made for brotherhood and union/ For equal laws to class and to communion' (*Poems*, p. 331).

McGee had planned his ballad-history of Ireland to kindle the Irish imagination to national enthusiasm through rhetorically selected history. 'The Summons of Ulster', written for this uncompleted project, is not about the Young Ireland canvass of Belfast, or not directly, but about the 1595 rebellion of Hugh O'Neill, Earl of Tyrone, in support of the imperiled heritage of Gaelic Ireland:

> Arm! arm! ye men of Ulster, for battle to the death!
> Arm to defend your fathers' fields, and shield your fathers' faith!
> They are coming! they are coming! the foe is gathering near!
> Arm for your rich inheritance, and for your altars dear!
>   (*Poems*, p. 301)

Ulster was rather improbably dragged into McGee's *Memoir of the Life and Conquests of Art MacMurrough, King of Leinster* (Dublin, 1847), the last volume in Duffy's Library of Ireland. This 'Irish hero of the Middle Ages' was enrolled in a national pantheon in which both Hugh O'Neill and Brien Boru had their place: 'Each kingdom [of Ireland] in turn made its stand until it came to Ulster's turn, where we find two heroes, in the same age [Hugh O'Neill and Hugh O'Donnell], nobly contending for the existence of their nation.'[93]

McGee seems here to endorse the specifically Catholic and Gaelic definition of the nation for which the O'Neill contended and this is read back into the triumph of Brien Boru at Clontarf, traditionally but anachronistically represented as a victory not only for the Gael against the foreigner but for Western Christendom. McGee even associates it with later Christian victories against the Turks despite the fact that the 'pagan' Danes fought for as well as against Brien and stayed on in Ireland after the battle. It is at this point that McGee's rhetorical history, modelled on Moore's *Irish Melodies*, parts company with the culturally pluralist contemporary political programme of Young Ireland which he simultaneously if inconsistently endorsed and promoted. The cultural interminglings and discontinuities of Irish history must bear much of the blame for this. But the discontinuities of McGee's own life are also relevant. The romantic Ireland of his writings was invented not on the shores of Carlingford Lough or in Dublin so much as in Boston and the British Museum. As with later Irish-American effusions, there was an imperfect fit with contemporary realities in Ireland. McGee was soon to return to America, and his literary nationalism froze into a self-sufficient Celtocentric myth constantly reiterated to provide a largely artificial identity for first- and second-generation Catholic Irishmen in the new world. The overrated anthology-pieces 'Salute to the Celt', addressed to the scattered Irish or 'sea-divided Gael', and 'The Celts', described imprecisely as a 'mighty race/ Taller than Roman spears', are the disappointing legacy of McGee's literary idealism (*Poems*, pp. 135f, 176f).

Young Ireland had split from O'Connell partly on the theoretical question of the admissibility of a recourse to arms. It soon became a more practical question. Though McGee resisted extremists such as Mitchel, who wanted to fight by any available means for radical land reform and an Irish republic, and insisted only on a return to legislative independence under the crown, he was eventually driven to take up arms. The example of the 1848 Paris Revolution, intemperate speeches and repressive government measures established a downward spiral of disaffection. McGee was arrested in Wicklow in July 1848 but released on bail. Almost immediately he went north, passing through

Belfast on his way to Glasgow. His mission was to co-ordinate promised support along the Clyde and embark armed volunteers at Greenock to sail to Sligo or to Killala, the French landing-place in 1798, to support a new armed struggle planned for August 1848. Unhampered by remarkably inefficient government surveillance McGee reached Glasgow and made some progress with his plans before he was recognized. He returned hurriedly to Ireland by way of England, avoided the two detectives looking for him in Belfast, and resumed the business of insurrection. The conspiracy was more imaginative than practical. McGee planned and plotted in Sligo and Donegal, dreaming of Owen Roe O'Neill and the United Irishmen and waiting for the West to be awake once more. He was disappointed. The rising came to nothing and McGee had to flee to America, disguised as a priest.[94]

McGee's ambition to forge national unity in diversity had little success in Ireland and even less in the United States, though it triumphed in Canada. In Boston once again, lecturing and writing about Ireland, he selected only those aspects of Irishness congenial to the overwhelmingly Catholic immigrant community among whom he had chosen to work. Even so, he failed to avoid controversy and disharmony. The liberal and possibly anti-papal taint of Young Ireland, placing national aspirations above ecclesiastical loyalties, had displeased Catholic Belfast and found no favour with the Irish-born Bishop (later Archbishop) Hughes of New York. McGee was attacked by the *Boston Pilot* which he had once edited. By 1852 he had become more conservatively Catholic, partly in response to continuing 'Know-Nothing' hostility, but his attacks on Mazzini and his ex-Young Ireland admirers lost him friends without appeasing Bishop Hughes. Later writings such as *A Catholic History of North America* (1855) express this new ultramontane religious conservatism and register incidental unease with liberal and officially secular America.[95]

Eventually McGee abandoned the USA for Canada. In his writing and in his public life he relived the aspirations of Young Ireland in a new context. He wrote *Canadian Ballads* (1858), proclaimed the possibilities of Canadian nationhood and national literature, and campaigned successfully for Canadian Confederation. This had the effect of harmonizing largely Protestant (including Ulster-Protestant) western Canada with the largely Catholic (including Irish-Catholic) east to form a new dominion under the British crown. Protestant and Catholic, Orange and Green, come together at a more personal level in McGee's collaboration and correspondence with the great John A.

Macdonald, closely associated with the Orangemen of Canada and the most famous advocate of Confederation.[96]

Despite the possibility of extremist violence latent in McGee's romantic nationalism, his natural conservatism reasserted itself in Canada. His hostility to the North American Fenian conspiracies reproduces his earlier opposition to Mitchel and the Young Ireland extremists. It procured his assassination. The Fenian executed for his murder may not actually have pulled the trigger: he was part of a conspiracy.[97] It was a sadly ironic death for the Young Ireland conspirator turned Canadian statesman. The contradictions of his career, rebel versus conservative, Moore versus O'Connell, romantic Celticist versus cultural pluralist, were symptoms of the confused identity of Victorian Ireland. His obituary notice in the *Montreal Gazette* called him 'the very apostle of peace' but he had neither found nor made peace in the land of his birth.[98]

CHAPTER 5

Revival Reviewed:

St John Ervine and James Joyce

————

HERE IS a striking contrast between the comparative failures of
Carleton and D'Arcy McGee and the resounding successes of
Yeats and Lady Gregory half a century later. This can be
related to a transformed political atmosphere: land reform and Home
Rule had now become serious possibilities and national hope gleamed
in the Celtic Twilight. By the end of the nineteenth century Ireland
began to take her place among the nations of the earth both politically
and culturally. In due course the mutually reinforcing processes of
national and literary revival came to a sudden, dramatic climax in the
terrible beauty of the Easter Rising of 1916.[1]

Or so the story goes. But the golden legend of triumphantly
rediscovered national identity has outlived its usefulness. It can now
be recognized that the writers of the Irish Literary Revival selected
ahistorical and particularist myths of identity which only reinforced
existing divisions in the country and postponed its coming of age as a
modern nation almost indefinitely.[2] The achievement of Yeats and
Lady Gregory is beyond question, but it is necessary to look more
critically at the fatally divisive cultural choices and consequences of the
Revival. These can be examined through the contrasting literary
careers of St John Ervine and James Joyce, a Belfast man and a
Dubliner, united, if in nothing else, in their complex disrespect for the
ambiguous achievements of Celtic revivalism.

The exiled Joyce looked outwards from Ireland and transformed the
contentious babble of Irish voices and identities into the masterly
polyphony of *Ulysses* and *Finnegans Wake*. The English-exiled Ervine
was gradually confined and limited by the strident confusion of a

disintegrated Ireland, partitioned into North and South, which infected his outlook even while imparting increasingly sectarian energy to it. Both writers became aware that the polemical assertion of identity damagingly forecloses on other possible identities and tends to deform both the individual imagination and the body politic.

Renewing national self-respect was a worthy object, but it was a dangerous strategy to introduce the habit of defining what was 'Irish' and 'national'. Too much was likely to be classified as 'unIrish'. The famous *Playboy* riots of 1907, when J. M. Synge's *Playboy of the Western World* was almost hissed off the stage of the Abbey Theatre as 'unIrish', were occasioned by the perceived insult to pure-minded Catholic-nationalist and heroic definitions of Irishness proffered by Synge's mock-heroic romantic realism. In later years Sean O'Casey's *The Plough and the Stars* and George A. Birmingham's *General John Regan* caused trouble in Irish theatres for similar reasons, though both were written by committed Irish nationalists. Yeats raged against the Dublin audiences as he was to rage against the Dublin shopkeepers. But the shopkeepers had their revenge in the puritanical censoriousness and actual literary censorship of post-Treaty Ireland which alienated and exiled Irish writers between the wars.

Synge's mock-heroic, and the sterner and more critical agrarian realism of dramatists such as Lennox Robinson, offended sections of the Irish public by demonstrating, with varying degrees of harshness, the inadequacy of the Celtic revivalist's romantic-heroic model of Irishness. This had been fashioned from a highly selective reading of ancient Irish materials first popularized by Standish Hayes O'Grady. His *History of Ireland: Heroic Period* (1878) was 'the start of us all', according to Yeats.[3] But O'Grady's engaging romantic history, based on bardic sources, owed more to his interest in Homeric epic than to critical scholarship. The example of Homer had led the German classical scholar Barthold Georg Niebuhr to describe epics as composed of matter 'which has . . . lived for centuries in popular songs and tales as common national property'.[4] This is a principal, but unacknowledged, source of the cultural-nationalist interest in folklore and Celtic myth as repositories of a recoverable national spirit. Behind Niebuhr lay the influence of Herder and German romanticism, and eighteenth-century Ossianism and European Celtomania lay behind that, but the revivalists were understandably reluctant to believe that their enthusiasm might itself have a history. O'Grady's sense of history was shaped by current affairs. His radical Toryism, influenced by Carlyle and Lord Randolph Churchill, encouraged an idealized vision of Anglo-Irish aristocratic landlordism (already discredited and obsolescent) which he felt could sustain the heroic energy he identified in Gaelic tradition. This did not attract Yeats at first but he came to believe in it in the new century, setting himself against the more democratic tendency of the age and driving a wedge between a mythical aristocratic Anglo-Ireland and the emerging Irish nation-state.[5]

The combination of aristocratic romanticism and *fin-de-siècle* aestheticism in the work of Yeats had the effect of separating Ireland from the modern world and from the popularist cultural pluralism of Young Ireland. Gavan Duffy and Yeats came sharply into conflict over Duffy's New Irish Library, intended to revive the Young Ireland Library of Ireland series of the 1840s to which both Carleton and D'Arcy McGee had contributed. The original model for the project, Brougham's utilitarian Library of Useful Knowledge, was an offence to Yeats' quasi-religious vision of spiritual renewal of Ireland and indicated too much traffic with the practical situation of Ireland past and present.[6]

In a sense, the issue between Yeats and Duffy simply reproduces the tension, long established in Irish tradition, between romantic idealism and pragmatic rationalism, between Moore and O'Connell. Within Young Ireland the division had been between the militant anti-English, anti-materialist John Mitchel and the more moderate and practical Duffy who lived to be knighted by Queen Victoria after a second, more successful, career in Australian politics. At another level the gulf between Duffy's populism and Yeats' prophetic vision draws attention to the distance between an increasingly urban, prosaic, bourgeois Ireland and an aesthetically self-conscious, sometimes arcane, literary culture.

But Yeats and Lady Gregory had their own brand of rural populism. Trinity College, urban and privileged, was its *bête noir*. Lady Gregory jeered at 'the Chinese Wall that separates Trinity College from Ireland'.[7] The slur was common at the time and still has some currency in the grumbling of Denis Donoghue.[8] There was some truth in it: Trinity was noticeably cool in the cause of Ireland's literary and political renaissance. But the dividing wall also tended to shut off the rest of Ireland from the cosmopolitan intellectual culture to which some at least at Trinity's protégés and the Anglo-Irish intelligentsia had always aspired. The legendary J. P. Mahaffy, eventually Provost of the College, was arrogantly dismissive of what he saw as the pretentiousness of the Celtic Revival, but his pioneering Greek scholarship earned him an international reputation as well as inspiring pupils such as the young Oscar Wilde. Mahaffy's pupil and colleague J. B. Bury, like Mahaffy the son of a Church of Ireland clergyman from rural Ulster, collaborated with his teacher in an edition of the *Hippolytus* of Euripides (1881) when still an undergraduate. After a glittering career at Trinity he eventually succeeded Lord Acton as Regius Professor of Modern History at Cambridge in 1902.

Bury can be seen as a kind of spiritual descendant of the Earl of Roscommon. His awe-inspiring output of self-consciously scientific scholarship covered the whole field of European history from the Roman Empire to the late Middle Ages. He seldom touched on Irish history as such but he stressed Ireland's participation in European movements. His small masterpiece of rationalist detachment, *The Life of St Patrick and his Place in History* (1905), presents the saint's life as a chapter in the story of Roman influence in the west.

The extent to which this broad perspective is unIrish is debatable. Ussher and Roscommon had found security amid Irish uncertainties in a comprehensive European vision. Bury believed in the ultimate unity of European history and in the possibility of charting European progress in reason and knowledge in works such as *The History of the Freedom of Thought* (1914). This recalls the work of another Trinity man, W. E. H. Lecky, historian not only of eighteenth-century England and Ireland (1892) but of European rationalism (1865) and European morals (1869). The old-fashioned Enlightenment values implicit in these ambitious essays in intellectual history are symptoms of the liberal, secular Protestantism to which Carleton aspired. Influenced by Gibbon (whom Bury edited), suspicious of ecclesiastical tyranny both Catholic and Protestant, Lecky and Bury were impatient with the divisions and narrow embittered provincialism of Victorian Ireland and found a way round them.

The quarrel between Revivalist Ireland and Trinity cosmopolitanism was most acute in Yeats' hostility to Edward Dowden, the Professor of English. There was an element of ungraciousness in this, almost family spite. Dowden was a family friend who had been at college with the poet's father. Yeats might well have followed his father and grandfather to Trinity but the fees would have been a problem and there was some doubt whether he could pass the entrance examination. Even so, he and his father often came to breakfast with Dowden. Professor Dowden was encouraging about young Willie's verses, and so was Professor Bury. It was at Dowden's house that Yeats met other young writers such as his future associates T. W. Rolleston and Douglas

Hyde.[9] Dowden had a Presbyterian father, an Anglican mother and a brother who became Bishop of Edinburgh, but he himself repudiated the sectarianism which often dogged orthodox religious belief in Ireland and found in Shelley, Shakespeare and Walt Whitman a kind of post-Christian substitute religion of the indomitable human spirit. He was a sensitive minor poet in his own right and his Browningesque dramatic monologues are still worth reading. But he could be a severe critic. He noted the rhetorical excess, sentimentality and technical inadequacy of much Irish writing in English and rather discouraged young writers from taking up Irish mythical or early historical subjects on the grounds of restricted appeal. Yeats aggressively disregarded the advice and attacked Dowden and Irish critics and professors in general for daring to prefer George Eliot to Samuel Ferguson.[10]

The cultural purism, or narrowness, of the Celtic Revival had really two aspects. One was a matter of taste and the other a matter of history. Dowden was afraid that an Irish national literature in English would be more national than literary. Yeats recognized the difficulty in his Preface to *A Book of Irish Verse* (1895; 2nd edition 1900) when he acknowledged both the national traditions of Thomas Davis and the aesthetic 'traditions of good literature, which are the morality of the man of letters', a formulation Dowden might have been proud of. The young Yeats had to convince himself that to the truly discerning national writing responsive to Celtic tradition would also be good writing.

In matters of cultural history, cultural patriots and Celtic revivalists were willing to concede nothing to the broader views of Trinity intellectuals. It was in the Trinity journal *Hermathena* that the indefatigable Mario Esposito published a series of very learned articles on medieval Irish literature.[11] But because his principal interest was in the Latin and Norman-French literature of medieval Ireland, not its Celtic traditions, his work attracted little attention. He also contributed to the Dublin journal *Studies*, but his quiet reflections on 'The Latin Writers of Medieval Ireland' (published in 1913) passed unnoticed, while in the same journal, in the same year, Patrick Pearse's 'Some Aspects of Irish Literature' flamboyantly proclaimed an exclusively Celtic literary culture in which Latin and Ireland's European heritage had no part.[12]

Celtic revivalism involved a wider world than some of its brasher publicists admitted. Celtic philology and scholarship had always been an international enterprise. The Trinity man Whitley Stokes, grandson of a United Irishman, inherited from his father and grandfather a characteristically Anglo-Irish gentlemanly interest in Irish antiquities. But this was transformed into a rigorous and formidable scholarship. He took lessons from John O'Donovan, editor of the *Annals of the Four Masters*, and acquired an enviable philological competence with the help of Zeuss's *Grammatica Celtica* (1853) and the German Sanskrit scholar Rudolph Siegfried, then an assistant librarian at Trinity. His professional career as a barrister took him to British India where he eventually became legal member of the Council, a position once held by Macaulay. His activities illustrate the multiple contexts, national and imperial, Irish and European, within which Irish cultural identity was explored. Stokes published his valuable edition of the *Fís Adamnain* ('Vision of Adamnan'), associated with the biographer and friend of St Columba, in Calcutta in 1870. He took advantage of his situation to consider the Irish language and Irish institutions in their Indo-European context. This was not an entirely new enterprise, since the philological and ethnological researches of James Cowles Prichard and others had already established Celtic membership of the Indo-European family. But the full institutional significance of this was not apparent until Stokes joined forces with the great English jurist and legal historian Sir Henry Maine. Maine's *Lectures on the Early History of Institutions* (1875) are dedicated to Stokes and incorporate a study of the ancient Irish Brehon laws with which Stokes assisted him. Ireland, England and India, represented by the ancient forms of their legal institutions, are brought closer together by Maine's comparative analysis. From this it emerges that apparent differences can be seen as differences in degree of development within the same Indo-European (or 'Aryan') culture common to the three countries. Technical detail acquires momentous significance. Maine's comparison of Irish and Germanic legal remedies for debt or other injury indicates a remarkable correspondence, 'almost enough by itself to destroy those reckless theories of race which assert an original, inherent difference of idea and usage between Teuton and Celt'.[13]

The common Aryan parentage of Teuton and Celt, or English and Hindoo, was convenient as a way of taking the sting out of colonial occupation and demonstrating an essential brotherhood between colonizer and colonized, but in Ireland at least this was to some extent already accepted and many of Ireland's national champions, such as Yeats and Parnell, were of Anglo-Irish descent. The 'reckless theories of race' Maine sensibly assailed were to lend bogus respectability to the racist attitudes of both 'Irish Ireland' cultural nationalists and the propagandists of the Third Reich.

Yeats himself never went to the extremes of 'Irish Ireland' cultural patriots such as D. P. Moran who attacked every aspect of Ireland's English and non-Celtic heritage. His later writing shows an increasing imaginative involvement with European perspectives. Even as a young man he indicates some awareness of Ireland's Indo-European identity. As a theosophist and romantic he was attracted by an apparently anti-materialist strand in both Indian and Celtic culture. In an early article entitled 'Irish Wonders' he claims boldly that 'Tradition is always the same. The earliest poet of India and the Irish peasant in his hovel nod to each other across the ages, and are in perfect agreement.'[14] Yeats' friend Charlie Johnston, son of the famous Orangeman William Johnston of Ballykilbeg, had helped to bring the East to Ireland, bypassing England, by founding the Dublin Theosophical Lodge in 1886. This allowed Yeats to meet the Bengali Brahmin Mohini Chatterji. In the very early Indian poems later collected in *Crossways* (1889) Yeats erected into a formal cult Chatterji's message of withdrawal into dreamy contemplation from the despised world of action.[15] Yeats' friend George Russell ('AE') wrote about the ancient Irish gods in an Asiatic, mystical vein which drew attention to Celtic links with the East, or so the poet Austin Clarke maintained.[16] But both Yeats and AE omitted Maine's middle term, the primitive Germanic traditions underpinning English institutions, themselves derived from Indo-European sources, because they were polemically insisting on difference from rather than similarity to a resented dominant culture.

The sometimes Indian, sometimes Celtic romanticism developed as a mode of escape from western materialism and, specifically, the industrialized society of England and (northern) Ireland, had the effect of encouraging cultural and political division in Ireland. It also resembled the late Victorian neo-romantic counter-culture of England associated with the anti-industrialism of William Morris. English materialism and philistinism were often (rather unfairly) identified with the historian Macaulay, whose Whig *History of England* presented scenes of protestant triumph in seventeenth-century Ireland which were frequently illustrated on the banners of nineteenth- and twentieth-century Orangemen. Macaulay had also championed the industrial revolution against romantic critics, such as Southey. William Morris's Romantic celebration of pre-industrial heroic simplicity appealed to Yeats, and Morris in his turn admired *The Wanderings of Oisin*. When the young Yeats was living in London he was a constant visitor to Morris's house.[17]

The romanticism of Morris and Yeats can be linked with contemporary European movements, drawing inspiration from Herder,
committed to recovering lost cultural, spiritual and national energies
by rediscovering vernacular tradition. The case of Iceland particularly
interested Morris. He visited the country in 1871 and soon after
commenced the study of Icelandic. By 1875, in collaboration with his
Icelandic tutor Eiríkr Magnusson, he had published the first of several
influential volumes of translations from the sagas under the title *The
Northern Love Stories*. The task was made easier by the pioneering
scholarship of the Icelander Gúdbrandr Vígfússon, who completed the
Oxford Icelandic-English dictionary in 1873. The Icelandic and Irish
experiences were not dissimilar, for Iceland was still under Danish
rule. But the growing consciousness of a prouder past, to which
Vígfússon's heroic lexicographical and editorial work on the sagas
contributed, eventually procured Home Rule for Iceland in 1904.[18]

The heroic Scandinavian past had already contributed to English
literary culture even before Morris's work. Bishop Percy and Vígfússon's
friend Thomas Carlyle had been interested not merely on grounds of
romantic primitivism but because the British Isles, including Ireland,
had participated in Scandinavian history and tradition. There had
been a Viking kingdom of York and a Viking kingdom of Dublin.
Yeats knew something about the revival of interest in Scandinavia not
only through his friendship with Morris but because he was a
neighbour of York Powell, Vígfússon's British collaborator. He
actually wrote to Douglas Hyde about the work of Powell and
Vígfússon in 1889.[19] But imaginatively and ideologically he turned his
back on Ireland's Scandinavian past. The Celtic revivalist myth of
Ireland could not cope with non-Celtic influences in early Ireland.

The different directions literary nationalism could have taken are
indicated in *The Revival of Irish Literature* (1894), a volume of
addresses delivered to the Irish Literary Society of London and the
Irish National Literary Society of Dublin. The extremist Douglas
Hyde spoke on 'The Necessity for De-Anglicizing Ireland' and linked
the rapid decline of the Irish language and culture by the nineteenth
century with earlier, less successful attempts to break the continuity of
Irish life, represented by 'the battleaxe of the Dane, the sword of the
Norman, the wile of the Saxon'. But Charles Gavan Duffy, the last
surviving Young Irelander, was less racially exclusive and less negative
about the Danes. The scholarly Danish-descended Dublin doctor
George Sigerson, author of *Poets and Poetry of Munster* (1860), which
anticipated Douglas Hyde's investigations of Gaelic poetry, reminded

Duffy of Ireland's complex past. He jocularly suggested ritually sacrificing Sigerson at Clontarf as a way of concluding Irish feuds and divisions ancient and modern. But on second thoughts he promised a pardon if Sigerson translated the sagas for Duffy's new Irish Library and so increased awareness of Norse Literature as it related to Ireland.[20]

Duffy and Sigerson contrived to be cultural pluralists as well as cultural patriots, aware of the false romantic-nationalist constructions of the Irish past in a way Hyde and Yeats chose not to be. Yeats rather ungenerously dismissed Sigerson as a timorous crank and an *ingénu*: he was baffled and perhaps disturbed by the extent and tendency of his erudition. Sigerson challenged the popular view that the Danes merely prefigured the Normans and the English as sworn enemies of incipient Irish nationality and dwelt on cultural links between the Northmen and the Irish.[21] But he made little impression on the Celtic racism of the literary revival. It was left to Joyce to revive Scandinavian Ireland, half-mischievously, in *Finnegans Wake*.

In a later volume, *Bards of the Gael and Gall* (1897), Sigerson stresses, indeed probably overstresses, the importance of Irish culture in Europe in the three centuries after the fall of Rome. He argues not for the splendid isolation of the Gael but for splendid permeation. His title and his dedication jointly to Gavan Duffy, a Gael, and Douglas Hyde, a Gall or foreigner of English descent, indicate a breadth of cultural vision for Ireland which Duffy welcomed and Hyde did not. Hyde's drastically Anglophobe *Literary History of Ireland* ignored Irish writing in English altogether, even very early work such as the medieval poem *The Land of Cokaygne*. Sigerson, however, was probably the first to note possible Celtic sources for the poem, indicating cultural syncretism even at an early period.[22]

The wilful myopia and exclusiveness of the Irish literary revival extended to the present as well as the past. Blindness to the Danes, despite Sigerson, was less serious, and less divisive, than the failure to comprehend or come to terms with north-eastern Ireland, only residually Celtic and with a culturally distinct industrial ethos. Hyde was unreasonable as well as inaccurate when he claimed that all Ireland was profoundly Celtic at the core 'in spite of the little admixture of Saxon blood in the north-east corner'.[23] Much can be forgiven the ardent propagandist eager to reassert the value of half-buried Irish tradition, but the bipolar rhetoric and the reduction of Anglo-Irish and Scots-Irish to mere Celtic anti-types have disastrously perpetuated misunderstanding and division. Cultural nationalism, partly inspired by Hyde's extremism, reached new heights of sublime silliness in an article by Peter McBrien on 'The Renascence of Ireland', published in 1919. This disowned the 'unGaelic constitutional movement of Molyneux, Grattan, O'Connell and Parnell' and the 'Teutonic ideals of the Thames', as well as the profoundly unIrish attitudes of 'those English Junkers, whose outpost still holds a bit of North-East Ulster'.[24] The description might fit a few of the largest Ulster landowners, but hardly the dour Presbyterian small farmers or the stubbornly independent-minded Belfast industrialists and artisans who had resisted Home Rule with such bitterness. It was perfectly possible to feel culturally remote from the Celtic Twilight or Lady Gregory's Kiltartan peasantry in St John Ervine's Belfast or Co. Down (or indeed in Joyce's Dublin) without being anti-Irish or having any sympathy for the 'Junker' arrogance of the old Protestant Ascendancy in its least attractive aspect. But few of the Celtic revivalists knew or wanted to know anything about non-Celtic Ulster and this attitude has bedevilled twentieth-century politics and hampered understanding of either the Irish or the British aspects of contemporary Ulster.

The disastrously selective revivalist myth of Ireland was reinforced by snobbery and inherited prejudice, at least in the case of Yeats. In old age he refused to endorse Maud Gonne's vendetta against the partition of Ireland, not because he had any respect for stubborn Ulster Unionists but because he found the inhabitants of the 'lost area' so disagreeable that he wanted nothing to do with them.[25] His grandfather had served as Rector of Tullylish, near Banbridge, in Co. Down, but had thought of himself as a sojourner in an alien province. Yeats himself had Ulster friends including AE, whom his father jovially dismissed as a 'Portadown Orangeman' (he was actually from nearby Lurgan), and Charlie Johnston, son of the Ballykilbeg Orangeman. But they were theosophists – hardly typical Ulstermen. When Yeats visited Johnston at his family home in Co. Down he complained that he could not find any folklore in the countryside '"among its half-Scotch people"'.[26] He cannot have looked very hard. Half-Scots Ulster, like the English philosophy of Newton and Locke, was an anti-type of the Yeatsian poetic imagination, its mythic status secure against the tyranny of fact.

The later Yeats could arise above prejudice and respect literary achievement whatever its origins. He wanted to include Ulster writers such as St John Ervine, whom he had once appointed to run the Abbey Theatre, and Forrest Reid the novelist in the Royal Irish Academy and the Irish Academy of Letters.[27] But Irish letters might have been better served if Yeats and the Celtic Revivalists had offered more enthusiastic support to the fledgeling Ulster Literary Theatre.[28] This had started rather tentatively in 1902 with a Belfast production of Yeats' *Cathleen ni Houlihan* in which the author showed little interest. His imagination lay in the rural west of Ireland and his practical interests in the Dublin theatre. For a time he tolerated the grim regionalist theatre of what he dubbed the 'Cork realists' and he accepted some of Ervine's early 'realist' Ulster plays for the Abbey, but he had little sympathy for Ulster cultural tradition at the points where it diverged from the heroic grandeur of Celtic myth or the folk-ways of the Celtic peasantry.

The domestic realism of the Ulster Literary Theatre, involving kitchen comedies and kitchen tragedies for the most part, was too prosaic for Yeats. But the most successful production, Gerald MacNamara's comedy *Thompson in Tir na nOg* (not published until 1918), drew attention to the absurdities of the Yeatsian heroic mode as well as well as of Ulster sectarianism. The play was originally written by request for Douglas Hyde's Gaelic League but was rejected as too disrespectful of Gaelic heroes.[29] A Portadown Orangeman (supposed to be the worst kind) wakes up in the Celtic otherworld among all-too-human legendary heroes. The farcical confusions and misunderstandings which follow depend on apparent parallels, unflattering to both sides, between the legendary Celtic cult of battle and the embattled posturings of the stage-Orangeman. MacNamara, whose real name was Harry Morrow, had shrewdly identified the insecure aggressiveness and militaristic bravado with which Protestant extremists in Ulster have regularly responded to cultural and political marginalization. He had also noticed the extent to which Celtic heroism and Protestant or Unionist intransigence could be reciprocal phenomena: cultural nationalism had begun to generate its counter-culture.

The Irish Literary Revival, generated by understandable hostility to the dominant London-centred metropolitan and cosmopolitan literary culture of Britain, overreacted badly. It depended far too much on what came to be dubbed 'peasant quality' in the theatre and a romanticized Celticism which excluded as 'unIrish' the contributions of Vikings, Normans, English and Scots to the composite identity of Ireland. Ernest Boyd, author of the contemporary survey *Ireland's Literary Renaissance* (1916), sourly noted the 'dour Protestantism', prudence and relative prosperity of rural Ulster in Rutherford Mayne's Ulster plays and contrasted it unfavourably with the 'soft Catholic atmosphere' in which Padraic Colum's writing was steeped.[30] This regionalist prejudice disguised as aesthetic preference, characteristic of the Revival, has left to the modern Irish writer, north and south, a contentious and disabling heritage. Fortunately, a more generous and stimulating understanding of the complex Irish literary tradition is afforded by the work of James Joyce. The Ulster writer St John Ervine is even more helpful as a mode of access to the cultural tensions which have been creatively explored and transformed by contemporary poets in the north of Ireland.

ST JOHN ERVINE (1883–1971)

Unlike Joyce, Ervine is now almost forgotten. But he left a bulky legacy of plays, novels, short stories, biographies, dramatic criticism and miscellaneous essays which had made his name in England and Ireland when Joyce was still almost unknown. There are English and Irish reasons for this reversal. Ervine practised obsolescent literary realism and social criticism in the English tradition of Dickens and Hardy and their successors H. G. Wells and Arnold Bennett. By 1919 Virginia Woolf was expressing influential dissatisfaction with Wells and Bennett. Modernist writers were developing techniques that went well beyond the methods and assumptions of the Victorian and Edwardian realists.[31] Politically, Ervine began as a Fabian radical and ended as a maverick conservative individualist, earning the disrespect of younger writers such as Day-Lewis and Louis MacNeice from the 1930s onwards.[32] In Ireland he had been a moderate nationalist with a very moderate sympathy for Celtic revivalism, but after Easter 1916 he gradually despaired of southern Ireland and cultural nationalism. With the rise of the Irish nation-state, which he disliked, it became difficult to sustain his sense of composite Irish and British identity. He pursued his career as an English and Ulster-regionalist writer in England and ensured his unpopularity in Dublin by aggressively espousing the cause of Ulster Unionism.

His worst enemy, however, was probably his own good-humoured relish for journalistic knockabout and critical coat-trailing. Soon after *Ulysses* was published, he robustly deplored Joyce's 'sewer-revelations' as the work of a 'Rabelais after a nervous breakdown'. This is unfair even to his own perception of Joyce. He admired the bold iconoclasm of Joyce's work which seemed to link him with Synge, Padraic Colum and Lennox Robinson in the worthwhile enterprise of demythologizing

Ireland's complacently sentimental national self-image.[33] From a different, more northerly, perspective Ervine tried to do the same. The best of his plays, such as *Mixed Marriage* (1911), and at least one of his novels, *Changing Winds* (1917), entertained cultural and social tensions arising out of the Irish experience without resorting to sentimental or simple-minded resolutions. Both *Mixed Marriage* and *Changing Winds* were in Joyce's library in 1920.[34]

Ervine's life and work illustrate in extreme form the problematic identity of the Irish writer in English. Born in Belfast, he was imaginatively involved with his birthplace all his life. But he left Ireland at the age of eighteen. His opportunities as a writer came only after he had settled in London. He joined the Fabian Society, which he later described as his university,[35] and met George Bernard Shaw and H. G. Wells. The romantic, rural and aristocratic tendencies of Irish letters, at least as indicated by Yeats and Lady Gregory, seemed poles apart from Wells' realistically rendered, lower-middle-class world of clerks and small shopkeepers dreaming of escape. Ervine had come to London as an insurance clerk, and his grandmother, whom he greatly admired, had been a small shopkeeper. He knew something of the Irish countryside, but it was Scots-settled north Down rather than the more romantic and Celtic remote west of Ireland. His literary options seemed to be either to write about English life or to develop some kind of Ulster regionalism as a counterpart to the ruralism, based on the west and south of the country, which was popular in literary Dublin.

In the event, he pursued both options with some success. His novel *Alice and a Family, a Story of South London* was published in 1915. In November 1915 the Abbey Theatre staged his most popular Irish play, *John Ferguson*, produced by Ervine himself, then manager of the theatre. *John Ferguson* was an Ulster regionalist tragedy parallel in some ways to the grimly unromantic tragedies of the 'Cork realists' such as Lennox Robinson, who had produced several of Ervine's earlier plays at the Abbey. But the play also had an English and a Scottish context. The simple dignity of the protagonist, a Scots-Irish small farmer, owes something to Hardy's Wessex and to the fiction of the Scottish 'Kailyard' school.

John Ferguson pursues the familiar Irish theme of oppression and insecurity on the land. It is set back in the 1880s, before effective land reforms such as the Wyndham Act (1903) had been introduced. The plot depends on old-fashioned, unreliable communications which prevent money arriving from America in time to satisfy a corrupt and rapacious neighbour who holds a mortgage on the farm. John

Ferguson finds himself unable to secure the farm for his family, though Fergusons have held it for many generations. This sounds rather like a tale by William Carleton, but there is a specifically Presbyterian dimension to the motif of generational continuity on the land. Continued Scots settlement in Ulster could be seen as an effect of the covenant relationship between God and His people, renewed from generation to generation as it had been with Abraham and Isaac and Jacob. But faith in the ancestral God, not to mention hope and charity, come under intolerable strain in the play. Ferguson's wife Sarah sees 'no sense or purpose' in their situation and urges a loveless marriage on their daughter Hannah to save the farm. Ferguson scrupulously insists Hannah should make up her own mind and piously claims that 'God never deserts His own people'.[36] But by the end of the play his unsatisfactory son Andrew, once intended for the Presbyterian ministry, has murdered the neighbour who holds the mortgage after he has apparently raped Hannah. Ferguson's stern Presbyterian integrity conflicts with family loyalties but he connives at his son's escape from justice. He still tries to insist that 'God knows better nor we do what's right to be done' but undermines his own assurance as he repeats from the Old Testament King David's heartbroken lament for his son Absalom.[37]

Hard times and Bible quotations are features of Scottish 'Kailyard' fiction as well as of Ervine's Ulster, and Ervine's self-reliant liberal theism in some ways resembles the humane modifications of severe Calvinist orthodoxy which lie behind J. M. Barrie's *Auld Licht Idylls* (1888) or S. R. Crockett's *The Stickit Minister* (1893). It was the literary fashion for many years to despise these 'Kailyard' works as sentimentally 'churchy' distortions of Scottish life,[38] but more appreciative recent criticism has noted how unPresbyterian attitudes keep breaking in.[39] Despite the grim and jealous God of the Old Testament and orthodox Scottish tradition, the Kailyard God is often shown to be 'more merciful than man'. Barrie's work, it was claimed, softened if it did not annihilate the 'doctrine of the Universal Depravity of the human Race'.[40] The emphasis was not on worthless sinners, helpless unless touched by divine grace, but on sinners who could succeed by their own efforts against the odds. S. R. Crockett's child-heroine Leeb (Elizabeth) McClurg valiantly organizes and supports the younger children of her neglected and orphaned family, advertising milk, eggs, firewood and sewing on a copybook page which has the heading 'Encourage Earnest Endeavour'.[41]

Ervine had a lot of respect for this quasi-Pelagian self-reliance. His novel *Alice and a Family* tells a story not unlike Crockett's: Alice, in her early teens, takes charge of the widowed Mr Nudd and his family and succeeds in her task through hard work and strength of character. Ervine's grandmother, deserted by her husband, had still managed to succeed as a shopkeeper, and his deaf-mute widowed mother had contrived to bring up her children despite every difficulty. Impressed by these examples, Ervine sometimes insisted on self-reliance as the supreme and characteristically Ulster virtue, whimsically suggesting that Pelagius was an Ulsterman.[42] In *John Ferguson* there is a Pelagian subtext which subverts the Presbyterian orthodoxy espoused by the protagonist. Ferguson in adversity relies on an inscrutable (and not very helpful) divine providence but his troubles can be attributed to bad management: no longer able to run the farm himself he has had to depend on his son Andrew who is a poor farmer. At the end of the play both Andrew and John Ferguson have to face up to the disaster that has come upon them and take some practical steps, but it is rather late for that.

The conviction that it was usually possible to do something to improve apparently intractable situations, and a corresponding hostility to wasted talent and opportunity, run through Ervine's life and work. A progressive, more or less secular Protestant like Carleton and Lecky (whose *History of European Morals* he had read), he was attracted by the scientific reformism of the Fabians and greatly admired the practical welfare work of the Salvation Army, eventually writing the life of its founder General Booth. A less sympathetic biography of Oscar Wilde convicted the dramatist of the ultimate sin against the Holy Ghost and Pelagius, not sodomy but squandering his talents.[43] The sectarianism and religious bigotry which had become ingrained in Belfast and rural Ulster during the nineteenth century seemed to defy improvement. But Ervine's early Irish plays, particularly *Mixed Marriage*, hint that the community contains some men and women (particularly women) of tolerant and practical good sense through whom a more generous attitude may eventually prevail.

Mixed Marriage, produced at the Abbey in March 1911, is set in Belfast. A strike is imminent (probably alluding to the great dock strike of 1907 in which Jim Larkin was prominent). It is shortly before 12 July, the day of the Orange processions. The plot centres on the wavering attitudes of John Rainey, a bitter, bullying Protestant, who is nevertheless open to reason. He is impressed by the argument of his son's friend Michael O'Hara, a Catholic socialist, that Protestant and Catholic workers' solidarity in the strike would represent 'a chance t' kill bigotry and make the men o' Belfast realize that onderneath the Cathlick an' the Prodesan there's the plain workin' man'.[44] Despite the efforts of the Protestant employers to play the Orange card and represent the strike as the work of Catholic Home Rulers, Rainey plans to speak in favour of the strike at his Orange Lodge. But he discovers his son is in love with the Catholic Nora Murray and atavistic sectarianism reasserts itself. The proposed 'mixed marriage', and the proposed meeting of minds in the strike, are abruptly dismissed as 'a Popish plot' (*Four Irish Plays*, pp. 32, 38). Healing love and workers' solidarity both come to grief: the play ends in a violent sectarian riot in which Nora is accidentally shot. But the play is not totally bleak: Mrs Rainey sets the tone near the beginning when, in the face of Catholic and Protestant hostilities, she tells her husband 'They'll have to mix in heaven, John' (*Four Irish Plays*, p. 3). The Dublin audience enjoyed the attack on Protestant attitudes in Belfast, but there were some misgivings about the implication that a mixed marriage might be a good thing.[45]

Mrs Rainey's common sense is shared by Mrs McClurg in the one-act play *The Orangeman* (1914). 'Do you think there's going till be Orangemen beating drums to the end of the world? I hope to my goodness, people'll have sense some day,' she says (*Four Irish Plays*, p. 113). There seems little prospect of it in the play. The Presbyterian sense of privileged continuity from generation to generation can be perverted into hereditary sectarianism. John McClurg's rheumatism threatens to keep him at home on the 'Twelfth', so to preserve the family tradition and keep Home Rule at bay through tribal sorcery he wants his son Tom to march in his place and beat the drum. But Tom rebels and kicks a hole in the drum.

Narrow sectarianism comes under fire again in *The Magnanimous Lover* (1912). The stage-directions specify a cottage interior festooned with biblical texts with a reproduction of the picture known as 'The Secret of England's Greatness' hanging on the wall. The same picture hung on the wall of John McClurg's Ballymacarrett home in *The Orangeman*. Even today it is a familiar image on Orange banners. The 'Secret' is the (Protestant) Bible. The original painting, by T. J. Barker, dates from the 1860s and now hangs in the National Gallery in London. It shows Queen Victoria bestowing a Bible on an unidentified kneeling figure, dark-skinned and exotically dressed, presumably some African prince accepting the religion and the associated imperial authority of an ever-greater Britain. Joyce was to make sardonic use of these political resonances in the Cyclops episode of *Ulysses*. But

PLATE 4   T. J. Barker, *Queen Victoria* ('The Secret of
England's Greatness')

Ervine's point is more moral than political. John McClurg's religion is
the secret of his own littleness, and it is the same with Henry Hinde,
the sanctimonious, would-be magnanimous lover. Hinde had fathered
Maggie Cather's illegitimate child ten years before the play begins.
Since then, while Maggie has had to cope with desertion and disgrace,
he has prospered as a shopkeeper in Liverpool and has been 'washed in
the Blood of the Lamb'. He returns with a proposal to save Maggie's
soul by marrying her and reconciling her to the Church she has
stopped attending. He also plans to 'wipe out some of the debt I owe to
God' by arranging for his child to be trained for the Christian ministry.
Maggie spiritedly refuses to let him salve his conscience at her expense.
Hinde's Calvinist, and Augustinian, sense of election by divine grace
into the blessings of salvation is seriously undermined by his Pelagian
impulse to try to save his own soul by a conscious act. Maggie,
Pelagian without pretence, robustly tells him, 'I'm not needing to
marry, but if I do, I'll marry to save my own soul, and not Henry
Hinde's' (*Four Irish Plays*, pp. 61, 70, 77).
    The play was not a critical success. The Dublin audiences, which

had rioted at Synge's *Playboy*, were encouraged to do their worst by a reviewer who complained that they had not hissed when the word 'whore' was used in the play, and another who claimed, 'The thing is too foul for dramatic criticism, and I am NOT a sanitary inspector.'[46] Ervine retaliated with his one-act play *The Critics* a year later. The setting is the foyer of the Abbey Theatre. The play which the assembled critics revile as 'unutterable stuff', a 'slur on the women of our country', turns out to be *Hamlet*. He had also written to the *Irish Times* with characteristically reckless gusto, robustly flailing the Dublin critics as hopelessly behind the times, 'exhausted men', 'symbols of the decadence of Dublin'. 'Wait, just you wait, you Dublin people, till Ireland has Home Rule, and we men from Ulster will put blood in your veins, and show you how to live.'[47]

It was still possible in those days to be both a nationalist and an Ulster patriot, though Ervine was one of the few who tried it. He was also, and simultaneously, an English progressive, a graduate of the 'Fabian nursery'. All these strands come together in his determined, unconventional, heroic women, representing the energy Ireland needed. Maggie Cather in *The Magnanimous Lover*, like Jenny Conn in the later play *Friends and Relations* (1947), owes something to theatrical tradition going back to Ibsen's Nora in *The Doll's House* (1879) or Shaw's outspoken 'new women' figures such as Vivie Warren in *Mrs Warren's Profession* (1894). But Maggie Cather and Jenny Conn and their sisters all derive from Ervine's dauntless grandmother. Their determination and their modern spirit are represented as a function of their region, the adventurous hardihood of north-east Ulster which has to contend with the sanctimonious humbug and bigotry of the same place. The novel *Mrs Martin's Man* (1914), based in some detail on his grandmother's experience, explores this endemic tension at length. Originally intended as another Ulster play for the Abbey, it was recast as a novel after Yeats severely criticized an early draft.[48] It has some good dramatic moments, such as the opening when Mrs Martin's man is just about to come back after sixteen years away. The reconciliation is not a success since Mrs Martin has learned to cope and run a business without him. The harshest criticism is reserved not for the sullen and graceless husband James, but for the respectable relations and the sanctimonious minister who try un-successfully to make James into a penitent prodigal son. Mrs Martin's response is stoicism, not prolix piety: 'She, too, had had longings, and she, too, had lost all that she had desired, but what was the good of mourning? Things happen, and they cannot be changed.'[49]

The constants of Ervine's varied output, fictional and dramatic, English as well as Irish, are stoical resolution and independence and a dramatically invaluable instinct for tension, usually resistance to conventional, traditional or familial expectation. These themes can probably be attributed to an ambivalent attitude to his birthplace, Ireland in general and north-east Ulster in particular. Irish habits and traditions, urban and rural, progressive, old-fashioned or atavistic, could seem appealing and appalling by turns, particularly when viewed from the safe distance of England. The Wellsian dream of escape which Ervine's triumphantly self-made literary career had enacted is explored in his semi-autobiographical novel *The Foolish Lovers* (1920).

John McDermot, the boy from Ballyards in Co. Down (clearly Newtownards), reluctantly decides to abandon his struggling literary life in London, comes home and manages to find romance in carrying on his mother's shop. This was the direction Ervine's life might have taken. But if the dream of escape comes to nothing that does not amount to an endorsement of provincial Ulster. John's truculent provincialism is derided and Ballyards is shown to be self-important and dominated by narrow Unionist prejudice. John's quixotic Uncle Matthew makes himself unpopular when he praises Parnell at the expense of Unionist politicians. Ervine too admired Parnell, never popular in Ulster, and wrote his biography.[50] Neither Matthew nor his late brother, John's father (modelled on Ervine's own father, whom he idealized but never knew), had paid any deference to the powerful local landlord Lord Castlederry (conflating 'Castlereagh' and 'London-derry'), a relic of old-fashioned 'Protestant Ascendancy'.

A later novel, *The Wayward Man* (1927), revisits the theme and the territory of *The Foolish Lovers* but finds a different and somehow equally disappointing resolution. Robert Dunwoody ran away to sea and when he comes back to Belfast he cannot reconcile himself to the shopkeeping life of his domineering mother and his shrewd businesslike wife. He is a more sympathetic version of Mrs Martin's man. His marriage disintegrates and he goes to sea again, though it almost breaks his mother's heart and his own. It might not have been altogether easy to live with Mrs Martin or Ervine's redoubtable grandmother.

Ambivalence about Belfast lies at the bottom of Ervine's English play *The Ship* (1922). First performed at the Liverpool Repertory Theatre, it is set in the shipbuilding town of Bigport which could easily be either Liverpool or Belfast. Arnold Bennett's Five Towns had encouraged Ervine to respond imaginatively to the energy and achievement of industrial Britain, including Belfast.[51] His shipbuilder protagonist John Thurlow, autocratic and obsessive, has affinities with Ibsen's Master Builder and even more with Dickens' elder Dombey: he tells his disaffected, Tolstoyan son that when he was a child, 'I didn't think of you as a child: I thought of you as a shipbuilder – the head of Thurlow's.'[52] The classic conflict of father and son is evenly balanced. The son, Jack, loathes machinery and seeks a return to nature as a farmer after he has seen the French countryside devastated by military technology during his time in the trenches. But the father's sense of the wonder and beauty of the technologically revolutionary ship *Magnificent* which he is building is not ridiculous. The apparently rather literary, rather formalized dramatic situation has urgent, ultimately Irish significance for Ervine because it reproduces the dilemma of Irish identity, rural or urban, pastoral or industrial, excluding or incorporating the smoke of Belfast. Ervine models the *Magnificent* on the Belfast-built *Titanic*. Jack is bullied into sailing on the ship on its maiden voyage in place of his father: he perishes when it strikes an iceberg and sinks in twenty minutes. Ervine seems to have sided with the southern Home Rulers against the Unionist shipbuilders and linen lords of industrial Belfast whose prosperity depended on links with industrial Britain. But the ending is ambiguous. Thurlow has lost a son and a ship, but his daughter is pregnant. Generational continuity, a Scots-Irish and Presbyterian obsession, seems to have revived, for better or worse. Thurlow's old mother urges him to build another ship since 'you can pass on your work to the next Thurlow'.[53]

Ervine's ambiguous feelings about Ireland and even about Belfast were reciprocated. An unkind letter in the *Irish Statesman* in 1929 concluded that 'Mr Ervine is not regarded as Irish by hosts of Belfast people'.[54] But Ervine could never think of himself as English either and was very proud of his Ulster accent. Though he became a member of the English literary establishment, serving as drama critic for the *Observer* and the BBC, Professor of Dramatic Literature at the Royal Society of Literature (1933–6), he sniped constantly at the English ruling classes and derided what he regarded as the colourless, indistinct, unvaried tones of the conventional English public school and Oxbridge accent.[55] His cheerful coat-trailing and sometimes outrageous polemic masked a certain social and cultural insecurity. At times he felt rather a misfit, and misfits keep recurring in his later comedies of English life. It was perhaps natural that he should write about Shylock, his own version of Joyce's Leopold Bloom.

Ervine's continuation of *The Merchant of Venice*, entitled *The Lady of Belmont* (1923), was dedicated to his Jewish friend Lewis Langner, a fellow-dramatist and founder of the New York Theatre Guild whose finances had been secured by the New York run of Ervine's *John Ferguson* and *Jane Clegg*. Shylock the despised but indispensable usurer has recovered his wealth, but he has still seen nothing of his estranged daughter Jessica and her growing family. He intervenes to save her marriage when she is about to commit adultery, not because he respects his son-in-law but because he cares about the idea of family: 'every Jew has a passion for posterity. How else could we have survived?'[56] The Old Testament God of succeeding generations, of Abraham and Isaac and Jacob, was known to Presbyterian Ulster as well as Israel. But the sense of a proud and distinctive people which goes with this Jewish God, tending towards Unionist intransigence or Zionism, is discouraged in the play. The last act rather degenerates into a Shavian debate between Portia and Shylock about the Jewish question. Portia steps out of character to express anti-Semitic commonplaces. She taunts the Jews with crucifying Christ and allowing themselves to become self-interested, rootless adventurers instead of establishing some settled community of their own. Shylock responds with a dignified cosmopolitan humanism which somehow reflects Ervine's tendency to affirm and generalize this specifically Ulster 'Pelagianism':

> We cannot go back, madam – we must go on and mingle with the world and lose ourselves in other men. I know that outward things pass and have no duration. There is nothing left but the goodness which a man performs.[57]

Behind this lie Ervine's anxieties about Ireland. The politics of separatism, whether Home Rule enthusiasm or Ulster Unionist resistance to it, thrust upon Irishmen sharp questions of identity of which Ervine was acutely conscious. But as a progressive Fabian he had felt that social and economic problems had moral priority, a view that underpins the unsectarian socialism in *Mixed Marriage*. His political study of *Sir Edward Carson and the Ulster Movement* (1915) tried to sidestep the problem of identity: 'There are not two Irelands and two kinds of Irishmen: there are four millions of Irish.'[58]

Shylock's sublimely simple ethical imperative, bypassing all the problems of race and identity, was not really available to Ervine himself in the period just before and after Easter 1916. He was managing the Abbey Theatre in Dublin and trying to maintain a wife and a home in England while some of the Abbey players drilled with the Citizen Army and he himself considered whether to enlist to fight in England's war in France. The confusion and bitterness of the time are reflected in his shapeless but revealing Irish and English novel *Changing Winds* (1917) and in the unhappy story of his management of the Abbey which has often been misrepresented.

Changing Winds takes its title from Rupert Brooke's sonnet 'The Dead', part of his famous '1914' sequence written shortly after the outbreak of war. Poem and novel alike invoke and memorialize an already distant Edwardian England, varied, vital, curiously unstable. For Brooke death in war procures glory and radiance, but for Ervine past vitalities and future death or glory are more problematic. His semi-autobiographical hero Henry Quinn, freed at last from irresolution, bewilderment, guilt and the fear of fear, leaves Dublin still smouldering after the Easter Rising to take his chance on the Western Front where two of his best friends have already died.[59] Rupert Brooke, whom Ervine had got to know in London early in 1913,[60] was a restless spirit like Ervine himself and like Ervine he had been involved with the Fabian Society. In the novel he appears as the Fabian poet Gerald Luke. Henry Quinn, who meets Wells and Shaw in Fabian circles just as Ervine had done, is Ulster-born. He is the son of a small landowner and unsuccessful barrister, a member of the Church of Ireland, who has retrieved his fortunes by marrying the daughter of a Belfast millowner. On the face of it this sounds like a symbolic marriage between Ireland's two Protestant communities and traditions, the English-descended landlords of the 'Protestant Ascendancy' and the largely Presbyterian 'Scots-Irish' who were well represented in mercantile Belfast. Unionists and Orangemen had been trying to promote this union since early in the nineteenth century and present-day Unionism derives from it. But Ervine undermines this possibility by making the elder Quinn an old-fashioned Tory paternalist disliking the unhealthy linen factory of his Belfast father-in-law and the sometime anti-Irish attitudes of the old 'Ascendancy' even though he is a staunch Unionist.

Henry Quinn's Irish career takes him to Trinity College, but he dislikes the unIrish ethos of the place of which Lady Gregory had complained and feels less at home in Dublin than in his northern birthplace, Ballymartin, or in Devon where he has been welcomed as a visitor. Inspired by progressive ideas, he plans a kind of Irish Fabian Society concerned with elementary education, wages and trade unions. He also sees himself as a Home Ruler. But he begins to realize the extent of Irish degradation, poverty and disease with a sinking heart.

He is stirred by the Gaelic League enthusiasm and messianic nationalism of his tutor John Marsh, a Patrick Pearse figure, but finds he cannot share them.

The other Ireland of the Belfast shipyards intrudes into the novel through the engineering enthusiasm of Quinn's friend Ninian Graham. The Easter Week heroism of John Marsh is balanced by the dedication of the marine engineer Tom Arthurs whose devotion to his craft was 'as pure as the devotion of a Samurai to the honour of Japan' (Book 1, chapter 9). This gestures in the direction of H. G. Wells' admiration for the Samurai, his models for the disciplined technocratic heroes of the new world-state envisaged in *A Modern Utopia* (1905). Curiously enough, Yeats also expressed his admiration for the Samurai, writing in 1916. He saw them as models for a different sort of modern hero, aristocratic warriors brought up on the Noh plays, combining military rigour and aesthetic discrimination.[61] This model would fit John Marsh. But Ervine avoids over-identification with either the Yeatsian or the Wellsian Samurai. The technocrat is not allowed to triumph: Tom Arthurs drowns when the *Gigantic* (clearly the *Titanic*) is sunk on her maiden voyage. Ervine seems to have been obsessed with the *Titanic*, a symbol of his fascinated unease about industrial Belfast. Tom Arthurs is clearly modelled on Thomas Andrews, the engineer who helped to build the ship and went down with her in 1912.[62]

Henry Quinn can hardly believe that a ship built in Belfast should have gone down so ignominiously, but his chastened Ulster pride finds no compensating glory in Dublin when he sees an unarmed policeman shot at the beginning of the Easter Rising. His mind dwells not so much on self-sacrificing heroism as on the rotting carcase of a horse killed in the disturbances but not removed. It is from a land of decay, squalor and disappointed hopes that he sets sail for the war in Europe.

The chaotic vividness of the novel, simultaneously documentary and fantasy, presenting the real Rupert Brooke in the title and his fictional counterpart in the text, self-indulgently rambling yet desperately pressured by contemporary history, can be attributed to undigested current affairs and to Ervine's own tense situation. He wrote the novel to support his wife in England while he went to war himself, as he told Shaw.[63] But he was unhappy about English military behaviour in Ireland before and during Easter Week and let it be known that he wanted to serve in an Irish rather than an English regiment (he was commissioned in the Royal Dublin Fusiliers).[64] Even so, he has been accused of insensitivity to the Irish ideals of the Abbey Theatre during his brief and difficult period as its manager.

This persistent imputation, and harsh comments on his 'reign of terror', derive from partisan hostility to the later Ervine. Because he came to despise De Valera and proclaimed himself an Ulster Unionist as a way of disowning De Valera's Ireland, it has been too easily assumed that he had always been a cantankerous Unionist bigot.[65] That he was high-handed, demanding and tactless as a manager there can be little doubt. But matters were desperate and the easy-going players were exasperating. Discipline and drive were urgently needed to keep the company from disaster. Miss Horniman's subsidy on which the Abbey had depended had been withdrawn in 1911. Irish-American hostility to *The Playboy* brought losses on the 1914 American tour. With the outbreak of war, audiences at home had dwindled. After the Easter Rising, the proclamation of martial law and the emptying of the Dublin theatres matters were so bad that Ervine had to resist suggestions that the players be disbanded and the theatre closed for the time being.[66] He had done his energetic best to keep things going, negotiating tours, organizing lectures and concerts, trying to let premises to avoid dependence on ungraciously offered subsidies in characteristically self-reliant fashion: 'If we can pay our way by our own exertions that, of course, is very much more desirable,' he told Lady Gregory.[67] His greatest success was with his own *John Ferguson* in November 1915, but, as he told Yeats the following March, he was busy with many other projects. He welcomed Lennox Robinson's new play *The White-Headed Boy* (eventually performed in December), admitted to stage-fright as he took the part of Hugh Rainey at short notice in a revival of his own play *Mixed Marriage*, suggested T. H. Nally's *The Spancel of Death* for Easter Week and adventurously proposed Milton's *Samson Agonistes*, perhaps, for later in the season.[68] This unIrish suggestion does not necessarily amount to an onslaught on the Irish idealism of the Abbey as it has been suggested. Lady Gregory had staged an adaptation of Molière and Yeats had rejected Cunninghame Graham's translation of an iconoclastic Spanish play, *La Vierge del Mar*, not because it was Spanish or had a Scottish translator but because it was not sufficiently supernatural and religious.[69] It is true that Ervine thought of the Abbey in a British as well as Irish context but this was simple prudence: unless the Abbey produced plays that could be taken on tour in England as well as Ireland it could not survive.

Many of the players were less concerned with prudence than with the possibly reviving cause of Ireland. It was in sorrow rather than in 'West Briton' wrath or indignation that Ervine wrote to Lady Gregory about the death of Shaun Connolly with the Citizen Army and the arrest and imprisonment of the young Arthur Shields.[70] Both men had acted in his own plays and he himself had taken Shields on again only a month before.

Distracted by the times, demoralized by low salaries and uncertain prospects, the players must have been as restless as Ervine himself in 1916. There seems to have been some contractual vagueness about rehearsals and the precise rights and responsibilities of manager and players which made a bad situation worse.[71] Matters came to a head in May 1916 when the players refused to fit in an extra Thursday afternoon rehearsal when they were on tour in Limerick (with *The Playboy*), even though this was the only way they could accommodate the hard-pressed leading lady. Ervine dismissed four of the company, with the backing of Yeats and Lady Gregory, but the players went on strike against his management. He eventually resigned in July 1916.[72]

This was the turning-point of Ervine's career. He went to the Western Front and was so severely wounded that a leg had to be amputated. Constant pain and the frustration of a once-active man, though endured with courage and cheerfulness, probably imparted an extra brusqueness to Ervine's public pronouncements and private grumblings, never tactful or diplomatic to start with.[73] The murderous violence of the Irish troubles after the world war was over sickened him. He condemned Black-and-Tans (British irregular forces) and Sinn Fein alike and stayed away from the country for a time because, as he told Shaw, 'the very thought of Ireland makes me feel like vomiting'.[74] As the years went by the twenty-six southern counties of Ireland, dominated by the Dublin which Ervine the northerner had always rather affected to scoff at, formed themselves into a new state dominated by Celtic enthusiasms and a conservatively Catholic social outlook.

Ervine had admired Shaw, though not uncritically, ever since he came to London, and Shaw responded by letting Ervine attempt his biography on the grounds that 'You will understand the Irish side of me better than anyone who is not Irish.'[75] Since Ervine's iconoclasm had been partly learnt from the sardonic author of *John Bull's Other Island* (1904), he jeered all the louder when Shaw took out Irish citizenship, apparently at the prompting of his romantic English wife. Ervine felt Ireland had degenerated into a land of 'bleating Celtic Twilighters, sex-starved Daughters of the Gael, gangsters and gombeen-men', no place for him or for Shaw: 'If anybody proposed to repatriate you in Ireland you would throw seventeen separate fits.'[76] In

1933 he told Sean O'Casey that the visionary nationalist George Russell ('AE') was disheartened by the new Ireland, 'a saddened man, a victim of the worst disillusionment that can befall any person, for he has seen his desire accomplished and wishes that it hadn't been.'[77]

This was an epitaph on Ervine's older nationalist self. By the 1920s he had concluded that the only way he could affirm his Irishness without espousing the narrowness of the new nation-state or repudiating Britain completely was to insist on the continuing Britishness and Irishness of his native Ulster at least. He became an Ulster Unionist and contributed to the articulation of a self-justifying sense of identity for the six northern counties which had accepted severance from the rest of Ireland to stay within the United Kingdom. His often ambivalent feeling for his own region passed over into an uncritical Ulster chauvinism shaped and limited by hostility to institutionalized Celtic and Catholic nationalism. There was an element of propaganda as well as of local patriotism in his little book *Ulster* (1926) written for the new Ulster Tourist Development Association.

Though he continued to visit Northern Ireland fairly regularly Ervine kept his home in Devon. He continued his career as an English and Ulster (no longer 'Irish') writer with English and Ulster successes. The Knightsbridge comedy *The First Mrs Fraser*, with Marie Tempest, was his first West End triumph in 1929. In 1937 up-to-the-minute social criticism and Edith Evans in the role of a progressive woman doctor made *Robert's Wife* one of the most acclaimed English plays. Amusing and well-crafted if unchallenging Ulster plays such as *Boyd's Shop* (1936) and *Ballyfarland's Festival* (1953) enjoyed great local popularity as live theatre and broadcast on the Northern Ireland Home Service of the BBC. Ervine's pleasant and still recognizably Ulster voice became familiar 'on the air' and his sometimes self-indulgent local-interest pieces in the *Belfast Telegraph* flattered the Ulsterman's self-esteem during the Depression and the war years.

But Ervine's Ulster loyalties were more discriminating than his bluff prose-style might suggest. The second world war consolidated the northern Unionist's sense of identity since the official neutrality of the Irish state separated the southern counties more than ever from self-consciously British Ulster, astonishingly productive of Belfast-built warships and British generals. Ervine's massive biography of the Ulster prime Minister Lord Craigavon (1949) pays some attention to this theme. It draws attention to, but does not fully endorse, the warrior-myth dear to the heart of Ulster Unionism, reacting against yet somehow parasitic upon the Celtic-revivalist warrior-myths of

Cuchulain and the Fianna exploited by Yeats and Patrick Pearse. Ulster's claims to British identity were – and are – deemed to have been vindicated by Ulster sacrifices in Britain's wars, notably the appalling casualties of the 'Ulster' division at the battle of the Somme in July 1916. Since the division had been recruited largely from the ranks of the illegal Ulster Volunteer Force formed to resist Home Rule in 1912 the Somme came to symbolize heroic and sacrificial 'loyalism', the terrible price Unionists were prepared to pay for union with Britain. But Ervine knew perfectly well that Ulster militarism was a recent development of the long tradition of Irish soldiering which contributed to Britain's war-effort during the first world war (and the second) irrespective of the politics of nationalism and Unionism. He pointed out that the Ulster division was not the only division to suffer at the Somme: the fourth division, including two battalions of Dublin Fusiliers (his own regiment), had also been present. One of the company commanders was the son of the nationalist leader, John Redmond. He survived, but all the other company commanders of his battalion were killed.[78]

The loyalist myth of the Somme, attacked in Frank McGuinness's play *Observe the Sons of Ulster Marching towards the Somme* (1986), includes ironies Ervine would have relished. A large painting of the Ulster division in action was commissioned by the (surviving) Ulster Volunteers and presented to the City of Belfast in 1918. It still hangs in Belfast City Hall. The painter, J. P. Beadle, was a distinguished military artist of partly Anglo-Indian background, which seemed appropriate since the already old-fashioned imperial ethos allowed Ulster Unionists to celebrate the idea of Britishness in a wide context. Even more appropriately, Beadle had married a Cope from Armagh and so had links with a long-established Anglo-Irish family.[79] But there were some lines of verse, unattributed, on the frame of the picture. The sentiments were unexceptionable, speaking of the fallen as inhabitants of 'Fame's eternal Camping-ground/ . . . The Bivouac of the dead'. But the words come from the Irish rather than the specifically Ulster tradition of battle. They were originally written for the Kentucky dead in the Mexican War of 1848 by Theodore O'Hara, whose father had left Ireland in a hurry in 1798 as a 'political exile'.[80]

Ervine's *Craigavon, Ulsterman* was uncritically applauded in the *Belfast Telegraph* and courteously regretted in the *Irish Times*.[81] It is a lengthy and sometimes cantankerous *apologia* for Ulster unionism, but even at his most partisan Ervine retains some nostalgia for his earlier and more generous nationalism. He suggests in passing that while the partition of Ireland may have been inevitable, the presence of Ulster Protestants in a Dublin parliament might have been in the best interests of the whole country and a useful check on what he regarded as the extremism of the Irish Prime Minister Eamon De Valera.[82]

Even as the biography was in preparation Ervine's persistent sense of the Irishness as well as the Britishness of Ulster led him into rather foolish controversy with his old friend Sean O'Casey. O'Casey had remained an Irish nationalist and had participated in the nationalist onslaught on the obdurate northern counties, denigrating Ulster culture in an article in *Time and Tide*. Ervine retaliated with a series of articles in the *Belfast Telegraph* with the splendidly coat-trailing title *Ulster, the Real Centre of Culture in Ireland*, reprinted as a pamphlet in 1944. By jeering at Pearse and attributing the greatness of Yeats to his Ulster mother Ervine convinced himself that Ulster had been the nursery of most of Ireland's literary talent. He cheated by insisting on a nine-county Ulster, the ancient geographical unit rather than the six counties of modern Northern Ireland, frequently called 'Ulster' for convenience. His meaningless list, ranging from William Carleton to Louis MacNeice, included nationalists as well as Unionists, the Young Ireland leader Gavan Duffy of Monaghan and the visionary agricultural reformer George Russell ('AE') from Lurgan. Such richness and variety, he implied, no longer flourished in the separated southern counties.[83]

Despite cheerful absurdities like this, Ervine was an Ulster Unionist only by default. The union he was committed to at the end of his career, as at the beginning, was the union of all civilized peoples incorporating the whole of Ireland and of Great Britain and the Commonwealth.[84] His rehabilitated Shylock, like Joyce's Leopold Bloom, gestured towards a cosmopolitan humanity through which one could at least dream of escape from the nightmare of a degraded and divided Ireland. But unlike Joyce, Ervine did not withdraw far enough from the place. His resentment of particularist nationalism stimulated only a corresponding Ulster narrowness which has harmed the reputation of a fine Irish writer.

JAMES JOYCE (1882–1941)

Joyce read Ervine's biography of Parnell and used it in *Finnegans Wake*.[85] Like Ervine, he had few illusions about contemporary

Ireland. But he was never remotely tempted by Unionism. He was an iconoclast and a natural heretic, but a Catholic nationalist heretic who repudiated ancestral allegiances without embracing their opposite. In any case, Unionism was strong only in Ervine's Ulster and Joyce had no Ulster connections, apart from a great-grandmother McCann. He had a poor opinion of the few Ulster Unionists he knew, perhaps visiting on all of them his resentment of the caution and cowardice of George Roberts. Roberts, an 'Ulster Scot', was manager of Maunsel & Co., a Dublin publishing house, and he had given Joyce a contract for *Dubliners* in 1909. But he seems to have regretted it, demanding extensive revisions, and eventually he refused publication.[86] But the crisis of identity, Irish or British, which Ervine eventually solved by turning Ulster Unionist, affected Joyce also as an Irish writer in English. He was only too aware of the English language as a partly alien idiom laden with the themes and cadences of the Elizabethans and the Victorians, Shakespeare and Walter Pater, Nashe and Newman.

The difficulty is confronted in *Portrait of the Artist as a Young Man*. The literary Stephen Dedalus, discussing a local usage with an English Jesuit, ruefully reflects: '"The language in which we are speaking is his before it is mine . . . His language, so familiar and so foreign, will always be for me an acquired speech".'[87] There can be no going back, however. Stephen will not learn Irish, the artificially revived speech of his country, nor dedicate his life to the seemingly thankless nationalist cause to atone for the weakness and folly of his ancestors who 'threw off their language and took another' (*Portrait*, p. 202). The nets of nationality and language threatening to ensnare the free spirit of the aspiring artist were both Irish and English, which is why in language as in life Joyce aspired to the cosmopolitanism so disdained by the patriots of the Irish Literary Revival. As he told Stefan Zweig, 'I'd like a language which is above all languages, a language to which all will do service. I cannot express myself in English without enclosing myself in a tradition.'[88]

In *Ulysses* Stephen Dedalus on Sandymount strand gets behind Ireland's more obvious and oppressive traditions as he meditates on the varied deposits chance and the past have left on Ireland's shores since Viking times, deposits which can speak for themselves: 'These heavy sands are language tide and wind have silted here.' Sentimental Celtic nostalgias, wafted on the airs of Tommy Moore's *Irish Melodies*, mingle audaciously with glimpses of Viking Dublin, the suppressed element of Ireland's romanticized past: 'Danevikings, torcs of tomahawks aglitter on their breasts when Malachi wore the collar of gold.'[89] The Citizen's allusion to 'Our Greater Ireland beyond the Sea' in the Cyclops episode of *Ulysses* (p. 270) invokes the diaspora of the famine and Thomas D'Arcy McGee's carefully nurtured notion of extended Irishness and the 'sea-divided Gael'. But behind this there lies the obscure legend of an overseas Ireland the Great, the mysterious Irland Hit Mikla or Hvitramannaland of Icelandic saga, testifying obliquely to the neglected Scandinavian component of Ireland's past.[90]

The Vikings are more prominent in *Finnegans Wake*, which is liberally sprinkled with Scandinavian allusions or 'Scandiknavery' (p. 47). The whole book is jestingly described as 'this Eyrawyggla saga' (p. 48), referring not only to earwigs and the doings of the egregious H. C. Earwicker but to the *Eyrbyggja Saga* which describes how the troublesome company of the undead at Frodis-water was finally dispersed by holding a court over them and passing judgment, which caused them all to walk out. Trouble from the insufficiently dead past and the necessity of decisive judgment are recurring Joycean themes. Bloom's dead son and Stephen's dead mother rise to disturb the living in *Ulysses*. In *Finnegans Wake* the dead and the living, past and present, Viking raiders and a contemporary Norwegian sea captain are all simultaneously present. The 'Ballad of Persse O'Reilly' which enacts the structurally crucial myth of the Fall and the fall of Humpty Dumpty alludes among much else to the 'black and tan man-o'-war' of the 'hammerfast viking' in Dublin Bay (p. 46). The 'Black-and-Tans' were the hated British anti-terrorist force in the recent troubles, but neither the ancient nor the modern disturbers of the Irish peace come in for condemnation as they would in nationalist discourse: the form of Joyce's narrative parodies and subverts the directed linearity and the purposeful recourse to sources and origins characteristic of tradition-seeking and of historical narrative. The origins of HCE are no more certain or secure than the Protean identities he manifests throughout the book, and 'offspring of vikings' is just one of many discarded 'theories from older sources' about his 'genesis' (p. 30).

Joyce took refuge from English and Irish tradition in Mediterranean lore as well as 'Scandiknavery'. He knew that the Homeric tradition of the wanderings of Odysseus (Ulysses in Latin versions) had been linked with Phoenicean voyages. General Vallancey's bizarre theories of the Phoenicean and so ultimately Semitic origins of Irish language and culture, which Joyce found it artistically appropriate to exploit, complete the imaginative linkages of the wandering Dublin Jew Leopold Bloom with the Homeric Ulysses. The Scythian (Hungarian) antecedents of Bloom and Molly Bloom's early days on Gibraltar, as much Iberian as British, help to liberate them and to liberate *Ulysses* from the constraints of Dublin's Irish and English traditions.[91]

But there is a residually English and Irish, even Anglo-Irish, aspect to the complicated revenge Joyce exacted upon the language of Shakespeare and upon the race of 'clodhoppers' who forsook Parnell. In the polysemous extravagance and dissolving identities of *Finnegans Wake* he finally subverted and repudiated tradition altogether, collapsing language and history into artful macaronic bricolage. But there are well-established Anglo-Irish precedents for at least some of what he tried to do. From Ussher to Oscar Wilde, Ireland within the Pale had been instructed or delighted by erudite cosmopolitan vistas, self-consciously literary sophistication and possible escape-routes from the nightmare of (Irish) history into historically displaced idealisms or dream-fantasies of dread and liberation. All could be said to derive from the insecurities of English-descended Protestants in Ireland, often proud, isolated and uneasy. Joyce's artistic aspirations promoted him into participation in this kind of insecurity: he had not been born into the 'Protestant Ascendancy', and he measured his distance from it when he found his Ulysses in the lower-middle-class life of Dublin,[92] but he saw himself as an aloof aristocrat of the imagination.

An early symptom of this is the undergraduate pamphlet 'The Day of the Rabblement' (1901), a challenge to Yeats in Yeats' own terms, attacking the Irish Literary Theatre rather unfairly for pandering to popular taste and complacent provincialism in its selection of plays. After all, it had been set up to oppose commercialism and vulgarity. There is a similar *hauteur* in *Portrait of the Artist*. The proud and lonely Stephen Dedalus proposes a distinction between language used in the tradition of the marketplace and literary language. His literary example is taken from Newman, whose 'cloistral silver-veined prose' (p. 175), well-bred and melancholy, is much admired. Newman's prose is one of the many samples from English literary history selected for parody in the 'Oxen of the Sun' episode in *Ulysses*. Newman and his writings, particularly his autobiography *Apologia pro Vita Sua* (1864), provide useful models for the isolated Joycean artist and priest of the imagination anxious to liberate himself from tradition. Newman had courageously forsaken the Anglican tradition in which he had grown up and prospered to pursue a new vocation as a Catholic priest. This had taken him to Dublin for a time, to run the new Catholic University which Joyce later attended. He had recorded his solitary spiritual pilgrimage in precise and flawless prose embodying a

challenging manifesto of his new convictions. The solitary young
Dedalus, trying to find phrases and images for his own developing
experience, muses also on the courtly traditions of Elizabethan song
and a little self-consciously dwells on Nashe's song from the allegorical
pageant *Summer's Last Will and Testament* with its hauntingly
beautiful line 'Brightness falls from the air' (*Portrait*, pp. 176, 232–4).
Yeats also had admired the song in his essay on 'The Symbolism of
Poetry' (1900), which may be where Joyce found it.

There is an element of ambivalent self-mockery in all this. The older
Joyce is reflecting sardonically on the fumblings of his literary
apprenticeship and the preciousness and conceit of his younger self.
But the haughty aloofness and isolations of the artist were sustained
into permanent exile and the writing of *Finnegans Wake*. In this he
resembled some of the proud, penurious and lonely Anglo-Irish writers
who found, or at least sought, their opportunities in England. The
Catholic Joyce was as much a displaced person as the Protestant
'downstart' Shaw, for instance, and had a rather similar, slightly
flyblown background of dissipated family fortunes and musical
culture. The language of the marketplace, of many marketplaces, was
incorporated into *Ulysses* and *Finnegans Wake*, but this was achieved
by withdrawing far enough from Dublin street-life to acquire some
artistic and imaginative purchase upon it.

The 'meere Irish' of sixteenth- and seventeenth-century colonial
discourse had long ceased to be feared and resented as a threat to
'civilization' and peaceful settlement in Ireland. But English-centred
and metropolitan cultural values had been rudely challenged by the
Celtic Revival which had revived a romantic and even sinister sense of
Celtic otherness, of marginalized but vital energies that could not
forever be suppressed. Daniel Corkery's famous book *The Hidden
Ireland* (1925) summed up not only a Celtic tradition but a tradition of
Celtic assertiveness going back to the early days of the Gaelic League.
Anglo-Irish intellectuals could respond to the challenge by becoming
revivalists themselves, or by shrinking a little more from the possibly
frightening new Ireland all around them. Hereditary Anglo-Irish fear
and bafflement, a sense that the nightmare of Irish history might never
end, provide a language of near-panic for the fledgling artist Stephen
Dedalus in an episode which grew darker as Joyce brooded on it. In
Stephen Hero, the earlier version of *Portrait of the Artist*, Stephen
laughs condescendingly at an army officer's story of an ignorant and
clownish peasant: fear of the 'other', the 'meere Irish', is well in control
if it can be dispelled in laughter. But in *Portrait of the Artist* the

episode is transformed. Like Synge in the Aran Islands, John Alphonsus Mulrennan has been to the west of Ireland and has tried to make contact with 'the hidden ways of Irish life' which Stephen had sensed as a provincial limitation upon his own aspirations (p. 181). The encounter with the Irish-speaking 'native' collapses into uneasy farce, the conversation in Irish rapidly changing to English to ensure communication. Stephen is disturbed rather than amused, for the Irish-speaker may be his enemy as an artist: 'I fear him, I fear his red-rimmed horny eyes. It is with him I must struggle all through this night till day come, till he or I lie dead' (*Portrait*, p. 225). For Stephen Dedalus such dread and hostility can only be resolved by an imaginative act, by reinventing Ireland from a distance The route to Tara, seat of ancient kings and mythic symbol of sovereignty over all Ireland, was the path of exile or, more prosaically, the sea-passage from Ireland to Holyhead.

Joyce's recurring themes of exile and escape to another country or into dream and reverie arise from a sense of spiritual and imaginative bankruptcy in his own country, an intuition that Irish tradition had already run its course. This intuition is developed in *Dubliners*. The first story, 'The Sisters', concerns the death of a strange priest. It begins, bleakly, 'There was no hope for him this time.' The child-narrator then embarks on oblique, frightened disclosures of paralysis and mental disturbance, 'something wrong with him'. The broken chalice which upset the priest and the 'idle chalice' laid on his breast in his coffin speak of a traditional religion fractured and drained of moral and spiritual energy. This sets the tone for the emptiness and lost opportunity of later stories. Drink, hollow rhetoric, failing light, sentimental tears and crippled emotions convey an unattractive atmosphere.

There is a political dimension to this, most apparent in 'Ivy Day in the Committee Room'. After the death of Parnell the prospect of Home Rule had seemed to recede again. The old 'Protestant Ascendancy' had been declining in power and influence as a result of land reforms and Gladstone's disestablishment of their Church and the long-term future was uncertain. But in Edwardian Ireland the march of history seemed for a time to have ground to a halt. This stagnation, as Joyce perceived it, was a challenge and an affront to both Catholic and Protestant providential history. Ever since Dan O'Connell Catholics had been encouraged to expect, even demand, progressive deliverance from evil and the Act of Union, not usually distinguished. Ever since Ussher Protestants had flattered and consoled themselves with a vision of progressive inroads upon Romanism and Irish darkness. Some, such as Lecky, had secularized this teleology into a progressive rationalism.

Joyce was sardonically aware of these rival patterns of history and unconvinced by either of them. He had a copy of Lecky's *History of European Rationalism* in Trieste,[93] but he did not really believe in it any more than he believed in a manifest destiny for his 'nation of clodhoppers'. He was seemingly indifferent to the moral and political history of his own times, unmoved by the making or breaking of nations, neutral to the point of offensiveness in two world wars, a European wanderer with none of the crusading zeal of 'fiery Columbanus', the Irish monk whom foolish Dedalus once hoped to emulate (*Ulysses*, p. 35). His sole concern was to survive and to promote his own art. Grand patterns were the achievement of art, not made by God or men in history, whatever Lecky might suggest to the contrary. Jeeringly he referred in *Finnegans Wake* to the 'slack march of civilisation' all too easily disrupted by 'unleckylike intoxication' (p. 438). The intoxicating confusions of *Finnegans Wake* resolve themselves not into linear narrative but cyclical patterns reflecting the Viconian view that history goes round in circles. Contending histories, identifying different modes of Irishness, are not so much reconciled as incorporated as dissonances into the polyphony of *Ulysses*.

History from a Protestant perspective is discussed in the early 'Nestor' episode by the sententious Ulster Protestant Mr Deasy. The Homeric Nestor had been the oldest and wisest Greek leader at Troy but Mr Deasy is an old fool. He proclaims that 'All history moves towards one great goal, the manifestation of God' (p. 28), but as the commentators have observed Joyce mischievously makes Deasy himself unreliable on historical matters. Not surprisingly, he fails to budge Stephen from his less optimistic convictions, borrowed from Jules Laforgue, that history is a nightmare.[94] Much later in the novel, in Nighttown, Deasy's history is brought into Joyce's ironic pattern as Stephen drunkenly murmers 'Moves to one great goal' but forgets about God (p. 459). Blake's revolutionary apocalyptic history in *The Marriage of Heaven and Hell*, a parodic inversion of Christian orthodoxy, lies closer to Stephen's heart, but this too is subverted. Stephen wildly smashes a chandelier and quenches 'Time's livid final flame' (p. 475), a phrase which had a more dignified context in Blake.

Drunk or sober, Stephen spends most of the novel trying to extricate himself from patterns of history and relationship, his mother's Irish Catholicism and his country's self-pitying involvement with imperial

Britain. He would not kneel down to pray for his mother on her deathbed when she asked him and is consequently haunted by his aunt's allegation that that proud refusal was what finally killed her (pp. 7, 35). When his mother rises accusingly from the dead in the disturbed fantasies of the Nighttown episode he echoes his defiance in *Portrait of the Artist* (p. 239) and intones 'non serviam' ('I will not serve') (p. 475). These are the words of the Vulgate traditionally attributed to Lucifer as the archetypal rebel against God. But in their biblical context the defiance is attributed to the apostate people of Israel, despoiled and assimilated by pagan Egypt and Assyria, denying their origins and their traditional pieties and allegiances (Jeremiah 2:17–28). The association of Ireland and Israel, sources of oppressive as well as oppressed identity, is a feature of seventeenth-century Gaelic-Irish poetry and of the Scots-Irish sense of being a covenanted people. Joyce knew enough about contemporary Judaism to realize its analogies with the burden of Irishness: Jewish religion, Jewish history and the pieties exacted by the Jewish sense of family, ancestry and origins were all deeply involved with each other and all were scorned and rejected in the act of apostasy. It was the same with Stephen's Irish apostasy, his repudiation of his mother's religion and the complex associated pieties which he had tried to escape by leaving Ireland.

Stephen's apostasy involves him in both Christian and Jewish heresy. He can no longer accept the traditional dogmas such as the creation of the world out of nothing, held up as an example of orthodoxy by Haines (p. 16). But on Sandymount Strand he audaciously thinks of himself as created out of nothing, an autonomous artist made and not begotten. This would conveniently sever him from the snares of family and background. There was a model available in the heretical Jewish Cabbalistic tradition. The Cabbalists had postulated not an ordinary human Adam but Adam Kadmon, an emanation of the creator God and himself an unconditioned creator of worlds to come. Adam Kadmon is adopted as a type of the free creative artist both here (p. 32) and in the boastful ramblings of H. C. Earwicker in *Finnegans Wake* (p. 546).

Like St John Ervine, oppressed by the narrowness of one of Ireland's other religions, Joyce was a natural heretic. But his heresy goes well beyond Ervine's whimsical Ulster Pelagianism. Joyce embraces and welcomes heresy as an aspect, almost a definition, of art. Pelagius is teasingly implicated in *Finnegans Wake* as a Pelagiarist (pp. 182, 525). Arius, Photius, Sabellius and Valentine are all mentioned in the opening episode of *Ulysses*. These heretics are part of the detritus of church history, outlawed and condemned by Catholic orthodoxy for unsound views on the nature of the Trinity. In Christian tradition the relationship between the Father and the Son had been notoriously prolific of heresies because of the confusing implications of identity-in-difference, priority and historical sequence entailed in the Father–Son metaphor. This provides a background for Stephen's musings on his problematic identity as a son unhappy about his Irish heritage, an artist in search of a spiritual father-figure. At one point he cavalierly simplifes the view of Sabellius as 'the Father was Himself His own Son' (p. 171), airily adduces Aquinas' refutation and bewilderingly develops the argument that in some sense it was because Shakespeare's own father had died that Shakespeare, no longer a son, could become a father and write *Hamlet*, liberated to perform the heroic Joycean task of generating timeless art out of personal history. As Stephen draws closer to Leopold Bloom, and eventually comes to play Telemachus to Bloom's Ulysses towards the end of the novel, the Father–Son metaphor of Christian orthodoxy is heretically translated into a metaphor of imaginative identity.

Joyce enjoyed himself brushing church history against the grain to resurrect heresies, but Stephen and Bloom have to negotiate partisan secular history as well. This is introduced by the aggressively Unionist, and anti-Semitic, Mr Deasy. He has his own paranoid version of the British imperial history in which Ireland was still (controversially) very much involved in 1904. Britain's recent imperial war in South Africa had been fought with the help of the Dublin Fusiliers. The enemy had been not only Boers but other Irishmen, anti-British nationalists enrolled into two small Irish brigades, one of which was commanded by John MacBride, husband of Yeats' beloved Maud Gonne since 1903. Irishmen were also prepared to fight British troops in Ulster, if necessary, to resist Home Rule. Mr Deasy vaguely quotes Lord Randolph Churchill's slogan 'Ulster will fight and Ulster will be right' (p. 29). The Homeric Nestor was an heroic survivor of earlier struggles, the only member of his family not to be slain by Heracles, and Mr Deasy also is represented as something of an archaic survival, harking back to the Act of Union and before. He claims descent from the Co. Down landowner Sir John Blackwood, alleging (quite wrongly) that Blackwood voted for the Union.

But Deasy wants to be Irish as well as British. He murmers vaguely, 'we are all Irish, all king's sons' and is concerned about cattle, important to the Irish economy since the legendary cattle-raid of Cuailgne celebrated in the Ulster Cycle. His curious letter for the press

on treating foot-and-mouth disease is based on an actual letter in the
Evening Telegraph on the same subject written in 1912 by Joyce's
friend in Trieste Henry Blackwood Price. Deasy's letter participates in
the long-standing Irish (particularly Anglo-Irish) resentment of harsh
British measures adversely affecting Irish trade. Instead of slaughtering
infected cattle and sustaining an economically damaging embargo to
the export of Irish cattle to England, the authorities would be better
advised to try a scientific cure for the disease which had had some
success in Austria, he suggests, much as Price, had done.[95] But Joyce
gives Deasy's letter a paranoiac edge not warranted by the original,
making him hint at possible conspiracy and intrigue on the part of
English economic interests. The Jews are blamed for the economic
malfunctions of Ireland's union with England of which this is an
example.

The Jews are blamed for most things in the 'Cyclops' episode when
the Citizen and other bystanders openly despise the inoffensive
Leopold Bloom. This allows Joyce to identify narrow Catholic
nationalism with Deasy's narrow Protestant Unionism, a witty effect
underlined as Bloom and Stephen find themselves united in their
estrangement from both these modes of Irishness. Deasy's attempt to
be British and Irish gets little sympathy. He is almost the sole
representative of awkward Ulster in the novel and Joyce finds it easy to
disown him. His last appearance is in the Nighttown episode: he is a
jockey, wearing a green jacket with orange sleeves symbolizing his
ambivalent Irishness, and he and his broken-winded nag Cock of the
North come last in the race (p. 467f).

For Stephen Dedalus and for Joyce, residually Catholic and
nationalist when confronted with Protestant Unionism, Deasy and
Deasy's Ulster represented in extreme form the heritage of sectarian
violence encumbering the artist and the free spirit in Ireland. But
partisan resentment of sectarian violence perpetrated by 'the other
side' was itself the bane of Irish life, stultifying the patriotism which
Joyce lampoons in the 'Cyclops' episode. The Homeric Cyclops had
only one eye, which Ulysses put out, and the pub talk about politics
manifestly lacks the clear vision and perspective of normal sight. The
discussion turns to flyblown ancient grievances against Bible-reading
Protestant aggressors in Catholic Ireland. The worst example is
'sanctimonious Cromwell and his Ironsides' who destroyed the town of
Drogheda and massacred the inhabitants. This leads into a newspaper
skit about the Bible and the Empire which the Citizen reads out to his
cronies. Similar political skits had actually appeared in the *United*

Irishman but Joyce makes this one up. It whimsically recounts the
meeting of the Alaki of Abeakuta, a visiting African potentate, with a
delegation of Manchester cotton magnates, and it reports the visitor's
statement that he treasures Queen Victoria's gift to him of a Bible, 'the
secret of England's greatness'. In 1904 there really was an Alake of
Abeokuta (Joyce's spelling is apparently at fault), one Ademola II
(1873–1962). He was not a Zulu, as the Citizen tells us, but a Yoruba,
chief of the Egba people of Western Nigeria. On 30 May 1904, shortly
before 'Bloomsday', he was formally received at Buckingham palace
where he mentioned the Bible presented by Queen Victoria (see
illustration 4, p. 181). The key phrase, 'the secret of England's
greatness', is not found in the press reports of the Alake's reception:
Joyce had supplied it from the title of a popular engraving which
showed Queen Victoria presenting a Bible to a subject prince. The
whole story seemed to bring the picture to life, particularly as the
Alake was described as richly dressed for his audience with the king,
just like the prince in the picture. It was actually the Alake's father,
Ademola I, who received the Bible from Queen Victoria, but Joyce
suppressed that trivial detail. Britain's relations with the Egba,
strained by the presence of French Catholic missionaries in competi-
tion with the Anglican mission station and the threat of a French
protectorate, had been placed on a secure footing with a treaty of
friendship and trade in 1893.[96] The combination of religion and trade
in the imperial enterprise is reflected in the invented detail of the
meeting with the Manchester cotton magnates and the Citizen's sour
comment 'Trade follows the flag' (p. 274). Joyce's contemporary St
John Ervine also made literary use of 'The Secret of England's
Greatness', as we have seen: in Protestant Ulster, last bastion of
British imperial sentiment and a beneficiary of imperial commerce, the
painting was often reproduced on Orange banners.

    The pomp and circumstance of Empire were part of popular
consciousness in England and Ireland at the time. Within recent
memory there had been Queen Victoria's Diamond Jubilee in 1897,
the coronation of King Edward VII and his state visit to Ireland
in 1903, occasioning nationalist protests organized by Arthur Griffith
and Maud Gonne.[97] Elgar was knighted in 1904 for celebrating
imperial Britain as a land of hope and glory. All this imperial glory
surfaces in *Ulysses* at the level of ironic fantasy. Leopold Bloom's
Nighttown experiences include a vision of himself as the great
reformer succeeding to an imperial crown in Dublin. The coronation
procession, magnificent but democratic, includes maharajas and the

Presbyterian moderator, Irish peers and chimneysweeps. Somehow, Bloom has become a successor both to King Edward (who makes a cameo appearance later in the episode) and to Charles Stewart Parnell, uncrowned king of Ireland, uniting and transcending imperial and nationalist traditions. He solemnly proclaims the new Bloomusalem and a utopia which is as much municipal as imperial. It combines, and so tacitly equates, the promises of local politicians, patriotic visionaries and newspaper advertisements. It outlaws religious discrimination, 'Tuberculosis, lunacy, war and mendicancy' as well as the hollow rhetoric of the 'Cyclops' episode: 'No more patriotism of barspongers and dropsical importers' (pp. 391–9). Sadly, the fantasy collapses into Bloom's habitual insecurity and alienation in the face of censorious Catholic Ireland and his masochistic and transsexual fantasies of humiliation take over.

Later on, anxious to avoid trouble with the drunken English soldiers Private Carr and Private Compton, Bloom mutters conciliatory remarks about the Royal Dublin Fusiliers in South Africa. His father-in-law Major Tweedy of the British Army drifts into consciousness, terrible in his moustache and medals, associated with the English heroism of Rorke's Drift or Waterloo (p. 486f). The Citizen and Major Tweedy, equal and opposite in their chauvinism, 'salute with fierce hostility'. Stephen, more Irish (despite himself) and less amiable than Bloom, is less conciliatory. The belligerent attitude of Britain's military representatives Carr and Compton is not encouraging. Compton moves the crowd back and calls for fair play in the approved British manner, but then urges Carr to 'make a bleeding butcher's shop of the bugger' (p. 487). The nightmare of history is somehow played out as black farce in Nighttown as reality and grotesque fantasy dissolve into each other. Stephen and Bloom are glad to escape.

But it is harder to escape from the pervasive national sentiment embodied in popular songs and ballads. The doomed heroism of the United Irishmen in 1798 had been celebrated in 'The Croppy Boy', one of the songs Joyce himself used to sing, and there are twelve references to it in *Ulysses*. In 1904 Dublin had very recent memories of the centenary of Robert Emmet's doomed insurrection of 1803, which had represented the last spasm of disaffection associated with 1798. The bard of the period was Tommy Moore, Robert Emmet's friend. It was difficult not to be reminded of Moore and his *Irish Melodies* in Edwardian Dublin. His statue stood, as it still does, near Trinity College, in the heart of Dublin. The arrogant young Stephen Dedalus projects upon it his disdain for slack, catchpenny sentimentality: 'sloth of the body and of the soul crept over it like unseen vermin, over the shuffling feet and up the folds of the cloak and around the servile head' (*Portrait*, p. 179f). But the disdain is a little brash and overstated, like Dedalus himself at this stage. The statue and 'Tommy Moore's roguish finger' are more genially treated in *Ulysses*, though Bloom's irreverent imagination cannot help reflecting 'They did right to put him up over a urinal: meeting of the waters' (p. 133). The allusion is to Moore's song about the vale of Avoca (on the Parnell estate in Co. Wicklow) where the sweet waters meet. Not surprisingly, in view of the extensive river symbolism in the book, this song is alluded to eleven times in *Finnegans Wake*.

The pattern of allusions to patriotic song in *Ulysses* almost amounts to a sardonically fractured version of the ballad history of Ireland which Thomas D'Arcy McGee had planned to write for Young Ireland.[98] 'She is far from the land where her young hero sleeps', Moore's song about Sara Curran, the betrothed of the doomed Robert Emmet, becomes a vague sentimental gesture in the 'Cyclops' episode, 'the Tommy Moore touch about Sara Curran and she's far from the land' (p. 251). Emmet's mythically resonant last words from the dock (which may have been invented by patriotic tradition)[99] prompted Moore's song 'O breathe not his name', but they are irreverently broken up by Bloom's flatulence in the 'Sirens' episode, surfacing among the casual bric-à-brac of unfocused consciousness:

> *When my country takes her place among*
> Prrpr.
> Must be the bur.
> Fff! Oo. Rrpr
> *Nations of the earth.*   (p. 238f)

Leopold Bloom happened to be born in Ireland but he inhabits the land of his own consciousness, the only country to which cosmopolitans and artists owe allegiance. Joyce makes the point by humanizing and personalizing shards of Irish tradition conveyed in Irish song, usually by Moore. The melancholy of Moore's 'The harp that once through Tara's halls' sounds in Bloom's inner ear with cloying hopelessness, 'The harp that once did starve us all' (p. 37). Earlier in life he had been involved in the penurious and tawdry world of musical theatre and alcoholic affability. His lost son Rudy and his decaying marriage give a sharp and poignant focus to the vague sense of loss and decay conveyed by patriotic song. Sentimental nostalgia floats free from its specific historical and political context, which in any case means little to the

Jewish Bloom. The Croppy Boy becomes a dead boy, not very bright, perhaps, rather than a martyr of 1798. The dead heroes of the past invoked in Moore's 'Forget not the field where they perished' are simply 'All gone', the specific battlefields and the lost causes alike forgotten (pp. 211, 238). The frequently cited last rose of summer, left to bloom alone, stands for Bloom's loneliness rather than Moore's melodious tears.

Bloom could have made something more positive out of Moore's materials. The whole spectrum of sentimentalized Irish history offers itself for comic treatment in the topical song (commissioned for a pantomime) which Bloom never finishes, a ditty entitled 'If Brian Boru could but come back and see old Dublin now' (p. 555). But Joyce succeeds where Bloom fails. The frequently sardonic juxtaposition of the topical and the mythical or traditional, Dublin in 1904 and Irish memories, preserved in song and story, stretching back to Celtic antiquity, has the effect of simultaneously activating and neutralizing the disruptive energies of Irish traditions and atavisms. In *Finnegans Wake* this project is carried forward with what often seems to be mock-heroic rigour and lunatic thoroughness.

There is something mechanical and factitious about the allusive comprehensiveness of *Finnegans Wake*. The bards of ancient Ireland and the nostalgia for them characteristic of the Celtic Twilight are dreamily, timelessly, comically conflated in the allusion to 'the twattering of bards in the twitterlitter between Druidia and the Deepsleep Sea' (p. 37). In the punning annihilation of distinctiveness historical and geographical difference simultaneously crystallize with false clarity and evaporate into the wordsmith's art with an unnatural inevitability. There is an inexorable pattern of fours suggested by the seventeenth-century *Annals of the Four Masters*, the four gospels (collapsed into 'Mamalujo', pp. 398, 476), Vico's three ages of history expanded to four to emphasize *ricorso* or recurrence, the four points of the compass and the four provinces of Ireland, the 'untired world of Leimuncononnulstria' (Leinster, Munster, Connaught and Ulster) (p. 229). This generates expectations of foursquare 'untirety' in the treatment of Ireland as of everything else. But Joyce's endlessly interwoven and overlapping schemata for *Finnegans Wake* mechanically infuse the deliberately overloaded language with structural significances at the expense of imaginative apprehension and coherence. Recognizable realities are subjected to an elaborate exercise in attribute-stripping to produce the brilliant fragments deployed and redeployed within the Joycean kaleidoscope.

The comic strategies of *Ulysses* constantly inflated or diminished personal and cultural idiosyncrasy, imperialist and nationalist attitudinizing, to the dimensions of farce, fantasy or stage-Irishness. But the more impersonal art of *Finnegans Wake* begins rather than ends in caricature and burlesque. Pattern rather than sardonic perception generates the discourse. In the fifteenth chapter we hear the voice of Matthew, one of the four evangelists, associated with the north and so with the northern province of Ulster.[100] In so far as this part of the book has an Irish dimension at all, it is an exercise in impersonating the stage Ulsterman, a figure introduced to the literary world in popular novels such as George A. Birmingham's *The Red Hand of Ulster* (1912) though the cheerful belligerence of St John Ervine also played a part. Matthew is a stern inquisitor with sharp vowels ('yu', 'yur'), crudely aggressive, darkly suspicious of 'paddyflaherty' and Catholics or 'RCs' (p. 250), identified as 'too farfar a cock of the north there, Matty Armagh' (p. 482). In *Ulysses* Mr Deasy rode a horse misnamed 'Cock o' the north', at least in the fantasy-world of Nighttown, but he had already deserved his hopeless nag by acting out the role of bluff yet uneasy Ulster Unionist bigot, dramatizing the economic and ideological tensions and contradictions of his politics.

Music and song are important in *Finnegans Wake* as in *Ulysses* as ways of identifying and negotiating Irish traditions. In *Finnegans Wake* the Orangeman's Lambeg drum and the grim economic prudence of the trueblue Ulster Scot are assumed rather than demonstrated as northern attributes. A song of romantic invitation with an Ulster accent produces grotesque caricature, promising 'Nine hundred and ninetynine million pound sterling in the blueblack bowels of the bank of Ulster' (p. 398). The three other provinces must also contribute their distinctive invitations to complete the pattern of the song, though this is more difficult since the other provinces, less sharply distinguished from each other in the crisis of Irish identity provoked by Home Rule and Celtic revivalism, were less vulnerable to parody and self-parody.

The pattern-making tyranny extends to, and depends on, trivial detail. The Dublin Fusiliers make a brief, inert appearance in the novel, not, as in *Ulysses*, in relation to Ireland's ambiguous involvement in England's Boer War but as a regiment from one of the four Irish provinces, part of a pattern completed by the Ulster Rifles, the Cork Militia and the Connaught Rangers (p. 451). The red hand of Ulster and the Latin motto of the city of Belfast occur in association with the northern Matthew (p. 521f), but this is partly to balance the repeated allusions to the Latin motto of the city of Dublin and partly to re-establish the idiom of heraldic language which Joyces' mentor Vico saw as the language of the second, heroic epoch of history.[101]

It would be unreasonable to complain about structurally necessary trivialization of the northern province when Joyce treats the rest of Ireland with comparable disrespect. But the accidents of geography ensured that the north-east of Ireland, 'lost' to Ireland by partition and virtually repudiated by the ruralist Celticizing national consciousness, should have remained largely unknown territory to Joyce, languishing on the outer fringes of his irreverent imagination. The northern writer could not benefit as directly as his southern brother from the laconic Joycean interrogation of Irish tradition and popular consciousness.

But other benefits were available. The strangeness of *Ulysses* and the formidable eccentricity of *Finnegans Wake* convey crucial insights. Joyce's subversions of the formal traditions and norms of narrative fiction demonstrated the limitations of linearity, the inadequacy of the personal, cultural or historical triumphalism or myth-making which myopically selects and charts royal roads to a distorted present and future. The dissolving reality-states of *Ulysses*, the dream-consciousness of *Finnegans Wake* and the radical instability of 'character' as traditionally understood in protean figures such as HCE are all somehow luminously Irish. Anglo-Irish insecurity in the nightmare of Irish history was often sublimated in cosmopolitan intellectual perspectives or displaced into the historically dislocated nightmare of Irish Gothic. Charles Maturin's *Melmoth the Wanderer* (1820) or the novels of Sheridan Le Fanu are good examples. *Finnegans Wake*, cosmopolitan in its linguistic register and Viconian historical perspective, is among many other things an exercise in comic Irish Gothic. It incorporates historical and literary violence and crime into bizarre fantasy. The Phoenix Park murders of 1882, when the Irish Chief Secretary and his Under-Secretary were assassinated, mingle with the plot of Le Fanu's *The House by the Churchyard* (1863), one of the few books owned by Joyce's father.[102] The fluid identities of the 'characters' of *Finnegans Wake* and Stephen Dedalus' search for a spiritual father and an identity are projections of the uncertain identity of the Irish writer in English, Irish, British, a citizen of the world and of his own imagination, a heretic in his own country and tradition yet profoundly shaped by his origins.

The importance of Joyce includes the sardonic publicity he gave to the different, interacting, traditions, popular and literary, English and Irish, imperialist and nationalist, which condition Irish identity.

Modern Irish writers, including the new generations hurt into poetry by problematic Ulster, owe him an immense debt. His cool virtuoso negotiation of Irish myth and tradition gives northern and southern authors an example and a model which can be extended and applied to their own time and place.

CHAPTER 6

Contemporary Ireland and the Poetics of Partition:

John Hewitt and Seamus Heaney

I N IRELAND, and in most other places, Joyce has become a patron saint of artistic liberation and creative renewal. He has confronted the modern writer, and the student of modernism, with epiphany, polyphony, internationalism, linguistic self-consciousness and the unimagined aesthetic possibilities of guilty sexuality and unremarkable urban life. The experimental fictions and bleakly echoing verbal structures of Samuel Beckett, or Flann O'Brien's disrespectful wit and brilliantly bewildering games played with time, writing and Irish expectations, especially in *At Swim Two Birds* (1939), are the most visible evidence of the stimulus and the burden of Ireland's Joycean heritage. But the poets have learnt from him too. Recent critical studies have drawn attention to the extent to which Joyce's sense of cultural disjunctions provided a route round and away from the powerful but intimidating presence of Yeats and unreconstructed Celtic revivalism.[1] For Irish writers Catholic adolescence and the Dublin streets can never be quite the same again since Stephen Dedalus passed that way. In national life and letters, wild and whirling words have become risky since the Citizen gave utterance in *Ulysses*, a departure indicated in the humane disenchantment with nationalistic rhetoric traced in Sean O'Faolain's short-story 'The Patriot' in *Midsummer Night Madness* (1932).

Joyce helped to bring Ireland and Irish writing to the world's attention and to create the audience that now reads Seamus Heaney in Caen and Connecticut. Ervine's literary fortunes seem to have splintered on the grim rocks of Ulster politics. But the contrast can mislead the literary historian. Every writer has some kind of involvement, however tense and difficult, with at least one community and with the traditions of feeling, thinking and writing which that community sustains and modifies as an aspect of its identity. These traditions outlive the individual writer, whether he has transformed them or simply acted and suffered as a symptom of them. St John Ervine can be seen as a symptom of the traditions, a product of the community, which later provoked the poetry of John Hewitt and Seamus Heaney, Michael Longley and Derek Mahon, Tom Paulin and Paul Muldoon. On this view Joyce's most immediate literary successors are the disenchanted urban Irish who share Dublin with him. The fragmented townscape of Thomas Kinsella's poem *Nightwalker* (1967) is one of the consequences.

St John Ervine ebulliently disagreed with his Belfast friends the writers John Boyd and Sam Hanna Bell: as men of the left, which Ervine had long abandoned, they would disclaim ideological continuity between his work and theirs. But all three were associated with the Northern Ireland region of the BBC which served the local community with broadcast talks, plays and features arising out of community concerns and a rich tangle of traditions. Sam Hanna Bell has reported affectionately on some of these in his book *Erin's Orange Lily* (1956) and rather more grimly in a series of Ulster historical novels from *December Bride* (1951) to *Across the Narrow Sea* (1987). John Boyd has dramatized community tensions in his published plays such as *The Flats* (1971) and helps to present the community to itself in his work with Belfast's Lyric Theatre. Neither is a direct literary disciple of Ervine but both operate within the same community and the same traditions.

The writer's relations with community and audience are complicated by the problems of contemporary Ireland, controversially partitioned into north and south. The compound divisions, religious and political, among and within the communities of the six northern counties, between Ulster and the rest of Ireland, between the various parts of Ireland and mainland Britain, ought perhaps to have isolated the Irish writer from any substantial audience anywhere. But this has manifestly not happened. Since the late 1960s, against a background of lively critical controversy[2] and more deadly political acrimony, Irish letters have positively flourished even in, perhaps particularly in, the troubled northern province. Irish writers are widely read and respected inside and outside their own country.

This involves some curious complexities. Traditional resentments of British, or more specifically English cultural, economic and political 'imperialism' have usually stopped well short of a boycott of English publishing houses, though Irish publishing north and south of the border has entered on a new and vigorous phase in recent years. The poet John Montague's collection *The Dead Kingdom* (1984) includes a poem called 'Border' and explores personal and political disruption and division. The geographical distribution of the expected readership encompasses the political divisions of the text: the book is published in the Irish Republic by the Dolmen Press (whose distinguished list includes the work of Thomas Kinsella), in Northern Ireland by the Blackstaff Press (John Hewitt's publishers) and in England by the Oxford University Press (who publish the poetry of Derek Mahon and Medbh McGuckian). There is a revealing, even embarrassing, overlap between two anthologies of the 1980s issued by leading English publishers: five of the ten poets in Paul Muldoon's *Faber Book of Contemporary Irish Poetry* (1986) also feature in Blake Morrison and Andrew Motion's *Penguin Book of Contemporary British Poetry* (1982). Seamus Heaney at least felt uneasy at being classified as a British poet, but in mainland Britain as in Ireland he is one of the best known of contemporary poets.

The modern Irish writer in effect mediates between two communities: a community of origin and the larger community which supplies the audience for his work. Seamus Heaney has paid repeated tribute to the influence upon him of the Monaghan writer Patrick Kavanagh,[3] and Kavanagh's fundamental community is the parish. This has encouraged Heaney to dwell on Mossbawn and Anahorish in his native Co. Derry, and Montague to hark back to Garvaghey in Co. Tyrone, the 'rough field' (in English translation) of his poetic sequence with that title published in 1972. John Hewitt identified himself and his poetry with the region of north-east Ulster, particularly Co. Down and Co. Antrim, where he spent much of his life. The city, whether the proletarian Dublin of James Plunkett's novel *Strumpet City* (1969) or the bomb-ravaged Belfast of Maurice Leitch's *Silver's City* (1981), represents another kind of community which has produced, and is reproduced, reflected or reinvented by, Irish writers. Sectarian politics and the sense of hereditary injustice or degradation have fractured geographical communities but encouraged an embattled tribalism with its own sense of communal hurt. This (characteristically Catholic) quality of feeling is registered in John Montague's collection of short stories *Death of a Chieftain* (1964) and the poems in *The Rough Field* (1972).

But these communities of origin may be largely unfamiliar to audiences made up of geographically dispersed and culturally various readers, listeners and theatre-goers. Authors have a complicated relation with such audiences in that as teachers, critics and commentators they are also partly identified with the audience-communities, and this feeds back into their own writing. The effect of this is to foster in readers and writers an often uneasy and unstable pluralism, a coming together of different strands of Irish tradition. This has always been a possibility, however tense and fraught, since the time when Archbishop Ussher chatted with Scots-Irish Presbyterian divines and corresponded with Celtic and Catholic antiquarians between visits to the Bodleian Library in England. But greatly improved educational opportunity and modern communications have involved more Irishmen than ever before in the possibilities of pluralism.

Even so, the fragility of the new pluralism can hardly be overstated. There is still little agreement about what Irish literature is and should be. The purist repudiation of the English language can still be encountered, notably in Michael Hartnett's *A Farewell to English* (1975). Where the Dublin poet Thomas Kinsella wilfully underrepresents recent Ulster poetry in *The New Oxford Book of Irish Verse* the northern poet Paul Muldoon, equally wilfully, includes only two writers from outside Ulster in his *Faber Book of Contemporary Irish Poetry*. The puritanical social and religious attitudes which once restricted creativity and upheld a literary censorship in the twenty-six southern counties have their present-day counterpart in the north: from time to time someone is bound to object to the use in Ulster schools of some text of an alleged libidinous, Catholic or nationalist tendency. Seamus Heaney's *Selected Poems 1965–1975* (1980) has proved a surprisingly controversial volume in certain quarters, though it is unlikely to be banned or burnt. The separateness of the communities of origin has increased with the partition of Ireland and the renewal of religious hostility. Joyce's Dublin of 1904 and the pubescent ordeals of Stephen Dedalus at his Jesuit school are at least as remote from the northern Protestant youth as the London of Arthur Morrison's *Tales of Mean Streets* (1894) or the adventures of Billy Bunter at Greyfriars School (first published in 1908).

This can be offset, or so one would like to think, by the respect good

Irish writers of all kinds have for each other and their distinguished predecessors. Northern poets have derived stimulus from the adroit ambivalences and evasions of the problematically Irish Louis MacNeice, born in Ulster though he would have preferred the west of Ireland, educated in England, vaguely classified as a 'sceptical Protestant' within the sectarian spectrum.[4] His little poem 'Snow', celebrating difference, excitedly juxtaposing 'snow and pink roses', is recalled in Derek Mahon's tribute of discipleship 'In Carrowdore Churchyard' which invokes 'The ironical, loving crush of roses against snow'. 'Snow' appears again, irreverently, in Paul Muldoon's poem 'History', which talks of having sex in 'the room where MacNeice wrote "Snow"/ Or the room where they say he wrote "Snow"'.[5] Muldoon also gives MacNeice the largest selection in the *Faber Book of Contemporary Irish Poetry*. But other Irish poets have not felt the anxiety of this influence. Seamus Heaney, from a Catholic background in rural Ulster, respected the poems but kept his distance from them, sensing that they 'arose from a mind-stuff and existed in a cultural setting which were at one remove from me and what I came from'.[6] John Montague, from a background similar to Heaney's, grudgingly includes only two MacNeice items in his *Faber Book of Irish Verse* (1974). Thomas Kinsella is only a little more generous in the *New Oxford Book of Irish Verse*. MacNeice felt cut off from both stridently Protestant industrial Ulster and the romantic Ireland of Catholic poverty and piety, a separation which began in an inherited distaste for Orange sectarianism and an embarrassed sense of hereditary Anglo-Irish privilege as a 'rector's son, born to the anglican order,/ Banned for ever from the candles of the Irish poor'.[7] A classical education at Marlborough and Merton and nurture in progressive and internationalist politics under the wing of the thirties literary left increased his distance from Irish traditions but did little to bring them into creative relationship.

The conflict of traditions can be illustrated in the disputed or ambiguous standing of other precursors of contemporary Irish writing. The picture is complicated by English, American and European influences, but Irish poets at least tend to respond most profoundly to other writers from their own place. Seamus Heaney has lived and worked on either side of the Irish border: his mentor Patrick Kavanagh, appropriately enough, was born in Co. Monaghan, one of the counties of the old province of Ulster now incorporated in the Irish Republic. Kavanagh is admired and respected, perhaps even overrated, on both sides of the border, but within the different discourse of mainland-dominated 'English' literature, in which Irish poets participate, he ranks as a minor figure. For some Irish writers he is the pioneer of a new order of Irish poetry after Yeats, marking a release from the limiting perspectives of cultural nationalism and undemocratic Anglo-Irishness and a fresh, visionary perception of black hills and small fields as important places.[8] But urban poets have been less impressed. John Hewitt, a meticulous craftsman himself and town-bred, tempered his praise of Kavanagh's vigour and piercing lyricism with severe technical criticisms of his risky, adventurous, uneven verse, vitiated perhaps by syntactic and rhythmic insecurity.[9]

For James Simmons, another northern poet, it is not Kavanagh but Hewitt himself who is 'the daddy of us all', 'good old John Hewitt',[10] a view courteously endorsed by Michael Longley in an obituary tribute.[11] But Hewitt is rather ostentatiously excluded from Muldoon's and Kinsella's recent anthologies and is only beginning to attract interest and attention outside Ulster.

Another controversial precursor, Austin Clarke, is an adroit metrist responsive to the intricate vowel-music of Gaelic poetic idiom, a Swiftian satirist and an exponent of the 'Celtic-Romanesque'. He has consistently articulated libertarian resentment of the new Irish state apparently dominated by a repressive, 'Jansenist' Catholicism, at least until shortly before his death in 1974. His antagonistic stance has been shared by other disaffected southern writers such as Sean O'Faolain, Liam O'Flaherty and Denis Devlin, while his revisionist Celticism parallels that of Frank O'Connor, translator of Brian Merriman's bawdy satire *Cúirt an Mheadhon Oidche* ('The Midnight Court'). In place of the reverential romantic and heroic appropriations of Gaelic tradition of the Celtic Revival Clarke has selected a wittier and more iconoclastic tradition typified by the medieval *Aislinge Mac Conglinne* ('The Vision of Mac Conglinne') which lies behind his comedy *The Son of Learning*. This tough-minded mode of Irishness has both exasperated and influenced Thomas Kinsella. He has criticized Clarke's narrowly focussed rage against Irish society and alienation from it, but this really reflects Kinsella's own differently morose relationship to contemporary Ireland and his sense of responsibility to (chiefly Gaelic) Irish tradition and the Irish past which coexists with a sense of hurt disjunction from it.[12]

The Dublin critic Maurice Harmon makes Clarke the first of his seven poets in a drastically selective anthology of *Irish Poetry after Yeats'* (1979). But further north Ulster poets have identified different concerns and antagonists and are involved with different traditions.

There has been plenty of northern injustice and philistinism to feed poetic angers. Tom Paulin, principal angry young man among the Ulster poets (though now teaching in England), has frequently resented Paisleyite fundamentalism and the politics of Unionism. But the chief adversary in the north is a Protestant, not a Catholic establishment, and this limits Clarke's influence and appeal among northern writers, particularly those upon whom Catholic and Gaelic traditions sit lightly. Only John Hewitt has shown a sustained interest in his work and his libertarian witness.[13] He does not feature in the Muldoon anthology though more contemporary than MacNeice or Kavanagh since he was still publishing important poems in the 1970s.

It is tempting to see the whole course of Irish writing since the death of Yeats as a sustained attempt to disown or escape from his overwhelming influence. For some at least, the significance of Yeats can be detached from the intrinsic excellence of his work. He has become the supreme representative figure of the 'colonist mentality',[14] the embodiment of a circumscribed and hybridized national culture. He has been blamed for the graciously moribund Anglo-Irish tradition which he partly invented and which the new middle-class Ireland has been anxious to proclaim dead and gone. Rumours of the death of Anglo-Irish literature on the Yeatsian model have been exaggerated, but the whispering campaign has been prompted by the political need to develop a differently-oriented sense of tradition in sympathy with the progressive formal detachment of the twenty-six southern counties from mainland Britain and residual English influences. The final stage of this process began two years before the death of Yeats with the promulgation of the effectively republican constitution of 1937, continued with the policy of neutrality in relation to Britain's enemies (and allies) during the second world war, and culminated in the official withdrawal from the British Commonwealth in 1949. Michael Harnett, born in 1941 into this self-consciously non-British Ireland, lampooned Yeats as the masterly chef who 'could raise mere stew to a glorious height', adding Gaelic flavouring and other ingredients to 'a simple Anglo-Saxon stock' to produce 'the celebrated Anglo-Irish stew'. More harshly Yeats appears as

> our bugbear Mr Yeats
> who forced us into exile
> on islands of bad verse.[15]

Different perspectives are available in Ulster where politics are still noisily but intimately involved with Britain. Paradoxically, Yeats seems to be more respected in the northern province which he made no attempt to dignify in verse. Perhaps it is easier to welcome a stranger for what he is than tolerate a neighbour for what he seems alarmingly to represent. For most Ulster people Yeats' romantic Ireland of peasants and gentry is a foreign country. But the early Yeats' dreamy responsiveness to landscape and natural beauty struck a chord with readers and poets all over Ireland. The Ulster poet R. N. D. Wilson registered the influence in fragile lyrics collected in *The Holy Wells of Orris* (1927). It was Wilson, rather than Yeats directly, who introduced the young John Hewitt to modern Irish poetry and domesticated Yeatsian rhythms and imagery in Ulster.[16] Edna Longley's critical study *Poetry in the Wars* (1986) adroitly traces the influence of Yeatsian syntax, imagery, music and public and personal rhetoric on Mahon, Heaney and MacNeice.[17] James Simmons mocks the blossoming Yeats industry which makes Yeats hated among schoolchildren, like Shakespeare, but he admits (rather lamely) 'that voice of Yeats still gives/ new friends old thrills'.[18] Seamus Heaney can select out of the variousness of Yeats a servant of the community and nature, a humane and exemplary poet separable from his 'great fur coat of attitude' and 'the domineering intellect and the equestrian profile.'[19]

Even in the south and west the Yeatsian Anglo-Irish tradition quietly lingers. The theme of the 'Big House', proud occupants in decline, painfully involved with yet separated from the rest of Ireland, still has literary currency, in elegy if not in contemporary record. It appears in Irish novels such as Molly Keane's *Good Behaviour* (1981) and William Trevor's *The Fools of Fortune* (1983). The Galway poet Richard Murphy, educated at Wellington, Oxford and the Sorbonne, is the finest, perhaps the last literary representative of stubborn Anglo-Ireland. Like Yeats, his roots are in the west of Ireland, and like Yeats he is the grandson of a clergyman of the Church of Ireland, on his father's side. His maternal grandfather, Thomas Ormsby, was also an Irish clergyman, but only after he retired from the British Army, Lieutenant-Colonel and DSO. The Colonel-rector's widow is recalled in her grandson's poem 'The Woman of the House'. Her possibly futile selflessness stands as an emblem of the benign paternalism of doomed Anglo-Ireland:

> She bandaged the wounds that poverty caused
> In the house that famine labourers built,
> Gave her hands to cure impossible wrong
> In a useless way, and was loved for it.[20]

Murray's father retired as Sir William Murphy KCMG after serving as
Governor of the Bahamas. Moved by post-colonial guilt as well as
nostalgia, Murphy dwells on Ireland's divided history since 'Aughrim's
great disaster'. His perspective is coloured both by his Anglo-Irish
heritage and by his anxious, willed sense of identity with the 'meere
Irish', particularly fishermen and islanders. His most ambitious poetic
sequence, *The Battle of Aughrim*, was commissioned by BBC Radio in
1968.

One of the readers was his friend Cecil Day-Lewis, then the English
poet laureate but born in Ireland in an Anglo-Irish rectory to a mother
remotely descended from Oliver Goldsmith. Day-Lewis's Anglo-
Irishness was to some extent the romantic fantasy of an insecure and
rootless poet since the family left Ireland when he was two, but it led to
some fine poems, including a Yeatsian meditation on Constance
Markievicz, 'Child running wild in woods at Lissadell', and some late
poems about rural landscapes and origins collected in *The Whispering
Roots* (1970). The (partly factitious) Irishness of the English poet
laureate demonstrates in extreme form the fluid identity of the modern
Irish (and English) poet.

The disputed status of MacNeice, Kavanagh, Hewitt, Clarke and
Yeats as precursors and models for the lively Irish poetry of the last
twenty years has been less divisive than it might appear. It is hard to
resist the glum realism of the Dublin poet and critic Eavan Boland
when she writes, 'Let us be rid at last of any longing for cultural unity,
in a country whose most precious contribution may be precisely its
insight into the anguish of disunity.'[21] But Ireland's most precious
contribution is probably its insight into the unending dialectic of
disunity and syncretism, tribalism and pluralism, in politics and
culture. Between the communities of origin and potentially pluralist
communities of reception modern Ireland interposes institutions
within which cultural and political tensions can be confronted,
mediated and brought into significant and energizing if not always
sympathetic relationship. Irish writers from different traditions often
know each other, particularly in Ulster. As Edna Longley has
observed, 'the notion of a community of the imagination is slightly less
bizarre in the context of Ulster than elsewhere'.[22] The institutions
which foster cross-cultural contact are the universities, the theatre, the
broadcasting companies, the Arts Councils and the little magazines.

There is often a certain overlap. Paul Muldoon, a graduate of The
Queen's University of Belfast, worked until recently for the BBC, like
Louis MacNeice before him. He has published many of his poems in

The Honest Ulsterman, a magazine founded by James Simmons in which poems by Tom Paulin, Derek Mahon, John Montague, Seamus Heaney and Michael Longley have also appeared. Michael Longley has worked for the Northern Ireland Arts Council since 1970 and is married to the critic Edna Longley who teaches English at Queen's, where Seamus Heaney was a colleague from 1966 to 1972. In 1970 the Arts Council arranged a series of poetry readings by John Hewitt and John Montague, juxtaposing different traditions under the title *The Planter and the Gael*. Hewitt had connections with Queen's before and after his long absence in Coventry as Art Director of the Museum and Art Gallery. While he was in Coventry he acted as poetry editor of the little magazine *Threshold* associated with Belfast's Lyric Theatre. This theatre has always welcomed poets: it was founded by Mary O'Malley in 1951 with encouragement from Austin Clarke and his Dublin Lyric Theatre Company. Its object was to foster, *inter alia*, the tradition of verse-drama which Clarke inherited from Yeats. Thomas Kinsella, poet and Dubliner, is a director. Both the theatre and the magazine have played host to Ireland's different traditions. Revivals of the plays of Yeats, Lady Gregory and O'Casey have alternated with work by Ulster dramatists such as John Boyd or Brian Friel. Friel is a founder of the Derry-based Field Day Theatre Company established in 1980 to produce his play *Translations*, which is an exploration of cultural tension and hostility. Field Day, whose directors include Tom Paulin, Seamus Deane and Seamus Heaney, has set out to stimulate discussion of cultural conflict in contemporary Ireland in response to the northern political crisis and has published several series of pamphlets by English and American as well as Irish authors.[23]

The northern crisis, or the 'troubles', has also been debated in *Threshold*, which has published contributions by important writers from all parts of Ireland since its foundation in 1957. In some ways it takes the place of the Belfast Arts magazines *Rann*, *Lagan* and *The Northman* published in the 1940s and early 1950s. But it is also a successor to the more ambitious and successful journal *The Bell* (1940–54), initially edited (from Dublin) by Sean O'Faolain. *The Bell* was friendly to northern writers despite increasing divisions between Ulster and the rest of Ireland during and after the second world war. It was impatient with narrow definitions of Irish cultural identity. In its crusading eclecticism and internationalism *The Bell* inherited the mantle of *The Irish Statesman* (1923–30), edited by Yeats' friend George Russell ('AE') which insisted against the dogmatism of 'Irish Ireland' and the sillier Celtic revivalists on the rich plurality of Irish cultural tradition.[24] Over nearly sixty years John Hewitt has had work published in all these magazines as well as in English journals such as *The Listener* and *The New Statesman*, participating, from a local Ulster base, in the complex evolving discourses of both Irish and English poetry. This has also been the pattern for the younger poets who have come to prominence in the last twenty years.

It is easy to exaggerate the significance in the general community of all these interactions. Universities, theatres and arts broadcasts, despite the best efforts of all concerned, reach a relatively small proportion of Irish society. Little magazines by definition have small circulations and Irish editors such as O'Faolain have usually been pessimistic about any impact they might have upon their society. But there is some evidence to suggest that cultural debate is beginning to reach a wider audience and to have some effect on the political process. Sensitive to this development, which it had helped to bring about, Field Day commissioned a contribution from the Unionist politician and lawyer R. L. McCartney. His essay on *Liberty and Authority in Ireland* (1895) makes an anti-nationalist case on grounds of individual freedoms, demonstrating the serious ideological differences under-pinning sectarian tension. Another Field Day contributor, Richard Kearney, has helped to make Dublin think about cultural aspects of Irish problems (not exclusively 'northern' problems) in the journal *The Crane Bag*. The most distinguished and influential cultural debater is probably the former Irish Prime Minister Dr Garret Fitzgerald whose 1982 Richard Dimbleby Lecture *Irish Identities* anticipated the pluralist aspirations of the New Ireland Forum Report (1984) and the bitterly controversial Anglo-Irish Agreement of November 1985. In Dublin and London as well as in Belfast there is now official recognition of the need to acknowledge 'a broader and more comprehensive Irish identity' and Dillon Johnson has noted the complicity of the poets in the traditions out of which this identity is constituted.[25]

But can the poets do anything to accommodate conflicting traditions to each other? Or should they? Can they aspire to be unacknowledged legislators of Ireland's peace? Politically committed critics such as Stan Smith and Seamus Deane have noted a political detachment from the 'troubles' among the Ulster poets. But there is always the danger that bad politics might be made worse by bad poems. Edna Longley has sensibly criticized the view that it is Seamus Heaney's job to be the bard and prophet of national emergency, exploring and articulating the tormented national psyche in some grand Yeatsian manner.[26] Heaney's own gestures in this direction, particularly in *North* (1975), have met with a mixed reception. But there is a tempting role-model available in the courageous and persistent Russian poets who irradiated private experience in the light of history and testified to humanistic values and an enduring sense of community in the face of an ideologically coercive utilitarian state. Both Tom Paulin and Seamus Heaney have written enthusiastically about Osip Mandelstam,[27] one of the heroes of witness of Henry Gifford's 1985 Clark Lectures *Poetry in a Divided World*.

This is a difficult matter. Poetic witness in times of historical crisis may enlighten, or merely hector at the expense of the poetry; and it may do no good anyway. W. H. Auden's glum reflection, conditioned by the 1930s but prompted by the death of Yeats, was that 'poetry makes nothing happen'.[28] John Hewitt (his exact contemporary) seems to be of the same mind, certain that in the northern crisis poetry has made no difference.[29] Poetry that tries to make a difference can be betrayed by its own indignation: it runs the moral and aesthetic risk of confirming or compounding bitterness and hatred, dividing and alienating its audience.

The problem is illustrated by Thomas Kinsella's poem 'Butcher's Dozen' (1972), a response 'with Anger at my heel' to the controversial findings of the Widgery Tribunal. This was an inquiry, conducted by the British Lord Chief Justice, into the circumstances of 'Bloody Sunday', 30 January 1972, when thirteen people were killed by British soldiers in Londonderry in the course of a riot sparked off by an illegal Civil Rights march. Widgery's conclusion that the soldiers acted in good faith and that there was no general breakdown of military discipline was received with incredulity and cynicism in some quarters.[30] Age-old distrust of English justice in Ireland had been vigorously revived even before Widgery reported and it was never likely that jesting Pilate's question 'What is truth?' would find any simple answers in the emotive tangle of political aggravation, confusion and misjudgement on all sides. But the facile rhymes and rhythms of Kinsella's pamphleteer doggerel reduces everything to the primitive dogmatic clarity of unreconstructed nationalist rhetoric:

> Yet England, even as you lie
> You give the facts that you deny.
> Spread the lie with all your power
> – All that's left, it's turning sour.[31]

The unpoliced frontier between humane outrage and sectarian rancour leaves poetry in danger.

There is a raw urgency about some of Padraic Fiacc's poems of the 'troubles', jaggedly confronting the reader with harsh metal and broken glass and a nine-year-old altar-boy shot dead by 'some trigger-happy cow-boy cop'.[32] But Fiacc's angry despairing verse-journalism does not cohere into sustained poetic vision. It provides a modicum of justification for an anonymous satirist's sweeping condemnation of recent northern poetry as 'Ulster-troubles-journalese', the amorphous work of 'pigmy bards' in unworthy succession to the allegedly glum and feebly topical Louis MacNeice: 'Thank God I'm not a rector's son.'[33] This is not to say that no worthwhile poetry has greeted the 'troubles'. Padraic Fiacc's excellent selection *The Wearing of the Black* (1975) includes good work by a wide range of poets from different generations, most of them already poets before the 'troubles' began. Roy Fuller courteously welcomed the volume for its 'indignation, concreteness and humanity [which] recall the best English poetry of the two world wars'.[34] But the analogy with hurt imaginations in England's external wars has limited application to internecine strife persisting in and through rather than over against the decencies of civilian life, dividing rather than uniting embattled communities, provoking a poetry of rage as well as or instead of pity.

At the other end of the spectrum there is the poetry of evasion and alienation, refusing rather than registering or negotiating the history of its time. Derek Mahon has been severely taken to task for this evasion by Stan Smith,[35] though he is hardly the typical figure in Ulster poetry that Smith implies. Mahon's alienation from Protestant and Unionist Belfast and Ulster, his sense that even the hills at the end of the streets (out of which Philip Larkin could make a poem)[36] cannot sustain an imagination recoiling into private space, is both a personal statement and a creative response to MacNeice's influential disgust with the sectarian city.[37] This places him against the trend of some of the best Eastern European writing which is beginning to make an impact in Ireland. Mahon's procedures run counter to the Acmeist poets such as Mandelstam or the disaffected symbolists such as Oscar Milosz (respectfully invoked by John Montague) whom the Polish-American Nobel Laureate Czeslaw Milosz aligns with the true mission of poetry, the 'passionate pursuit of the Real', compounded of fraternity with the past and moral engagement with the great human family.[38] Mahon seems more at home with Mallarmé and Rimbaud. He invokes Constantin Cavafy's poem 'Waiting for the Barbarians' which Milosz respects, but the barbarians range uneasily from gallowglasses to spiritually impoverished suburbanites. Mahon translates the Greek not into Anglo-Irish but into the discourse of fastidious personal alienation and withdrawal.

For Seamus Deane the extremes of withdrawal and involvement can be formulated as the dialectic of a poetry of denial and a poetry of commitment, represented by the wildly eclectic quicksilver shape-changing and elusiveness of Paul Muldoon on the one hand, and the sternly politicized work of Tom Paulin on the other.[39] Paulin is nostalgic for a romanticized version of eighteenth-century Protestant Republicanism and William Drennan's Ulster, pitting himself against contemporary Ulster Unionism in the sharp accents of another St John Ervine, unaware of the extent to which he resembles Ervine in the contentious obstinacy he derives from the cross-grained community he addresses.

Between these extremes the contemporary Irish poet is awkwardly poised. The matter of Ireland, disparaged by Kavanagh as 'the Irish thing', has limited and limiting imaginative substance: a partitioned and divided country ultimately weakens rather than stimulates the poetic (and political) imagination. Edna Longley may be too harsh when she suggests that the 'psychic hinterlands' of the Irish mentality may be imaginative dead ends,[40] but Irish poetry, Irish writing, can and does have other interests. The familiar themes of history's nightmare, heroism and the Gael, the land and the anguish of a nation powerless to be born, oppressive holiness and psychosexual maiming, had urgency in Liam O'Flaherty or Frank O'Connor but in the 1980s they have become just a little flyblown. There are, and always have been, other possible conjunctions between the inner life and the business of being Irish, perceptible at the level of tone, diction and form as much as content.

To take one example, the elegant classicism of Michael Longley is manifest not only in invocations of Circe and Narcissus or reworkings of Homer or Propertius but in the containment of disturbance in formally shaped poems about birds and visited places:

> A place of dispersals
> Where the wind fractures
> Flight-feathers, insect wings
> And rips thought to tatters
> Like a fuchsia petal.[41]

This conveys an intellectually achieved serenity characteristic of the Anglo-Irish tradition, well represented in the Olympian classical and historical scholarship of Bury and Mahaffy at Trinity College, Dublin, where Longley also read classics.

Longley's friend from schooldays, Derek Mahon, commands classical resonances from a similar background, but to more ironic effect: a chorus from Sophocles' *Antigone* celebrating the wonders of the world sardonically introduces 'Glengormley', post-heroic and suburban, where Mahon grew up. In 'Heraclitus on Rivers' Heraclitean flux sweeps away the permanence of love and poetry and personality itself.[42]

There is yet another kind of classicism in the poems of the Presbyterian romantic W. R. Rodgers. Ovidian legend helps to structure an exuberant eroticism in fruitful tension with an inherited (and professed) Calvinist sense of the special responsibility of consecrated life. The turbulent, torrential rhetoric of *Europa and the Bull and Other Poems* (1952), drawing attention to its own energies, has been plausibly linked with the enthusiastic, evangelical mode of preaching within the Irish Protestant dissenting tradition. The contrasting quietness and formal precision of John Hewitt can be associated with the more austerely rationalist tendency within the same tradition.[43]

Even without direct access to the 'matter of Ireland' the dialectic of disunity and harmony, aggression and peace within Irish culture can be displaced into creative conflicts of voice and attitude between different poets representing different traditions and even within the consciousness and the work of the individual poet. These conflicts are estabilshed or exacerbated through the poet's endless, uneasy, oscillation between restrictive (but also stimulating) community of origin and potentially pluralist audience which may, or may not, serve in its turn as a new community of origin. Two contrasting poets, from different generations and traditions, will serve to indicate the range of possibilities: John Hewitt, of nonconformist parentage and 'planter' stock, and Seamus Heaney, who acknowledges the 'slow obstinate Papish burn' of his poetry.[44]

JOHN HEWITT (1907–87)

The success of the recently established John Hewitt International Summer School perhaps signals the beginnings of posthumous fame, but for most of his long life Hewitt's work was respected but not widely

read, little known outside his native Ulster. He was relatively
neglected by critics and anthologists (except for Geoffrey Grigson),
overshadowed by his contemporaries Auden and MacNeice in his early
career, less conspicuous than the younger Ulster poets such as Seamus
Heaney or Paul Muldoon in the last twenty years. His verse and prose
repay attention not only for their intrinsic virtues of clarity, humanity
and painful honesty about divided Ireland but for the extent to which
they introduce and promote a non-Celtic, non-romantic mode of
relating to the landscape, history and culture of an Irish region too
long neglected by literary fashion.

Hewitt was born in Belfast, the son of Robert Hewitt, a teetotal
Methodist schoolteacher of angular integrity and radical educational
outlook. Robert Hewitt was much influenced by the liberation ideals of
A. S. Neill, controversial founder of Summerhill, and John Hewitt's
humane liberalism owes something to the same source: as he says in a
wryly confessional poem,

> I should have made it plain that I stake my future
> on birds flying in and out of the school-room window.[45]

Hewitt was never baptised because his father resented the overbearing
attitude of the local minister who was also manager of the Agnes Street
Methodist Primary School, where he was principal. This non-baptism
symbolically inaugurated the conscientious freethinking of the poet's
adult life: 'and from that day I've stood outside the creeds.'[46]

But the old Belfast joke about Protestant atheists and Catholic
atheists has some truth in it: Hewitt was a Protestant and Methodist
atheist affected almost despite himself by his background. He was a
dissenter even from Dissent, liberal and radical through and beyond
the generous humanity of his parents' religion. Irish Methodism cuts
across divisions between planter and Gael, Anglo-Irish and Scots-
Irish. Eighteenth-century Wesleyan evangelists preached effectively in
Irish as well as English. Wesley himself came frequently to Ireland and
preached in the open air to the Catholic communities of the south of
Ireland as well as to the Protestant communities in the north.
Methodism attracted converts all over Ireland lapsed from or
indifferent to their hereditary religious allegiances.[47] This may have
something to do with the exemplary record of present-day Irish
Methodists in pioneering ecumenical understanding and addressing
the problems of a divided society in the midst of sectarian violence.[48]
Certainly liberal Methodism helped deliver John Hewitt at an early age

from the worst extremes of Ulster tribalism and Protestant bigotry. It is not altogether fanciful to see connections between popular Methodist hymns, carefully shaped to embody and reinforce religious orthodoxy for a worshipping community, and Hewitt's poems, usually plain and accessible, well crafted to embody more humanistic pieties for a divided community. Hewitt can sound like Ervine's decent secular protestant Mrs Martin:

> there's no hope save in enduring and trying by small
> gestures of love and pity to publish the habit
> of mercy from man to man.
> ('The Habit of Mercy', *Collected Poems*, p. 105)

Hewitt's sonnet sequence *Kites in Spring. A Belfast Boyhood* (1980) is something of a lay-sermon. It reviews his peaceful middle-class childhood from the perspective of renewed communal violence in Belfast and other parts of Ulster. The anti-sectarian theme is much more prominent than in an earlier prose autobiography covering the same ground.[49] The golden age of childhood acquires added lustre from the belief – or illusion – that early in the century, despite incidental ancestral bigotries, a 'tolerant and just society' was still in prospect.[50] Loving one's neighbour could help to bring it about. Friendship with Willie Morrissey, the Catholic boy next door, was an initiation into another culture, Hewitt now realizes, and he entitles the sonnet 'The Irish Dimension' (*Kites in Spring*, p. 56). His title is a political catch-phrase of the 1970s and 1980s in the continuing debate on the future of problematically Irish and British Ulster. Hewitt's father accepted his Catholic neighbours and stayed faithful to the Irish National Teachers' Organization, which included Catholic teachers, even when a Protestant Ulster Teachers' Union was founded after the partition of Ireland:

> that they were teachers was to him enough,
> to sect or party singularly blind.
> ('Going up to Dublin', *Kites in Spring*, p. 57)

But sect and party still intruded. One grandfather had been an Orangeman, until his Lodge introduced strong drink. On the twelfth of July each year, to the sound of fife and drum, the Orangemen marched through streets festooned with bunting, as they still do. The obtrusive rhythms and colours of the tribal festival are reflected in the terse images, regular beat and insistent rhymes of Hewitt's sonnet 'The Twelfth of July'. The billowing banners are described with terse economy: they include 'The Secret of England's Greatness', or 'Queen hands a Bible to a turbaned black', but the resonances of circumscribed Protestantism and imperialism interrogated by Ervine and Joyce are not explored. The poem is less dull and prosaic than many of the other sonnets in the sequence because of a covert imaginative sympathy with its subject. Hewitt's well-drilled verse with its sober, purposeful diction actually rather resembles a parade of dark-suited marching Orangemen when the bands have stopped playing. But the quiet manner is often deceptive. The implied sense of involvement with the tribe, more explicit in the adjacent poem 'The Eleventh Night' describing how 'we' built bonfires to be lit on the eve of the 'Twelfth', is in fact problematic. Unspoken differences of class and culture separate the liberal schoolmaster's son, the observer, from the 'boys about my size' who grip the 'taut strings' of the banners. The need to tether the swaying silks, the strain of the taut strings, impart an element of tension and just-contained risk which answer to the wary insecurity and latent defensive violence of Ulster 'loyalists' and Orangemen:

> Their painted banners flaunt the bearded faces
> of founding fathers, flicker an array
> of famous fighters in embattled places
> like Derry, Enniskillen, Dolly's Brae,
>
> (*Kites in Spring*, p. 45)

The verse is less innocent than it seems. It articulates an aggressive and edgy heritage. The heavy rhythm and oppressive alliteration harshly assimilate 'founding fathers' to 'famous fighters' and implicate them in the arrogance of 'flaunt' and the nervousness of 'flicker'. The syntax seems to give autonomy to the 'array/ of famous fighters' apparently flickering on their own, but 'flicker' is unconventionally transitive: it is the tribal banners which awkwardly, even disturbingly, cause the flickering. The 'embattled places', rhyming with Victorian 'bearded faces', are momentarily, comfortably, part of the past until the next line brutally specifies 'Derry', scene of battles in the Bogside and the shootings of 'Bloody Sunday' in 1972 as well as of the seventeenth-century siege.

Appalled by the 'troubles', the 'tragic confusion of this heart-breaking present' as Hewitt put it in 1972, he wrote poems in the 1970s offering not so much solutions as 'intuitions, intimations, imaginative realisations, epiphanies' in response to a harsh heritage.[51] Under this Wordsworthian and Joycean pressure isolated fragments of childhood experience acquired, or had thrust upon them, an extra burden of significance. The poetic results were rather mixed. The sinking of the *Titanic* which had obsessed St John Ervine ought to be important as a warning to misplaced pride. But the poetry sinks too, to awkwardness and bathos: 'drowned now her hundreds, she'd not sail again' ('Late Spring, 1912', *Kites in Spring*, p. 36). The Easter Rising of 1916, noticed in a poem in the 1976 collection *Time Enough*, might perhaps have prompted poetry in the grand Yeatsian manner. But it was not actually very important to him at the time, and in any case Hewitt disliked grand manners. The real subject of the poem is not 1916 but the pernicious connection, as Hewitt sees it, between the patriotic legend of 1916 and the continuing urban violence of the 1970s. A more convincingly personal revelation, a moment of vision rather than intellectualized reflection, is achieved in 'Encounter Nineteentwenty'. The young Hewitt has been dribbling a football along the street, all on his own, when he collided with a 'stiffly striding man' and glimpsed a rifle held under his coat. In time the rifle has come to represent 'the shape of fear that waits each Irish child', but the solitary footballer grown into the liberal poetic dreamer is still isolated, racing 'to secure my sad unchallenged goal', implicated in communal hurt but embarked on a bleak, unfrequented, personal route out of it.[52]

This draws attention to Hewitt's painful, sometimes arrogant, loneliness as a leftish secular Protestant in conservative Ulster. He felt intellectually and imaginatively identified with a community and a region at the same time as he experienced moral revolt against the indigenous political and religious culture with its inherited polarities. 'I have turned to the landscape because men disappoint me,' he wrote in 1949 ('The Ram's Horn', *Collected Poems*, p. 61). His comment on the cultural and ideological isolation of the poet William Allingham in Donegal applies equally to himself: 'he found himself, by his unorthodox theological and political ideas, driven to become even more alone.'[53] Even the natural world involved rejection and unbridge-able difference: the hedgehog, rolled up in a ball as a protection against human presence, epitomized 'the world of things I know and do not know' though the hedgehog was 'a fellow creature native to my sod' ('Hedgehog', *Collected Poems*, p. 86).

The Worldsworthian and regional impulse in Hewitt's poetry, enthusiastically commended in Howard Sergeant's *The Cumberland*

Wordsworth (1950), produced some of his best work, but it did not make him belong. In 'O country people' (1950) he wryly acknowledged the 'high wall' that still separated him from the Antrim hill farmers he had got to know at weekends and in his holidays (*Collected Poems*, p. 69f). The title of his most extended nature-poem 'Conacre' (1943) signals impermanence: it is the term for seasonal letting of land in the Irish land system. With characteristic honesty Hewitt admitted to himself

> You would escape from brick but not too far.
> You want the hill at hand familiar,
> the punctual packet and the telephone,
> that you may not be lonely when alone.
>   (*Collected Poems*, p. 40)

A later, less successful sequence entitled 'Freehold' (1946) largely fails to make good its claim to a more permanent tenure. At best Hewitt can identify and take possession of rare moments outside time and history such as the day in wartime when he visited the apple-growing area of Co. Armagh where the first Irish Hewitts had settled:

> Once walking the country of my kindred
> up the steep road to where the tower-topped mound
> still hoards their bones, that showery August day
> I walked clean out of Europe into peace.[54]

   Philosophically rejecting the refuge or consolation of a transcendental religion, confined to awkward Ireland in the 1940s by the hazards of war, Hewitt looked for hidden peace and vitality in the Ulster countryside and the buried local traditions of dialect verse and Protestant radicalism. The quest for a hidden Ulster as a model for a better future involved conscious distancing from other Irish modes of tradition-making: Hewitt wanted to invent something distinct from Daniel Corkery's eighteenth-century Gaelic Munster or Yeats' aristo-cratic Anglo-Ireland which was different also from the militarist Ulster of the new Unionist mythology, the land of the heroes of the Somme and the generals of England's wars. A cultural tradition partly mediated through Scots-Irish dialect was an effective way of demonstrating differences between potentially radical Ulster and the moribund Anglo-Irish 'Protestant Ascendancy'. Indignantly repudiating J. C. Beckett's formulation 'We Englishmen born in Ireland', Hewitt retorted, 'Call an Ulster Scot an Anglo-Irishman and see what happens.'[55] Samuel Ferguson assumes importance for Hewitt's purposes not as a Celtic revivalist and Yeatsian precursor but as an Ulster poet who could write ballads in the vernacular on Ulster themes and recognized his non-English identity – which Hewitt shared – as 'an Irishman of Ulster Planter stock' ('The course of writing in Ulster', *Ancestral Voices*, p. 60f).

Hewitt's rather lonely quest for a distinct cultural and linguistic tradition within an intimately knowable locality had non-Irish antecedents. The cultural but not political separatism of Mistral and the Félibrige in Provence offered one model. Closer to home there was the radical Scottish revivalism of Lewis Grassic Gibbon and Hugh MacDiarmid typified by their eccentric anthology *Scottish Scene* (1934). There was also the quieter English regionalism of the poet Norman Nicholson, who shared St John Ervine's respect for Arnold Bennett's Five Towns novels as a model for the regional writer.[56] Hewitt's heroic researches into unpromising materials provoked affectionate derision. His brother-poet and critic Roy McFadden invented a poetic ledger-clerk from Aughnacloy, Samuel James Megarrity, who had no idea that he would be posthumously claimed for 'Ulster Literature'.[57] But a more typical figure for Hewitt's Ulster tradition was James Hope, the Presbyterian weaver of Templepatrick, a United Irishman held up to Ulster socialists as an exemplar in the struggle for economic justice, his prose style favourably contrasted with that of the English bourgeois apologist 'marzipan Macaulay' ('James Hope, Weaver, of Templepatrick', *Ancestral Voices*, pp. 133–7).

There are democratic and radical themes (amid much else) in the dialect verse and more conventional work of the artisan poets of place whom Hewitt investigated for his unpublished MA thesis (1951). Generous selections from their work are included in his anthology *Rhyming Weavers* (1974). Though the conservative William McComb, whom Hewitt brusquely dismisses, was probably more popular in his day in Ulster, prominence is given to James Orr of Broadisland, Ballycarry, and James Campbell of Ballynure, both of them United Irishmen in 1798. A little later the Industrial Revolution transformed the textile industry in rural Ulster. Weavers' earnings and status declined sharply. Their verse sounded the note of poverty and Luddite indignation. Hewitt's regionalism, socialism and sense of the poet's public responsibility have their ideal counterpart in this brief historical moment. But soon the 'Rhyming Weavers fell silent/ when they flocked through the factory door' ('A Local Poet', *Time Enough*, p. 36).

Pre-industrial nostalgia and romantic ruralism are forms of escape for the modern urban poet and Hewitt was too puritanical, too honest, to escape for very long. Social conscience, sharpened by the hunger-marching 1930s, would always pull him back to economic realities and contemporary life:

> Then I remembered that the nature-poet
> has no easy prosody for
> class or property relationships,
> for the social dialectic.[58]

The socioeconomic dialectic of the leftist poet in effect reformulates the age-old dialectic confronting the Irish writer, the dialectic of the Planter and the Gael, in that economic relations are partly determined by land distribution which in its turn derives from resented colonial settlement. Hewitt's response to the nativist myth of dispossession is a kind of environmental legitimation, a sense that long-continued settlement on the land brings assimilation to it and a shared identity with even longer-settled peoples weathered and moulded by the same place. In 'The Colony' he sees the planters and colonists from whom he claims descent as Romans in ancient Britain:

> the rain against the lips, the changing light,
> the heavy clay-sucked stride, have altered us;
> we would be strangers in the Capitol;
> this is our country also, nowhere else;
> and we shall not be outcast on the world.
>
> (*Collected Poems*, p. 79)

The obstinate rhythms of rootedness and the truculent tone lay claim to Irish identity in the teeth of particularist Celtic and Catholic nationalism. But Hewitt places too much reliance on the mute eloquence of Ulster landscapes which say more to poets than to politicians. He confessed in 1944 that

> Because I paced my thought by the natural world . . .
> I found myself alone who had hoped for attention.
>
> (*Collected Poems*, p. 47)

The voice of the nature poet needed to be joined by other voices for Hewitt's radicalism to gain a hearing. The scholarly tones of the local art historian and the secular witness derived from identification with the Irish and British traditions of religious dissent imparted colour and urgency to his writing. For many years he worked in the Belfast Museum and Art Gallery and produced pioneering studies such as 'Painting and Sculpture in Ulster' (1951), reprinted in *Ancestral Voices*. The local artist William Conor (1881–1968), whose work is well represented in the Belfast Art Gallery, provided an early and enduring influence, genially presenting the 'pity and the laughter of the poor', the colour and quality of life in the textile mills and the shipyard irradiated by neighbourly cheerfulness, the best self of self-tormenting urban Ulster.[59] Scots, English and Irish elements come together in Hewitt's definition of the 'ideal Ulsterman' (*Ancestral Voices*, p. 8). All three countries contributed to his notion of a composite radical tradition friendly both to 'the people' and to art and letters with which he could identify his own stance. A little detached in his ex-Methodism, he felt able to ignore the more institutional aspects of Ulster Presbyterianism and to select from it the liberal, even radical impulse expressed in the United Irishmen and the nineteenth-century Tenant Right campaigns. In the 1930s, in the intervals of work with the Left Book Club, the Belfast Peace League and the British Civil Liberties Union, he was a frequent speaker at the Sunday afternoon meetings held in York Street Non-Subscribing Presbyterian Church. These meetings, open to all creeds and classes, discussed a wide range of issues in a long-established Presbyterian tradition of free enquiry.[60] Thomas Drennan, father of the poet, had ministered in another Presbyterian church in Belfast where he had inaugurated a rationalist, non-Trinitarian (or 'non-subscribing') tradition which the congregation still honours. William Drennan was admired by Hewitt as much for his radical politics as his poetry. Both Drennans identified with English Dissenters such as Joseph Priestley and this points to a different strand in Hewitt's self-fashioned intellectual pedigree. Radical Dissenters such as the Quaker George Fox, the Digger Gerrard Winstanley, author of *The Law of Freedom* (1652), or the poet and artist William Blake coexist with the Donegal Deist John Toland and more secular radicals such as William Cobbett and William Morris in Hewitt's personal myth. In a late poem, 'Roseblade's Visitants and Mine', these radical champions haunt the poet as ghostly mentors (*Freehold*, p. 34).

Another Irish radical, closer to Hewitt's own time and background, was George Russell ('AE'), poet, painter, economist and prophet, a fellow Ulsterman whose father attended primitive Methodist services in Lurgan. Russell was a mystic and a visionary, which Hewitt was not, but he was also a practical reformer, an active campaigner for agricultural co-operatives. Russell and Hewitt shared a commitment to social justice and a sense of necessary connection between literature and socio-economic realities. For many years Russell had edited the farming paper *The Irish Homestead* (the 'Pigs' Paper'), finding space in it for literature including early work of Joyce. When this passed over into the more ambitious *Irish Statesman* in 1923 literary discussion and new writing were welcomed from the newly separated six northern counties and elsewhere. Hewitt's first published poem, 'Christmas Eve', appeared in *The Irish Statesman* in 1929 and he treasured the badly typed letter of acceptance from AE which warned him to steer clear of the influence of the American poet Vachel Lindsay (*Ancestral Voices*, p. 150).

Lindsay's interests ran parallel to Hewitt's, so the influence was seductive. Like Hewitt, Lindsay had come under the spell of William Morris, with a strong sense of the healing importance of art in the community. His enthusiastic populism was registered in the vigorous rhythms of his poem for the people's champion William Jennings Bryan ('Bryan, Bryan, Bryan, Bryan') and in 'General William Booth Enters into Heaven' (to be sung to the tune of 'The Blood of the Lamb'). Hewitt's 'Christmas Eve' is about the different kinds of Christmas music, the formal harmonies of the celestial orchestra and the heavenly host, encountered in vision in the stillness of a starlit night, and the more democratic drumming of the Salvation Army accompanying 'the hoarse hosanna gospel shout'. Like Lindsay's 'General William Booth' (founder of the Salvation Army), Hewitt's poem reproduces the heavy drum-beats in emphatic stresses, reinforced by alliteration:

> A big boy beat on a thundering drum
> and a thin man screacht of the Kingdom Come,
> and a redfaced man, covered over with braid,
> knelt in the slush, and prayed . . . and prayed . . .[61]

The near-rhyme of 'beat' and 'screacht' signalling a counterpoint of shrill message and resonant accompaniment and the flamboyant juxtaposition of messy slush and gorgeous braid resist easy sympathy but demand attention. Hewitt the secular Protestant, like St John Ervine, was attracted by the social outreach and unstuffy popular appeal of the Salvationists. His respectable grandmother had once scandalized the family by stepping out boldly behind a Salvation Army band, an episode commemorated in a much later poem, 'A Victorian Steps Out' (*Collected Poems*, p. 130). The contrast is not just between the ethereal music of unworldly religion and the crudely vital music of suffering humanity; it is also the contrast of bourgeois refinement and the harsh world of the poor and downtrodden. The Salvation Army and the Orange Order (both inescapable in a Belfast childhood) march to the same stirring rhythms, but this time the shrinking middle-class observer is invited into the celebration.

The poem heralds both the technical competence and the conscientious if willed democratic concern of much of Hewitt's later work. The poet's relations with 'the people', however identified, were always dutiful and difficult even apart from the special problems posed by the people of Ireland. 'Anti-Promethean Ode' (1933), published in *The Listener*, sets out to be a classic statement of 1930s poetic radicalism, urging the lonely intellectual to make common cause with struggling humanity:

> Leave now the crest of thought's high secrecy,
> and the scarce breathable air.

The purpose of poetry, it emerges, is didactic and slightly Methodistical, to encourage men to

> walk kindlier, follow more lasting good,
> and build again ramparts of brotherhood.

Such poetry demands everyday imagery, but the invitation to come down from the mountain-tops to 'fields and habitable places' is curiously unattractive, as if social imperatives and the imagination were uneasy companions. In place of the 'frenzied rhetoric/ of toppling crags and elemental skies' there is only a rather suburban Wordsworthianism forcing undemonstrated connections between accessible nature and the multitude:

> Go back and use your eyes
> on hedgehid speedwell or clipped garden rose,
> on hearts and faces of dull common people.[62]

The difficult adjustment of individual voice to poetic theme is managed more successfully in Hewitt's first important Irish poem, 'Ireland', first published in 1932 and placed at the beginning of the *Collected Poems*. The poetic 'I' and the 'dull common people' of the poet's country are elided into 'We Irish', and divisions between poet and people, planter and Gael, politics and nature are closed over in an angry rhetoric of self-denunciation. Where Berkeley and Yeats after him could use the phrase 'We Irish' with pride and a magnificent disregard for problems raised and questions begged Hewitt uses it to condemn pride and self-imposed problems alike:

> We Irish pride ourselves as patriots . . .
> We Irish vainer than tense Lucifer
> are yet content with half-a-dozen turf,
> and cry our adoration for a bog.

The narrow, divisive myth of Ireland as rural and heroically Celtic had intensified if anything in the aftermath of partition which cut off the six northern counties least conveniently assimilable to the myth. Hewitt, surprisingly, seems to be accepting the myth despite the Ulsterman's sense of non-Celtic distinctiveness:

> We were the keltic wave that broke over Europe
> and ran up this bleak beach among these stones:
> but when the tide ebbed were left stranded here . . .

In fact the myth has been turned against itself. The relatively unfamiliar spelling 'keltic' conforms to the Greek *keltoi* used by Herodotus and others to denote an ancient European people;[63] it bypasses the Latin- and French-derived form 'Celtic' and by extension the French romantic Celticism of Thierry and Renan, De Jubainville and the *Revue Celtique* which lay behind the Irish Celtic Revival. Hewitt proposes an alternative Celtic myth of provincial stagnation: the Celt metonymically stands for the whole Irish population only because he too is an immigrant and settler, type of later (and earlier) immigrants, marooned on an island with which he has no intimate connection at least to begin with. Ireland's geographical position to the far west of Europe places it at the extreme limit of early population movements, uncontaminated but unrefreshed by frequent contact with a wider world, its people sour and bitter, frustrated and self-deceived in their attachment to an unrewarding soil and climate:

We are not native here or anywhere . . .
and what we think is love for usual rock
or old affection for our customary ledge,
is but forgotten longing for the sea
that cries far out and calls us to partake
in his great tidal movements round the earth.

(*Collected Poems*, p. 11f)

There are other, later strategies for momentarily containing fractured
Ireland within a unitary rhetoric. Easygoing Protestant and Catholic
liberals, casually amiable to each other, are harshly condemned, side
by side, as 'coasters', morally accountable for the renewed sectarian
violence of 1969.[64] The parallel of Roman colony and planted Ireland,
to which Hewitt constantly reverts, involves 'civilized' settlers confronting dispossessed 'barbarians'. But just who are the barbarians?
'The Roman Fort' (1971) was prompted by seeing a modern
reconstruction, carried out by soldiers, of the timbered gateway to an
old Roman fort which had protected the Fosse Way against (British)
barbarians. The same soldiers were likely to be sent to Northern
Ireland, a 'beleaguered colony' notorious for its 'stubborn barbarians',
not clearly identified as Protestant or Catholic, planter or Gael, since
none has a monopoly of barbarism or civilized behaviour.[65]

Hewitt is not impervious to the mystique of Celtic Ireland, but he
links Celtic myth, the Irish landscape and Irish prehistory in
idiosyncratic ways. The prominence in Celtic tradition of Finn and
Oisin and the Ulster cycle could hardly be altogether ignored by an
Ulsterman. In fact, the legendary contention between Oisin and
Patrick, heroic paganism and Christian Ireland, preserved in the
Agallamh na Senorach or 'Colloquy of the Ancient Men', is a
convenient parable. Denied promotion in Belfast because of political
and sectarian prejudice (or so he always maintained), Hewitt
eventually moved to Coventry and left behind a 'creed-haunted
Godforsaken race' ('An Irishman in Coventry', *Collected Poems*,
p. 111). Oisin the revenant from the pagan past, 'warrior and bard'
unsubdued by Patrick, is both a model and a challenge for Hewitt. The
old traditions seem irrelevant to Hewitt's modern anxieties, yet Oisin
with his tales of passion and action stands for irreducible true poetry
('Homestead', *Collected Poems*, pp. 64f, 67). According to local
tradition Oisin is buried in Glenaan in the Antrim Glens. While the
standing stones of 'Ossian's Grave' have been assigned by scholars to a
pre-Celtic sun-worshipping people, as Hewitt acknowledges, this does

not matter: a pre-Christian sense of the numinous persists. There is an
interesting parallel with the Scottish regionalist fiction of Lewis
Grassic Gibbon. In *A Scots Quair* (1932–4) it is the mysterious
prehistoric standing stones among the remembered hills of the Mearns
which embody ultimate continuities in a harshly divided society
('Ossian's Grave, Lubitavish, Co. Antrim', *Collected Poems*, p. 106).

Despite the distractions of contemporary Ireland Hewitt the nature
poet is able to identify and respond to the ancient sense of mysterious
virtue and healing in natural things. This was the old faith 'before
Saint Patrick came', documented in the researches of the Belfast-based
geographer E. Estyn Evans.[66]

> The healing well by Rathray's cliff
> that answers to the tide,
> the blessings of the gentle bush
> deep in my pulse abide.
> ('Rite; Lubitavish, Glenaan', *Collected Poems*, p. 87)

The 'gentle bush' is the 'fairy thorn' of Irish folklore. The term 'gentle'
attractively combines 'absence of harshness' with the special Irish
sense of 'enchanted'. In this poem Hewitt's habitual gravity relaxes a
little as he thinks of an older and better Ireland more whimsically
recalled by earlier Ulster poets such as William Allingham (in 'The
Fairies') and Samuel Ferguson (in 'The Fairy Well of Lagnanay'). But
there is a darker aspect to the folklore of the countryside which Hewitt
relates to the anarchic energies of his country in 'The Swathe Uncut'
(1943). Local tradition suggests that the wayward spirit of the corn is
left in the last swathe to be cut and must be ritually slain and 'safely
brought/to some known corner of beneficence' to protect next year's
ploughing and sowing. Ireland itself, 'sundered to the west', can be
seen as the last swathe uncut in modern Europe. The language in
which the analogy is proposed is benign, seemingly an endorsement of
Celtic nationalist intuitions of the ancient freedoms of the Gael
untrammelled by Roman conquest: Ireland is

> the blessed wheat
> wherein still free the gentle creatures go
> instinctively erratic, rash or slow,
> unregimented, never yet possessed.
> (*Collected Poems*, p. 30)

But the context, and the larger context of the sceptical, rational, non-Celtic tradition with which Hewitt identifies himself, yield ironies beneath the bland surface. The spirit of the corn is both goddess and vulnerable fugitive, a lively free spirit and a threat to the future. The wayward fancy of the poet can celebrate what the poet in his more responsible aspect must sternly repudiate, ritually put to death and place under social discipline. The discipline of Hewitt's regular, rhymed iambic verse contains the anarchic energies of instinct and 'erratic', 'unregimented' creatures: the harmlessness of 'gentle' could conceal the social danger associated with irresponsible magic of 'gentle' in its Irish sense. 'Rash' and 'slow' could be indulgent towards a precarious vitality, or progressively intolerant of atavistic recklessness. The rationalist reformism of Carleton's largely secular Protestantism in tension with the older Ireland of his childhood is delicately reproduced in the ambiguities of the poem.

Hewitt's imaginative sympathy with an older Ireland, however circumscribed by progressive and iconoclastic rationalism, gives emotional authority to his characteristic refrain 'I am of the Irishry/ by nurture and by birth' ('Rite; Lubitavish, Glenaan', *Collected Poems*, p. 87), his obstinate, truculent response to the old-fashioned racial exclusiveness of unreconstructed Celtic nationalism. Human as well as natural sympathy with the life of the land is another way of spanning differences and acquiring that ultimate, elusive sense of belonging to which Hewitt and most Ulster Protestants defensively lay claim in the face of aggressive Catholic nationalism. When Hewitt's great-grandmother died of the 'famine fever', catching the infection after helping a starving man who had travelled all the way from the 'stricken west', that fatal gesture of solidarity 'Conscribed me of the Irishry forever'.[67] 'Irishry' was the often contemptuous term used for recalcitrant natives or 'Wilde Irish' at the time of the sixteenth- and seventeenth-century plantations but the poet of planter stock is glad, even anxious, to claim the label. The younger poet, in 'Conacre', had tentatively commented,

> This is my home and country. Later on
> perhaps I'll find this nation is my own
> (*Collected Poems*, p. 41)

The older poet, thinking of his great-grandmother, responded a little over-eagerly that 'in that woman's death I found my nation' ('The Scar', *Out of My Time*, p. 40).

But it is as a nature poet rooted in a particular landscape rather than as a slightly defensive humanitarian burdened by history that Hewitt is most successfully an Irish poet. His most ambitious attempt to combine these different modes is an early dramatic poem, *The Bloody Brae*. This was written in 1936, broadcast as a radio play in 1954, performed by the Lyric Players in Belfast in 1957 and first published in the same year. It is another lay-sermon, a 'plea for tolerance' which Hewitt near the end of his life felt was 'still valid after nearly 50 years'.[68] Appropriately, it draws on Ireland's different literary traditions, local, national and metropolitan. Like Austin Clarke, Yeats's successor in developing the Irish verse-drama, Hewitt had been interested in the now-forgotten historical verse-dramas of the 'Georgian' poet Gordon Bottomley. He tried to domesticate the form to accommodate a persistent Co. Antrim legend about sectarian murder at the Gobbins, on the coast at Islandmagee, during the 1641 rebellion. There seems to be little historical foundation for the story, though the present writer's father recalls hearing it from his grandmother. But the bitterly divisive heritage of the seventeenth century which the legend encapsulates has come down to Catholics and Protestants in Ulster and in Ireland as a whole.

The play is set in the early eighteenth century and opens with talk of ghosts on a bare roadside above a cliff. A solitary old man, John Hill, is overheard in conversation with the ghost of Malcolm Scott, his comrade in the grim times of the 1640s. On a wild night, seventy years before, acting under orders as troopers, Hill and Scott drove some harmless Catholic women over the cliff to their deaths. Hill is guiltily aware that one of them was a neighbour, Bridget Magee, and that her baby perished with her. The Magees had worked the land alongside the fields where Hill and his planter father and grandfather had lived and laboured and become Irish. Scott is unrepentant, but Hill passionately regrets the mercy and pity he withheld and wants to meet the ghost of Brigid Magee to ask her pardon. She comes and she forgives him, but urges him to abandon his solitude and preach reconciliation to all he meets, a challenge from which he shrinks.

The strengths of the play are in its concreteness which refuses to allow the nightmare and the healing of the past to be disengaged from present realities. The eerie atmosphere and the frightening noises of the night are reduced to the precision of

> the heifers nosing the bushes, the soughing trees,
> the round stone falling with a spatter of mould.

Ancestral ghosts themselves are rendered familiar as precursors in the business of farming in a particular place, spirits whose presence lingers and enriches the earth to which they gave 'the shape and pattern of use, of sowing and harvest'. Whin bushes and jagging thorns by the roadside help to connect a painful past with an actualized present. Sharp speech unevenly sprinkled with dialect forms gives some local reality and dramatic life to the formal moral dialectic of hatred and mercy:

> Mercy's gone done and fellowship's flung in the sheugh,
> and every time he rises he's dunted back.
>
> (Freehold, pp. 49, 50, 58)

The strongly realized sense of place has survived catastrophe and seventy years and will endure. But there is a desperate, unstable tension and fragility about the reconciliation of murderer and victim, both withdrawn from their society, both holding back from full accord, which Hewitt does not dare to resolve into either sentimental harmony or renewed tragedy.

A different kind of reconciliation, a sense of harmony with past and present and with Ireland itself, is glimpsed in the sharp precision of Hewitt's best nature poetry, tautly constrained by conservative verse-forms. Some of the best moments of 'Conacre' are sudden disclosures of colour, light and texture. The city does not thrill the poet's senses,

> whereas the heathered shoulder of a hill,
> a quick cloud on the meadow, wind-lashed corn,
> black wrinkled haws, grey tufted wool on thorn,
> the high lark singing, the retreating sea –
> these stab the heart with sharp humility. . .
>
> (Collected Poems, p. 34f)

Such keen intimations of natural beauty disturbed the labours of the ancient Irish monastic scribes and moved them to terse 'glosses' or occasional poems in the margins of their manuscripts. Hewitt is linked with them and with Ireland in a kindred responsiveness. Thomas Kinsella, poet and translator deeply committed to the Gaelic tradition from which Hewitt seems remote, has translated some of the best of these glosses and has demonstrated in his own poems, such as 'Wyncote, Pennsylvania: A Gloss', how that particular mode of consciousness can persist.[69] Hewitt takes an early Irish 'gloss', which includes the first known literary allusion to Belfast Lough, and by disregarding the metrical and phonetic structure of the original he brilliantly condenses it into the seventeen syllables of a Japanese haiku:

> Across Loch Laig
> the yellow-billed blackbird
> whistles from the blossomed whin.
> ('Gloss: On the Difficulties of Translation', *Out of My Time*, p. 19)

Seamus Heaney, another poet of the land moulded by different Irish traditions, quoted the same poem (apparently in his own translation) in a broadcast talk on Irish nature poetry and noted Hewitt's haiku comparison with approval.[70] John Montague, another poet who would claim to be more Gael than Planter, translated it for his *Faber Book of Irish Verse* (1974). Many years earlier Frank O'Connor included it among his translations from the Irish prepared with Yeats at his elbow.[71] But Hewitt is less moved by solidarity with Irish poets than by the connection with his native place. The Irish language is no longer the language of Hewitt's region. But the physical features of the land persist, and in place of Kinsella's brooding sense of 'gapped' tradition and discontinuity Hewitt can acknowledge the difficulties of translation but still find a regional idiom which responds to and identifies the images without letting them escape into conventional metropolitan poetic diction. If he were a straightforward English poet,

> I should
> have to substitute
> *golden* for *yellow*
> and *gorse* for *whin*,
> this last is the word we use
> on both sides of Belfast Loch.
> (*Out of My Time*, p. 19)

The 'we' signals the unity and identity which Hewitt has always sought in his native place. Though 'whin' appears in the *Oxford English Dictionary* it is more common in northern, Scottish and Scots-influenced Ulster usage. In the *Scottish National Dictionary* (1931–76), itself a symptom of the growing regionalist consciousness which Hewitt tried to promote in Ulster, there is a lengthy entry on 'whin'. This includes examples from the Co. Down historical fiction of W. G. Little, dwelling on the United Irishmen and the stirring times of 1798 to which Hewitt himself often returned in imagination. The different peoples of Ulster with their divided history, the country people of the Glens of Antrim, the prosperous businessmen living along the Co. Down shore of Belfast Lough, the Catholics and the Protestants, the Gaels and the Planters, now have the same word and always had the same rich yellow blossom. For Hewitt it was at least a beginning.

SEAMUS HEANEY (1939–   )

The land that grows whins links Hewitt with Seamus Heaney. Heaney's first collection, *Death of a Naturalist* (1966), drew an enthusiastic welcome from Hewitt in the *Belfast Telegraph*. He praised Heaney as an 'authentic countryman' who could find energetic language and concrete imagery for the objects and processes of the farm but imaginatively reached beyond them. Hewitt did not expect Heaney to stay with the land. But in and around the occasional poems, the elegies and sophisticated parables of Heaney's latest collection *The Haw Lantern* (1987) there are still 'briars coiled in ditches', 'Hard green plums' and 'the flanks of milking cows'. Heaney's poetic development and his developing sense of relationship with the traditions of writing available to the Irish poet have brought different perspectives upon the same places. Some early poems had drawn attention to the famine, the supreme crisis in the tangled history of the land, and it was through contact with Ireland's vexed history that Hewitt thought Heaney might 'broaden his range and our imaginative state'.[72]

Heaney's later poems have indeed grappled variously and often indirectly with the complex heritage of the poet and his country, but this has only been part of the story. For Heaney's concern has been the pursuit of poetry itself. There is no Catholic tradition of lay-preaching, and in all his sophisticated negotiations of his identity as Irish Catholic and English poet in British Ulster Heaney's humanitarian decency has not lured or inspired him to the lay sermons and calls to righteousness which are sometimes too near the surface in Hewitt's work. Heaney pays tribute to Hewitt for achieving 'the kind of authority without dogma that poets stand for',[73] which is at least partly true, but this reflects Heaney's poetic objectives rather than Hewitt's.

This poetic difference further complicates the differences of generation and community separating the two men. There are also differences of temperament and outlook between the isolated art-gallery man and literary archaeologist and the more gregarious teacher of English and professional writer early encouraged in the craft of verse by Philip Hobsbaum and the Belfast university wits he gathered round him.[74] But there are points of contact which have to do with shared territory and a parallel though different engagement with both English and Irish writing. Both admired the Belfast painter Colin Middleton, and Heaney's early poem 'In small townlands' is a bold attempt to reproduce Middleton's idiosyncratic way of seeing local landscape (see Plate 5).[75] Later on, Middleton provided the illustrations for Heaney's translation *Sweeney Astray*. Both poets have responded to the richness of local speech and country crafts and traditions. The Catholic inheriting nationalist traditions is aware of the hostile pressure of Protestant and Unionist attitudes which would marginalize him in Ulster just as the secular Protestant of planter stock is on the defensive against the more extreme nationalists who might question his credentials as an Irishman. Each is aware of a violent heritage. Each appropriates from Wordsworth, or Robert Frost, or Yeats, poetic strategies for confronting and affirming identity.

Heaney is more literary and more securely Irish than Hewitt. Hewitt left Belfast for a civic post in Coventry; Heaney left it to write poetry in Wicklow and Dublin. Hewitt had admired the poetry Robert Frost wrote about New England: Ulster and New England were both once British colonies where settlers had to come to terms with an unfamiliar territory (*Ancestral Voices*, p. 121). But Heaney the Catholic farmer's son, native rather than colonist, had no need to talk his way into relationship with the land: for better or worse, his traditions were deeply rooted in it. For him Frost indicated a way of seeing rather than a way of belonging. Some of the early poems in *Death of a Naturalist* may have been suggested by important moments in Frost's work. 'After apple-picking' in *North of Boston* (1914) contributes to Heaney's 'Blackberry-picking' an almost surreal clarity of visual perception and remembered sensation. But where Frost's verse is spare Heaney allows his poem to be invaded and overcrowded with colour, taste and texture, preparing not for Frost's haunted sleep after apple-picking but for a recurring dismay as the berries rotted and the glutted senses found 'A rat-grey fungus, glutting in our cache' (*Death of a Naturalist*, p. 20).

Both Frost and Heaney liked looking into wells, seeking more than a reflection. But Frost's 'For once then, something' in *New Hampshire* (1923) is limited, precise and occasional, registering a glimpse of something white beyond the reflection, where Heaney's 'Personal Helicon' is habitual and elegiac, constructing out of different occasions a poetic sensibility, responsive to darkness and damp smells, which has persisted at the level of imagination beyond immediate sensation. The passage from sensation to recollection and reverie, the sense of distance from vividly remembered natural scenes, signals both the 'Death of a Naturalist' of Heaney's title and the Wordsworthian matrix of much of his poetry of the land. The allegiance is half-ironically acknowledged in an epigraph from *The Prelude* set at the head of the later poem 'Singing School', Heaney's study of the growth of an Ulster Catholic poet's mind in a sectarian but not overtly violent society. Wordsworth's lines apply quite neatly to a rural Ulster childhood in the 1940s and 1950s:

> Fair seedtime had my soul, and I grew up
> Fostered alike by beauty and by fear:
> Much favoured in my birthplace . . .[76]

Early in the 1960s, when Heaney was teaching English in a school and starting to write the poems published in *Death of a Naturalist*, he also contemplated a postgraduate thesis on Wordsworth's educational ideas.[77] The fear as well as the beauty of Wordsworth's formative years was important to Heaney, particularly in the title-poem of *Death of a Naturalist*. But as Nicholas Roe has argued,[78] the poet is not released from his fears by any integrative or redemptive strategy of the kind Wordsworth absorbed from Milton and protestant theology. In Heaney and Heaney's Ireland the horrors do not go away. The sickening, threatening frogs or 'slime kings' seem to have little connection with 'the warm thick slobber/ Of frogspawn that grew like clotted water' in the festering flax-dam. The process of decay attracts a language of unnatural relish and celebration ('Bubbles gargled delicately, bluebottles/ Wove a strong gauze of sound around the smell') unassimilable to the shrinking horror with which the poem ends (p. 15f).

The onomatopoeic 'slap' and 'plop' of the frogs, and the consonantal densities and phonetic self-consciousness characteristic of Heaney's verse, can be attributed to (or blamed on) the influence of Hopkins. The early commitment to a 'subject-matter that is rural, ungenteel and treated with force'[79] can be attributed to the influence of Ted Hughes. The whole enterprise of *Death of a Naturalist* can be attributed to the inspiration of Patrick Kavanagh who taught Heaney that Irish poetry could be made out of the apparently unremarkable acres of home. But Heaney's work builds upon and goes beyond all these early influences as it creatively incorporates and exploits aspects of other writers, Joyce, Dante, Osip Mandlestam and Czeslaw Milosz among them. In his best work external influences, the pressures of literary traditions, the pressures of contemporary violence in Ulster, facilitate rather than confine the poetry, encouraging intuitive access not to wisdom or peace, necessarily, but to disturbing, atavistic energies which can be too easily identified with the totality of the Irish experience.

The sometimes misguided praise heaped upon Heaney, particularly after the publication of *North* (1975), testifies to the danger as well as the power of his work. He is not, and was not meant to be, Ireland's national poet. Robert Lowell, who should have known better, welcomed 'a new kind of political poetry by the best Irish poet since W. B. Yeats'.[80] But the implied senatorial status and lordly authority is more a temptation than an attitude. Heaney's search for 'images and symbols adequate to our predicament' (*Preoccupations*, p. 56) has not achieved or even attempted transcendence of that predicament. It has drawn him away from Burke, Berkeley and Byzantium, down into the bog which has become for him a kind of Irish collective unconscious, a sometimes dark and vicious place.

Born near Castledawson but outside the walls of the Chichester–Clarke demesne (home of a future Unionist Prime Minister), Heaney has always measured his distance not merely from Protestant Unionism but from the accents and attitudes of Yeatsian Anglo-Ireland. He is both more democratic and more sectarian. A guest in alien, mellow Gloucestershire, remote from the 'scraggy farm and moss' of his birthplace, he feels, 'I might as well be in Coole Park'.[81] The old-fashioned elegance of Anglo-Irish discourse is exuberantly challenged by the farm-boy who

> innovated a South Derry rhyme
> With *hushed* and *lulled* full chimes for *pushed* and *pulled*.
> Those hobnailed boots from beyond the mountain
> Were walking, by God, all over the fine
> Lawns of elocution.

> ('Singing School', *North*, p. 64)

The implied disrespect to caste and privilege belongs to what Heaney called 'the slightly aggravated young Catholic male' aspect of

·rament rather than the private rural sensibility distilled into well-made poems.[82] Heaney's early journalism for the *New n*, reviewing books on progressive education and folklore, g the liberal atmosphere of the newly vigorous cultural life of keeps the aggravated Catholic in check without suppressing ıl causes of aggravation such as Orange marches and the rise ısley and his *Protestant Telegraph*. But two years later the ırbances and resentments which accompanied the civil rights ·t increased his sense of aggravation and solidarity with his ıle, Ulster's Catholic minority.[84] In 'The Unacknowledged ˍgıslator's Dream' in *North*, Heaney self-mockingly acknowledges the temptation to be Red Shelley, to pursue revolutionary fantasies of liberation, swinging into the Bastille like Tarzan ('My wronged people cheer from their cages', *North*, p. 56).

This mild sectarian inflammation leads to imaginative polarization. Non-Catholic Ulster is resented rather than fully explored in Heaney's Ulster Poetry. It manifests itself mainly in the unattractive form of Orange extremism, as in the early poem 'Docker' (*Death of a Naturalist*, p. 41). The patriarchal Protestant neighbour in 'The Other Side' is different, but his Bible-steeped discourse, 'that tongue of chosen people', hints at obnoxious privilege in the hinterland of social decency. There is no easy intercourse and no common language except talk of the weather and the price of grass-seed.[85]

But Heaney himself has broad literary sympathies. The Tyrone dialect-verse of Rev. W. F. Marshall (1888–1959), novelist and historian of Presbyterian Ulster, enjoyed enormous local popularity and still does. As a child Heaney could recite Marshall's 'Me an' me Da'.[86] Despite religious differences, Marshall's world of muddy townlands and poor farms is recognizably Heaney's own. The ill-treated farm girl in Marshall's ballad of 'Sarah Ann' who shouted 'I wunthered [wintered] in wee Robert's, I can summer anywhere' lies behind Heaney's poem 'Servant Boy' and his title *Wintering Out*: like Heaney himself at the time, the boy is 'wintering out/ the back-end of a bad year' (*Wintering Out*, p. 17).[87] Occasionally, Heaney imaginatively incorporates the Calvinist rigour and the dour purposefulness of the Ulster Scot, qualities which have often found expression in engineering triumphs and the world of ships and ship-building with which St John Ervine engages. In Conrad's novella *Typhoon* (1903) the unlikely hero of the storm is the steadfast unimaginative Captain MacWhirr from Belfast. In Heaney's 'Holding Course', a tender poem about the renewal and resilience of love, Heaney entreats

Think of me as your MacWhirr of the boudoir,
Head on, one track, ignorant of manoeuvre.[88]

A granite chip from Joyce's Martello Tower stands for some of the same qualities in 'Shelf Life': it is an 'Aberdeen of the mind', 'a Calvin edge in my complaisant pith'.[89]

But Heaney ranges beyond sectarian imaginative allegiances largely through topography and the phonetic resources of poetic language. He learnt Irish at school and Anglo-Saxon at university and relishes the sounds and poetic idiom of both languages. In a piece of whimsy tailor-made for the *Guardian* Heaney once wrote, 'I think of the personal and Irish pieties as vowels, and the literary awareness nourished on English as consonants' ('Belfast', *Preoccupations*, p. 37). Consonants cut off and limit vowel sounds but they also make them into syllables and speech. Ulster dialect speech is particularly given to stressing the harsher consonants (especially *k*), and the intricate vowel-patterns of traditional Gaelic poetry have long given way in Irish verse to the English rhythms which once depended, in Anglo-Saxon poetry, on alliterating consonants. Heaney's conceit of the complementariness of imaginative substance and poetic expression yields up a partly unconscious political and racial tension:

> Our guttural muse
> was bulled long ago
> by the alliterative tradition . . .
> ('Traditions', *Wintering Out*, p. 31)

But where Kinsella and Montague are disposed to bitterness and regret for a lost culture among the bare fields and ancient place-names of the Irish countryside Heaney revels in the vowel-music of 'Moyola', a river name which is almost onomatopoeic, and the rich sounds of 'Toome', 'Broagh', 'Derrygarvey'. He responds also to the consonants of English speech prominent in some planter names like 'Castledawson', with its hard initial letter, imparting form and limitation, almost a metaphor of 'ascendancy'. Both vowels and consonants are needed to let the historically moulded Irish landscape speak itself ('A New Song', *Wintering Out*, p. 33).

The different strains of Irishness congregate in the Boyne valley, which contains the site of pre-Celtic decorated passage-graves at Newgrange. Later the place became the numinous burying-place of the Dagdae in Celtic myth. Later still the area became a hallowed place for Orangemen because of King William's famous victory in 1690. In

'Funeral Rites', in *North*, Heaney tries to impart dignity to the daily
horror of 'neighbourly murder' by imagining a great funeral procession
assembling from all over the country, culminating in a ceremonial
burial in 'the great chambers of the Boyne' which will unite the dead
with the immemorial Irish past (*North*, p. 16f). Something of the same
idea lies behind 'In Memoriam Francis Ledwidge'. Ledwidge was a
Catholic poet who came from the Boyne valley and died in Britain's
cause in the first world war despite his sympathy for the cause of Irish
nationalism. For Heaney he is 'our dead enigma', representing the
continuing paradoxes of partly British Ireland, marching to war 'from
Boyne water' but no Orangeman, 'Though all of you consort now
underground'.[90]

In life, if not in death, there are still divisions, and Heaney
constantly returns to them. The Protestant revolutionary Wolfe Tone
is seen as remote from the people he wanted to lead, Heaney's people.
Heaney makes him say

> I affected epaulettes and a cockade,
> wrote a style well-bred and impervious
> to the solidarity I angled for,
> and played the ancient Roman with a razor.
> ('Wolfe Tone', *Haw Lantern*, p. 44)

Paradoxically there is no unity among Irishmen in their perception of
the United Irishmen. Broadly speaking there are two traditions, a
northern and Protestant one, favoured by Protestant liberals such as
John Hewitt, and a southern and Catholic one favoured by Heaney
which responds to the different, more sectarian nature of the military
campaign outside Ulster. Heaney's friend Thomas Flanagan, the
Irish-American scholar-critic and novelist, has enshrined the southern
tradition in his novel *The Year of the French* (1979) in which the action
does not extend to Ulster. But Heaney is aware of the northern
tradition as well. A print of High Street, Belfast, in 1786 is poetically
recreated in terse lines: 'The edged gloom of arcades' frames a scene
not yet darkened by the disasters of 1798; liberal and radical hope still
flourishes. Persistent alliteration on hard *t* as well as liquid *l* and the
sharp smell of salt water penetrate the period-piece with an unexpected
crisp regret:

> It's twenty to four
> On one of the last afternoons
> Of reasonable light.

PLATE 5   Colin Middleton, *September Evening, Ballymote* (see p. 242)

Smell the tidal Lagan:
Take a last turn
In the tang of possibility.
('Linen Town', *Wintering Out*,
p. 38)

But poem and possibility are frail and delicate by comparison with
'Requiem for the Croppies', written in 1966 in indirect commemoration
of the 1916 Easter Rising (*Preoccupations*, p. 56). The rebels carried
barley in their pockets to eat on the march, and the summer after they
were mown down at Vinegar Hill the barley sprouted. Heaney sees in
this renewal a powerful metaphor for the persistent renewals of armed
struggle for Irish nationhood, including the apparently disastrous
Easter Rising. The poem begins with loose, fragmented syntax and
rhythms disturbed out of iambic regularity to register the desperate,
improvised movements of the doomed insurgents: 'We moved quick
and sudden in our own country.' The phrase 'in our own country',
emphatic at the end of the line, is covertly resentful: retreat is easier
over familiar territory, but why should people be hounded by superior
military force in their own country? Spare diction and verse-form
impose pattern and authority and a terrible poetic logic on the
confusion. The poem discloses itself as a formally rhymed sonnet, its
final image defying the emphatic rhyme-word 'grave':

The hillside blushed, soaked in our broken wave.
They buried us without shroud or coffin
And in August the barley grew up out of the grave.[91]

Whatever the disaster the blood-soaked land itself is vital and
indomitable. As Tertullian had said, 'The more ye mow us down, the
more we grow.'[92] Heaney, like Thomas Moore and all poets of Irish
insurgency, knew that the blood of the martyrs was the seed of the
church. Patrick Pearse's powerful and appalling rhetoric of blood-
sacrifice warming the heart of the earth is not too far away.

Even before the renewal of sectarian violence in Ulster Heaney had
located a dangerously potent idiom of romantic irrationalism. In his
early poetry poets, water-diviners, trench-digging farmers and potato-
gatherers share an intuitive, sometimes quasi-sexual and procreative
relationship with the wet earth and the Irish bogs, layered with
history: the bitterness and pain involved in that intimacy is made
explicit in 'At a potato digging'. The freshly dug potatoes are 'live

skulls, blind-eyed': the harshly contrived metaphor signals a rather laboured cinematic transition as the image resolves into actual skulls, the present dissolves into the haunting past of the Irish potato famine. The 'Wicker creels' and 'higgeldy lines' of the modern potato-pickers become the 'higgledy skeletons' and 'wicker huts' of starving Irishmen. The fruitful earth, ritually honoured by kneeling, grateful labourers, changes from 'the black/ Mother' to 'the bitch earth' and finally 'the faithless ground' (*Death of a Naturalist*, pp. 31–3).

The faithless ground was soon the setting for renewed violence. In 1969, at the beginning of the Ulster troubles, the Danish archaeologist P. V. Glob's book *The Bog People* became available in English translation. Heaney was fascinated. He had found a new way of approaching the violence and the dark gods of his native place. Connections between Danish bogs and Irish bogs were not too difficult to establish. Though Glob concentrated on the discovery of well-preserved bodies in the bogs of central Justland he also referred to similar discoveries elsewhere, including an Irish one which lies behind Heaney's poem 'Bog Queen' (*North*, p. 32). Some of the bodies seemed to have been ritually sacrificed. 'Tollund man', found with a rope still found his neck, may have been buried as bridgegroom to the powerful fertility goddess Nerthus. Nerthus is glossed as 'Earth Mother' ('Terra Mater) by Tacitus,[93] and the name may be of Celtic origin: Welsh *nerth* and Irish *neart* both denote 'strength' or 'power'. More to the point, perhaps, and more grimly, sectarian killings in rural Ulster could be seen to resemble ritual killings in central Jutland two thousand years before. Heaney began his poem 'The Tollund Man' with the cheerful tourist's ambition: 'Some day I will go to Aarhus', but concluded more bleakly:

> Out there in Jutland
> In the old man-killing parishes
> I will feel lost,
> Unhappy and at home.
> (*Wintering Out*, p. 47f)

The parish which inspired Patrick Kavanagh to poetic vision is darkened with history and murder.

Heaney tries to contain this unhappy and uncomfortable insight within a framework balancing light and dark, rational and atavistic impulses. The poems 'Antaeus' and 'Antaeus and Hercules' which begin and end the first section of *North* seem at first to be naive homage to Yeats and the Celtic Revival. As Yeats had said,

John Synge, I and Augusta Gregory, thought
All that we did, all that we said or sang
Must come from contact with the soil, from that
Contact everything Antaeus-like grew strong.[94]

But Heaney had already observed that contemporary Irish writers
were wary of sticking too close to the soil and the peasantry: it was an
invitation to be patronized.[95] Antaeus, son of Poseidon and Earth, lost
his strength when 'Sky-born' Hercules lifted him clear of the ground,
defeating 'black powers/ feeding off the territory' and leaving only
dreams of loss, subject-matter for elegists and 'pap for the dispossessed'.
Hercules is the dispossessor, the rational, modernizing, colonizing
presence, but the poem accepts his triumph and has little tenderness
for what he has overthrown. It was time to grow up: 'Antaeus, the
mould-hugger,/ is weaned at last' ('Hercules and Antaeus', *North*,
p. 52f). But the imagination still lags behind modern consiousness.
   The dark, disturbing atavisms associated with the earth, released
into consciousness by the Danish bog-people, can be related to the
whole sweep of Irish history. The Viking god Njǫrd, important to
seafarers, represented a later, attenuated version of Nerthus. Viking
Ireland, ignored by Celtic Revivalists but artistically exploited by
Joyce, furnished Heaney with more images of beauty and endemic
violence, sometimes fastened to Ulster placenames like Strangford and
Carlingford, 'Strang and Carling fjords' ('Funeral Rites', *North*,
p. 17). Heaney's appeal to the Vikings seems to echo the young artist
Stephen Dedalus's appeal to the mythic Dedalus, 'Old father, old
artificer':

> Old fathers, be with us.
> Old cunning assessors
> of feuds and of sites
> for ambush or town.
('Viking Dublin: Trial Pieces', *North*, p. 24)

Sixteenth-century colonizing rapacity, seventeenth-century strife, the
Act of Union with England, the proud aggressive masculinity of
contemporary Ulster protestantism, the casualties of the 'troubles', can
all be linked with the boggy Irish landscape penetrated, if not
necessarily violated, by imperial England. The poem 'Ocean's love to
Ireland', overloaded with significance, starts from Sir Walter Ralegh's
urgent sexual possession of a court lady, described by John Aubrey,

but makes this a metaphor for the possession and ruin of Ireland, disappointed both by her poets and by Spain (*North*, p. 46f).

Heaney's voyeuristic excesses in *North* extend to imaginative complicity with endemic violence and 'tribal, intimate revenge' ('Punishment', *North*, p. 38) and metaphorical indulgence of a debased male sexuality. The reader has some sympathy with the Ulster poet Ciarán Carson's harsh verdict on Heaney: 'an anthropologist of ritual violence'.[96] Heaney was unhappy himself about the relations between poetry and strife. 'Exposure', the last poem in *North*, is an uneasy meditation on poetic responsibility. Heaney had already moved from Belfast to Wicklow after 'wintering out' in the midst of the Ulster troubles. His sense of himself as an 'inner emigré', weighing his 'responsible *tristia*', may reach back to Ovid on the coast of the Black Sea, at odds with imperial Rome, but it probably relates also to the disaffection of Russian poets such as Osip Mandelstam whose poems of exile were also given the title of *Tristia*.[97] It is easy to make too much of the move to Wicklow, to link it with the grander exiles of Joyce or Dante. But Heaney has decamped voluntarily. He sees himself, surrounded by dripping trees, as a 'wood-kerne/ Escaped from the massacre', escaped from the polarizing demands of the 'troubles' upon members of the Ulster Catholic community: 'I am neither internee nor informer' (*North*, p. 72f). But he still affirms a tribal identity: he may have been influenced by John Montague's *The Rough Field*, illustrated with woodcuts from John Derricke's *A Discovery of Woodkerne* (1581), which laces embittered meditation on the situation of the disadvantaged Ulster Catholic with fragments from the harsh past, including the barbarous Elizabethan wars when the great Hugh O'Neill was defeated:

> A messenger from the Pale
> Found the hunted rebel
> Living, like a wood kerne,
> In the water meadows near
> His broken coronation stone.[98]

Heaney had praised Montague's celebration of 'tribal consciousness'[99] but there is a wilful naiveté about his own gesture towards the wood-kerne and his tribe: wood-kernes on the run could not write much poetry.

Heaney's later poetry can be seen as a sustained effort of adjustment to the potentially conflicting challenges of Ireland and poetry. The

'Glanmore Sonnets' included in *Field Work* were also published separately under the title *Hedge School*, suggesting both learning from nature, perfecting 'A voice caught back off slug-horn and slow chanter' ('Glanmore Sonnets' 2, Field Work, p. 34), and the disadvantaged schooling of the Irish poor. For the modern Irish nature poet, nature has to adapt itself to elegy and pain. Heaney's second cousin Colum McCartney, victim of a random sectarian shooting in 1975, brought Heaney's imagination back to 'The lowland clays and waters of Lough Beg', close to Heaney's birthplace, where he and his cousin had walked together in the mist and dew of early morning ('The Strand at Lough Beg', *Field Work*, p. 17). The poem and the bereavement haunted Heaney. Eventually, in the ghostly sequence 'Station Island', he faced his cousin's shade and heard him – made him – say that the poet had ' "whitewashed ugliness" ' and ' "saccharined my death with morning dew" ' (*Station Island*, p. 83).

The poet was less than fair to himself. His best elegies are neither sentimental nor gruesome. They explore a changed mode of consciousness of the withdrawn presence, living now only in memory and imagination. He writes about his mother's death:

> The space we stood around had been emptied
> Into us to keep, it penetrated
> Clearances that suddenly stood open.
> ('Clearances', *Haw Lantern*, p. 31)

Unlike Kinsella in his notorious and deliberately tasteless 'Butcher's Dozen', Heaney does not directly confront the horror and anger of Derry's Bloody Sunday. But in the aftermath a pub bombing took the life of a friend of his, a fisherman who

> drank like a fish
> Nightly, naturally
> Swimming towards the lure
> Of warm lit-up places . . .

'Casualty' begins and ends by recreating the man rather than his senseless death. Heaney had been out in his boat and 'I tasted freedom with him' (*Field Work*, p. 23f). The elegies for Robert Lowell, the musician Sean O'Riada, the murdered social-worker Sean Armstrong, are celebrations of creative life and achievement. Death has no dominion.

In among the dripping trees and varied light of the Wicklow countryside, the poetry of *Field Work* reaches toward harmony and peace, but the resolution is personal and literary rather than directly political. The achieved love celebrated in the last of the 'Glanmore Sonnets' emerges through a dream which mingles memory and the moss of Donegal with Shakespearian and Celtic lovers and Wyatt's love-lyric 'They flee from me who sometime did me seek' which itself passes from the dream to the reality of love. In 'The Harvest Bow' memory and art, the art which plaited the harvest bow and the poet's art, weave images which signify beyond language and silence and justify the quotation from Coventry Patmore, 'The end of art is peace' (*Field Work*, p. 58). Heaney had found his quotation in Yeats' *Explorations* and used it again as his epigraph for his prose-collection *Preoccupations*.

Dante is perhaps the supreme poet of peace and love, but the *Inferno* and the *Purgatorio* come before the *Paradiso*. Before rising to heaven the poetry engages with the bitterness, division and pain of history, including the recent Florentine history in which Dante himself had acted and suffered. One of the most horrible episodes of the *Inferno* is the discovery of Ugolino gnawing at the head of Archbishop Roger and Ugolino's story of betrayal, imprisonment, starvation and cannibalism. Even Ireland could hardly compete with the horror. Heaney translates this tale at the end of *Field Work*. It is an introduction to his own *Purgatorio*, a series of disquieting confrontations with his own personal and literary antecedents, set at St Patrick's Purgatory on Station Island in Lough Derg. The ambitious aping of Dante is sustained into intermittent approximations to Dante's *terza rima*, though Heaney still clings to informal speech rhythms and his less demanding rhymes (aba cdc to Dante's aba bcb), sensitive to the different phonetic structure of English, somehow disclose a less ordered, more atomistic culture.

Order and freedom are in tension in the *Station Island* collection. The third section, after the actual 'Station Island' sequence, is entitled 'Sweeney Redivivus'. Dante and Sweeney, the sober religious poet and the mad king cursed by St Ronan, driven to fly away over the mountains, can be seen as opposite poles of poetic possibility. There are allusions to both in the same poem, 'The Strand at Lough Beg', in *Field Work* (p. 17). Slightly mischievously, Heaney makes Sweeney a prototype of Stephen Dedalus, a figure of the displaced artist quarrelling with the constraints of religion, politics and domestic life. Even more mischievously, but instructively, Heaney also notes

Sweeney's Ulster origins but easy affinities with both western Scotland and southern Ireland and observes that the whole story may have a British original.[100]

The tension between Dante and Sweeney, responsibility and the free creative imagination, surfaces in 'Station Island' itself. Heaney's visitants include family, clergy, representatives of local and tribal ties on the one hand and artists such as Joyce on the other, not to mention a mysterious free spirit and Sabbath-breaker called Simon Sweeney. Other poems in the same volume approach the same dilemma. In 'Away from it All' the lobster forked out of the tank, out of its element but still protected by its shell, epitomizes a debate about aloofness and engagement, poles of a tension between which the poet is left to struggle like the lobster. A passage quoted directly from the autobiography of Czeslaw Milosz, writing about his ambivalent attitude as an idealistic young poet to materialism and the historical process, is used, rather mechanically, to crystallize the discussion (*Station Island*, p. 16f).[101] The Sweeney poem 'The First Flight' seems to admonish the over-involved poet of *North* and to encourage him to stretch his wings in proud Joycean independence:

> I was mired in attachment
> until they began to pronounce me
> a feeder off battlefields
>
> so I mastered new rungs of the air
> to survey out of reach
> their bonfires on hills . . .
>
> (*Station Island*, p. 102f)

The theme of Sweeney and the theme of the Lough Derg pilgrimage are themselves meeting-places for many Irish writers, among whom Heaney defines his literary identity. William Carleton's anti-Catholic account of his own Lough Derg pilgrimage is both iconoclastic and vividly responsive to human particulars. Modern poems by Denis Devlin and Patrick Kavanagh, on the other hand, testify to specifically Catholic disenchantments. Heaney's concern is neither formal piety nor scepticism but the pursuit of his own poetic voice. Carleton's ghost appears early in the sequence: Heaney makes him a harsher, angrier, more devious and opportunist version of himself, a man who had participated as a 'turncoat' propagandist in sectarian politics but who had also lived in fear of Orange drums and guns after dark. As a parting shot Carleton sends the ambitious poet who once wrote *Death of a Naturalist* back to his roots, tribal as well as rural:

> We are earthworms of the earth, and all that
> has gone through us is what will be our trace.
>   (*Station Island*, p. 66)

The other voices of the sequence are milder. Kavanagh makes a brief appearance to relieve solemnity and impart colloquial energy: in his day some pilgrims used to come 'on the hunt for women' (p. 74). A different challenge to solemnity and poetic anxiety comes from a friend of Heaney's youth murdered in the 'troubles'. Heaney's habitual guilt-feelings surface: 'forgive my timid circumspect involvement', to which the friend retorts ' "Forgive/ my eye," he said, "all that's above my head." ' (p. 80) But guilt and self-contempt will not go away.

Dante's experience of Purgatory was progressive, and so is Heaney's. After darkness and guilt come the possibilities of forgiveness and renewal, though Heaney's only sin is poetic worry. He meets with a confessor and his (pleasantly poetic) penance is to translate from St John of the Cross the 'Song of the soul that is glad to know God by faith'.[102] Heaney's final deliverance is artistic rather than religious. Joyce is almost as brusque as Carleton, and more effective, because he tells the poet what he needs to know and believe. Closer to the Irish language than Joyce ever was, Heaney was fascinated by the passage in *Portrait of the Artist* in which Stephen Dedalus muses on the strangeness of English as a medium for the Irish whose ancestral speech is a different language. A key sentence from this was used as an epigraph in *Wintering Out* ('The Wool Trade', p. 37) and it is acclaimed here as a revelation, 'the collect of a new epiphany'. The refurbishing of Joyce's own religious metaphor of 'epiphany' is slyly appropriate in the metaphoric purgatory of 'Station Island', but it is a little overstated and Joyce jeers, 'Who cares?' In a pastiche not of Joyce but of Joyce's brash protagonist Stephen Dedalus, the Joyce of the poem mingles colloquial terseness with far-fetched metaphors of creative individuality, telling Heaney that 'That subject people stuff', the tired old debates about 'Irish Ireland', need not concern him and he should strike out on his own.

Sweeney was famous for striking out on his own. The legend was already a thousand years old, a fragment of historical tradition moulded and magnified by the literary imagination, when some time in the 1670s a Sligo scribe wrote the manuscript which is the basis of

Heaney's translation. Between Sweeney and Heaney there are inter-
posed not only the scholarship of the Celtic Revival which led to J. G.
O'Keefe's Irish Texts Society edition (1913) but other Irish writers
fascinated with the wild freedoms of madness and escape, cold to the
chillingly pious ascetic St Ronan who cursed aggravating Sweeney
with madness. George Moore had been at odds with Catholic
orthodoxy in the name of his art ever since the short stories of *The
Untilled Field* (1903). Years later, he told Austin Clarke that the
Sweeney story had inspired half of his medieval Irish picaresque novel
Ulick and Soracha (1926).[103] Clarke himself caught the madness and
violence of Sweeney in a wild rain-soaked landscape in his poem 'The
Frenzy of Suibhne' in *The Cattledrive in Connaught* (1925) and
returned to the theme in his late poem 'The trees of the forest', the
trees among which the stricken Sweeney wanders. There is a sense in
which the maverick Catholic poet stays with the aggravated and
aggravating Sweeney through his long career.[104] The mingling of
Joycean escape from obligation into creative innovation and the flights
of mad Sweeney which pervade *Station Island* is most apparent in the
mad games with fiction and reality which are enacted in the partly
Joycean novel by Flann O'Brien *At Swim-Two-Birds* (1939). The
bizarre title comes from a literal translation of one of Sweeney's
resting-places on the Shannon and the Sweeney story is presented
in the wild and whirling words of a rhetorical translation of the
seventeenth-century text as one element, one form of narrative, in the
multi-layered texture of the novel. More recently John Montague and
Paul Muldoon have found Sweeney poetically useful: Sweeney is one
of the many disguises of Paul Muldoon's preposterous shape-changer
Gallogly in *Quoof* (1983), but Muldoon has Heaney very much in
mind.

In this company Heaney offers some experiments in poetic
ventriloquism in 'Sweeney Redivivus', the last section of *Station
Island*. But the idea of Sweeney is more interesting than these oblique,
obscure lyrics complaining about 'The Scribes' or registering scattered
intuitions and perceptions. Hopping madly from tree to tree,
observing and resenting from the air or from outside, which is what
Sweeney has to do, is not the ideal condition of the liberated
imagination.

Though Heaney's Joyce in *Station Island* tells Heaney not to be so
earnest, good advice for 'Station Island' at least, Heaney is more
impressive in a mood of settled gravity than he is on the Sweeney trail.
Perhaps Ireland is best looked at not from trees and recreated Irish

legend but from the perspective of parable. There are several strange
parables in *The Haw Lantern*. Perhaps the most intriguing is 'Parable
Island', written for the novelist William Golding's seventy-fifth
birthday. Golding can be seen as a moralist and a fabulist. *Lord of the
Flies* (1954) is set on the uninhabited island of juvenile fiction
throughout the ages, though what happens there is an adult story of
evil and corruption among children. *The Inheritors* (1955) imagines
and explores neanderthal consciousness and behaviour under threat
from *homo sapiens* as a dark commentary upon ourselves. Poets can be
fabulists too. In 'Parable Island' a strange 'island' already inhabited by
a strange people comes under anthropological scrutiny. The 'islanders'
insist they live on an island though their country has a land frontier like
the would-be self-contained six counties of Northern Ireland. Heaney's
preoccupation with place-names in *Wintering Out* is extended to his
imaginary country: the people are now 'an occupied nation' and
occupiers and natives have different names for the same geographical
features. Heaney hints at but does not endorse a dream of unity which
might be the nativist fantasy of a Celtic revivalist or the syncretic
aspiration of a liberal optimist: the 'forked-tongued natives', culturally
bilingual and devious in their occupied condition, secretly believe in
prophecies of

> a point where all the names converge
> underneath the mountain and where (some day)
> they are going to start to mine the ore of truth.

The nicely judged postponement of 'some day', emphasized by the
lame syntax of 'going to start to mine', drily measures the distance
between dream and reality. Prophetic truth has always been elusive
and controversial in Ireland and in the other territories of the mind,
the blighted Europe of Milosz and Mandelstam, where Heaney's
imagination now travels. Archaeologists and scholars, who are 'like the
subversives and collaborators' of European wars and revolutions,
dispute the significance of evidence from the past, since the past can be
shaped and interpreted as a tool of ideology. There is a fine ambiguity
about the alleged 'autochthonous tradition' of a single bell-tower

> which struck its single note each day at noon
> in honour of the one-eyed all-creator.

In the country of the blind the one-eyed man is king, and the limited
vision of the Cyclopean Citizen in *Ulysses* is perhaps darkly implied.

But perhaps it never really was like that. Perhaps such traditions are necessary illusions, imaginative legitimations of collective hopes and fears. The islanders have other stories, including the one about the man convinced that the completed Panama Canal would drain away the ocean 'and the island disappear by aggrandizement', an irrational fear with its own internal logic which somehow resembles provincial attitudes in Ulster, hostile to what goes on 'across the water' or 'down south', resisting the larger unities of 'Britain' or 'Ireland', let alone 'Europe' (*Haw Lantern*, p. 10f).

Parable provides a liberating approach to the guilty dialectic of commitment and the untrammelled imagination, illiterate fidelities or tribal atavisms and rational articulation, Carleton and Joyce. Traditions invented in parables can be enjoyed and disowned without personal or social damage. Like Czeslaw Milosz, Polish Catholic poet and cosmopolitan humanitarian, Heaney travels between two worlds, not just bitter rural Ireland and the international literary community but history and poetic truth. Like Osip Mandelstam he follows the 'grain of the ordinary'[105] to root his fantasy and imaginative exploration in palpable realities. The sting of oppression and the tang of rich early experience continue to energize his poetry.

The fine sonnet sequence 'Clearances', a formal tribute to his mother who died in 1984, reinvents the shared life of mother and son in childhood, and peacefully revisits the territory of *Death of a Naturalist*. The first sonnet is self-consciously a genre piece, a legacy like 'silver and Victorian lace'. A Victorian great-grandmother who had become a Catholic had a stone thrown at her the first Sunday she went to Mass. The crow shouted 'Lundy', a synonym for 'traitor' in Protestant and Unionist Ulster after the governor who proposed to surrender beleaguered Derry in 1689. But the seventeenth-century heritage of violence and tribal mistrust is somehow accepted and contained in the strange last line of the poem, 'The exonerating, exonerated stone' (*Haw Lantern*, p. 25). Christ ironically suggested that someone without sin should cast the first stone, but stones get thrown anyway: this stone testifies laconically to communal sin, the danger and distinction of crossing tribal boundaries, the acceptable pain of witness.

Pain is one of the constants of Irish literary history and of the Irish experience. The myths and realities of conquest and dispossession, iconoclastic progressive enlightenment and particularist national self-discovery, have painfully divided Irishmen from each other and from aspects of their complex heritage and interacting traditions. The articulation of tradition itself sharpens the pain of division. Ussher's scholarly commitment to the Irish past was prompted by an aggressively Protestant churchmanship which reinforced religious hostilities. Heaney's slightly aggravated Catholic consciousness resisted and resented obtrusively Protestant and British elements in Irish tradition, which has provoked sectarian resentment in its turn, if only from Ian Paisley.[106] Thomas D'Arcy McGee tried to make the best of Ireland's different traditions and ended up pleasing nobody, except the people of Canada. But the pursuit of tradition and identity can also bring healing. To find his own voice, to discover who he is, the Irish writer and the Irishman must understand and come to terms with past and present, predecessors and peers, the project of Heaney's 'Station Island'. As the best work of Heaney and Ussher, James Joyce and Thomas Moore has demonstrated, Irish identities and the traditions of Irish writing acquire ultimate significance and meaning not in aggressive relation to each other and problematic Ireland but in the context of the wider world, English-speaking, European, cosmopolitan, in which good Irish writing is produced and valued and Irishmen and their country can earn respect.

Notes

CHAPTER I

Tradition, Ireland, Literature

1 Revisionist historical scholarship is reviewed by T. W. Moody, 'Irish history and Irish mythology', *Hermathena* 124 (1978), 7–24, and embodied in R. F. Foster, *Modern Ireland 1600–1800* (London: Allen Lane, 1988); for the new literary history, see F. S. L. Lyons, *Culture and Anarchy in Ireland 1890–1939* (Oxford: Oxford University Press, 1979); W. J. McCormack, *Ascendancy and Tradition in Anglo-Irish Literary History 1789–1939* (Oxford: Oxford University Press, 1985); and Seamus Deane, *Celtic Revivals* (London: Faber, 1985).

2 Useful guides include A. Norman Jeffares, *Anglo-Irish Literature* (London: Macmillan, 1982); Robert Hogan (ed.), *The Macmillan Dictionary of Irish Literature* (London: Macmillan, 1979); Maurice Harmon, *Select Bibliography for the Study of Anglo-Irish Literature and its Backgrounds* (Dublin: Wolfhound, 1977).

3 Walter Benjamin, *Illuminations*, trans. Harry Zohn (London: Collins/ Fontana, 1973), p. 260; Michel Foucault, 'Nietzsche, genealogy, history', in *Language, Counter-Memory, Practice*, trans. D. F. Bouchard and Sherry Simon (Ithaca, N.Y.: Cornell University Press), pp. 139–164.

4 See e.g., John Healy, *The Life and Writings of St Patrick* (Dublin: M. H. Gill, 1905) (Catholic); and J. H. Todd, *St Patrick. Apostle of Ireland* (Dublin: Hodges, Smith, 1864) (Protestant).

5 W. B. Yeats, '"I am of Ireland"' and 'The Statues', *Collected Poems*, 2nd edition (London: Macmillan, 1950), pp. 303f, 375.

6 See R. F. Foster, 'History and the Irish Question', *Transactions of the Royal Historical Society*, 5th ser., 33 (1983), 176, 191.

7 *Henry V*, II. ii. 116, in Thomas Flanagan, *The Irish Novelists 1800–1850* (New York: Columbia University Press, 1959).
8 John Cronin, *The Anglo-Irish Novel I: the Nineteenth Century* (Belfast: Appletree, 1980), p. 18.
9 Richard Kearney (ed.), *The Irish Mind* (Dublin: Wolfhound, 1985), pp. 9f, 37.
10 'Tradition and the individual talent' (1919), *Selected Essays*, 3rd edition (London: Faber, 1951), pp. 13–22.
11 *Transatlantic Review* 1 (January 1924), 94f; 'What is a Classic?' (1944) and 'Virgil and the Christian world' (1951), in *On Poetry and Poets* (London: Faber, 1957), pp. 70, 130.
12 *Transatlantic Review* 1, p. 96.
13 Benjamin, *Illuminations*, p. 255.
14 See William Thomas, 'John Stuart Mill and the uses of autobiography', *History* 56 (1971), 341–59.
15 Eric Hobsbawm and Terence Ranger (eds), *The Invention of Tradition* (Cambridge: Cambridge University Press, 1983); Raymond Cocks, *Foundations of the Modern Bar* (London: Sweet & Maxwell, 1983), chapter 7.
16 Discussed in Frank Kermode, *Forms of Attention* (Chicago: Chicago University Press, 1985) and *The Art of Reading* (Cambridge, Mass.: Harvard University Press, 1983), esp. pp. 170–80; see also James Barr, *Holy Scripture: Canon, Authority, Criticism* (Oxford: Oxford University Press, 1983).
17 See e.g., Holly Goulden and John Hartley, '"Nor should such topics as Homosexuality . . ."', *Literature Teaching Politics* 1 (1982), 4–20; W. V. Spanos, 'The Apollonian investment of modern humanist education' (I), *Cultural Critique* 1 (Fall 1985), 7–72.
18 Raymond Williams, *Marxism and Literature* (Oxford: Oxford University Press, 1977), Part I, chapter 3 'Literature'.
19 Gilles Deleuze and Félix Guattari, *Kafka: Pour une littérature mineure* (Paris: Minuit, 1974); David Lloyd, *Nationalism and Minor Literature: James Clarence Mangan and the Emergence of Irish Cultural Nationalism* (Berkeley: University of California Press, 1987).
20 J. D. Y. Peel and T. O. Ranger (eds), *Past and Present in Zimbabwe* (Manchester: Manchester University Press, 1983).
21 Donald Denoon and Adam Kuper, 'Nationalist historians in search of a nation. The "New Historiography" in Dar es Salaam', *African Affairs* 69 (1970), 329–49.
22 Nicholas Canny, 'The formation of the Irish mind: religion, politics and Gaelic Irish literature 1580–1750', *Past and Present* 95 (May 1982), 92.
23 Hans-George Gadamer, *Truth and Method*, Trans. W. Glen-Doepel, 2nd edition (London: Sheed & Ward, 1979), p. 420.
24 Alan Bliss, *Spoken English in Ireland, 1600–1740* (Dublin: Dolmen, 1979) pp. 11–30.

25 J. C. Beckett, 'The Irish writer and his public in the nineteenth century', *Yearbook of English Studies* 11 (1981), 103.

26 J. C. Beckett, *The Anglo-Irish Tradition* (London: Faber, 1976), p. 131f, though Beckett for one is a little unhappy with any use of the term 'Anglo-Irish Literature'.

27 Northrop Frye, *Anatomy of Criticism* (1957) (Princeton, N.J.: Princeton University Press, 1971), pp. 52–67, 327.

28 Hobsbawm and Ranger, *The Invention of Tradition*, p. 7f.

29 See, e.g., Ernest Boyd, *Ireland's Literary Renaissance* (Dublin: Maunsel, 1916); Richard Fallis, *The Irish Renaissance. An Introduction to Anglo-Irish Literature* (Dublin: Gill & Macmillan, 1978); Roger McHugh and Maurice Harmon, *A Short History of Anglo-Irish Literature* (Dublin: Wolfhound, 1982).

30 John Eglinton, *Anglo-Irish Essays* (Dublin: Talbot, 1917), p. 9.

31 John Eglinton, *Irish Literary Portraits* (London: Macmillan, 1935), p. 6f.

32 Joseph Hone and M. M. Rossi, *Bishop Berkeley* (London: Faber, 1931).

33 'Irish Letter', *The Dial* 82 (May 1927), 407f.

34 *Anglo-Irish Essays*, p. 4.

35 G. B. Shaw, Preface to *John Bull's Other Island* (1904), *Prefaces* (London: Constable, 1934), p. 443f.

36 *Irish Statesman* 1 (no. 1) (15 September 1923), 9.

37 James Esse, 'Literature and life. An interview with Mr James Stephen', *Irish Statesman* 1 (no. 2) (22 September 1923), 48–50.

38 Discussed in F. S. L. Lyons, *Ireland since the Famine*, 2nd edition (London: Collins/ Fontana, 1973), pp. 230–3.

39 See McCormack, *Ascendancy and Tradition*, esp. pp. 78–80.

40 Jawaharlal Nehru, *An Autobiography* (London: John Lane, 1936), p. 426f.

41 Douglas Hyde, 'The necessity for de-Anglicising Ireland', in C. G. Duffy et al., *The Revival of Irish Literature and other Addresses* (London: Unwin, 1894).

42 Douglas Hyde, *A Literary History of Ireland* (London: Unwin, 1899), pp. 554, 619f.

43 St John Ervine, *Ulster, the Real Centre of Culture in Ireland* (1944), reprinted from the *Belfast Telegraph*, a reply to Sean O'Casey.

44 See Terence Brown, *The Whole Protestant Community*, Field Day Pamphlet no. 7 (Derry, 1985). For a sympathetic but critical historical survey, see Rory Fitzpatrick, *God's Frontiersmen: the Scots-Irish Epic* (London: Weidenfeld & Nicolson, 1989).

45 D. W. Miller, *Queen's Rebels: Ulster Loyalists in Perspective* (Dublin: Gill & Macmillan, 1978).

46 Seamus Heaney, 'Singing School', *North* (London: Faber, 1975), p. 65.

47 Seamus Heaney, *An Open Letter*, Field Day Pamphlet no. 2 (Derry, 1983).

CHAPTER 2

Seventeenth-century beginnings: *Archbishop Ussher and the Earl of Roscommon*

1　Seamus Deane, *A Short History of Irish Literature* (London: Hutchinson, 1986), chapter 2, 'The formation of the Anglo-Irish literary tradition'; A. Norman Jeffares, *Anglo-Irish Literature* (London: Macmillan, 1982), chapter 2; Patrick Rafroidi, *L'Irlande et la romantisme* (Paris: Editions Universitaires, 1972), p. 7; Richard Fallis, *The Irish Renaissance. An Introduction to Anglo-Irish Literature* (Dublin: Gill & Macmillan, 1978).

2　David Cairns and Shaun Richards, *Writing Ireland: Colonialism, Nationalism and Culture* (Manchester: Manchester University Press, 1988); St John D. Seymour, *Anglo-Irish Literature, 1200–1582* (Cambridge: Cambridge University Press, 1929).

3　A. T. Q. Stewart, *The Narrow Ground. Aspects of Ulster, 1609–1969* (London: Faber, 1977); P. J. Corish, 'The origin of Catholic nationalism', in *A History of Irish Catholicism* (Dublin: Gill & Macmillan, 1967–　), vol. 3, fasc. 8 (1968), p. 57.

4　Oliver MacDonagh, *States of Mind. A Study of Anglo-Irish Conflict 1780–1980* (London: Allen & Unwin, 1983), p. 1.

5　Aodh De Blácam, *Gaelic Literature Surveyed* (Dublin: Talbot Press, 1929), p. 217.

6　For a selection of this poetry, see Seán Ó Tuama and Thomas Kinsella (eds and trans.), *An Duanaire 1600–1900: Poems of the Dispossessed* (Portlaoise: Dolmen Press, 1981).

7　Brian Ó Cuiv, 'The Irish language in the early modern period', in T. W. Moody, F. X. Martin and F. J. Byrne (eds), *Early Modern Ireland 1534–1691* (*A New History of Ireland* vol. 3) (Oxford: Oxford University Press, 1976), p. 511; J. R. R. Adams, *The Printed Word and the Common Man. Popular Culture in Ulster 1700–1900* (Belfast: Institute of Irish Studies, The Queen's University, 1987), p. 23.

8　See Paul Walsh, 'The Great Book of Lecan', in *Irish Men of Learning* (Dublin: At the Sign of the Three Candles, 1947), pp. 102–18.

9　De Blácam, *Gaelic Literature*, p. 80.

10　Geoffrey Keating, *History of Ireland*, ed. and trans. D. Comyn and P. S. Dinneen, 4 vols (London: Irish Texts Society, 1902–14), I, p. 153; see also IV, p. 401.

11　Keating III, pp. 5, 301; II, p. 11.

12　See D. Berman and A. Harrison, 'John Toland and Keating's *History of Ireland* (1723)', *Donegal Annual* (1984), 25–9.

13　Diarmaid Ó Catháin, 'Dermot O'Connor, translator of Keating', *Eighteenth Century Ireland* 2 (1987), 69.

14　Marsh's Library MS Z3.1.17.

15 John Lynch, *Cambrensis Eversus*, ed. and trans. Matthew Kelly, 3 vols (Dublin: Celtic Society, 1848), esp. I, pp. 183–5; 209.

16 Discussed by Benignus Millet, 'Irish literature in Latin 1550–1700', in Moody, Martin and Byrne, *Early Modern Ireland*, p. 574.

17 See R. B. Walsh, 'John O'Donovan, the man and the scholar', in C. J. Byrne and Margaret Harry (eds), *Talamh an Eisc. Canadian and Irish Essays* (Halifax, Nova Scotia: Nimbus Publishing, 1986), pp. 119–39.

18 Aodh De Blácam, *Gaelic Literature*, p. 219.

19 See Paul Walsh, *Irish Men of Learning*, p. 270.

20 Canice Mooney, OFM, 'Father John Colgan, OFM, his work and times and literary milieu', in Terence O'Donnell, OFM (ed.), *Father John Colgan, OFM, 1592–1658* (Dublin: Assisi Press, 1959), p. 18.

21 Thomas Dempster, *Historia Ecclesiastica Gentis Scottorum* (Bononiae [Bologna], 1627), pp. 227–32, 42f.

22 Published at Lyons, 1639: see Canice Mooney, OFM, 'The writings of Father Luke Wadding, OFM', *Franciscan Studies* 18 (1958), 231.

23 Brendan Jennings, OFM (ed.), *Wadding Papers 1614–38* (Dublin: Irish MSS Commission, 1953), p. 552.

24 David Rothe, *Hibernia Resurgens, sive Refrigerium Antidotale. Adversus Morsum Serpentis Antiqui* (Rouen: Nicolaus le Brun, 1621), pp. 301f.

25 G. F. Veridicus Hibernus, *Hiberniae sive Antiquioris Scotiae Vindicia* (Antwerp, 1621), p. 62 (my translation).

26 Sir James Ware, *De Scriptoribus Hiberniae* (Dublin, 1639), p. 42; John Colgan, *Triadis Thaumaturgae* (Louvain, 1647), pp. 255, 582, 598.

27 J. T. Leerssen, 'Antiquarian research: patriotism to nationalism', in C. J. Byrne and Margaret Harry (eds), *Talamh an Eisc*, pp. 71–83.

28 See Jennings (ed.), *Wadding Papers*, p. 169.

29 See P. J. Corish, 'Two contemporary historians of the confederation of Kilkenny, John Lynch and Richard O'Ferrall', *Irish Historical Studies* 8 (March 1953), 217–36; the epigraph for Lynch's *Alithinologia* (1644) comes from Psalm 49: 20–1 (Vulgate) (Psalm 50 in the Authorized Version).

30 Trinity College MS 664 f.209b.

31 For a sketch of the history of the MS, see Thomas D'Arcy McGee, *A Memoir of the Life and Conquests of Art MacMurrough* (Dublin: J. Duffy, 1847), pp. 145–7.

32 See W. S. Gibson, *Bruegel* (London: Thames & Hudson, 1977), pp. 178–80; V. Väänänen, 'Le fabliau de Cocagne', *Neuphilologische Mitteilungen* 48 (1947), 19–47.

33 See St J. D. Seymour, *Anglo-Irish Literature 1200–1582*, p. 103; Mercier, *The Irish Comic Tradition*, pp. 16–18, 214–17.

34 British Library MS Landsdowne 418ff. 91–3; 88: see the published *Catalogue of Lansdowne MSS*.

35 Bodleian MS Rawlinson B.480.

36 Walsh, *Irish Men of Learning* p. 84.

37 Bodleian MS Ir. e.l is a later copy, dated *c*.1700.
38 See the Preface to Edward Lhuyd, *Archaeologia Britannica* (Oxford, 1707). Plunket's MS Dictionary is in Marsh's Library, MS Z4.2.5.
39 Trinity College MS 664 ff.121–7: 'Ex libro Ric. Creagh de Lingua Hibernica'.
40 Rothe to Wadding, 20 July 1631, in Brendan Jennings (ed.), *Wadding Papers*, p. 552.
41 Lynch, *Cambrensis Eversus* I, p. 185.
42 See Daniel Droixhe, *La Linguistique et l'appel de l'histoire (1600–1800)* (Geneva: Droz, 1978).
43 T. Ó Raifeartaigh (ed.), *The Royal Irish Academy. A Bicentennial History 1785–1985* (Dublin: Royal Irish Academy, 1985), p. 170.
44 Jerome, Epistola 18 'Ad Damasum Papam, De Seraphim et Calculo', in Migne, *Patrologia Latina* 22, col. 365; Dante, *De Vulgari Eloquentia* I, chapter 6. In *Paradiso* 26. 124–6 Dante suggests Adam's language had disappeared before Babel.
45 Adrianus Srieckus, *Originum Rerumque Celticarum et Belgicarum Libri XXIII* (Ypres, 1614).
46 Sir James Ware, *De Hibernia et Antiquitatibus ejus, Disquisitiones* (London: 1654), p. 10f.
47 *Calendar of State Papers (Ireland) 1592–6*, ed. H. C. Hamilton (London: HMSO, 1890), p. 311; *Wadding Papers*, pp. 170, 173.
48 See James Knowlson, *Universal Language Schemes in England and France, 1600–1800* (Toronto and Buffalo: Toronto University Press, 1975), pp. 9f, 76–86.
49 Knowlson, *Universal Language Schemes*, p. 10f.
50 See G. H. Turnbull, *Hartlib, Dury and Comenius. Gleanings from Hartlib's Papers* (Liverpool: Liverpool University Press, 1947), pp. 24, 156, 206, 222.
51 T. C. Barnard, 'The Hartlib Circle and the origins of the Dublin Philosophical Society', *Irish Historical Studies* 18 (1974), 56–71.
52 See K. T. Hoppen, in *Irish Historical Studies* 20 (March 1976), 40–8; Nicholas Canny, *The Patriot Earl. A Study of the Social and Mental World of Richard Boyle, first Earl of Cork* (Cambridge: Cambridge University Press, 1982), p. 146f.
53 T. C. Barnard, 'Miles Symner and the New Learning in seventeenth-century Ireland', *Journal of the Royal Society of Antiquaries of Ireland* 102, part 2 (1972), 137, 142; E. S. Shuckburgh, *Two Biographies of William Bedell* (Cambridge: Cambridge University Press, 1902), p. 109f; Gilbert Burnet, *Life of William Bedell, DD*, 3rd edition (Dublin, 1758), p. 61.
54 James Knowlson, *Universal Language Schemes* p. 10; Vivian Salmon, *The Works of Francis Lodwick* (London: Longman, 1972), p. 16.
55 [T. C. Croskery], 'Irish Massacres of 1641', *Edinburgh Review* 160 (October 1884), 523.

56 For a lucid brief account, see J. C. Beckett, *The Making of Modern Ireland 1603–1923* (London: Faber, 1966), chapter 3.

57 See Aidan Clarke, 'The genesis of the Ulster Rising of 1641', in Peter Roebuck (ed.), *Plantation to Partition* (Belfast: Blackstaff, 1981), pp. 30–6.

58 Alan Gailey, 'The Scots element in north Irish popular culture', *Ethnologia Europaea* 8 (1975), 5.

59 Finlay Holmes, *Our Presbyterian Heritage* (Belfast: Presbyterian Church in Ireland, 1985), chapter 1; Miller, *Queen's Rebels*, p. 14f.

60 Ó Tuama and Kinsella, *An Duanaire*, pp. 104–9; see also J. T. Leerssen, *Mere Irish and Fíor-Ghael* (Amsterdam and Philadelphia: Benjamins, 1986), p. 217.

61 John Milton, *Observations on Ormond's Articles of Peace with the Irish Rebels and on a Representation of the Scotch Presbytery of Belfast* (1649), discussed in W. R. Parker, *Milton, a Biography*, 2 vols (Oxford: Oxford University Press, 1968), I, pp. 356–9.

62 Suggested to me by Angus Ross.

63 Sir John Temple, *The Irish Rebellion* (London, 1646), p. 2.

64 Lord Anglesey, *Letter . . . to the Earl of Castlehaven* (1681) (Delmar, New York: Scholar's Facsimiles and Reprints, 1974), p. 3of.

65 Miller, *Queen's Rebels*, p. 18f.

66 Thomas Witherow, *Historical and Literary Memorials of Presbyterianism in Ireland (1623–1731)* (London and Belfast: William Mullan, 1879); Andrew Stewart, *History of the Church of Ireland, after the Scots were Naturalized*, printed as an appendix to Patrick Adair, *A True Narrative of the Rise and Progress of the Presbyterian Church in Ireland*, ed. W. D. Killen (Belfast: C. Aitchison, etc., 1866), p. 319.

67 Adair, *A True Narrative*, p. 9.

68 Ibid., p. 6.

69 D. W. Miller, 'Presbyterianism and "modernization" in Ulster', *Past and Present* 80 (August 1978), 66–90.

70 Quoted in J. Seaton Reid, *History of the Presbyterian Church in Ireland (1834–53)*, 3 vols (Belfast: William Mullan, 1867), I, p. 372.

71 See J. M. Barkley, *Handbook to the Church Hymnary, Third Edition* (London, etc.: Oxford University Press, 1979), pp. 96, 158.

72 Holmes, *Our Presbyterian Heritage* p. 44.

73 See Miller, 'Presbyterianism and "modernization"', p. 83f.

74 Patrick Walker, *Six Saints of the Covenant*, 2 vols (London: Hodder, 1901), I, p. 66, Alexander Peden, *The Lord's Trumpet Sounding an Alarm against Scotland* (1682) (Glasgow, 1779), pp. 11, 31.

75 See *Cogadh Gaedhel re Gallaibh* ('The war of the Irish against the foreigners'), ed. J. H. Todd (London: Rolls Series, 1867), p. 11.

76 James Ussher, 'Refutation of J. H. [John Harrison] his Opinion, that ye World Should End AD 1630' (*c*.1615), Bodleian MS Add. C.301 ff. 95–7.

77 C. R. Elrington, *The Life of James Ussher DD* (Dublin: Hodges & Smith, 1847), p. 21f; see, e.g., Thomas Rymer, *The Whole Prophecies of Scotland, England, Ireland, France and Denmark . . . [and] Bishop Ussher's Wonderful Prophecies of the Times* (Edinburgh [?1810]).

78 N. French, *The Bleeding Iphigenia* (1675), quoted in Corish, 'The origins of Catholic nationalism', p. 58.

79 T. J. Dunne, 'The Gaelic response to conquest and colonisation: the evidence of the poetry', *Studia Hibernica* 20 (1980), 7–30; Nicholas Canny, 'The formation of the Irish mind: religion, politics and Gaelic Irish literature 1850–1750', *Past and Present* 95 (May 1982), 91–116.

80 Rev. J. C. MacEarlean, SJ (ed. and trans.), *Poems of David Ó Bruadair*, 3 vols (London: Irish Texts Society, 1910), I, p. xxi.

81 Quoted in Leerssen, *Mere Irish and Fíor-Ghael*, p. 232f.

82 Robin Flower, 'Ireland and medieval Europe', *The Irish Tradition* (Oxford: Oxford University Press, 1947), pp. 107–41.

83 See Michael Hartnett (trans.), *Ó Bruadair* (Dublin: Gallery Books, 1985), p. 14.

84 Cecile O'Rahilly (ed.), *Five Seventeenth-Century Political Poems* (Dublin: Institute for Advanced Studies, 1952), esp. pp. 12–32.

85 Ó Tuama and Kinsella, *An Duanaire*, p. 91.

86 David Ó Bruadair, 'Caithreim Taidhg' ('The Triumph of Tadhg'), *Poems*, trans. J. C. MacEarlean, III, p. 129.

87 Ó Bruadair, *Poems* I, pp. 37–9.

88 See N. J. A. Williams (ed.), *Pairlament Chloinne Tomáis* (Dublin: Institute for Advanced Studies, 1981), pp. xlviii–lii.

89 The MSS include British Library Add. MS 29614 f.38^v and Royal Irish Academy MS 23 M 31 p. 23 which contain substantially the same marginal glosses.

90 Ó Bruadair, *Poems* II, pp. 98–101; Royal Irish Academy MS 23 L 37 p. 220.

91 Royal Irish Academy MS 24 L 11; see Brian Ó Cuív (ed.), *Párliament na mBan* (Dublin: Institute for Advanced Studies, 1952), pp. xxxiv, 53.

92 P. O'Dinneen (ed.), *Danta Sheaffraidh Uí Donnchadha* (Dublin: Gaelic League Publications, 1902), p. 8.

93 See Norman Sykes, 'James Ussher as churchman', *Theology* 60 (1957), 54–60, 102–11; R. Buick Knox, *James Ussher, Archbishop of Armagh* (Cardiff: University of Wales Press, 1967) (the only modern book on Ussher); Hugh Kearney, in *Scholars and Gentlemen* (London: Faber, 1970), pp. 67–77.

94 Edward Gibbon, *Decline and Fall of the Roman Empire* (1776–88), ed. J. B. Bury, 7 vols (London: Methuen, 1896–1900), IV, chapter 37, p. 62n; James Boswell, *Life of Johnson* (1791) (London: Oxford University Press, 1970), p. 448; H. Trevor-Roper, 'James Ussher,

Archbishop of Armagh', in *Catholics, Anglicans and Puritans* (London: Secker & Warburg, 1987), pp. xii, xiii, 142.

95 See Thomas D'Arcy McGee, *Irish Writers of the Seventeenth Century* (Dublin: J. Duffy, 1846), pp. 45–61; Charles Gavan Duffy proposed Ussher's body should be brought back to Ireland where it could be properly honoured (see *Irish Statesman* 6 (4 September 1926), p. 712); Douglas Hyde, *A Literary History of Ireland* (London: Unwin, 1899), p. 620.

96 Benignus Millett, in T. W. Moody, F. X. Martin and F. J. Byrne (eds), *Early Modern Ireland 1534–1691*, (Oxford: Oxford University Press, 1970, p. 568.

97 See W. B. Wright, *The Ussher Memoirs* (Dublin: Sealy, Bryers & Walker, 1889).

98 See R. Parr, *The Life of . . . James Usher* (London: Nat. Ranew, 1686), pp. 1–3; R. Parr (ed.), *A Collection of Three Hundred Letters [of] . . . Usher* (London: Nat. Ranew, 1686), p. 1f (Ussher to Stanihurst, n.d.).

99 R. O'Ferrall and R. O'Connell, *Commentarius Rinuccinianus* (1658), 6 vols (Dublin: Stationery Office, 1932–49), I, p. 242.

100 C. R. Elrington, *The Life of James Ussher* (Dublin: Hodges & Smith, 1847), pp. 11–13.

101 S. Schoenbaum, *Shakespeare's Lives* (Oxford: Clarendon Press, 1970), pp. 122–4, 460, 739; R. C. Bald, *John Donne: a Life* (Oxford: Clarendon Press, 1970), pp. 22–5; W. R. Parker, *Milton: a Biography* I, (Oxford: Oxford University Press, 1968), pp. 4, 658.

102 *Commentarius Rinuccinianus* I, p. 242.

103 See R. Mant, *A History of the Church of Ireland* (London: J. W. Parker, 1840), pp. 422–8.

104 James Ussher, 'The effect of a speech delivered by the Lo[r]d Primate before the Lo[r]d Deputy', Trinity College, Dublin, MS 842, esp. ff. 173–4, 176–8, 187–8. The speech is published in part in N. Bernard (ed.), *Clavi Trabales* (London, 1661) (as 'The Duty of Subjects to supply the King's Necessities') but the discussion of Irish appointments and economic matters is omitted.

105 Knox, *James Ussher*, p. 16.

106 See Hugh Kearney, *Strafford in Ireland 1633–41* (Manchester: Manchester University Press, 1959), pp. 112–8.

107 See James Ussher, *The Reduction of Episcopacy unto the form of Synodical Government received in the ancient Church* (1641), in *The Whole Works*, ed. C. R. Elrington, 17 vols (Dublin: Hodges & Smith, 1829–64), vol. XII; Knox, *James Ussher* pp. 23, 185, 177–9.

108 T. K. Lowry (ed.), *The Hamilton Manuscripts* (Belfast: Archer & Sons [1867]) p. 5; John Bruce (ed.), *Correspondence of King James VI of Scotland* (London: Camden Society, 1861), pp.xlii–xliv.

109 See Walter J. Ong, *Ramus, Method, and the Decay of Dialogue* (Cambridge, Mass.: Harvard University Press, 1958); for a summary of

revisionist scholarship see Brian Vickers, *In Defence of Rhetoric* (Oxford: Oxford University Press, 1988), pp. 475f.

110 See P. A. Duhamel, 'Milton's alleged Ramism', *PMLA* 67 (1952), 1035–53; Kathleen M. Swaim, *Before and After the Fall* (Amherst, Mass.: University of Massachusetts Press, 1986), esp. chapter 3 'Lapsarian logic'.

111 Kearney, *Scholars and Gentlemen*, pp. 68–70.

112 Trevor-Roper, *Catholics, Anglicans and Puritans*, pp. 125–9.

113 Bodleian MS Barlow 13, ff. 80–84.

114 Kearney, *Scholars and Gentlemen*, pp. 66, 69f.

115 McCormack, *Ascendancy and Tradition in Anglo-Irish Literary History*.

116 *Commentarius Rinuccinianus* I, 193–8, citing P. O'Sullevan, *Historiae Catholicae Iberniae Compendium* (Lisbon, 1621).

117 James Ussher, *Discourse of the Religion Anciently Professed by the Irish and British* (London: R. Young for Partners of the Irish Stocke, 1631), p. 128.

118 Ibid., p. 114.

119 Aubrey Gwynn, SJ, 'Archbishop Ussher and Fr Brendan O'Connor', in *Father Luke Wadding*, ed. Franciscan Fathers, Killiney (Dublin: Clonmore and Reynolds, 1957), pp. 263–75.

120 Jennings (ed.), *Wadding Papers*, pp. 280f, 289, 304, 606.

121 Gwynn, 'Archbishop Ussher', p. 267.

122 *Calendar of State Papers (Ireland) 1633–1647*, ed. R. P. Mahaffy (London: HMSO, 1901), p. 371.

123 *Commentarius Rinuccinianus* I, p. 243.

124 *Calendar of State Papers (Ireland) 1615–25*, ed. C. W. Russell and J. P. Prendergast (London: Longmans, 1880), p. 631.

125 For a useful modern account, see J. M. O'Donnell's article 'Gottschalk', in the *New Catholic Encyclopaedia* (New York: McGraw-Hill, 1967).

126 *Calendar of State Papers (Ireland) 1625–32*, ed. R. P. Mahaffy (London: HMSO, 1900), p. 618.

127 Joannes Scotus, *De Divina Praedestinatione*, esp. 3.6, in Migne, *Patrologia Latina* 122, col. 368.

128 James Ussher, *Gotteschalci . . . Historia*, chapter 9 in *Whole Works* IV, p. 112f; Ussher also published two of Erigena's letters in his *Veterum Epistolarum Hibernicarum Sylloge* (Dublin: Stationers' Company, 1632), pp. 57f, 58–64.

129 James Ussher, *Discourse of Religion*, Dedication, sig.A3.

130 James Ussher, *Britannicarum Ecclesiarum Antiquitates* (Dublin: Stationers' Co., 1639), chapter 8; the origins of Pelagius are discussed in J. Ferguson, *Pelagius* (Cambridge: W. Heffer, 1956), p. 39.

131 Gibbon, *Decline and Fall*, chapter 31, citing *Britannicarum Ecclesiarum Antiquitates*, chapters 8–12.

132 James Ussher, *Answer to a Challenge made by a Jesuit* (1625) (London: R. Young for Partners of the Irish Stocke, 1631), p. 581.

133 Sermon on Revelation 21:8, *Whole Works* XIII, p. 108.
134 Hubert Butler, *Escape from the Anthill* (1985) (Mullingar: Lilliput Press, 1986), p. 2.
135 See E. A. Strathmann, *Sir Walter Ralegh. A Study in Elizabethan Skepticism* (New York: Columbia University Press, 1951), esp. pp. 24–7.
136 For Rabbi Kattina in the Talmud, see *Sanhedrin* 97a; *Rosh Hashanah* 31a. Rabbi Kattina is cited by the influential Renaissance commentator Benedictus Pererius, *Commentariorum et Disputationum in Genesim Tomi Quattuor* (Cologne, 1601), p. 83. For Luther and Melanchthon, see J. M. Headley, *Luther's View of Church History* (New Haven and London: Yale University Press, 1963), pp. 109–11. The background to Ussher's project is discussed in James Barr, 'Why the world was created in 4004 BC: Archbishop Ussher and biblical chronology', *Bulletin of the John Rylands Library* 67 (Spring 1985), 575–608.
137 Discussed in Arnold Williams, *The Common Expositor* (Chapel Hill, N.C: North Carolina University Press, 1948), p. 63.
138 *Rosh Hashanah*, 11a; James Ussher, *The Annals of the World* (London, 1658), p. 1.
139 See P. O'Sullevan, *Archicomigeromastix, sive Jacobi Usherii Heresiarchae Confutatio*, included in his *Patritiana Decas* (Madrid: F. Martinez, 1629).
140 See G. T. Stokes, 'St Fechin of Fore and his monastery', *Journal of Royal Society of Antiquaries of Ireland* 22 (1892), 1–12, esp. p. 6; J. T. Leerssen, 'Archbishop Ussher and Gaelic culture', *Studia Hibernica* 22–3 (1982–3), 50–8, esp. p. 52.
141 Ussher to Sir Robert Cotton, 22 March 1628, *Whole Works* XV p. 428; Ware to Ussher, 21 September 1627, *Whole Works* XVI, p. 461.
142 Leerssen 'Archbishop Ussher', p. 52.
143 Matthew Kelly, Introduction to John Lynch, *Cambrensis Eversus*, I, p. iv.
144 Sykes, 'James Ussher as churchman', p. 104.
145 Ussher, *Whole Works* XV, pp. 463–76, 485; Elrington, *Life of Ussher*, p. 118; see W. O'Sullivan in *Irish Historical Studies* 16 (September 1968), 215–19.
146 Bedell to Samuel Ward, 14 November 1630, *Tanner Letters*, ed. Charles McNeil (Dublin: Stationery Office, 1943), p. 98.
147 *Tanner Letters*, p. 98.
148 Bedell to Ussher, 18 September 1630; Parr, *Life of . . . Ussher*, p. 453.
149 'Orders and directions concerning the State of the Church of Ireland . . . A[nn]o 1623', Marsh's Library MS Z3.1.3, p. 27; see [Christopher Anderson], *A Brief Sketch of Various Attempts that have been made to diffuse a knowledge of the Holy Scriptures through the medium of the Irish Language* (Dublin, 1818), pp. 11, 13.
150 Parr, *Life of Usher*, pp. 90f.

151 Alexander Gordon, 'James Ussher', *Dictionary of National Biography*.
152 P. O'Sullivan Beare (also known as O'Sullevan), *Zoilomastix* (1625), discussed in T. W. Moody, 'Early Modern Ireland', Introduction to Moody, Martin and Byrne, *Early Modern Ireland*, p. lvii.
153 See G. E. C., *The Complete Peerage*, revised edition, 13 vols (London: St Catherine's Press, 1910–40), XI, s.c. Roscommon and IV, s.c. Dillon, for detailed accounts.
154 Samuel Johnson, 'Roscommon', *Lives of the English Poets* ed. G. B. Hill, 3 vols (Oxford: Clarendon Press, 1905), I, p. 228n.
155 D. M. Stuart, 'Roscommon of the unspotted bays', *English* 1 (1936), 141.
156 *Calendar of State Papers (Ireland) 1633–47*, p. 350.
157 *Tanner Letters*, p. 339.
158 Dr George Hakewell to Ussher, 16 July 1628; Dr John Prideaux to Ussher, 27 August 1628, in James Ussher, *Whole Works* XV, pp. 417, 419.
159 See J. T. Leerssen, 'On the edge of Europe: Ireland in search of oriental roots, 1650–1850', *Comparative Criticism* 8 (1986), 91–112, esp. 95–100; N. Vance, 'Irish literary traditions and the Act of Union', in Byrne and Harry (eds), *Talamh an Eisc*, p. 37f.
160 Alexander Pope, *Imitations of Horace*, Epistle 2.1.213f.
161 Earl of Roscommon, *Essay on Translated Verse* 2nd edition (London: Jacob Tonson, 1685), p. 8.
162 Discussed by Stuart, 'Roscommon', p.449.
163 Johnson, *Lives of the English Poets* I, p. 231.
164 J. Addison, 'An account of the greatest English poets' (1694), *Works*, 6 vols (London: Henry G. Bohn, 1888–92), I, p. 26.
165 Johnson, *Lives of the English Poets* I, p. 234.
166 See the Introduction and notes in *The Poems of Alexander Pope* vol. I, ed. E. Audra and A. Williams (London: Methuen, 1961).
167 See L. A. Elioseff, *The Cultural Milieu of Addison's Literary Criticism* (Austin: Texas University Press, 1963), p. 206n.
168 See, e.g, Samuel Cobb, *Discourse on Criticism and of Poetry* (1707), cited in Elioseff, *Cultural Milieu*, p. 35.
169 Pope, *Essay in Criticism*, pp. 713–28.
170 See Carl Niemeyer, 'The Earl of Roscommon's academy', *Modern Language Notes* 49 (1934), 432–7.
171 Dryden, 'To the Earl of Roscommon, on his Excellent Essay on Translated Verse', 28f.
172 Ibid., 45f.
173 Earl of Roscommon, Epilogue to *Alexander the Great* in *Poems* (*The British Poets* vol. 20) (Chiswick: C. Whittingham, 1822), p. 278.
174 Johnson, *Lives of the English Poets* I, p. 231.

CHAPTER 3

The eighteenth century and beyond: *William Drennan and Thomas Moore*

1 See, e.g., Donald L. Torchiana, *W. B. Yeats and Georgian Ireland* (Evanston, Ill.: North Western University Press, 1966).
2 Daniel Corkery, *The Hidden Ireland. A Study of Gaelic Munster in the Eighteenth Century* (Dublin: M. H. Gill, 1925).
3 R. B. McDowell, *Ireland in the Age of Imperialism and Revolution, 1760–1801* (Oxford: Clarendon Press, 1979), pp. 468–70; Patrick Macrory, *The Siege of Derry* (Oxford: Oxford University Press, 1988), p. 121n.
4 J. R. R. Adams, *The Printed Word and the Common Man*, p. 6; see also Sean Connolly, 'Popular culture in pre-famine Ireland', in C. J. Byrne and Margaret Harry (eds), *Talamh an Eisc, Canadian and Irish Essays* (Halifax, Nova Scotia: Nimbus Publishing, 1986), p. 15.
5 See Jacqueline Hill, 'Popery and Protestantism, civil and religious liberty: the disputed lessons of Irish history 1690–1812', *Past and Present* 118 (February 1988), 96–129, esp. pp. 102f, 119.
6 William Crawford, *History of Ireland from the Earliest Period to the Present Time*, 2 vols (Strabane, 1783), I, p. 91.
7 Ibid., II, p. 382f.
8 Capel Molyneux, *An Account of the Family and Descendants of Sir Thomas Molyneux* (Evesham, 1820), p. 61f.
9 O'Flaherty to Samuel Molyneux, 9 April, 1708, Molyneux Papers, Southampton City Record Office, D/M.1/2, p. 45. The Molyneux–O'Flaherty letters are now available in the microfiche edition of *The Papers of the Dublin Philosophical Society*, ed. K. T. Hoppen (1982), pp. 1540–662; see *Analecta Hibernica* 30 (1982), 151–248.
10 Molyneux, *Account*, p. 8; *A Catalogue of the Library of the Honble Samuel Molyneux* (1730), p. 51.
11 Percy to John Pinkerton, 11 February 1786, *The Correspondence of Thomas Percy and John Pinkerton*, ed. Harriet Harvey Wood (New Haven and London: Yale University Press, 1985), p. 66f.
12 W. J. McCormack, *Ascendancy and Tradition in Anglo-Irish Literary History, 1789–1939* (Oxford: Oxford University Press, 1985).
13 See J. G. Simms, 'The case of Ireland stated', in his *War and Politics in Ireland 1649–1730* (London: Hambledon Press, 1986), p. 255f.
14 See Gerard O'Brien, 'The Grattan Mystique', *Eighteenth Century Ireland* 1 (1986), 177–94.
15 See Angus Ross, 'The Hibernian patriots' apprenticeship', in Clive T. Probyn (ed.), *The Art of Jonathan Swift* (London: Vision Press 1978), p. 89f; D. A. Downie, 'Swift's politics', in H. J. Real and H. J. Vienken

(eds), *Proceedings of the First Münster Symposium on Swift* (Munich: Wilhelm Fink, 1985), esp. p. 56.

16 Adams, *The Printed Word and the Common Man*, p. 85.

17 Molyneux, *Account*, p. 102.

18 Thomas D'Arcy McGee, *Irish Writers of the Seventeenth Century* (Dublin: J. Duffy, 1846), p. 227.

19 See A. A. Luce and T. E. Jessop (eds), *The Works of George Berkeley*, 9 vols (London: Nelson, 1948–57), I, pp. 146, 151, 154f, 225–7.

20 See A. A. Luce, *The Life of George Berkeley* (London: Nelson, 1949), pp. 31, 33, 190–92.

21 W. B. Yeats, Introduction to J. M. Hone and M. M. Rossi, *Bishop Berkeley* (London: Faber, 1931), pp. xv, xvi; Berkeley's phrase 'We Irish men' cannot sustain the full burden of nationalism Yeats thrusts upon it: see *Philosophical Commentaries*, *Works* I, pp. 47, 123f.

22 J. W. Stubbs, *The History of the University of Dublin* (Dublin: Hodges, Figgis, 1889), p. 283f.

23 G. Berkeley, *The Querist*, Q.191; *A Word to the Wise* (1749) in *Works* VI, pp. 120, 235.

24 Louis Cullen, 'Catholics under the Penal Laws', *Eighteenth Century Ireland* I (1986), 23–36.

25 S. Ó Tuama and T. Kinsella (eds and trans), *An Duanaire 1600–1900: Poems of the Dispossessed* (Portlaoise: Dolmen Press, 1981), p. 195; Royal Irish Academy MS 23 A 45, p. 52.

26 See P. S. Dinneen and Tadhg O'Donoghue (eds and trans), *Dánta Aodhagáin Uí Rathaille* (1900) (London: Irish Texts Society, 1911), esp. pp. xv–xx, 33, 172–5, 232–5.

27 The poem, by Michael McCarthy or Dermot O'Sullivan, was written some time (soon?) after 1715: see British Library Add. MS 29614 f.55ᵛ.

28 Maynooth MS 3b.16 p. 36, published in T. F. O'Rahilly, *Búrdúin Bheaga. Pithy Irish Quatrains* (Dublin: Browne & Nolan, 1925), p. 26.

29 Royal Irish Academy MS 23 B 37 p. 13; Trinity College, Dublin, MS H.5.3 p. 84: the English, Irish and Latin versions are all printed in O'Rahilly, *Búrdúin Bheaga*, p. 9.

30 Royal Irish Academy MS 23B 37, p. 17.

31 Quoted J. T. Leerssen, *Mere Irish and Fíor-Ghael* (Amsterdam and Philadelphia: Benjamins, 1986), p. 284.

32 See R. J. Dickson, *Ulster Emigration to Colonial America 1718–1775* (1966) (Belfast: Ulster Historical Foundation, 1976), esp. p. 31.

33 Quoted in J. M. Barkley, *A Short History of the Presbyterian Church in Ireland* (Belfast: Presbyterian Church in Ireland [1959]), p. 41.

34 *Memoir* prefixed to John Toland, *A Critical History of the Celtic Religion* (London: Lackington [?1740]).

35 See J. C. Beckett, *Protestant Dissent in Ireland 1687–1780* (London: Faber, 1948); Thomas Witherow, *Historical and Literary Memorials of Presbyterianism in Ireland (1623–1731)*; Peter Brooke, *Ulster Pres-*

byterianism: the Historical Perspective 1610–1970 (Dublin: Gill & Macmillan, 1987), chapter 4.

36 Records of the Presbytery of Antrim vol. 2 (1783–1817), Public Record Office of Northern Ireland T.1053/1, p. 28.

37 Records of the General Synod of Ulster 1691–1830, 3 vols (Belfast: Synod of Ulster, 1898), III, p. 157.

38 Records of the General Synod III, p. 208.

39 D. A. Chart (ed.), The Drennan Letters (Belfast: HMSO, 1931), pp. 125, 127, 130.

40 Drennan to Mrs M. McTier (his sister), ? August 1785, Drennan Letters p. 34.

41 McDowell, Ireland in the Age of Imperialism and Reform pp. 255–64, 431–3.

42 Finlay Holmes, Our Presbyterian Heritage (Belfast: Presbyterian Church in Ireland, 1985), p. 67.

43 The best account is still W. R. Scott, Francis Hutcheson (Cambridge: Cambridge University Press, 1900).

44 Donald Winch, Adam Smith's Politics (Cambridge: Cambridge University Press, 1978), chapter 3.

45 Garry Wills, Inventing America: Jefferson's Declaration of Independence (Garden City, N.Y.: Doubleday, 1978); Adrienne Koch, The Philosophy of Thomas Jefferson (Gloucester, Mass.: Peter Smith, 1943), pp. 15–17, 138.

46 Records of the Presbytery of Antrim vol. 2, p. 26.

47 See Caroline Robbins, The Eighteenth-Century Commonwealthman, 2nd edition (Cambridge, Mass.: Harvard University Press, 1961); M. A. Stewart, 'John Smith and the Molesworth Circle', Eighteenth Century Ireland 2 (1987), 89–102.

48 I. Ehrenpreiss, Swift: the Man, his Works and the Age, 3 vols (Cambridge, Mass. and London: Harvard University Press, 1962–83), III, pp. 129, 287f.

49 Francis Hutcheson, A Short Introduction to Moral Philosophy (Glasgow, 1747), pp. 303f, 310.

50 Scott, Francis Hutcheson, p. 28.

51 Seamus Deane, The French Revolution and Enlightenment in England (Cambridge, Mass. and London: Harvard University Press, 1988), pp. 15–18.

52 See F. P. Canavan, The Political Reason of Edmund Burke (Durham, N.C.: Duke University Press, 1960), p. 56; B. T. Wilkins, The Problem of Burke's Political Philosophy (Oxford: Clarendon Press, 1967), p. 68f.

53 Wills, Inventing America p. 150.

54 See J. I. Maguire, 'The Church of Ireland and the "Glorious Revolution of 1688"', in A. Cosgrove and D. McCartney (eds), Studies in Irish History presented to R. Dudley Edwards (Dublin: U.C.D., 1979), pp. 137–49.

55 Jonathan Swift, *Poems*, ed. Harold Williams, 2nd edition, 3 vols (Oxford: Clarendon Press, 1958), III, p. 812.

56 Jonathan Swift, 'A Serious Poem upon William Wood . . .', *Poems* I, p. 333.

57 See Alan Bliss, *Spoken English in Ireland, 1600–1740* (Dublin: Dolmen Press, 1979), p. 217.

58 Jonathan Swift, *Prose Works*, ed. H. Davis et al., 14 vols (Oxford: Basil Blackwell, 1939–68), IV, p. 18.

59 Swift, *Prose Works* IV, p. 232; Daniel Droixhe, *La Linguistique et l'appel de l'histoire* pp. 131, 144; Norman Vance, 'Celts, Carthaginians and Constitutions', *Irish Historical Studies* 22 (March 1981), 216–38.

60 Vivien Mercier, 'Swift and the Gaelic tradition', in A. N. Jeffares (ed.), *Fair Liberty was all his Cry* (London: Macmillan, 1967), pp. 279–89.

61 See Alan Bliss's Introduction to his edition of *A Dialogue in Hybernian Stile* (Dublin: Cadenus Press, 1977), pp. 50–4.

62 See Andrew Carpenter and Alan Harrison, 'Swift's "O'Rourke's Feast" and Sheridan's "Letter": early transcripts by Anthony Raymond', in H. J. Real and H. J. Vienken (eds), *Proceedings*, pp. 27–46.

63 Discussed, e.g., in Arthur E. Case, *Four Essays on 'Gulliver's Travels'* (Gloucester, Mass.: Peter Smith, 1958), pp. 82–4.

64 *Gulliver's Travels* Book 1, chapter 4; R. Barry O'Brien (ed.), *Autobiography of Wolfe Tone 1763–1798*, 2 vols (Dublin: Maunsel, [1893]), p. 77.

65 Bliss, Introduction to *A Dialogue in Hybernian Stile*, p. 38.

66 The best account of his career is the Introduction to *The Letters of Charles O'Conor* ed. C. Coogan Ward and R. E. Ward, 2 vols (Ann Arbor, Mich.: University Microfilms International, 1980).

67 Catherine A. Sheehan, 'The contribution of Charles O'Conor of Belanagare to Gaelic scholarship in eighteenth-century Ireland', *Journal of Celtic Studies* 2.2 (December 1958), 219–37.

68 See Walter J. Love, 'Charles O'Conor of Belangare and Thomas Leland's "Philosophical History of Ireland"', *Irish Historical Studies* 13 (March 1962), 1–25.

69 Brooke's pamphlets are discussed in R. B. McDowell, *Irish Public Opinion 1750–1800* (London: Faber, 1944), pp. 11, 23.

70 See Robert E. Ward, 'A letter from Ireland: a little-known attack on David Hume's *History of England*', *Eighteenth-Century Ireland* 2 (1987), 196f.

71 Charles O'Conor, *Dissertations on the History of Ireland* (Dublin: Faulkner, 1766), p. 95.

72 [Charles O'Conor and John O'Curry], *Observations on the Popery Laws* (Dublin: T. Ewing, 1771), p. 53; Demosthenes, *De Corona*, 194; Plato, *Republic* 6. 488; Livy 8. 13–18.

73 *Letters* II, 198.

74 *Transactions of the Royal Irish Academy* 1 (1786–7), Antiquities section, pp. 17–24.

75 G. W. Dunleavy and J. E. Dunleavy (eds), *The O'Conor Papers. A Descriptive Catalogue* (Madison, Wisc.: University of Wisconsin Press, 1977), p.xxf.

76 O'Raifeartaigh (ed.), *The Royal Irish Academy* pp. 13, 42.

77 Thomas Davis, 'Irish music and poetry', reprinted from *The Nation* in *Prose Writings*, ed. T. W. Rolleston (London: Walter Scott [1890], p. 189.

78 Thérèse Tessier, *La Poésie lyrique de Thomas Moore (1779–1852)* (Paris: Didier, 1976), p. 135 notes 38 of Bunting's tunes used by Moore; Drennan's 'Branch of the Sweet and Early Rose' appears in Bunting's *General Collection of the Ancient Music of Ireland* (Dublin, 1809), p. 22f.

79 Thomas Moore, *Poetical Works* (London: Longmans, 1869), p. 163n.

80 *Irish Book-Lover* 5 (1914), 143; Robert Farren, *The Course of Irish Verse in English* (London: Sheed & Ward, 1948), p. 9.

81 See, e.g., John Hewitt, 'The course of writing in Ulster', *Rann* 20 (June 1953), 46.

82 Drennan's autobiographical statement was never delivered in court but he published it in *Fugitive Pieces in Verse and Prose* (Belfast: F. D. Finlay, 1815), pp. 192–7.

83 *The Drennan Letters*, p. 60.

84 John Rivers, *Louvet: Revolutionist and Romance-Writer* (London: Hurst & Blackett, 1910), pp. 245–7.

85 Adams, *The Printed Word and the Common Man*, p. 86.

86 See Maurice Colgan, 'An Enlightenment solution to the Irish problem', in *Studies in Voltaire and the Eighteenth Century*, ed. T. Besterman, 152 (1976), 485–96, esp. p. 493.

87 William Drennan, *Glendalloch and Other Poems*, 2nd edition (Dublin: W. Robertson, 1859), p. xiv.

88 Quoted in Frank MacDermot, *Theobald Wolfe Tone* (London: Macmillan, 1932), p. 80.

89 [William Drennan], *Letters of an Irish Helot* (Dublin: J. Chambers, 1785), pp. 7f, 11).

90 See, e.g., Francis Dobbs, *A Concise View from History and Prophecy of the Great Predictions in the Sacred Writings* (London, 1800), pp.viii–xxi, 116f, 268f.

91 Drennan to Rev. W. Bruce, 6 July 1782, Public Record Office of Northern Ireland D.553/2; *Fugitive Pieces*, pp. 60–2.

92 See J. R. Watson (ed.), *Pre-romanticism in English Poetry of the Eighteenth Century* (London: Macmillan, 1989).

93 William Drennan, *De Venaesectione in Febribus Continuis* (Edinburgh, 1778), p. 43.

94 The poem Drennan translated, Tibullus 3.19 (sometimes numbered 4.3), is no longer attributed so confidently to Tibullus, though there is no agreement on the matter.

95 William Drennan (trans.), *The Electra of Sophocles* (Belfast, 1817), pp. 16, 78; compare lines 1503–10 of the Greek text.

96 McCormack, *Ascendancy and Tradition*, pp. 19f, 31, 41, 50; Deane, *Celtic Revivals*, pp. 23f, 27.

97 See T. H. D. Mahoney, *Edmund Burke and Ireland* (Cambridge, Mass.: Harvard University Press, 1960), esp. p. 181.

98 Stanley Ayling, *Edmund Burke: his Life and Opinions* (London: John Murray, 1988), pp. 257, 263.

99 [James Porter (ed.)], *Paddy's Resource, or the Harp of Erin, attuned to freedom* (Dublin [?1795]), p. 122.

100 McDowell, *Irish Public Opinion 1750–1800*, p. 210.

101 [J. Edkins (ed.)], *A Collection of Poems* (Dublin: M. Graisberry, 1801), pp. 181, 34, 135.

102 Marianne Elliott, *Partners in Revolution. The United Irishmen and France* (New Haven and London: Yale University Press, 1982), p. 129.

103 Drennan, *Glendalloch*, p. 47.

104 Marilyn Butler, *Maria Edgeworth. A Literary Biography* (Oxford: Clarendon Press, 1972), pp. 95f, 198.

105 *The Irish Unitarian Magazine and Bible Christian* 2 (1847), 328.

106 '"I found myself alone"', BBC (N. Ireland) television broadcast on John Hewitt, 6 December 1987.

107 William Hazlitt, in *The Spirit of the Age* (1825), *Complete Works*, ed. P. P. Howe, 21 vols (London: Dent, 1930–4), XI, p. 174.

108 James and Horace Smith, *Rejected Addresses* (1812) (London: Methuen, 1904), p. 36.

109 James Joyce, *Finnegans Wake* (London: Faber, 1939), p. 492.

110 See Matthew J. C. Hodgart and Mabel P. Worthington, *Song in the Works of James Joyce* (New York: Columbia University Press, 1959), pp. 9–11.

111 W. B. Yeats, 'Modern Irish poetry', Introduction to *A Book of Irish Verse* (1895), 2nd edition (London: Methuen, 1900), p. xviiif.

112 Patrick Kavanagh, 'A Wreathe for Tom Moore's Statue', *Collected Poems* (London: Martin Brian & O'Keefe, 1972), p. 88.

113 Thomas Kinsella, Introduction to *The New Oxford Book of Irish Verse*, p. xxvi.

114 See, e.g., Hoover H. Jordan, *Bolt Upright: The Life of Thomas Moore*, 2 vols, Salzburg Studies in English 33 (1975); Thérèse Tessier, *La Poésie lyrique de Thomas Moore (1779–1852)* (Paris: Didier, 1976); Terence de Vere White, *Thomas Moore, the Irish Poet* (London: Hamish Hamilton, 1977); Robert Welch, *Irish Poetry from Moore to Yeats* (Gerrads Cross: Colin Smythe, 1980); Wilfred S. Bowden (ed.), *The*

Journal of Thomas Moore (Newark, Delaware: University of Delaware Press, 1983–[in progress]).

115 Tessier, *La Poésie*, p. 399.

116 John Hewitt, *Collected Poems* (London: Macgibbon & Kee, 1968), p. 112.

117 [Thomas Moore], 'Boyd's translations from the Fathers', *Edinburgh Review* 24 (November 1814), 58–72; 'The state of Protestantism in Germany', *Edinburgh Review* 54 (September 1831), 238–55.

118 Farren, *The Course of Irish Verse in English*, pp. 4–7; de Vere White, *Tom Moore* p. 76; Moore, *Poetical Works* p. 168.

119 G. K. Chesterton, *Ballad of the White Horse* (1911) (London: Methuen, 1914), Book 2, p. 35.

120 Thomas Moore, 'Extract from a Poem in Imitation of Ossian', *The Press*, 19 October 1797, discussed by Tessier, *La Poésie*, pp. 2, 18; Alphonse de Lamartine, 'Pieces Datées (Vers Inspirés d'Ossian)' (?January 1808), *Oeuvres*, ed. M.-F. Guyard (Paris; Pléiade, 1965), p. 1603; cf. pp. 378, 592; Augustin Thierry, *Dix ans d'études historiques* (1835), 11th edition (Paris: Furne, 1868), pp. 121, 125.

121 See [Francis Jeffrey in] *Edinburgh Review* 8 (July 1806), 456–65; compare *Blackwood's Edinburgh Magazine* 4 (October 1818), 1–5.

122 P. B. Shelley, *Adonais* (1821), 269.

123 See Samuel Whyte, *Poems on Various Subjects*, 3rd edition (Dublin, 1795), which contrives to incorporate information about the school.

124 In *The Oxford Book of Greek Verse*, ed. Gilbert Murray et al. (Oxford: Clarendon Press, 1946), p. 185f.

125 J. M. Edmonds (ed. and trans.), *Elegy and Iambus with the Anacreontea*, 2 vols, Loeb series (Cambridge, Mass.: Harvard University Press, 1931), II, p. 26f.

126 Edmonds, *Elegy and Iambus*, pp. 34–7.

127 Thomas De Quincy, *Autobiography from 1785 to 1803* (1853), *Collected Writings*, ed. David Masson, 14 vols (Edinburgh: A. & C. Black, 1889–90), I, p. 223.

128 John Philpot Curran, *Speeches* (Dublin: Stockdale [1808]), pp. 5, 28.

129 Richard Holmes, *Shelley: the Pursuit* (London: Weidenfeld & Nicolson, 1974), pp. 117–28.

130 See Norman Vance, 'Text and tradition: Robert Emmet's speech from the dock', *Studies* 71 (1982), 185–91.

131 See, e.g., Job 38: 25–8; Hosea 14: 5–7; Zechariah 8: 12.

132 Hector Berlioz, *Memoirs, 1803–65*, trans. Rachel and Eleanor Holmes (1932) (New York: Dover, 1966), p. 107.

133 *Edinburgh Review* 29 (November 1817), 1–35, p. 1.

134 de Vere White, *Thomas Moore*, p. 235.

135 Voltaire, *Les Guèbres*, in *Oeuvres Complètes: Théâtre*, vol. 6 (Paris: Garnier, 1866), p. 566.

136 Preface to *Les Guèbres*, p. 489.
137 Sir William Jones, *Asiatick Researches* (1794) in *Works*, 13 vols (London, 1807), III, pp. 34f, 125; see also E. S. Shaffer, *'Kubla Khan' and the Fall of Jerusalem* (Cambridge: Cambridge University Press, 1975), pp. 116–19.
138 See *Catalogue of Books the Property of the late Thomas Moore, Esq., presented to the Royal Irish Academy*, Appendix (1858) to *Proceedings of the Royal Irish Academy* 6 (1853–7), pp. xxviii, xlix, xlii.
139 Tessier, *La Poésie*, p. 232f.
140 P. A. Murray in *Dublin Review* 10 (May 1841), 429–50; G. Crolly in *Dublin Review* 34 (March 1853), 104–35.
141 Justin McCarthy, *Reminiscences*, 2 vols (London: Chatto & Windus, 1899), II, p. 99f.

CHAPTER 4

The literatures of Victorian Ireland: *William Carleton and Thomas d'Arcy McGee*

1 W. B. Yeats, 'To Ireland in the Coming Times', *Collected Poems*, p. 57.
2 W. B. Yeats, *Memoirs*, ed. D. Donoghue (London: Macmillan, 1972), p. 211.
3 Malcolm Brown, *The Politics of Irish Literature* (London: Allen & Unwin, 1972), p. 47.
4 John Wilson Foster, *Fictions of the Irish Literary Revival. A Changeling Art* (Syracuse, N.Y.: Syracuse University Press, 1987).
5 See, for example, Barry Sloan, *The Pioneers of Anglo-Irish Fiction, 1800–1850* (Gerrads Cross: Colin Smythe, 1986).
6 See, e.g., W. J. McCormack, *Sheridan Le Fanu and Victorian Ireland* (Oxford: Clarendon Press, 1980), pp. 11f, 51, 205.
7 Oliver McDonagh, *The Hereditary Bondsman. Daniel O'Connell, 1775–1829* (London: Weidenfeld & Nicolson, 1988), p. 165f, 42f, 61.
8 *Dublin University Magazine* 25 (January 1845), 11; *Blackwood's Edinburgh Magazine* 33 (January 1833), 87.
9 Finlay Holmes, *Henry Cooke* (Belfast: Christian Journals, 1982), pp. 5, 64, 88f.
10 John Giffard to Sir Robert Peel, 19 March 1816, Peel Papers, British Library Add. MS 40253 f. 258.
11 Quoted in Sir James O'Connor, *History of Ireland 1798–1924*, 2 vols (London: E. Arnold, 1925), I, p. 226.
12 Quoted (from *Dublin University Magazine* 7 (1836)) in A. Mac-Lochlainn, 'The racism of Thomas Davis', *Journal of Irish Literature* 5 (May 1976), 114.
13 *Quarterly Review* 124 (April 1868), 444.

14 McCormack, *Sheridan Le Fanu*, p. 101.

15 Holmes, *Henry Cooke*, p. 148.

16 Ibid., p. 115f.

17 J. S. Reid, *Seven Letters to the Rev. C. R. Elrington* (Glasgow, 1849); Robert Allen, *James Seaton Reid* (Belfast: William Mullan, 1951), pp. 131–4.

18 Thomas Witherow, unpublished autobiography (1888), the Presbyterian Historical Society, Belfast, p. 40.

19 Thomas Witherow, *Historical and Literary Memorials of Presbyterianism in Ireland (1623–1731)*, p. 230.

20 *Banner of Ulster*, 14 June 1842, p. 4.

21 Desmond Bowen, *The Protestant Crusade in Ireland* (Dublin: Gill & Macmillan, 1978), p. 275.

22 Allen, *James Seaton Reid*, pp. 135–7; Holmes, *Henry Cooke*, pp. 157–60.

23 See *Hansard*, 3rd ser., 60 (1842), cols 69, 900, 1008f, 1092, 1181.

24 Holmes, *Henry Cooke*, pp. 64–6.

25 Holmes, *Our Presbyterian Heritage*, p. 130. I am very grateful to Rev. Dr T. H. Mullen of Coleraine for information about Tenant Right and Presbyterian support for it.

26 Devon Commission Minutes of Evidence, *Reports from Commissioners* (London: HMSO, 1845), vol. 19, witness 105 (John Andrews), q. 42.

27 Devon Commission, *Reports* vol. 19, witness 138, qq. 63, 39.

28 R. J. Gregg, 'The Scotch-Irish dialect boundaries in Ulster', in Martyn F. Wakelin (ed.), *Patterns in the Folk Speech of the British Isles* (London: Athlone Press, 1972), pp. 109–39.

29 [Gilbert Frazier], 'Irish-American literature', *New England Magazine* 2, (June 1832), 491.

30 See Ivan Herbison, 'David Herbison – the Bard of Drumclug and his community, 1800–1880', *Mid-Antrim 1983* Ballymena: Mid-Antrim Historical Group, 1983), pp. 102–30. I am grateful to Ivan Herbison for discussing his ancestor with me.

31 Witherow, *Autobiography*, pp. 3, 37.

32 See Bowen, *The Protestant Crusade in Ireland*, esp. p. 89.

33 Quoted in S. P. Kerr, *The Church of Ireland in Belfast 1800–70*, Edinburgh M. Phil. thesis, 1978, p. 206.

34 See William Gibson, *The Year of Grace* (Edinburgh, 1860) (the fullest account) and Isaac Nelson, *The Year of Delusion. A Review of the Year of Grace* (Belfast, 1860–2). Pamphlets and other printed materials relating to the Revival can be found in the Henry Collection in the Library of the Queen's University, Belfast and in the Linenhall Library, Belfast.

35 See Finlay Holmes, 'Ulster Presbyterianism and Irish nationalism', *Studies in Church History* 18 (1982), 541.

36 Ian R. K. Paisley, *The 'Fifty Nine' Revival* (1958), new edition (Belfast: Martyrs' Memorial Free Presbyterian Church, 1981).

37 *Flora Verner; or, the Sandy Row Convert. A Tale of the Belfast Revival* (Belfast, n.d.) (there is a copy in the Henry Collection).

38 John Edgar, *Temperance and Revival in Ulster*, 2nd edition (n.p., 1861), p. 9.

39 Kerr, *The Church of Ireland in Belfast* pp. 148–50.

40 Rev. F. J. Porter, *The Prophet Deceived . . . An Epistle to an Enemy of Revivals*, 2nd edition (Londonderry, 1860), p. 3; Anon., *Another Stone in the Temple* (Belfast, 1859), pp. 1–2.

41 John Fullarton, 'Sketches of Ulster poets: life and writings of Thomas Beggs', *The Ulster Magazine* 2, no. 18 (June 1861), 240–9.

42 Witherow, *Autobiography*, pp. 80–2.

43 Thomas Witherow, *Derry and Enniskillen in the Year 1689* (1873), 4th edition (Belfast: William Mullen, 1913), p. 372.

44 There is a fairly literal English version of the poem, under the title 'Mag Uidhir's winter Campaign', by Thomas Kinsella in his *New Oxford Book of Irish Verse*, pp. 159–61.

45 James Clarence Mangan, 'O'Hussey's Ode to the Maguire', in Kinsella, *New Oxford Book of Irish Verse*, p. 277.

46 Francis Davis, 'To the Rev. J. Radcliffe', *Miscellaneous Poems and Songs* 2nd edition (Belfast: John Henderson, 1852), pp. 74–6.

47 Sloan, *The Pioneers of Anglo-Irish Fiction*, p. 237.

48 Francis Davis, 'A Song of Eighteen Hundred and Forty Eight', *Lispings of the Lagan* (Belfast: John Henderson, 1849), p. 18f.

49 John Hewitt, '"The Northern Athens" and after', in J. C. Beckett et al., *Belfast: the Making of the City 1800–1914* (Belfast: Appletree, 1983), p. 75.

50 William McComb, *Poetical Works* (London, Edinburgh and Belfast, 1864), pp. 359f, 330.

51 William Johnston, *Diary*, 6 October 1847 (unpaginated), Public Record Office of Northern Ireland D.880/2/1.

52 William Johnston, *Diary*, 25 August 1857, 6 March 1858; for an account of the anti-Catholic background to *Westward Ho!*, see Norman Vance, *The Sinews of the Spirit* (Cambridge: Cambridge University Press, 1985), pp. 86–90.

53 William Johnston, *Diary*, 17 and 23 January 1856; Thomas Babington Macaulay, *The History of England from the Accession of James II*, chapter 14.

54 W. B. Yeats, Introduction to *Stories from Carleton* (London: Walter Scott [1889]), p. xvi.

55 John Montague, 'Tribute to William Carleton', *The Bell* 18 (April 1952), 13.

56 Donald Davie, *The Heyday of Sir Walter Scott* (London: Routledge, 1961), pp. 81, 92–9; Walter Allen, *The English Novel* (Harmondsworth: Penguin Books, 1958), p. 131.

57 See, e.g., Benedict Kiely, *Poor Scholar: A Study of the Works and Days*

of William Carleton (1794–1869) (London: Sheed & Ward, 1947); André Boué, *William Carleton*. *Romancier Irlandais* (Paris: Publications de la Sorbonne, 1978); Barbara Hayley, *Carleton's Traits and Stories and the Nineteenth Century Anglo-Irish Tradition* (Gerrards Cross: Colin Smythe, 1983).

58 [Patrick Aloysius Murray], 'Traits of the Irish peasantry', *Edinburgh Review* 96 (October 1852), 384–403.

59 William Carleton, Preface (1830) to *Traits and Stories of the Irish Peasantry*, Complete edition (London: Routledge [1893]), p. [vii].

60 D. J. O'Donoghue, *The Life of William Carleton*, 2 vols (London: Downey & Co., 1896), II, p. 106f.

61 William Carleton, Preface to *Valentine McClutchy* (Dublin: James Duffy, 1847),. pp. vi, vii.

62 William Carleton, *The Emigrants of Ahadarra* (London and Belfast: Simms & McIntyre, 1848), p. 288.

63 See Joseph Lee, *The Modernisation of Irish Society 1848–1918* (Dublin: Gill & Macmillan, 1973).

64 See Emmet Larkin, 'The devotional revolution in Ireland, 1850–75', *American Historical Review* 77 (1972), 625–52.

65 Thomas Davis, 'Habits and character of the Irish peasantry', *Literary and Historical Essays* (Dublin: James Duffy, 1846), p. 209.

66 Boué, *William Carleton*, p. 345.

67 D. D. R. Owen, *The Vision of Hell: Infernal Journeys in Medieval French Literature* (Edinburgh and London: Scottish Academic Press, 1970), p. 37f; G. P. Krapp, *The Legend of St Patrick's Purgatory* (Baltimore, Md: John Murphy Co., 1900).

68 William Carleton, 'A pilgrimage to St Patrick's purgatory', *Christian Examiner* 6 (April 1828), 268.

69 Ibid., p. 353.

70 [William Carleton], *Father Butler* (Dublin: William Curry, 1829), p. [iii].

71 Davie, *The Heyday of Sir Walter Scott*, p. 92.

72 William Carleton, *Autobiography* (London: McGibbon & Kee, 1968), p. 212.

73 Interview in *Irish Times*, 17 January 1973.

74 J. Wilson Foster, *Forces and Themes in Ulster Fiction* (Dublin: Gill & Macmillan, 1974), p. 8.

75 Gregg, 'The Scotch-Irish dialect boundaries in Ulster'.

76 Carleton, *Autobiography* pp. 44, 60; *Records of the General Synod of Ulster* III, p. 306. I am grateful to Mrs Margaret Reid of the Presbyterian Historical Society of Ireland for tracing the elusive Mr Wylie for me.

77 Terence Brown, 'The Death of William Carleton, 1869', *Hermathena* 110 (1970), 81–5.

78 J. H. Todd (ed. and trans.), *Cogadh Gaidhel re Gallaibh* (London:

Rolls Series, 1867), p. 11; Eugene O'Curry, *Lectures on the Manuscript Materials of Ancient Irish History* (Dublin, 1861), pp. 399–402.

79 Keith Thomas, *Religion and the Decline of Magic* (London: Weidenfeld & Nicolson, 1971), p. 398.

80 Bowen, *The Protestant Crusade in Ireland*, p. 64.

81 See Isabel Skelton, *The Life of Thomas D'Arcy McGee* (Gardenvale, Canada: Garden City Press, 1925), the fullest biography.

82 Thomas N. Brown, 'The Irish layman', in *The United States of America*, vol. 6, fascicle 2 (1970) of P. J. Corish (ed.), *A History of Irish Catholicism* (Dublin: Gill and Macmillan, 1967–), pp. 45–97, esp. pp. 59–77; Carl Ballstadt, 'Thomas D'Arcy McGee as a father of Canadian literature', *Studies in Canadian Literature* 1 (1976), 85–95; Germaine Warkentin, 'D'Arcy McGee and the critical act', *Journal of Canadian Studies* 17 (Summer 1982), 119–27. For these last two references and for other bibliographical guidance I am indebted to Margaret Harry of St Mary's University, Halifax, Nova Scotia, where there is to be a D'Arcy McGee Chair of Irish Studies.

83 Yeats, *Memoirs*, p. 211.

84 C. Chenevix Trench, *The Great Dan. A Biography of Daniel O'Connell* (London: Cape, 1984), pp. 120, 276f.

85 See Hugh Brogan, *The Pelican History of the United States of America* (1985) (Harmondsworth: Penguin Books, 1986), pp. 312f, 316, 414.

86 Quoted in Skelton, *Life*, p. 17.

87 Thomas D'Arcy McGee, *Historical Sketches of O'Connell and his Friends* (1845) 3rd ed. (Boston: Donahoe & Rohan, 1845), p. 15.

88 *Eva Macdonald. A Tale of the United Irishmen and their Times* (Boston: Brainard, 1844). The work was never reprinted and the only surviving copy known to me is in the New York Public Library.

89 *Poems*, ed. Mrs J. Sadlier (New York: Sadlier, 1869), p. 450.

90 *The Irish Writers of the Seventeenth Century*, Duffy's Library of Ireland (Dublin: James Duffy, 1846).

91 McGee to O'Brien, 9 September 1847, O'Brien papers, National Library of Ireland MS 439 no. 1985.

92 Skelton, *Life*, p. 104f.

93 *Memoir of the Life and Conquests of Art McMurrough, King of Leinster*, Duffy's Library of Ireland (Dublin: James Duffy, 1847), p. xxiii.

94 For McGee's autobiographical narrative of his adventures see Appendix V of Denis Gwynn, *Young Ireland and 1848* (Cork and Oxford: Cork University Press, 1949), pp. 318–21.

95 Skelton, *Life*, pp. 166, 192–9; Brown, 'The Irish layman', pp. 63–72.

96 The letters, dated 1863–8, are in the Public Archives of Canada with copies in the Vanier Library, Concordia University, Montreal, McGee MSS Group 1A, 8. I am grateful to Judy Appleby of the Vanier Library, the best single source of McGee materials, for this information. For Macdonald, Orangeism and Confederation. see W. L. Morton, *The*

Critical Years: the Union of British North America 1857–1873 (Toronto: McClelland & Stewart, 1964) esp. pp. 86f, 89.

97 For the fullest discussion of this and the Canadian career see T. P. Slattery, *The Assassination of D'Arcy McGee* (Toronto and Garden City, N.Y.: Doubleday, 1968).

98 Fennings Taylor, *The Hon. Thomas D'Arcy McGee. A Sketch of his Life and Death* (Montreal: John Lovell, 1868), p. 53.

CHAPTER 5

Revival reviewed: *St John Ervine and James Joyce*

1 See W. I. Thompson, *The Imagination of an Insurrection* (New York: Harper, Row, 1967).

2 See Seamus Deane, 'The literary myths of the revival', *Celtic Revivals* pp. 28–37; George Watson, *Irish Identity and the Literary Revival* (London: Croom Helm, 1979).

3 W. B. Yeats, *Memoirs*, ed. D. Donoghue (London: Macmillan, 1972), p. 59.

4 B. G. Niebuhr, *History of Rome*, trans. J. C. Hare and C. Thirlwall (Cambridge: Cambridge University Press, 1828–42), I, p. 166.

5 John Kelly, 'Choosing and inventing: Yeats and Ireland', in G. Dawe and E. Longley (eds), *Across a Roaring Hill: the Protestant Imagination in Modern Ireland* (Belfast: Blackstaff, 1985), pp. 8, 16.

6 See Appendix to *Collected Letters of W. B. Yeats*, ed. J. Kelly and E. Domville, vol. I (Oxford: Oxford University Press, 1986), p. 483f.

7 Lady A. Gregory (ed.), *Ideals in Ireland* (London: At the Unicorn, 1901), Preface, p. 9.

8 Denis Donoghue, 'T.C.D.', *We Irish: Selected Essays* (Brighton: Harvester Press, 1986), pp. 169–75.

9 Joseph Hone, *W. B. Yeats 1865–1939* (1943) (Harmondsworth: Penguin Books, 1971), pp. 41, 45f.

10 Review article (October 1886) quoted by R. Ellmann, *Yeats: the Man and the Masks* (1948) (Oxford: Oxford University Press, 1979 edn), p. 47.

11 See, e.g., 'Notes on medieval Hiberno-Latin and Hiberno-French literature', *Hermathena* 36 (1910), 58–72.

12 Mario Esposito, 'The Latin writers of medieval Ireland', *Studies* 2 (1913), 495–521; Patrick Pearse, 'Some Aspects of Irish Literature', *Studies* 2, pp. 810–22.

13 H. Maine, *Lectures on the Early History of Institutions* (London: John Murray, 1875), p. 282f. See also Raymond Cocks, *Sir Henry Maine. A Study in Victorian Jurisprudence* (Cambridge: Cambridge University Press, 1988). I am grateful to Raymond Cocks for drawing my attention to this aspect of Maine's work.

14 Review in *The Providence Sunday Journal*, 7 July, 1889, reprinted in *Letters to the New Island*, ed. H. Reynolds (Oxford: Oxford University Press, 1934), p. 204.

15 See F. F. Farag, 'Oriental and Celtic elements in the poetry of W. B. Yeats', in D. E. S. Maxwell and S. B. Bushrui (eds), *W. B. Yeats: Centenary Essays* (Ibadan: Ibadan University Press, 1965), p. 46.

16 AE, *House of the Titans* (1934) discussed by Austin Clarke, 'Anglo-Irish poetry', in J. E. Caerwyn Williams (ed.), *Literature in Celtic Countries* (Cardiff: University of Wales Press, 1971), p. 156.

17 *Collected Letters of W. B. Yeats*, vol. I, pp. 23, 32, 106, 128.

18 See Gunnar Karlsson, 'Icelandic nationalism and the inspiration of history', in R. Mitchison (ed.), *The Roots of Nationalism* (Edinburgh: John Donald, 1980), pp. 77–89.

19 *Collected Letters of W. B. Yeats* vol. I, p. 189.

20 Hyde, 'The necessity of de-Anglicising Ireland'; Sir C. G. Duffy, 'Books for the Irish people': Sir C. G. Duffy et al., *The Revival of Irish Literature and Other Addresses* (London: Unwin, 1894), pp. 128, 56f.

21 Yeats, *Memoirs*, p. 53; G. Sigerson, 'Irish literature: its origin, environment and influence', in *The Revival of Irish Literature*, pp. 93–9.

22 G. Sigerson, *Bards of the Gael and Gall. Examples of the Poetic Literature of Eirinn* (London: Unwin, 1897), pp. 91, 145, 197–200.

23 Hyde, 'The necessity for de-Anglicising Ireland', p. 159.

24 Peter McBrien, 'The Renascence of Ireland', *Studies* 8 (March 1919), 47f.

25 Oliver Edwards, 'W. B. Yeats and Ulster; and a thought on the future of the Anglo-Irish tradition', *The Northman* 13, no. 2 (Winter 1945), 16.

26 Ibid., p. 17.

27 W. B. Yeats, *Letters*, ed. A. Wade (London: Hart Davis, 1954), pp. 717, 801.

28 See D. E. S. Maxwell, *A Critical History of Modern Irish Drama 1891–1980* (Cambridge: Cambridge University Press, 1984), p. 16.

29 Sam Hanna Bell, *The Theatre in Ulster* (Dublin: Gill & Macmillan, 1972), p. 43.

30 Ernest Boyd, *Ireland's Literary Renaissance* (1916) (Dublin: Allen Figgis, 1968), p. 368.

31 Ervine pays tribute to Wells and Bennett in *Some Impressions of My Elders* (London: Allen & Unwin, 1923); Virginia Woolf disparages them in 'Modern Novels' (1919; later collected as 'Modern Fiction') and 'Mr Bennett and Mrs Brown' (1924), in *Collected Essays*, 3 vols (London: Hogarth Press, 1966), II, p. 105; I, pp. 319–37.

32 Sean Day-Lewis, *Day-Lewis* (London: Unwin, 1982), pp. 96, 102; W. H. Auden and Louis MacNeice, *Letters from Iceland* (London: Faber, 1937), p. 252.

33 Ervine, *Some Impressions* pp. 191, 51.

34 R. Ellmann, *The Consciousness of Joyce* (London: Faber, 1977), p. 108.
35 Ervine to Shaw, 18 May 1926, Shaw Papers vol. 26, British Library Add. MS 50533 f. 140.
36 St John Ervine, *John Ferguson* (London: Allen & Unwin, 1915), p. 13, 8f.
37 Ibid., p. 113.
38 See, e.g., George Blake, *Barrie and the Kailyard School* (London: Arthur Barker, 1951), p. 43.
39 See Eric Anderson, 'The Kailyard School', in Ian Campbell (ed.), *Nineteenth-Century Scottish Fiction* (Manchester: Manchester University Press, 1979) and F. R. Hart, *The Scottish Novel* (Cambridge, Mass.: Harvard University Press, 1978), pp. 116, 122, 131.
40 Endpaper of J. M. Barrie, *Auld Licht Idylls*, 10th edition (London: Hodder & Stoughton, 1896).
41 S. R. Crockett, *The Stickit Minister and Some Common Men* (1893), 11th edition (London: Unwin, 1895), p. 212.
42 Pelagius is claimed for Ulster, e.g. by the sensible Adam Bothwell in Ervine's Ulster comedy *Friends and Relations* (London: Allen & Unwin, 1947), p. 83.
43 St John Ervine, *God's Soldier: General William Booth* (London: Heinemann, 1934); *Oscar Wilde: a Present Time Appraisal* (London: Allen & Unwin, 1951), pp. 30, 163.
44 St John Ervine, 'Mixed Marriage', in *Four Irish Plays* (London and Dublin: Maunsel, 1914), p. 11.
45 See Robert Hogan et al., *The Rise of the Realists 1900-1915 (The Modern Irish Drama*, vol. 4) (Dublin: Dolmen, 1979), pp. 120-3.
46 W. J. Lawrence, in *The Stage*, 24 October 1912, p. 6; 'Jaques', in *Irish Independent*, 18 October 1912, p. 6; see Hogan et al., *The Rise of the Realists*, p. 200.
47 Quoted in Hogan et al., *The Rise of the Realists*, p. 202.
48 John Boyd, 'St John Ervine. A biographical note', *Threshold* 25 (Summer 1974), p. 105. The play is incorrectly identified as *The Orangeman* in Hogan et al., *The Rise of the Realists*, p. 327, which quotes Ervine's chastened reply to Yeats's kindly letter of rejection.
49 St John Ervine, *Mrs Martin's Man* (London and Dublin: Maunsel, 1914), p. 312.
50 St John Ervine, *Parnell* (London: Ernest Benn, 1925).
51 Ervine, *Some Impressions of My Elders*, p. 71.
52 St John Ervine, *The Ship* (London: Allen and Unwin, 1922), p. 33.
53 Ibid., p. 78.
54 *The Irish Statesman* 12 (17 August 1929), 470f.
55 See, e.g., stage-direction for *The First Mrs Fraser* (London: Chatto, 1929), p. 9: 'Ninian, despite his fine Scottish name, has a conventional English public school accent: colourless, unvaried, with flattened vowels and elided consonants.'

56 St John Ervine, *The Lady of Belmont* (London: Allen & Unwin, 1923), p. 93.

57 Ibid., p. 94.

58 St John Ervine, *Sir Edward Carson and the Ulster Movement* (Dublin: Maunsel, 1915), p. 16.

59 St John Ervine, *Changing Winds* (Dublin: Maunsel, 1917), Book 3, chapter 14.

60 See Christopher Hassall, *Edward Marsh, Patron of the Arts: a Biography* (London: Longmans, 1959), pp. 207, 211.

61 W. B. Yeats, Introduction to E. Fenollosa and Ezra Pound, *Certain Noble Plays of Japan* (1916), reprinted in Ezra Pound and E. Fenollosa, *The Classic Noh Theatre of Japan* (New York: New Directions, 1959), p. 161f.

62 Ervine discusses the *Titanic* at perhaps irrelevant length in *Craigavon: Ulsterman* (London: Allen & Unwin, 1949), pp. 216–18.

63 Trooper St John Ervine to Shaw, 9 November 1916, British Library Add. MS 50533 f. 117.

64 Ervine to Mrs H. Sheehy-Skeffington, 9 August 1916, National Library of Ireland MS 22279 (iv).

65 See Hugh Hunt, *The Abbey* (Dublin: Gill & Macmillan, 1979), p. 111; and Dawson Byrne, *The Story of Ireland's National Theatre* (Dublin: The Talbot Press [1929]), p. 111.

66 Ervine to Lady Gregory, 5 May 1916, Berg Collection, New York Public Library, 64B 8959.

67 Ervine to Lady Gregory, 11 May 1916 (Berg).

68 Ervine to Yeats, 9 March 1916 (Berg), printed in R. J. Finneran et al. (eds), *Letters to Yeats*, 2 vols (London: Macmillan, 1977), II, pp. 322–4.

69 Lennox Robinson, *Ireland's Abbey Theatre* (London: Sidgwick & Jackson, 1951), p. 102 (adaptations of Maeterlinck, Sudermann, Hauptmann, Strindberg were also staged between 1907 and 1913, Robinson, p. 207f); Cedric Watts and Laurence Davies, *Cunninghame Graham, a Critical Biography* (Cambridge: Cambridge University Press, 1979), p. 187.

70 Ervine to Lady Gregory, 11 May 1916 (Berg).

71 W. F. Bailey to Yeats, 9 June 1916 (Berg).

72 Ervine to Lady Gregory, 22 May, 29 May 1916 (Berg); Ervine to W. F. Bailey, 6 July 1916; W. F. Bailey to Ervine, 7 July 1916; W. F. Bailey to Lady Gregory, 11 July 1916 (National Library of Ireland MS 13068 (18)).

73 John Boyd in conversation with the present writer, Belfast, 20 March 1987: I am grateful to John Boyd for sharing with me his memories of his friend.

74 Ervine to Shaw, 13 August 192?3, British Library Add. MS 50533 ff. 137–8.

75 St John Ervine, *Bernard Shaw. His Life, Work and Friends* (London: Constable, 1956), p. [vii] (Foreword).

76 Ibid., p. 110; Ervine to Shaw, 16 February 1932, British Library Add. MS 50533 f. 145.

77 Ervine to O'Casey, 14 November 1933, National Library of Ireland MS 27031.

78 Ervine, *Craigavon*, p. 325.

79 For Beadle, see *Who's Who*, 1917 edition. I am grateful to Jenny Spencer Smith of the Department of Fine Art, National Army Museum, for information on painter and painting.

80 See R. B. Wilson, 'Theodore O'Hara', *The Century Magazine* 40 (1890), 106–10.

81 'Biography of a man of destiny', *Belfast Telegraph*, 18 August 1949, p. 4; 'The Bitter Word', *Irish Times*, 20 August 1949, p. 4.

82 Ervine, *Craigavon*, p. 325.

83 St John Ervine, *Ulster, the Real Centre of Culture in Ireland* (Belfast, 1944), pp. 4, 6, 7, 10, 11.

84 Ervine, *Craigavon*, p. 612.

85 J. S. Atherton, *The Books at the Wake* (London: Faber, 1959), pp. 100f, 134. I am indebted to this pioneering work for many points in this discussion.

86 Richard Ellmann, *James Joyce* (Oxford: Oxford University Press, 1959), pp. 324f, 339.

87 James Joyce, *A Portrait of the Artist as a Young Man* (1916) (Harmondsworth: Penguin Books, 1960), p. 188f.

88 Ellmann, *James Joyce*, p. 410.

89 James Joyce, *Ulysses* (1922), ed. H. Gabler (Harmondsworth: Penguin Books, 1986), p. 37.

90 Irland Hit Mikla ('Ireland the Great') is discussed in Thomas D'Arcy McGee, *A History of the Irish Settlers in North America* (1851) (Boston: Donahoe, 1852), pp. 20–2, 239f. For a detailed account, see my essay 'Irish literary traditions and the Act of Union', in *Talamh an Eisc: Canadian and Irish Essays*, p. 40 and nn.

91 Michael Seidel, *Epic Geography: James Joyce's 'Ulysses'* (Princeton, N.J.: Princeton University Press, 1976), citing Victor Bérard, *Les Phéniciens et l'Odyssée* (Paris, 1902–3).

92 Ellmann, *James Joyce*, p. 3.

93 Ellmann, *The Consciousness of Joyce*, p. 133.

94 Weldon Thornton, *Allusions in 'Ulysses'* (Chapel Hill, N.C.: University of N. Carolina Press, 1968), p. 38f. I have made extensive use of this book in this section.

95 The text of Price's letter is given in Ellmann, *James Joyce*, p. 336f.

96 *Irish Daily Independent*, 31 May, 1904, p. 6; *Times*, 31 May, 1904, p. 6; Walter Schwartz, *Nigeria* (London: Pall Mall Press, 1968), p. 74;

Robert Smith, *Kingdoms of the Yoruba* (London: Methuen, 1969), pp. 183f, 186.

97 Lyons, *Ireland since the Famine*, p. 255.

98 See Matthew Hodgart and Mabel P. Worthington, *Song in the Works of James Joyce* (New York: Columbia University Press, 1959) for a detailed account.

99 Discussed in my essay 'Text and tradition: Robert Emmet's speech from the dock', *Studies* 71 (1982), 185–91.

100 See John Gordon, *Finnegans Wake: A Plot Summary* (Dublin: Gill & Macmillan, 1986), p. 245f.

101 See Atherton, *The Books at the Wake*, pp. 32–4.

102 McCormack, *Sheridan Le Fanu and Victorian Ireland*, pp. 14, 16; Atherton, *The Books at the Wake*, pp. 110–13.

CHAPTER 6

Contemporary Ireland and the Poetics of Partition: *John Hewitt and Seamus Heaney*

1 Dillon Johnston, *Irish Poetry after Joyce* (Notre Dame, Indiana: Notre Dame University Press, 1985); Robert Garratt, *Modern Irish Poetry. Tradition and Continuity from Yeats to Heaney* (Berkeley: University of California Press, 1986), chapter 3.

2 Polemically reviewed in W. J. McCormack, *The Battle of the Books* (Mullingar: Lilliput, 1986); see also Edna Longley, *Poetry in the Wars* (Newcastle upon Tyne: Bloodaxe, 1986).

3 Seamus Heaney, 'From Monaghan to Grand Canal', *Preoccupations* (London: Faber, 1980); 'The Placeless Heaven: another look at Kavanagh', *The Government of the Tongue* (London: Faber, 1988).

4 Stan Smith, *Inviolable Voice. History and Twentieth-Century Poetry* (Dublin: Gill & Macmillan, 1982), p. 189.

5 Louis MacNeice, 'Snow' (1935), *Collected Poems*, ed. E. R. Dodds (London: Faber, 1966), p. 30; Derek Mahon, 'In Carrowdore Churchyard', *Poems 1962–1978* (Oxford: Oxford University Press, 1979), p. 3; Paul Muldoon, 'History', *Why Brownlee Left* (London: Faber, 1980), p. 27.

6 *The Government of the Tongue*, p. 8.

7 Louis MacNeice, 'Carrickfergus', *Collected Poems*, p. 69.

8 Michael O'Loughlin, *After Kavanagh. Patrick Kavanagh and the Discourse of Contemporary Irish Poetry* (Dublin: Raven Arts Press, 1985), pp. 7, 27.

9 John Hewitt, 'The Cobbler's Song: a consideration of the work of Patrick Kavanagh', *Threshold* 5 (1951), 42–54.

10 James Simmons, 'Flight of the Earls now leaving', *Judy Garland and the Cold War* (Belfast: Bickerstaff, 1976), p. 3.

11 *Belfast Telegraph*, 29 June, 1987.

12 Discussed in Garratt, *Modern Irish Poetry*, esp. pp. 192–6.

13 See, e.g., John Hewitt, 'Austin Clarke 1896–1974', *Threshold* 25 (1974), 3–6.

14 Seamus Deane, 'Yeats and the idea of revolution', *Celtic Revivals*, p. 49; see also O'Loughlin, *After Kavanagh*, p. 18.

15 Michael Hartnett, *A Farewell to English*, enlarged edition (Dublin: Gallery Books, 1978), pp. 64, 65.

16 John Hewitt, 'Journey of discovery into the literature of Ulster', *Belfast Telegraph*, 24 November 1958.

17 Longley, *Poetry in the Wars*, esp. pp. 176f, 156, 83, 227.

18 James Simmons, 'For the centenary', *Judy Garland and the Cold War*, p. 5.

19 Heaney, 'Yeats as an Example?', *Preoccupations*, p. 112.

20 Richard Murphy, 'The woman of the house', *Sailing to an Island* (London: Faber, 1963), p. 38.

21 Eavan Boland, 'The weasel's tooth', *Irish Times*, 7 June 1974, p. 7.

22 Edna Longley, 'Pigs and trees, stars and horses', *The Crane Bag* 3 (Spring 1979), p. 57.

23 The earlier pamphlets have been published as a book, *Ireland's Field Day*, with an afterword by Denis Donoghue (London: Hutchinson, 1985); see also McCormack, *The Battle of the Books*, chapter 6, 'Having a Field Day'.

24 See Terence Brown, *Ireland: a Social and Cultural History 1922–79* (Glasgow: Fontana, 1981), pp. 120, 201f.

25 *New Ireland Forum Report* (Dublin: Stationery Office, 1984), p. 32; Johnston, *Irish Poetry after Joyce*, p. 272.

26 Longley, *Poetry in the Wars*, p. 168f.

27 Tom Paulin, 'The writer underground', *Ireland and the English Crisis* (Newcastle upon Tyne, 1984), pp. 70–2; Seamus Heaney, 'Osip and Nadezhda Mandelstam', *The Government of the Tongue*, pp. 71–88.

28 W. H. Auden, 'In memory of W. B. Yeats', *Collected Shorter Poems* (London: Faber, 1969), p. 142.

29 John Hewitt in '"The Crane Bag" and the North of Ireland', *The Crane Bag* 4 (1980–1), 102.

30 For a detailed, if hardly impartial, account, see Samuel Dash, *Justice Denied. A Challenge to Lord Widgery's Report on 'Bloody Sunday'* (New York: International League for the Rights of Man, 1972).

31 Thomas Kinsella, *Fifteen Dead* (Dublin: Dolmen, 1979), p. 15.

32 Padraic Fiacc, 'Elegy for a "Fenian Get"', *The Selected Padraic Fiacc* (Belfast: Blackstaff, 1979), p. 45.

33 The Master of Dark Truth, *De Lycanthropia: Satire I of Onegin in Ulster* (Athenis Hiberniae [Belfast], 1984), stanzas 2–5.

34 *Times Literary Supplement*, 17 January, 1975, p. 50.

35 Smith, *Inviolable Voice*, p. 189.

36 Philip Larkin, 'The Importance of Elsewhere', *The Whitsun Weddings* (London: Faber, 1971), p. 34.

37 Louis MacNeice, 'Autumn Journal' (1938), XVI, *Collected Poems* pp. 131–4.

38 Czeslaw Milosz, *The Witness of Poetry* (Cambridge, Mass.: Harvard University Press, 1983), p. 37.

39 Seamus Deane, *A Short History of Irish Literature* (London: Hutchinson, 1986), p. 244.

40 Longley, *Poetry in the Wars*, p. 188.

41 Michael Longley, 'Landscape', *Poems 1962–1983* (Edinburgh: Salamander Press, 1985), p. 126.

42 Mahon, *Poems 1962–1978*, pp. 1, 107.

43 J. W. Foster, '"The Dissidence of Dissent": John Hewitt and W. R. Rodgers', in Gerald Dawe and Edna Longley (eds), *Across a Roaring Hill: the Protestant Imagination in Modern Ireland* (Belfast: Blackstaff, 1985), p. 156.

44 Seamus Heaney, 'Unhappy and at home', interview with Seamus Deane, *The Crane Bag* 1 (Spring 1977), 62.

45 John Hewitt, 'Because I Paced my Thought' (1944), *Collected Poems* (London: McGibbon & Kee, 1968), p. 47.

46 John Hewitt, 'Outside the creeds', *Kites in Spring: A Belfast Boyhood* (Belfast: Blackstaff, 1980), p. 23.

47 F. Jeffery, *Irish Methodism* (Belfast: Epworth House, 1964), pp. 18f, 30f, 190.

48 See, e.g., E. Gallagher and S. Worrall, *Christians in Ulster, 1968–1980* (Oxford: Oxford University Press, 1982).

49 John Hewitt, 'Planter's Gothic: an essay in discursive autobiography' (1953), in *Ancestral Voices. The Selected Prose of John Hewitt*, ed. Tom Clyde (Belfast: Blackstaff, 1987).

50 Hewitt, 'A happy boy', *Kites in Spring*, p. 1; Ervine's bleak *Mixed Marriage* offers a much less optimistic view of the same period in Belfast.

51 John Hewitt, 'No rootless colonist', *Ancestral Voices*, p. 156.

52 John Hewitt, *Time Enough* (Belfast: Blackstaff, 1976), p. 18.

53 Introduction to *The Poems of William Allingham* (Dublin: Dolmen, 1967), p. 18.

54 John Hewitt, 'Townland of peace', *No Rebel Word* (London: Frederick Muller, 1948), p. 22; this section appears in altered form in a revised version of 'Freehold' included in Hewitt's last collection, *Freehold and other Poems* (Belfast: Blackstaff, 1986), p. 13.

55 *Lagan* 2 (1945), 47 (Beckett); *Lagan* 3 (1945), 96 (Hewitt).

56 John Hewitt, 'Regionalism: the last chance' (1947); 'No rootless colonist' (1972) (reviewing his regionalist activities in the 1940s), *Ancestral Voices* pp. 133–7, 152–7.

57 Roy McFadden, 'Postscript to Ulster regionalism', *A Watching Brief* (Belfast: Blackstaff, 1979), p. 3.

58 John Hewitt, 'Below the Mournes in May', *The Rain Dance* (Belfast: Blackstaff, 1978), p. 35.

59 John Hewitt, 'William Conor, RHA, 1881–1968', *The Rain Dance*, p. 7; see also his essay 'Conor's art', in Judith C. Wilson, *Conor* (Belfast, 1981), pp. 107–27.

60 Alan Warner, Introduction to *The Selected John Hewitt* (Belfast: Blackstaff, 1981, p. 4f; Louis Gilbert, 'John Hewitt – "A tremendous man" ', *Belfast Telegraph*, 3 November 1987.

61 John Hewitt, 'Christmas Eve', *The Irish Statesman* 13 (21 December, 1929), 310f.

62 *Listener*, 12 July, 1933: Poetry Supplement, 'Nine Poems', p. 1.

63 Herodotus 2.33; see also Xenophon, *Hellenica* 7.1.20.

64 John Hewitt, 'The Coasters', in *An Ulster Reckoning* (1971), (privately printed) and *The Selected John Hewitt*, pp. 41–3.

65 John Hewitt, 'The Roman Fort' (1971), *Out of My Time* (Belfast: Blackstaff, 1974), p. 38.

66 E. Estyn Evans, *Irish Heritage* (Dundalk: Dundalgan Press, 1942), esp. pp. 168, 176.

67 John Hewitt, 'The Scar' (1971), *Out of My Time*, p. 40: the poem is writtten for Padraic Fiacc, the Catholic Irish poet.

68 John Hewitt's letter to the present writer, 31 July 1985.

69 Kinsella (ed.), *The New Oxford Book of Irish Verse*, pp. 30, 373.

70 Seamus Heaney, 'The god in the tree: early Irish nature poetry' (1978), *Preoccupations*, p. 181.

71 Frank O'Connor, *Kings, Lords and Commons* (Dublin: Gill & Macmillan, 1970), p. 27.

72 John Hewitt, in the *Belfast Telegraph*, 19 May 1966.

73 Seamus Heaney, 'The Poetry of John Hewitt' (1972), *Preoccupations*, p. 210.

74 See 'The Belfast Group: a symposium', *Honest Ulsterman* 53 (November–December 1976), 53–63.

75 Seamus Heaney, 'In small townlands', *Death of a Naturalist* (London: Faber, 1966), p. 54; John Hewitt, *Colin Middleton* (Belfast: Arts Council of Northern Ireland [1975]).

76 William Wordsworth, *The Prelude* (1805 version) 1, 305–7, quoted in Seamus Heaney, *North* (London: Faber, 1975), p. 62, as an epigraph for 'Singing School'.

77 Neil Corcoran, *Seamus Heaney* (London: Faber, 1986), p. 20.

78 Nicholas Roe, 'Wordsworth at the Flax Dam', unpublished paper read at the 1985 Belfast IASAIL Conference. I am grateful to Dr Roe for giving me a copy of his paper.

79 Roland Mathias, 'Death of a naturalist', in T. Curtis (ed.), *The Art of Seamus Heaney* (Bridgend: Poetry Wales Press, 1982), p. 16.

80 Robert Lowell in 1975, cited in Neil Corcoran, *Seamus Heaney*, p. 35.

81 Seamus Heaney, 'A Peacock's Feather', *The Haw Lantern* (London: Faber, 1987), p. 38f.

82 'Unhappy and at home', interview with Seamus Deane, *The Crane Bag* 1 (1977), 61.

83 Seamus Heaney, 'Kicking against the code', *New Statesman*, 12 November 1965, p. 748; 'Jacob and Josie', *New Statesman*, 17 June 1966, p. 899; 'Out of London: Ulster's Troubles', *New Statesman*, 1 July 1966, p. 23f.

84 Seamus Heaney, 'Old Derry's walls', *Listener*, 24 October 1968, pp. 521–3.

85 Seamus Heaney, 'The Other Side', *Wintering Out* (London: Faber, 1972), pp. 34–6.

86 Robert Buttel, *Seamus Heaney* (Lewisburg: Bucknell University Press, 1975), p. 25.

87 W. F. Marshall, *Livin' in Drumlister* (Belfast: Blackstaff, 1983), p. 73; Seamus Heaney, 'Mother Ireland', *Listener*, 7th December 1972, p. 790.

88 Seamus Heaney, *The Haw Lantern*, p. 41; Conrad's Belfast seaman, taciturn and unimaginative, derives from a familiar stereotype, even caricature, of the Ulster Protestant.

89 Seamus Heaney, *Station Island* (London: Faber, 1984), p. 21.

90 Seamus Heaney, *Field Work* (London: Faber, 1979), p. 59f; see also Heaney's article 'The Labourer and the Lord' (Ledwidge and Lord Dunsany), *Listener*, 28 September 1972, p. 55f.

91 Seamus Heaney, *Door into the Dark* (London: Faber, 1969), p. 24.

92 Tertullian, *Apologeticum* 50 ('Plures efficimus quoties metimur a vobis, semen est sanguis Christianorum').

93 Tacitus, *Germania* 40.2.

94 W. B. Yeats, 'The Municipal Gallery revisited', *Collected Poems*, p. 369.

95 Seamus Heaney, 'Celtic fringe, Viking fringe', *Listener*, 21 August 1969, p. 255, discussed by Blake Morrison, *Seamus Heaney* (London: Methuen, 1982), p. 36.

96 Quoted in Corcoran, *Seamus Heaney*, p. 34.

97 Ibid., p. 125.

98 John Montague, *The Rough Field* (1972) (Portlaoise: Dolmen, 1984), p. 37.

99 Seamus Heaney in *Listener*, 26 April 1973, p. 55of.

100 Seamus Heaney, *Sweeney Astray* (Derry: Field Day, 1983), Introduction, p. viii.

101 Czeslaw Milosz, *Native Realm* (1968) (London: Sidgwick & Jackson, 1981), p. 125.

102 For the original Spanish, and a perhaps less felicitous translation, see Roy Campbell's *Poems of St John of the Cross* (1951) (Glasgow: Collins, 1979), pp. 44–7.

103 Austin Clarke, *A Penny in the Clouds* (London: Routledge, 1968), p. 210.

104 Austin Clarke, *Collected Poems* (Dublin: Dolmen, 1974), pp. 131–4, 507–9.

105 Heaney, *The Government of the Tongue*, p. 78, of Mandelstam.

106 Corcoran, *Seamus Heaney*, p. 31.

Note on Unpublished Sources

This study draws mainly on published sources which are indicated in the references. But it has also benefited from unpublished materials, including academic dissertations and documents illustrating aspects of the life and work of particular writers. Since these are not mentioned in the references unless directly quoted or referred to I have compiled the list below both in acknowledgement and as a guide to further research.

THESES

Atfield, Joy Rosemary, *'The End of Art is Peace': Creative Tensions in the Poetry of Seamus Heaney*, University of Sussex DPhil, 1989.

Brooke, Peter, *Controversies in Ulster Presbyterianism, 1790–1836*, University of Cambridge PhD, 1980.

Curley, Patrick G., *Northern Irish Poets and the Land since 1800*, Queen's University of Belfast MA, 1977.

Kerr, S. P., *The Church of Ireland in Belfast 1800–1870*, University of Edinburgh MPhil, 1978.

Leonard, D. W., *John Mitchel, Charles Gavan Duffy and the Legacy of Young Ireland*, University of Sheffield PhD, 1975.

O'Brien, George, *Life on the Land: the Inter-relationship between Identity and Community in the Irish Fiction of Maria Edgeworth, William Carleton and Charles Lever*, University of Warwick PhD, 1979.

Whelan, Irene, *New Lights and Old Enemies: the 'Second Reformation' and the Catholics of Ireland, 1800–35*, University of Wisconsin (Madison) MA, 1983.

MANUSCRIPTS

Archbishop Ussher

Dublin: Trinity College MSS, esp. MS 842.
Oxford: Bodleian MSS, particularly 'Usseri Collectanea', 8 vols (MSS Add.
C. 296–300; Add. A. 379–80; Auct. T. 5. 30); MS Barlow 13. (These
include miscellaneous writings and collections of theological, historical and
geographical materials.)

William Drennan

Belfast: Public Record Office of Northern Ireland: originals and typescript
transcripts of the Drennan Letters (1776–1819), of which only a selection
has been published.

Thomas D'Arcy McGee

Dublin: National Library of Ireland: William Smith O'Brien Papers (which
include twenty-two letters from McGee to O'Brien, relating to Young
Ireland).
Montreal: Vanier Library, Loyola Campus, Concordia University: Copies of
McGee letters, including those relating to 1841–50 and those among the
John A. MacDonald Papers in the Public Archives of Canada.

St John Ervine

Dublin: National Library of Ireland: Abbey Theatre Papers 1915–16 (MS
13068 (17, 18)); Ervine–Sean O'Casey correspondence 1928–34 (MS
27031).
London: British Library: Shaw Papers vol. 26 (Ervine–Shaw correspondence
1916–41) (Add. MS 50533).
New York: Berg Collection, New York Public Library: Ervine–Lady Gregory
correspondence, 1916.
Bloomington, Indiana: Indiana University Library: Ervine MSS, 1914–57,
particularly Ervine's Journal (1 January–2 February 1939).

General

Belfast Public Record Office of Northern Ireland: Diary of William
Johnston of Ballykilbeg; Records of the Presbytery of Antrim.
Presbyterian Historical Society: Autobiography of Rev. Dr Thomas
Witherow (1888).

Dublin   Marsh's Library: Geoffrey Keating, *A Defence of the True History of Ireland* (English translation).
Trinity College: MS 664 (includes summary of Richard Creagh, *De Lingua Hibernica*).
Royal Irish Academy: MSS include invaluable collections of seventeenth- and eighteenth-century poetry in Irish, some with English glosses or parallel English stanzas.
London   British Library: MS Harley 913; MS Landsdowne 418. Both include medieval texts of Irish provenance, some in English.
Oxford   Bodleian Library: MS Rawlinson B.480, Dubhaltach MacFirbhsigh, *Ughdair na h-Erend* ('Authors of Ireland') (1656).
Southampton   City Record Office: Molyneux Papers, including Molyneux-O'Flaherty letters.

Select Bibliography of Primary Texts

Untranslated Irish and Latin texts have been omitted, together with many older texts now hard to come by. In some cases I have in the references cited editions which are earlier and less accessible than those listed here.

ANTHOLOGIES

An Duanaire. 1600–1900. Poems of the Dispossessed, ed. and trans. S. Ó Tuama and T. Kinsella (Portlaoise: Dolmen, 1981).

A Book of Irish Verse, ed. W. B. Yeats, 2nd edition (London: Methuen, 1900).

Kings, Lords and Commons. An Anthology from the Irish, trans. Frank O'Connor (Dublin: Gill & Macmillan, 1970).

The New Oxford Book of Irish Verse, ed. T. Kinsella (Oxford: Oxford University Press, 1986).

The Penguin Book of Irish Verse, ed. B. Kennelly (Harmondsworth: Penguin Books, 1970).

Allingham, William, *Poems*, ed. John Hewitt (Dublin: Dolmen, 1967).

Carleton, William, *Autobiography*, intro. Patrick Kavanagh (London: MacGibbon & Kee, 1968).

Carleton, William, *The Black Prophet*, intro. Timothy Webb (Shannon: Irish University Press, 1972).

Carleton, William, *Traits and Stories of the Irish Peasantry* (London: Routledge, [1893]).

Clarke, Austin, *Collected Poems* (Dublin: Dolmen, 1974).

Dillon, Wentworth, 4th Earl of Roscommon, *An Essay on Translated Verse and Horace's Art of Poetry Made English* (London: Scolar, 1971).

Drennan, William, *Fugitive Pieces in Verse and Prose* (Belfast: F. D. Finlay, 1819).

Drennan, William, *The Drennan Letters*, ed. D. A. Chart (Belfast: HMSO, 1931).

Ervine, St John G., *Changing Winds* (Dublin: Maunsel, 1917).

Ervine, St John G., *The Foolish Lovers* (London: Collins, 1920).

Ervine, St John G., *Mrs Martin's Man* (London and Dublin: Maunsel, 1914).

Ervine, St John G., *The Wayward Man* (London: Collins, 1927).

Ervine, St John G., *Selected Plays*, ed. John Cronin (Gerrards Cross: Colin Smythe, 1988).

Heaney, Seamus, *Death of a Naturalist* (London: Faber, 1966).

Heaney, Seamus, *Door into the Dark* (London: Faber, 1969).

Heaney, Seamus, *Fieldwork* (London: Faber, 1979).

Heaney, Seamus, *The Government of the Tongue* (London: Faber, 1988).

Heaney, Seamus, *The Haw Lantern* (London: Faber, 1987).

Heaney, Seamus, *North* (London: Faber, 1975).

Heaney, Seamus, *Preoccupations: Selected Prose 1968–1978* (London: Faber, 1980).

Heaney, Seamus, *Station Island* (London: Faber, 1984).

Heaney, Seamus, *Sweeney Astray* (London: Faber, 1984).

Heaney, Seamus, *Wintering Out* (London: Faber, 1972).

Hewitt, John, *Ancestral Voices: the Selected Prose of John Hewitt*, ed. Tom Clyde (Belfast: Blackstaff, 1987).

Hewitt, John, *Collected Poems* (London: MacGibbon & Kee, 1968).

Hewitt, John, *Freehold and Other Poems* (Belfast: Blackstaff, 1986).

Hewitt, John, *Kites in Spring. A Belfast Boyhood* (Belfast: Blackstaff, 1980).

Hewitt, John, *Loose Ends* (Belfast: Blackstaff, 1983).

Hewitt, John, *Mosaic* (Belfast: Blackstaff, 1981).

Hewitt, John, *Out of My Time: Poems 1967–1974* (Belfast: Blackstaff, 1974).

Hewitt, John, *The Rain Dance* (Belfast: Blackstaff, 1978).

Hewitt, John, *Time Enough* (Belfast: Blackstaff, 1976).

Hutcheson, Francis, *Collected Works*, 7 vols (Hildesheim: Georg Olms, 1971).

Joyce, James, *Dubliners* (London: Triad Grafton, 1977).

Joyce, James, *Finnegans Wake* (London: Faber, 1939).

Joyce, James, *Portrait of the Artist as a Young Man* (London: Triad Grafton, 1988).

Joyce, James, *Ulysses*, ed. Hans Gabler (Harmondsworth: Penguin Books, 1986).

Kavanagh, Patrick, *Collected Poems* (London: Martin Brian & O'Keefe, 1972).

Kinsella, Thomas, *Fifteen Dead* (Oxford: Oxford University Press, 1979).

Kinsella, Thomas, *Nightwalker and Other Poems* (Dublin: Dolmen, 1968).

Longley, Michael, *Poems 1963–1983* (Harmondsworth: Penguin Books, 1986).

McGee, Thomas D'Arcy, *Irish Writers of the Seventeenth Century* (New York: Lemma Publishing, 1973).

McGee, Thomas D'Arcy, *Poems*, ed. Mrs J. Sadlier (New York: Sadlier, 1869).

MacNeice, Louis, *Collected Poems*, ed. E. R. Dodds (London: Faber, 1966).

Mahon, Derek, *Poems 1962–1978* (Oxford: Oxford University Press, 1979).

Montague, John, *The Rough Field* (Portlaoise: Dolmen, 1984).

Moore, Thomas, *Irish Melodies*, music arr. M. W. Balfe (London: Novello, 1923).

Moore, Thomas, *Poetical Works*, ed. A. D. Godley (Oxford: Oxford University Press, 1910).

Muldoon, Paul, *Why Brownlee Left* (London: Faber, 1980).

Paulin, Tom, *The Liberty Tree* (London: Faber, 1982).

Swift, Jonathan, *Complete Poems*, ed. Pat Rogers (Harmondsworth: Penguin Books, 1983).

Swift, Jonathan, *Prose Works*, ed. H. Davis et al., 14 vols (Oxford: Basil Blackwell, 1939–68).

Ussher, James, *The Whole Works*, ed. C. R. Elrington and J. H. Todd, 12 vols (Dublin: Hodges & Smith, 1829–64).

Yeats, W. B., *Collected Poems* (London: Macmillan, 1988).

Yeats, W. B., *Memoirs*, ed. Denis Donoghue (London: Macmillan, 1988).

Index

Abbey Theatre (Dublin), 177, 179, 185, 187–9
Abeokuta (Nigeria), 202
Abernethy, Rev. Dr John, 75–6, 89
Adair, Rev. Patrick, 33
Addison, Joseph, 59, 60, 73
'AE' see Russell, George
Agallamh na Senorach ('Colloquy of the Ancient Men'), 3, 235
Aislinge Mac Conglinne ('Vision of MacConglinne'), 2, 105, 214
Allen, Walter, 137
Allingham, William, 132, 227, 236
American Declaration of Independence, 77
Anacreon, 106–7
Angelesey, Arthur Annesley, Earl of, 33
Anglican (or Protestant episcopal) Church in Ireland, 29, 43, 69, 70, 74–5, 79, 128, 130; see also 'Protestant Ascendancy'
Anglo-Irish Agreement (1985), 14, 219
Anglo-Irish attitudes, 10–11, 51–2, 69, 74, 167, 207
'Anglo-Irish literature', concept of, 11–12
Annals of the Four Masters, The, 22–

3, 37, 54, 67–8, 205
Aquinas, St Thomas, 200
Arnold, Matthew, 104, 123, 130, 159
Arius, 199
Aryan culture see Indo-European culture
Ashton, John, 66
Aubrey, John, 251
Auden, W. H., 220, 224
Aughrim, battle of, 66, 217

Barrie, J. M. 178
Barthes, Roland, 11
Beadle, James Prinsep, 191
Becanus, J. G., 21
Beckett, J. C., 7, 228
Beckett, Samuel, 2, 209
Bedell, William, Bishop of Kilmore, 29–30, 54–5
Beggs, Thomas, 131
Belfast Peace League, 231
Bell, Sam Hanna, 210
Belloc, Louise Swanton, 103
Beresford, Lord John George, Archbishop of Armagh, 125
Benjamin, Walter, 1, 4, 159
Bennett, Arnold, 176, 183
Berkeley, George, Bishop of Cloyne, 2, 10, 70–2, 116, 234

Berlioz, Hector, 103, 111
Birmingham, George A. (Rev. J. O.
　Hannay), 166, 206
Black, Rev. Dr Robert, 75
Blacker, Colonel William, 137
Blair, Rev. Robert, 33–4
Blake, William, 198, 231
'Bloody Sunday', 220, 226
Bochart, Samuel, 58–9
Boehme, Jacob, 29
Boland, Eavan, 217
Book of Invasions, The (*Leabhar
　Gabhála*), 23
Bottomley, George, 238
Boyd, Ernest, 175
Boyd, John, 210, 218
Boyne, battle of, 66, 246–7
Brehon Laws, 170
Brigid, St, 23, 24–5
Brooke, Charlotte, 68, 85
Brooke, Henry, 83–4
Brooke, Rupert, 186
Brown, Rev. Dr John, 127
Brown, Terence, 86
Browne, Sir Thomas, 53
Bruce, Rev. William, 75
Bunting, Edward, 87, 102
Bunyan, John, 116
Burke, Edmund, 10, 65, 78, 96–9
Burke, Richard, 97
Burns, Robert, 127, 134
Bury, John Bagnell, 52, 168, 223
Butler, Hubert, 52
Butler, Marilyn, 99
Butler, Samuel, 38
Byron, Lord, 105–6

Cabbalism, 29, 199
Cairns, David, 17
Camden, William, 20, 81
Campbell, James, 229
Canny, Nicholas, 6
Carleton, William, 36, 120, 121, 124,
　131, 135, 136–53, 154, 167, 178–9
　192, 255–6; language in, 143–5;
　opportunism of, 137; religion of,
　141–2; reputation, 136–7; social

displacement of, 140; and Caesar
　Otway, 142; and 'modernization',
　140–1; and Presbyterians, 146–8;
　and 'prophecy', 149–50, 152–3;
　and Yeats, 136–7; *Art Maguire*,
　143, 151; *The Black Prophet*, 150–
　1, 153; *The Emigrants of
　Ahadarra*, 140, 149; *Fardorougha
　the Miser*, 151; 'Father Butler',
　143; *Parra Sastha*, 142–3;
　'Pilgrimage to St Patrick's
　Purgatory', 142; 'Poor Scholar',
　139; *Rody the Rover*, 143; *Tales
　and Sketches*, 141; *The Tithe
　Proctor*, 143, 149; *Traits and
　Stories of the Irish Peasantry*, 136,
　139, 144–5, 149; *Valentine
　McClutchy*, 143, 147–8; *Willy
　Reilly*, 152
Carlyle, Thomas, 166, 172
Carson, Ciarán, 252
Castlehaven, James Touchet,
　Earl of, 33
Catholic Church in Ireland,
　devotional revolution in, 140–1;
　racial and political tension in, 25;
　and Irish nationalism, 3, 163; and
　'prophecy, 152; and Ussher, 45–8,
　54
Catholicism, 23, 36, 41, 42, 65, 71,
　72, 90–1, 112, 115, 134, 155–6,
　163, 201, 213, 223, 224, 225, 245
Cavafy, Constantin, 221
Celtic Revival *see* Irish Literary
　Revival
Charlemont, James Caulfeild, Earl of,
　67, 85
Charles I, 32, 42
Chatterji, Mohani, 171
Chaucer, Geoffrey, 38–9
Chesterton, G. K., 104
Churchill., Lord Randolph, 166, 200
Civil Rights movement in Ulster, 220
Clarke, Austin, 171, 214, 238, 257
Cobbett, William, 231
Cokaygne (Cocaigne), Land of, 26,
　105, 173

Colgan, John, 23, 25
Colum, Padraig, 175
Columba (Columkille), St, 23, 149, 152
Comenius (Komensky), J. A., 29–30
Conor, William, 231
Conrad, Joseph, 245
Cooke, Rev. Dr Henry, 122, 124–5, 126, 134, 137
Corkery, Daniel, 12, 65, 196, 228
covenanting, in Scotland and Ireland, 14, 31–2, 62, 125
Cowley, Abraham, 106–7
Craigavon, James Craig, Viscount, 190–1
Crawford, Rev. William, 67–8
Creagh, Richard, Archbishop of Armagh, 27–8
Crockett, Samuel Rutherford, 178
Crolly, George, 117
Cromwell, Oliver, 2, 15, 19, 56, 136, 201
Cronin, John, 2
Croskery, Rev. Thomas, 31
Cuchulain, 1, 38, 191
Curran, John Philpot, 109

Danes (including Vikings), 36, 96, 111, 173, 193–4, 250–1
Dante Alighieri, 2, 3, 28, 142, 254–5
Davie, Donald, 137, 144
Davis, Francis, 132–4
Davis, Thomas, 11, 86–8, 119, 121, 124, 141, 157–8, 160, 169
Day-Lewis, Cecil, 176, 217
Deane, Seamus, 17, 78, 96, 218, 219, 222
De Blácam, Aodh, 19
Defoe, Daniel, 61
Deleuze, Gilles, 5
Dempster, Thomas, 23–5, 50
De Quincey, Thomas, 109
Derry, Siege of, 66, 131, 226, 259
De Valera, Eamon, 19, 188, 192
Devlin, Denis, 214, 255
Devon Commission, 126–7
Dickens, Charles, 103, 176, 184

Dickson, Rev. Dr William Steel, 75, 114
Dobbs, Francis, 91–2, 105
Donatus, St, of Fiesole, 24–5
Donne, John, 41–2, 50
Dowden, Edward, 168–9
Downham, George, Bishop of Derry, 42, 45
Doyle, J. W., Bishop of Kildare, 152
Drennan, Rev. Thomas, 76, 88–9, 231
Drennan, William, 70, 76, 86–101, 119–21, 132–3, 222, 231; critical neglect of, 86–7, Presbyterianism of, 86–9; and Burke, 96–9; and Catholics, 90–1; and Davis, 86–7; and Gray, 92–3; and Horace, 93; and Juvenal, 97–9; and Milton, 92–3; and Moore, 87, 100–2, 108; and Pope, 94–5; and Sophocles, 93–4; and Tibullus, 93, 108; and United Irishmen, 86, 87, 90, 92, 94; *Belfast Monthly Magazine*, 100; *Fugitive Pieces in Verse and Prose*, 87, 90, 91, 93, 97–8, 99; 'Glendalloch', 94–6; *Letters of an Irish Helot*, 86, 89, 91, 92; *Letters*, 88; 'The Wake of William Orr', 88, 99
Drew, Rev. Dr Thomas, 129
Duchal, Rev. James, 77, 89
Duffy, Charles Gavan, 157, 160, 167, 172–3, 192
Dury, John, 30, 44
Dyer, John, 95

Easter Rising (1916), 165, 187, 227, 249
Edgeworth, Maria, 89, 99–100, 120, 137
Edgeworth, Richard, 89, 99–100
Edkins, Joshua, 98
Edward VII, 202–3
Eglinton, John (W. K. Magee), 10, 52
Elgar, Sir Edward, 202
Eliot, T. S., 2, 3, 5, 14

Elizabeth I, 29
Elrington, Rev. C. R., 55, 125
Emmet, Robert, 109–10, 112–13, 203–4
Encyclopédie, L', 79
English language, cultural imperialism and, 11–12, 81, 212
Enniskillen, siege of, 66, 131, 226
Erasmus, 38
Erigena, Johannes Scotus, 2, 24, 49–50
Ervine, St John Greer, 13, 165, 174–5, 176–92, 193, 199, 202, 210, 222, 225, 226, 229, 232, 245; career 176–7; critical reputation 176, 192; and Fabianism, 177, 185–6; and Irishness, 184, 194; and Joyce, 176–7; and O'Casey, 192, 194; and regionalism, 176–7; and sectarianism, 179–80; and self-reliance ('Pelagianism'), 178–9, 181; and Shaw, 177, 187–8; and Ulster Unionism, 190–1; *Alice and a Family*, 177, 179; *Boyd's Shop*, 190; *Changing Winds*, 177, 186–7; *The Critics*, 182; *The First Mrs Fraser*, 190, 287 n.; *The Foolish Lovers*, 183; *Friends and Relations*, 182; *John Ferguson*, 177, 179, 185, 188; *The Lady of Belmont*, 184–5; *The Magnanimous Lover*, 180–2; *Mixed Marriage*, 177–8, 179–80; *Mrs Martin's Man*, 182; *The Orangeman*, 180; *Robert's Wife*, 190; *Sir Edward Carson*, 185; *The Ship*, 183; *The Wayward Man*, 183
Esposito, Mario, 169
Evangelical Revival in Ulster (1859), 129–31
Evans, Estyn, 236
Evans, Edith, 190

Fallis, Richard, 17
famine, 139, 150–1, 237, 241
Farren, Robert, 88, 104
Faulkner, George, 71

Fenianism, 164
Ferguson, Sir Samuel, 119, 123–4, 158, 169, 229, 236
Fiacc, Padraic, 221
Field Day Theatre Company, 218–19
Finn, 20, 235
Finnerty, Peter, 109
Fitzgerald, Lord Edward, 2, 110
Fitzgerald, Dr Garret, 219
Fitzsimons, Henry, S. J., 41
Flagerty, Cornelius, 27
Flanagan, Thomas, 2, 247
Flower, Robin, 37
Foster, John Wilson, 119
Foucault, Michel, 1, 15, 159
Fox, George, 231
French, Nicholas, Bishop of Ferns, 36
Friel, Brian, 218
Frost, Robert, 242 f.
Frye, Northrop, 7
Furneaux, Philip, 89

Gadamer, Hans-Georg, 6
Gaelic League, 127, 175, 187, 196
Gaelic poetry, 36–40, 72–4, 132, 239–40, 246; *see also* Ó Bruadair, Ó Dálaigh, Ó hEoghusa, Ó Mealláin, Ó Rathaille
Gibbon, Edward, 40, 50
Gibbon, Lewis Grassic (James Leslie Mitchell), 229, 236
Gibson, Rev. William, 131
Giffard, John, 122–3
Gifford, Henry, 220
Giraldus Cambrensis, 20–2, 33
Glob, P. V., 250
Golding, William, 258
Goldsmith, Oliver, 10, 217
Gonne, Maud, 174, 200, 202
gothic, Irish versions of, 207
Gottschalk of Orbais, 48–50
Grattan, Henry, 70, 85, lo6, 109
Gray, Thomas, 92–3, 95
Gregory, Lady Augusta, 10, 165, 167, 188–9
Grey, Betsy (Bessie), 135

Griffith, Arthur, 202
Grigson, Geoffrey, 224
Grotius, Hugo, 44
Guattari, Félix, 5

Hall, Mrs S. C., 141
Hamilton, James, later Viscount
    Claneboy, 44, 88
Hanmer, Meredith, 21
Hanna, Rev. Hugh, 129
Hardy, Thomas, 176–7
Hartlib, Samuel, 30
Hartnett, Michael, 212, 215
Hazlitt, William, 102
Heaney, Seamus, 2, 14–15, 210–13,
    218, 219–20, 240, 241–60; and
    Carleton, 121, 255–6; and
    Catholicism, 223, 244–5, 260; and
    Dante, 252, 254–5; and Hewitt,
    241–2; and Hopkins, 243; and
    Joyce, 251, 256, 258–9; and
    Kavanagh, 213, 243–4, 256; and
    Mandelstam, 220, 252, 259; and
    Wordsworth, 243; and Yeats, 244;
    Death of a Naturalist, 242–4, 259;
    Field Work, 253–4; *Haw Lantern*,
    247, 253, 258–9; *North*, 220, 244–
    5, 250–2; *Station Island*, 253,
    255–7; *Sweeney Astray*, 242, 257;
    Wintering Out, 245–6, 249, 256,
    258
Herbison, David, 127–8
Herder, Johann Gottfried, 166, 172
Herodotus, 234
Herrick, Robert, 106
Hewitt, John, 14, 127, 211, 214, 216–
    17, 218–19, 220, 223–41, 242, 247;
    loneliness, 227; Methodist origins,
    224–5; and Celts, 234–7; and
    countryside, 230, 233, 239–41; and
    Drennan, 88, 100; and Moore, 103;
    and radical tradition, 231–2; and
    regionalism, 229–30, 240; and
    Rodgers, 223; and Wordsworth,
    227–8; 'Anti-Promethean Ode',
    233; *Bloody Brae*, 238–9;
    'Christmas Eve', 232; 'The

Colony', 230; 'Conacre', 228, 237,
    239; 'Freehold', 228; 'Ireland',
    234–5; *Kites in Spring*, 225–7; *Out
    of My Time*, 237; *Rhyming
    Weavers*, 229; 'The Swathe
    Uncut', 236–7; *Time Enough*, 227,
    230
Hobsbaum, Philip, 242
Hobsbawm, Eric, 8
Hogg, James, 147
Homer, 166, 194, 198, 200–1, 222
Home Rule, 13, 165, 180, 182, 185,
    206
Honest Ulsterman, The, 218
Hope, James, 229
Horace, 59–60, 81, 93
Hughes, Ted, 243
Hull, Eleanor, 88
Hutcheson, Francis, 76–9, 88, 90,
    114
Hyde, Douglas, 12, 14, 40, 54, 169,
    172, 174–5

Ibsen, Henrik, 182, 184
Iceland, cultural nationalism in, 172
Indo-European culture, 170–1
Irish language, 28–9, 27, 81–2; and
    Hebrew, 28; poetry in *see* Gaelic
    poetry; printing in, 20, 27; and
    Ussher, 54–6; *see also* Gaelic
    League
Irish Literary Revival, anticipated in
    late eighteenth century, 82; and
    cosmopolitanism, 167–70, 175;
    divisive particularism of, 165, 173;
    and Ervine, 165, 187, 189; and
    India, 171; and Joyce, 165, 196,
    205; and Ulster, 174–6; *see also*
    Gaelic League; Gregory; Hyde;
    Yeats
Irish music, 83, 87
Irish Penny Journal, The, 142
Irving, Edward, 105

James II, 136
Jefferson, Thomas, 77
Jerome, St, 28, 39, 50

John of the Cross, St, 256
Johnson, Samuel, 40, 60–1
Johnston, Charlie, 171, 174
Johnston, Rev. John (?), 30
Johnston, William, of Ballykilbeg, 135–6, 146, 171
Jones, Sir William, 113
Joyce, James, 2, 12, 165, 174, 176, 192–208, 226, 251, 256, 259; and Dublin, 12, 202, 205; and English language, 193, 195; and identity of the Irish writer, 207; and Irish Literary Revival, 165, 196, 205; and Moore, 102, 104, 193, 203–5; and Newman, 195–6; and 'Protestant Ascendancy', 195; 'The Dead', 104; *Dubliners*, 193, 197; *Finnegans Wake*, 2, 102, 173, 192,, 194–5, 198, 205–7; 'Ivy Day in the Committee Room', 197; *Portrait of the Artist*, 193, 195–7, 199, 256; 'The Sisters', 197; *Stephen Hero*, 196; *Ulysses*, 2, 193–5, 198–205, 207, 258
'Junius', Letters of, 91
Juvenal, 97–9

Kafka, Franz, 5
'kailyard', fiction, 177–8
Kames, Henry Home, Lord, 77
Kavanagh, Patrick, 102, 211, 213–14, 222, 243–4, 250
Keane, Molly, 216
Kearney, Hugh, 45
Kearney, Richard, 2, 219
Keating, Geoffrey, 21–2, 37, 67
Kingsley, Charles, 136
Kinsella, Thomas, 17, 72, 102, 210–14, 218, 220, 239–40, 246, 253
Kirkpatrick, Rev. Dr James, 75–6

Lamartine, Alphonse de, 104
Lament for Art O'Leary, The, 74
land, problems of the, 120, 126–7, 139, 149; reform, 162, 165, 177
Langner, Lewis, 184–5
language, as vehicle of Irish tradition, 6

Lanigan, Dr John, 67–8
Larkin, Philip, 221
La Touche, James Digges, 141
Laud, William, Archbishop of Canterbury, 43, 49, 56
Lecky, W. E. H., 65, 168, 179, 198
Ledwidge, Francis, 247
Leerssen, J. T., 8, 25
Le Fanu, Joseph Sheridan, 207
Left Book Club, 231
Leitch, Maurice, 211
Leland, Thomas, 83
Lhuyd, Edward, 27
Lindsay, Vachel, 232
Linen Hall Library (Belfast), 100
literature, concepts of, 7–8
Little, W. G. 240
Livingston, Rev. John, 34–5
Livy, 84–5
Lloyd, David, 5
Lloyd George, David, 17
Locke, John, 69, 71, 89, 114
Longley, Edna, 216–17, 218, 219, 222
Longley, Michael, 214, 218, 222–3
Louvet, Jean-Baptiste, 89
Lowell, Robert, 244, 253
Lynch, John, 21, 22, 25, 28, 54
Lyric Theatre (Belfast), 218

Macaulay, Thomas Babington, 11, 136, 171
MacBride, John, 200
McBrien, Peter, 174
Mac Caghwell (or Mac Aingil), Aodh, 27
McCartney, R. L., 219
McComb, William, 132, 134–5, 141, 229
McCormack, W. J., 46, 96
MacDiarmid, Hugh (Christopher Murray Grieve), 229
Macdonald, John A., 163–4
McFadden, Roy, 229
Mac Firbhisigh, Dubhaltach, 27
McGee, Thomas D'Arcy, 26, 70, 117, 153–64, 167, 194, 204; American misfortunes, 163; Canadian

success, 163–4; career, 154–5, 163–4; death, 164; and Moore, 155–7, 162; and O'Connell, 154–7, 159; and tradition-seeking, 159; and Ulster, 159–62; *Catholic History of North America*, 163; 'The Celts', 162; *Eva Macdonald*, 157; *History of the Irish Settlers in North America*, 155–6; *Irish Writers of the Seventeenth Century*, 158–9; *Memoir of Art McMurrough*, 161–2; 'Salute to the Celt', 162; 'The Summons of Ulster', 161; 'To the River Boyne', 161

McGuckian, Medbh, 211
McGuinness, Frank, 191
McHenry, James, 127
MacIlwaine, Rev. William, 129
MacNamara, Gerald (Harry Morrow), 175
MacNeice, Louis, 176, 192, 213, 217, 221, 224
Madden, Samuel, 71
Magee, William, Archbishop of Dublin, 129
Mahaffy, Sir John Pentland, 167–8, 223
Mahon, Derek, 146, 210–11, 213, 221–2, 223
Maine, Sir Henry, 170
Mandelstam, Osip, 220
Mangan, James Clarence, 5, 119, 132
Markievicz, Constance, 217
Marsh, Narcissus, Archbishop of Dublin, 69
Marshall, Rev. W. F., 146, 245
Martial, 73
Mathew, Father Theobald, 128–9
Maturin, Charles, 113, 207
Maupassant, Guy de, 12
Mayne, Rutherford (Samuel Waddell), 175
Mazzini, Giuseppe, 160, 163
Mercier, Vivien, 2, 181
Merriman, Brian, 105, 214
Methodism in Ireland, 128, 224–5
Michelburn, John, 66–7

Middleton, Colin, 242, 248
Millais, Sir John Everett, 136
Miller, D. W., 34
Milosz, Czeslaw, 220, 255, 259
Milosz, Oscar, 221
Milton, John, 32, 42, 43–4, 45, 60, 62, 92–3, 106, 188
Mistral, Frédéric, 229
Mitchel, John, 70, 122, 160, 162, 167
Molesworth, Robert, Viscount, 77, 79
Molyneux, Sir Capel, 70
Molyneux, Samuel, 68–9, 71
Molyneux, William, 68–71, 89, 114, 159
Montague, John, 137, 211, 212, 221, 240, 246, 252, 257
Montgomery, Rev. Henry, 100, 122
Moore, George, 257
Moore, Thomas, 68, 84, 86–7, 100–17, 119–21, 133–4, 155–7, 162, 249; Catholicism of, 112, 114–16; conservative hostility to, 111; eclecticism of, 114–15; identities of, 103; reputation, 102–3, 111; romanticism, 108–11, 113; satirical writing, 105–6; and Anacreon, 106–7; and Berlioz, 103, 111; and Byron, 105–6; and Dickens, 103; and Drennan, 87, 108, 110–12; and Emmet, 109–10, 112–13; and Joyce, 102, 104, 193, 203–5; and Ossian, 104; and Shelley, 105; and Southey, 105–6; and Tibullus, 108; *The Epicurean*, 116–17; *Irish Melodies*, 87, 102–3, 106, 108, 116; *Lalla Rookh*, 111–14; 'The Petition of the Orangemen of Ireland', 115; *Sacred Songs*, 116–17
Moran, Denis Patrick, 11, 171
Morgan, Lady Sydney, 113
Morris, William, 171–2, 231–2
Morrison, Blake, 211
Moryson, Fynes, 21
Motion, Andrew, 211
Muldoon, Paul, 211–13, 217, 257
Murphy, Richard, 216–17
Murray, Patrick Aloysius, 117, 137, 145
Mythological Cycle, 9

Nashe, Thomas, 196
Nation, The, 132
Nehru, Jawaharlal, 12
Neill, A. S., 224
New Ireland Forum Report, 219
Newgrange (Co. Meath), 2, 246
Newman, John Henry, 195–6
Nicholson, Norman, 229
Northern Ireland *see* Ulster

O'Brien, Flann (Brian O'Nolan), 209, 257
O'Brien, William Smith, 160
Ó Bruadair, Daibhi, 37–9
O'Carolan, Turlough, 83
O'Casey, Sean, 166, 190, 192
Ó Clérigh, Michael, 22–3, 27, 54
O'Connell, Daniel, 73–4, 87, 121, 122–3, 126, 137, 141, 197
O'Connor, Frank (Michael Francis O'Donovan), 12, 240
O'Conor, Charles, 68, 82–6
O'Curry, Eugene, 73, 158–9
O'Curry, Dr John, 84
Ó Dálaigh, Peadar Dubh, 74
O'Donnell, Rory, 19, 38
O'Donovan, John, 22, 158–9, 170
O'Faolain, Sean, 12, 209, 214, 218–19
O'Flaherty, Liam, 12, 214
O'Flaherty, Roderic, 22, 68–9, 72, 83
O'Grady, Standish Hayes, 166
O'Halloran, Dr Sylvester, 68
O'Hara, Theodore, 191
Ó hEoghusa (O'Hussey),Eochaidh, 132
Oisin *see* Ossian
Ó Mealláin, Fear Dorcha, 32
Ó Neachtain, Tadhg, 82
O'Neill, Hugh, 19, 38
Orangeism, 66, 130, 135–6, 179–80, 202, 206, 225–6, 245; in Canada, 164
Ó Rathaille, Aogán, 73
Orr, James, 229
Orr, William, 99
Ossian (or Oisin), 3, 20, 84, 98, 104, 134–5, 166, 235
O'Sullevan Beare, Philip, 46, 56
Ó Tuama, Seán, 72
Otway, Rev. Caesar, 142
Ovid, 223, 252

Paine, Tom, 77–8, 82, 92, 121
Paisley, Rev. Dr Ian R. K., 129, 245, 260
Párliament na mBan ('Parliament of Women'), 39
Parliament of Clan Thomas, 38–9
Parnell, Charles Stewart, 117, 148, 192, 195, 197, 203
Parnell, Thomas (poet), 95
Parnell, Thomas, (of Sunday School Society), 148
'Pastorini' *see* Walmisley
Patmore, Coventry, 254
Patrick, St. 1, 3, 23, 168, 235–6
Paulin, Tom, 14, 88, 215, 218, 220, 222
Pearse, Patrick, 1, 36, 169, 187, 191, 192, 249
Peden, Rev. Alexander, 35–6
Pelagius, 50, 179, 199
Penal Laws, 72
Percy, Thomas, Bishop of Dromore, 68, 82, 172
Petrie, George, 158
Pezron, Paul-Yves, 81
Phoenix Park murders, 207
Photius, 199
Plunkett, James, 211
Pope, Alexander, 94, 95
popular culture, 37, 66; *see also* 'prophecy'; Ulster dialect
Powell, York, 172
Presbyterianism, 14, 33–6, 62, 65, 74–6, 86–9, 124–6, 135, 146–8; *see also* covenanting
Preston, William, 98
Prichard, James Cowles, 170
Priestley, Rev. Dr Joseph, 89, 231
printing in Ireland, introduction of, 20; in Irish language, 27
Propertius, 222

'prophecy', 35–6, 105, 135, 149–50, 152–3
'Protestant Ascendancy', 12, 13, 65, 69, 76, 125, 174, 183, 195, 197, 228; and Burke, 96; and Moore, 115
Protestantism, 20, 41, 43, 66–7, 115, 128, 129, 135, 198, 201, 224, 225, 245; *see also* Anglican Church; Evangelical Revival; Methodism; Orangeism; Presbyterianism
publishing in Ireland, 211

Rafroidi, Patrick, 17
Ralegh, Sir Walter, 52, 251
Ramsey, Allan, 127
Ramus, Petrus (Pierre de la Ramee) and Ramism, 44–6
Raymond, Anthony, 81
rebellion, in 1641–2, 30–1; in 1798 *see* United Irishmen; in 1803 *see* Emmet; in 1848 *see* Young Ireland Rising; in 1916 *see* Easter Rising
Redmond, John, 191
regionalism, 175, 176–7, 229–30, 240
Reid, Forrest, 174
Reid, Rev. James Seaton, 43, 125
Reid, Thomas, 114
Richards, Shaun, 17
Robertson, Thomas, 98
Robinson, Lennox, 166, 176–7, 188
Rodgers, W. R., 223
Roe, Nicholas, 243
Roscommon, Wentworth Dillon, Earl of, 56, 57–63, 65, 80, 168; family of, 57–8; Irishness of, 59–60, 62–3; prescriptiveness of, 59–61; and Addison, 60; and Dryden, 57, 61; and Horace, 59–60; and Pope, 57, 59–61; and Ussher, 56, 58, 60, 63; *Essay on Translated Verse*, 57, 59, 60–1
Rothe, David, Bishop of Ossory, 24, 28, 47
Rousseau, Jean Jacques, 89
Rowan, Archibald Hamilton, 109
Rowe, Nicholas, 106
Royal Irish Academy, 85–6

Russell, George ('AE'), 171, 174, 190, 192, 218, 231–2
Russell, Lord John, 104, 150

Sabellius, 199–200
St Anthony's College (Louvain), 22–3
St Isisdore's College (Rome), 24
St Patrick's Purgatory (Co. Donegal), 138, 142, 254
Salvation Army, 179, 232–3
Scaliger, Joseph Justus, 28, 52–3
Schlegel, August Wilhelm von, 159
Scott, Sir Walter, 62, 121, 136
Scottish Enlightenment *see* Hutcheson; Smith, Adam; Stewart
Scotus, Johannes Duns, 24
Scrieckus (Schrieck), Adrianus, 28
'Secret of England's Greatness' (painting), 180–1, 202, 226
sectarianism, 128–9, 135–6, 179–80, 201, 211–12, 220, 238
Sergeant, Howard, 227
Seymour, St John D., 17
Shakespeare, William, 2, 17, 41, 169, 200
Shaw, George Bernard, 11, 177, 182, 186, 196
Shelley, Percy Bysshe, 105, 109, 169, 245
Sheridan, Denis, 82
Sheridan, Richard Brinsley, 82
Sheridan, Thomas (the younger), 82, 106
Sherlock, William, 61
Sidney, Algernon, 97
Sigerson, Dr George, 172–3
Simmons, James, 214, 216, 218
Sirmond (Sirmondus), Jacques, 49
Smith, Adam, 77–8
Smith, Horace and James, 102
Smith, Stan, 219, 221
Somme, battle of, 191
Sophocles, 93–4, 223
Southey, Robert, 105–6, 171
Spenser, Edmund, 17, 21
Stafford, Sir Thomas, 25–6

Stanihurst, Richard, 20, 21, 22, 28, 41–2
Stephens, James, 11
Stewart, Dugald, 77, 88, 100
Stillingfleet, Edward, Bishop of Worcester, 68
Stokes, Whitley (Celtic scholar), 169–70
Stokes, Whitley (Dean of Trinity College), 109
Strafford, Thomas Wentworth, Earl of *see* Wentworth
Sweeney (Suibhne) legend, 254–7
Swift, Jonathan, 10, 33, 70–1, 77, 79–82, 97
Synge, Edward, later Bishop of Elphin, 77–8
Synge, John Millington, 166, 182, 197

Tacitus, 250
Tanzania, 6
Tara (Co. Meath), 98
Taylor, Jeremy, Bishop of Down and Connor, 50
Tempest, Marie, 190
Temple, Sir John, 32–3
Temple, Sir William, 33
tenant right (in Ulster), 126–7, 231
Tertullian, 249
Thierry, Augustin, 104–5, 119, 234
Threshold, 218
Tibullus, 93, 108
Toland, John, 21, 67–8, 74–5, 77, 91, 95, 231
Tone, Theobald Wolfe, 82, 86, 90, 97, 247
Towgood, Rev. Micaiah, 75, 89
Trevor, William, 216
Trinity College, Dublin, 10, 41, 43–6, 71, 115, 167–9
Turgenev, Ivan, 12

Uí Dhonnchadha, Sheaffraidh, 39–40
Ulster, and Irish cultural identity, 13, 124, 192, 230, 237; and philistinism, 130–1, 159; plantation of, 19; Unionism in, 190–1, 193, 201, 206, 215, 244
Ulster Cycle, 9, 200, 235
Ulster dialect, writing in, 127–8, 132, 229–30
Ulster Literary Theatre, 175
Ulster 'troubles', 219–21, 224, 225, 235, 251–3; *see also* 'Bloody Sunday'; Orangeism; sectarianism
Union, Act of (1800), 120, 140, 197; 200
United Irishmen, 76–7, 85, 86, 87, 90, 92, 94, 109, 121–2, 154–5, 203, 231, 240, 247; *see also* Drennan; Tone; Vinegar Hill
Ussher, Henry, Archbishop of Armagh, 29, 41
Ussher, James, Archbishop of Armagh, 12, 21, 27, 29–30, 34–6, 40–56, 57–8, 60, 63, 67–9, 125, 159, 168, 197, 212, 260; ancestry, 40–1; conflicting loyalties of, 42–3, 56; sermons, 50–1 and biblical chronology, 40, 52–3; and episcopacy, 43–4; and insecurity, 51–2; and Irish church history, 47–8, 52, 56; and Irish language, 54–6; and Laud, 49, 56; and predestination controversies, 48–50; and Ramism, 45; and Richelieu, 48; and Roman Catholic Church, 45–8, 54

Valentine (heretic), 199
Vallancey, Major-General Charles, 81, 83, 194
Vance, Rev. Patrick, 75
Vico, Giambattista, 198, 205, 207
Victoria, Queen, 134, 167, 180–1, 202
Vígfússon, Gúdbrandr, 172
Vikings *see* Danes
Vinegar Hill, battle of, 249
Virgil, 2, 3, 61
Voltaire (François Marie Arouet), 103, 112, 121
Volunteers, the (in 1780s and 1790s),

75–6, 85, 89, 91, 99, 109
von Ranke, Leopold, 4
Voss (Vossius), Gerhard Jan, 49

Wadding, Father Luke, 24–5, 47–8
Walker, Joseph Cooper, 83
Walmisley, Rev. Charles ('Pastorini'),
    152–3
Ware, Sir James, 21, 23, 24–5, 26–7,
    54, 67–8, 159
Warner, Ferdinando, 83
Wellington, Arthur Wellesley, Duke
    of, 134
Wells, H. G., 176–7, 186–7
Wentworth, Thomas, Earl of
    Strafford, 31, 56–7
'West Britonism', 123, 146
Whyte, Samuel, 106
Wilde, Oscar, 137, 168, 179
Wilkins, John, 29
William III, 2, 246
Williams, Raymond, 5
Wilson, R. N. D., 216

Winstanley, Gerrard, 231
Witherow, Rev. Dr Thomas, 33, 125,
    128, 131, 136
Woolf, Virginia, 176
Wordsworth, William, 108–9, 227–8

Yeats, William Butler, 1, 10, 63, 65,
    88, 102, 119–20, 136, 165–75, 187,
    188–9, 191, 195–6, 215–16, 218,
    234, 244, 250–1, 254; and
    Carleton, 136–7; and eighteenth-
    century Ireland, 65; and Heaney,
    244; as precursor of recent Irish
    poetry, 215–17, 219; and Ulster,
    174–5, 216
Young Ireland, 86–7, 117, 121, 132–
    3, 160; *see also* Davis, Thomas;
    Duffy; McGee; Mitchel
Young Ireland Rising, 162–3

Zimbabwe, 5
Zoroastrianism, 112–13